AMERICA'S MODERN WARS

Understanding Iraq, Afghanistan and Vietnam

CHRISTOPHER A. LAWRENCE

The Dupuy Institute

CASEMATE

Philadelphia & Oxford

Published in the United States of America and Great Britain in 2015 by
CASEMATE PUBLISHERS
908 Darby Road, Havertown, PA 19083
and
10 Hythe Bridge Street, Oxford, OX1 2EW

ISBN 978-1-61200-278-1
Digital Edition: ISBN 978-1-61200-279-8

Cataloging-in-publication data is available from the Library of Congress and
the British Library.

10 9 8 7 6 5 4 3 2 1

Printed and bound in the United States of America.

For a complete list of Casemate titles please contact:

CASEMATE PUBLISHERS (US)
Telephone (610) 853-9131, Fax (610) 853-9146
E-mail: casemate@casematepublishing.com

CASEMATE PUBLISHERS (UK)
Telephone (01865) 241249, Fax (01865) 794449
E-mail: casemate-uk@casematepublishing.co.uk

Contents

Dedication

This book is dedicated to my father, Colonel William A. Lawrence, who served two tours in Vietnam. It is also dedicated to all those who died in the Vietnam War, including his friends Captain Robert Maluenda Caliboso and Major Robert William Arnold. It is unfortunate that the sacrifice of almost 60,000 U.S. servicemen and women had not been better used to educate future generations on the problems of fighting insurgencies.

Acknowledgments

I would like to thank all the people who helped me in the various insurgency studies. First and foremost are my predecessors at *The Dupuy Institute*, the late Colonel Trevor N. Dupuy (USA) and Major General Nicholas Krawciw (USA, ret). If not for them, I would not have been in a position to do this work to begin with.

All of our work came about as a result of a series of government contracts. Therefore, of equal importance are E. B. Vandiver, former Director of the Center for Army Analysis (CAA) and Andrew Marshall, Office of the Secretary of Defense, Net Assessment. Also of importance is the contractual support we received from the Central Intelligence Agency (CIA), courtesy of the National Intelligence Council (NIC). In particular, I would like to thank Major General John R. Landry (USA, ret.), military advisor to the NIC.

This work could not have been done without the able assistance of the staff and consultants of *The Dupuy Institute*. They include Richard C. Anderson, Alexander Dinsmoor, C. Curtiss Johnson, L. Jay Karamales, Nicolas Klapmeyer, Ciro Pabon, Dr. Victoria Plamadeala-Johnson, Nicolas Reinhart, Dr. Dmitri Ryabushkin, Susan Sims, Blair Trimble, Eugene Visco and Dr. Shawn Woodford. As this book was based upon a series of a dozen reports that we did, almost by default some sections of this book were effectively co-authored by our staff, especially Curt Johnson and Richard Anderson.

We would also like to thank others who helped along the way, including Dr. Andrew Birtle, Dr. Ivo Feierabend, Dr. Andrew D. Hossack, Dr. Michael Spagat, Robert Smith and Chad Yost.

Introduction

When we found those boys in that bunker with their equipment, it became a whole new ballgame. The way these guys fight is different than the insurgents.—PFC Troy Langley, TF 2-2, 1st Inf. Div., during the Second Battle of Fallujah, November 2004[1]

On 4 April 2004, the U.S. Armed Forces deployed 2,000 troops around the smallish city of Fallujah in Iraq. This was a turning point in a developing insurgency in Iraq. Four days earlier, on 31 March 2004, four American contractors had been ambushed and killed as their convoy passed through the town. They were then pulled from their SUVs by a crowd, and their bodies burned; two of the bodies were hung on a bridge in the center of town. The gruesome ambush was tailor-made for television, and of course, images of it were broadcast around the world. Until that point, the developing Iraqi insurgency, which some U.S. leaders denied *was* an insurgency, had cost the U.S. 304 troops killed in combat over approximately 11½ months.[2]

The U.S. felt it had to respond and that response was to take Fallujah. Earlier that week the U.S. Army had also lost five soldiers in nearby Habbaniya, but it was the broadcast deaths of four U.S. Blackwater contractors that galvanized the administration to take in a city and against an insurgency that it previously all but ignored.

To accomplish this, the U.S. Marine Corps initiated *Operation Vigilant Resolve*. On the night of 4 April, Fallujah was surrounded by about 2,000 troops, including Iraqi allies. The Marines attacked the following day, and after three days of fighting, had secured about a quarter of the city. They then declared a ceasefire and began negotiations with various Iraqis in the area. Their own Iraqi allies had deserted at the start of the fight, and so a new Iraqi militia was formed to police Fallujah. On 1 May, the U.S. forces withdrew from Fallujah, handing over control of the city to the thousand or so new militiamen. The First Battle of Fallujah was a confused, unresolved affair that had cost the U.S. at least 39 killed.[3] For all practical purposes, it was an insurgent victory. Other areas of Iraq erupted at the same time, resulting in some 126 U.S. combat casualties for the month. The previous month U.S. combat losses had only been 35 killed.[4]

Meanwhile, in the comfortable, idyllic offices of *The Dupuy Institute*, I hammered out an unsolicited proposal entitled "Proposal for Casualty Estimation in the Iraq War." It was emailed to the U.S. Army's Center for Army Analysis (CAA) on 20 April 2004. The director of CAA, E. B. "Van" Vandiver, immediately responded and the contracting process was initiated.

At *The Dupuy Institute* we had been watching the developing Iraq situation with some concern. We noted the statement of General Eric Shinseki on 25 February 2003, that the U.S. needed several hundred thousand troops to occupy Iraq. We noted the deployment initially of less than 125,000 troops into Iraq. This deployment did not include either of our two military police brigades.

The U.S. invasion of Iraq, *Operation Iraqi Freedom*, began on 19 March 2003. The violence of the conventional the war effectively ended on 14 April 2003, after a loss of 103 killed in combat and 27 non-combat deaths.[5] During the following four weeks, there were only four U.S. troops killed in action in Iraq. From the middle of May until the middle of July (two months), the combat was slightly more intense— 31 combat deaths. Still, we remained concerned.

On 17 July 2003, I requested that my office manager start assembling a database of U.S. losses in Iraq, as "I don't think this is over yet." Nine months later, I was ready to send out a proposal to look further into what we might be facing in Iraq. The contract for that work was awarded effective 24 August 2004.

But, the battles for Fallujah were not over. The U.S. again moved against the city on 7 November This time, in a well-telegraphed offensive, U.S. forces first surrounded the city using over 10,000 Marines and Army troops under command of the Marine Corps. The insurgents left a holding force in the city, while many fled elsewhere. The U.S. initiated its attack, *Operation Phantom Fury*, the following day. Fallujah was entered carefully and each block was systematically cleared while the insurgents bravely fought a futile defense. By 12 November, it was claimed that the U.S. held 80 percent of the city.[6] The process was continued until December 23, when the last major combat occurred, and the city was brought under U.S. control. Fallujah had been cleared and the U.S. had proven itself victorious in conventional warfare once again. There were 95 U.S. soldiers and Marines killed in the fighting, and 560 were wounded. Our allied Iraqi forces lost 11 men, with 43 wounded. The Iraqi insurgents had lost 1,350 killed (U.S. claim) and 1,500 captured.[7] The U.S. began pulling forces out of Fallujah in January 2005, but maintained control of the city through the autumn of 2007.

The counterinsurgent leadership pounced on this news to proclaim victory in Fallujah as early as 15 November 2004. This included the interior minister of Iraq, and the commander of the 1st Marine Expeditionary Force (MEF), Lt. General John F. Sattler. By 19 November, the MEF commander was effectively declaring victory in

Iraq. "We feel right now that we have . . . broken the back of the insurgency, and we have taken away this safe haven."[8] The optimism now was not just a political face-saving effort on the part of U.S. senior civilian leadership but included the declarations from many elements of the U.S. military, including the chairman of the Joint Chiefs of Staff, the senior command in Iraq and the commanding general at Fallujah.

General Sattler continued, explaining that the insurgency, in losing Fallujah, had lost "your location and your means for command and control,"

> [Y]ou lose your lieutenants, which we have taken out of the Zarqawi network over the course of the last almost three months on a very precise basis. . . . And you also lose the turf where you're operating, the town that you fell comfortable moving about in, where you know your way about. Now you're scattered. I believe, I personally believe, across the country, this is going to make it very hard for them to operate. And I'm hoping that we'll continue to breath down their neck.[9]

It was a part of a repeated effort by some in the U.S. military to try shape the war into the war that they wanted to fight, as opposed to recognizing what type of war they were fighting.

Meanwhile, at *The Dupuy Institute*, we were putting the final touches on our Iraq casualty estimate and conducted our first brief of our estimate on 28 December 2004. This estimate would lead to an extended series of studies, first on Iraq, then later on researching insurgencies in general and analyzing their basic nature. The final step in this process, tying all the work together in this book, was begun in September 2009.

NOTES

1. Jackie Spinner and Karl Vick, "Troops Battle for Last Parts of Fallujah." *The Washington Post* (14 Nov. 2004), A01.
2. From *The Dupuy Institute's* Iraq Casualty Data Base (ICDB). This is the total killed in combat from 15 Apr. 2003, through 31 Mar. 2004.

   Specific denials included a statement by Defense Secretary Donald Rumsfeld in a Pentagon press conference on 7 Apr. 2004. In response to a reporter's comment that "U.S. forces are fighting pitched battles with both Sunni and Shia in many cities in Iraq today," Rumsfeld asserted: "You say 'pitched battles'. . . . [T]he number of people that are involved in those battles are relatively small. And there's nothing like an army or a major, large elements of hundreds of people trying to overthrow or to change the situation. You have a mixture of a small number of terrorists, a small number of militias, coupled with some demonstrations and some lawlessness." See Jim Lehrer, Online newsletter, *Iraq: Military Briefing* (Apr. 7, 2004).
3. The 1st Marine Div. stated that by 13 Apr. 2004, 39 Marines and soldiers had died in the fighting for Fallujah, along with an estimated 600 enemy fighters. See Jonathan F. Keiler, "Who Won the Battle of Fallujah?" The Naval Institute *Proceedings* (January 2005). The U.S. lost 126 troops in combat in Iraq in Apr. 2004.

4.   From *The Dupuy Institute's* ICDB, as are all subsequent tabulations of losses in Iraq.
5.   We record 130 killed in the conventional phase of the war (19 Mar.–14 Apr. 2003), 27 of these were non-combat deaths. There were also 31 allied troops killed, of which 12 were non-combat deaths. The first casualties in the operation were incurred on 21 Mar. 2003. The last casualties occurred on 14 Apr. 2003, with one U.S. combat loss and five non-combat losses. During the next nine days, there were no combat deaths among U.S. or allied forces.

     An alternate end date for the conventional phase of the war (and the one most commonly used) is 1 May 2003, when Pres. George W. Bush announced that "major combat operations in Iraq have ended."
6.   Spinner and Vick, *op. cit.*
7.   These estimates are from Wikipedia. During November and December, the U.S. lost of total of 183 troops in combat in Iraq, along with 26 non-combat deaths. According to another published source (Keiler), U.S. casualties in *Operation Phantom Fury* were 51 killed and 425 seriously wounded. Iraqi losses were 8 dead and 43 wounded and as many as 1,200 insurgents were killed.
8.   Rowan Scarborough, "U.S. Declares Insurgency 'Broken'; Military also Says Bin Laden is Cut Off." *The Washington Times* (19 Nov. 2004).
9.   *Ibid.* At the time, Zarqawi was the leader of Al-Qaeda in Iraq, one of the primary terrorist groups among the insurgents.

CHAPTER 1

The Iraq Casualty Estimate

Q: *Mr. Rumsfeld, some experts are saying the insurgency in Iraq could last 10 years or more. Is this possible, in your estimation?*
SEC. RUMSFELD: *Who are these experts?*
Q: *It's all over CNN . . .*
SEC. RUMSFELD: OH, CNN—COME NOW.

—From a news conference of 21 September 2004[1]

In December 2004 and January 2005, *The Dupuy Institute* presented two briefings at the Center for Army Analysis (CAA) that declared as its salient points that the insurgency in Iraq was a major insurgency, that it would last around 10 or so years, and that it may cost the U.S. 5,000 to 10,000 killed.

The U.S. began its war with Iraq on 19 March 2003, and invaded Iraq the following day, initially with 92,000 U.S. and 20,000 allied troops. By the middle of April, Iraq had been completely occupied by the United States, and the war appeared effectively over. From 15 April through 15 June 2003, the U.S. lost 58 soldiers, only 14 of them from combat.

But, things did not remain so peaceful for long. The U.S. lost 28 soldiers from combat in July 2003 and 126 in April 2004. By 31 December 2004, the war had gone on for 21 months, and U.S. casualties in the war were around 1,335 soldiers killed, 1,038 of them from combat.[2] There were 153,000 American and 25,000 allied troops deployed in Iraq at that time.[3]

Our briefings were given at CAA (Center for Army Analysis) on 28 December 2004 and again, in final form, on 31 January 2005. As of December 2011, the war had gone on for 105 months (8.7 years), and U.S. casualties had risen to 4,485 fatalities—3,436 of them from combat. Counterinsurgent forces in Iraq in December 2007 included 160,000 U.S. troops, 10,961 allied troops and 161,380 Iraq National Government troops. It only became significantly lower in 2010. Unfortunately, we feel we were pretty close to correct on this one.

In 2004 our slides further went on to estimate that the insurgent force strength was probably between 20,000 to 60,000 full and part-time insurgents. While we stated that is was a major insurgency, we did note that it was of medium intensity. This was relative to other insurgencies in our data base. We noted that U.S. commitment can be expected to be relatively steady throughout this insurgency and will not be quickly replaced by indigenous forces.

We had additional operational caveats, in that we assumed no major new problems in the Shiite majority area. We also noted that we considered the insurgency to be a regional or factionalized insurgency and that it must remain that way (emphasis was in the original briefing). A copy of this briefing slide is provided in Appendix I.

This effort began with a contract awarded on 24 August 2004. *The Dupuy Institute* had four months to come up with a reasonable and analytically-sound casualty estimate for a developing insurgency. This had not been done before in the analytical community.[4]

The Dupuy Institute's methodology, as always, is first focused on data collection. If we were going to create an estimate, it was going to be based upon something tangible. Before we could estimate casualties, we had to achieve some understanding of the basic nature of insurgencies, and where Iraq fit relative to them.

The Dupuy Institute compiled data on 28 post-World War II insurgencies to serve as the basis for our analysis. These cases included not only large and famous insurgencies like Vietnam, Algeria and Indochina but also many smaller and more obscure cases. They were selected based on five requirements: 1) the conflict must have been post-World War II; 2) it had to have lasted more than a year (as was already the case in Iraq); 3) it had to be a developed nation intervening in a developing nation; 4) the intervening nation had to be supporting or establishing an indigenous government (which also provided troops—in this case the indigenous government could also be a colonial government); and 5) there had to be an indigenous guerilla movement (although it could be receiving outside help). A few of the conflicts we selected did not entirely meet the criteria, but at least we had a good starting point. There were only a few post-World War II conflicts meeting the criteria that were not selected.

A few simple initial cuts at the data yielded some truly frightening trends. First, we looked at the area, in square kilometers, of the countries in which the insurgencies occurred and compared that to the outcomes of the insurgency. Using our 28 cases, we found that when insurgencies occurred in small countries, the insurgents won only 14% of the time. In medium-size countries, they only won 43% of the time. In large countries, they won 71% of time. Now, this result got our attention for a few reasons. First, it is rare with social science or historical data to get clear, obvious patterns than imply a cause-and-effect relationship. Second, it raised the question as to whether there was a cause-and-effect relationship. Third, Iraq was a large country! Fourth, and oddest of all, we were not aware of anyone else finding this obvious correlation, which took us only one evening to ferret out.

Encouraged with this first result, we continued down this path, looking at population versus winner, population density versus winner, border area versus winner, type of government of intervening force on winning and duration, degree of outside support on winning and duration, the political concept behind the insurgency on winning and duration, orderly versus disorderly insurgencies on winning and duration, intervening force size versus winner, counterinsurgency force size versus winner, insurgent force size versus winner, casualty rates versus winner, force ratio versus winner, and duration versus winner.

This only took a couple of weeks and startled us not only with our results but also in that we were able to get clear results so easily. We scheduled our first briefing with the government less than a month after the contract had been awarded. That turned out to be the morning after the Labor Day weekend, with the expected contingent of sleepy senior analysts and military officers. By the time we had gone through the data that was later used to create this chart, we had their attention.

One of our briefing slides showed ten factors and rated each low, medium or high. They were country area, population, border length, outside support, political concept, orderliness, intervening force size, insurgent force size, casualty rate, and force ratios. We then divided our 28 cases into each of the three categories based upon their values. From there we calculated what percent of those cases the insurgents won. For example we had seven countries with an area of 9,250 to 131,940 square kilometers. In those seven cases, the insurgents won once (or 14% of the cases). For countries with an area of 162,460 to 212,380 (what we categorized as our medium case), the insurgents won 43% of the time (again only seven cases). For those countries with an area of 290,079 to 2,381,740 (our high case), the insurgents won 71% of the time (14 cases). Iraq fell into the "high" category, meaning that among our data set, it was categorized as a large country.

Now, does this mean that if you fight an insurgency in a large country, you have a 71% chance of losing? No. What it means is that in the 14 cases in which we had a cuntry that we defined as "large," the insurgents won in 10. This is cold comfort.

The data on population gets harsher. In the seven cases in which insurgencies were fought in countries with a population of 9,529,000 or higher, the insurgents won in all seven cases! The population of Iraq at the time was around 24,000,000. The same situation showed up concerning border length.

So we broke out each of the ten factors into three categories. This created the following chart based upon the percent of insurgent wins among the cases in each category:

CATEGORY	LOW	MEDIUM	HIGH
Country Area	14%	43%	71%
Population	27	40	100
Border Length	18	63	78
Outside Support	56	54	33
Political Concept	0	75	50
Orderliness	73	36	33
Intervening Force Size	50	39	71
Insurgency Force Size	22	47	86
Casualty Rate	40	86	50
Force Ratios	0	66	47

We then compared where Iraq stood in comparison to these 28 cases. In the case of country area, it was in the high category, where in 71% of the cases the insurgents had won. In case of population, it was also in the highest category, where in all cases the insurgents won. In the case of border length, it fell in between the medium and high category. As these had 63% and 78% of the cases ending with insurgent victory, this also was not encouraging. Looking at only these three geographic comparisons, this did not look positive for the U.S. counterinsurgency operations in Iraq (see Appendix I for copy of briefing slide).

The same negative outlook was provided with the factors that looked at force strength and force ratios. In those cases where the intervening force size was greater than 95,000, the insurgents won in 71% of those cases. We had well over 100,000 troops in Iraq, and it was proving not to be enough. In those cases where the insurgent force size was greater than 50,000, the insurgents won in 86% of the cases. We had estimated 20,000 to 60,000 insurgents based upon their level of activity. The U.S. also fell in the medium category for casualty rate and the medium category for force ratios. In both of these cases, this was the worst category to be in.

We looked three more conceptual measures, degree of outside some (rated as primarily indigenous, some outside support and considerable outside support), political concept of the insurgency (rated as limited developed political thought, central political idea and overarching idea), and the orderliness of the insurgency (rated as disorderly, directed and orderly). Again, Iraq fell into the worst category in two of those three comparisons.

In nine of the ten categories, Iraq fell into the worst category. As one colonel sitting at the table said, "This is a hell of a briefing to wake up to after a long weekend."[5]

Still, one can go too far in assuming the worst here. Correlation is not causation. Like any complex social science problem, there are a wide variety of effects that could be interacting to create such a result and most likely there were. It was going to take more time, effort and examples to say much on the subject with authority. However, from the initial limited data collection (and limited analysis), we provided them with ten telling points:

1. It is difficult to control large countries
2. It is difficult to control large populations
3. It is difficult to control an extended land border

In retrospect, this seems obvious. At the time, September 2004, the administration was still talking about the effort in Iraq as pretty much just cleaning up a bunch of "dead-enders."[6] The U.S. Army (or perhaps more correctly, the Bush administration) had deliberately gone in with limited force and with no intention of remaining for a long time.

4. "Limited outside support" does not doom an insurgency
5. "Disorderly" insurgencies are very intractable and often successful insurgencies (for example the USSR in Afghanistan)
6. Insurgencies with a large intervening forces (above 95,000) are often successful insurgencies
7. Higher combat intensities do not doom an insurgency.

Now, these next four points require some explanation. *The Dupuy Institute* had to decide what the degree of outside support for an insurgency was. There was an impression, based upon the U.S. experience in Vietnam, that the really dangerous insurgencies were the ones that had a Ho Chi Minh trail running through hundreds of miles of jungles with a steady flow of trucks and people coming down it.[7] This is learning from a single example. The rest of the world provides a very different story than what one might derive from studying that one case.

For example, in our 28 cases, those insurgencies that we coded as "primarily indigenous" were winning more often than not, while the ones that were coded as having "considerable outside support" were winning just one-third of the time. This is counter-intuitive. It does not mean that providing more support to an insurgency weakens it. But, it does mean that an insurgency that does not have the equivalent of a Ho Chi Minh trail is still a problem to be taken seriously. At the time, the administration kept repeating that Iraq is not Vietnam.[8] This was true. This did not mean that it was not a serious problem.

The discussion of "disorderly" insurgencies again harkens back to the lessons that were learned or learned incorrectly from Vietnam. In Vietnam, we faced an insurgency that was centrally commanded and centrally controlled. It had a military structure and a parallel over-watching political structure. It was about as tightly controlled and commanded as any major insurgency has been. In Iraq, in September 2004, we did not really know who we were even fighting, let alone if there was something that began to resemble a central command. So, to attempt to address this dichotomy, we came up with three poorly-chosen terms to describe the range of organization: these were orderly, directed, and disorderly.

Orderly insurgencies have a military-like structure or communist party-type structure. They are tightly-structured, highly-disciplined, obedient to rules of behavior, conduct, and the chain of command. Examples are the various communist-led insurgencies in Indochina, and those with a clear military-like structure throughout their organization.

Directed insurgencies or centrally-directed are insurgencies with clear leadership and direction but without the disciplined command structure of a communist-led and/or a militarily-based insurgency. In some instances, locally-raised and led units acknowledge central command of their actions, but may also act independently.

Disorderly insurgencies, which invariably include those with multiple factions, are insurgencies that are either multi-faceted, with many commanders or no clearly predominant commander, or which exhibit a lack of organizational discipline, as for example Afghanistan versus the Soviet Union or the Mau Mau revolt. They were often characterized by intra-factional or inter-factional conflict.

Now, the first interesting point to make about these 28 cases is that disorderly insurgencies were the most common type of insurgency. It made up 11 of our cases. These are almost the norm. Highly structure insurgencies ("orderly") like Vietnam were the exception. The other interesting point is that the insurgents won 73% of the disorderly cases!

A good example of one of these "disorderly" insurgencies was that of the Afghan mujahedeen versus the Soviet Union from 1979–1989. The Afghan insurgents functioned in at least ten major factions. Seven of them were nominally allied and under control of a Peshawar-based council. Three major Shiite factions operated outside the control of that council. Within the council, the factions were divided by ethnicity, politics and some good old-fashioned feuding. The factions occasionally engaged each other during the insurgency, sometimes independently organized ceasefires with the Soviet Union or the Afghan government, and openly warred against each other once the Soviet Union pulled out. Obviously, the lack of a single central command did not undercut the insurgency to the point where it was not effective. I suspect if that was the case, then they would have felt the need to organize better. A disorderly insurgency can be very dangerous and hard to suppress.

Point number six, insurgencies with a large intervening forces (above 95,000) are often successful insurgencies, is one of considerable controversy and not one that I think has been fully or properly explored. In the 28 cases we looked at, larger insurgencies tended to win. It did not matter whether this was measured by size of the intervening force, size of the counterinsurgent force, or size of the insurgent force. If these forces were large, the insurgencies tended to win. More specifically, insurgencies with an intervening force size of 95,000 or higher (of which we had seven cases) won 71% of the time. Those insurgencies with an insurgent force size of 50,000 or higher (also seven cases) won 86% of the time. This does not mean that the size of the force led to the insurgency winning. The virulence of the insurgency may have been factor that led to both its size and its success. But, it is an interesting correlation.

There is talk in the analytical community that sometimes the size of the intervening force fuels the insurgency.[9] We don't know the basis for this. We haven't seen any analysis that establishes such a cause-and-effect relationship. Still, this statement continues to be repeated. It was stated by people attending our briefings in 2004 and 2005. While the data appear to support this supposition, we feel it is still basically unsupported, and we do not think that it is a major factor in determining the success or failure of an insurgency. Still, people grabbed onto that point often in our briefings.

Point number seven we will gloss over for now. The relationship between casualty intensity and outcome is one that we will explore in depth later. For this estimate, it was not an issue other than that we were comfortable that the loss rates we were seeing in Iraq were not a primary driver of the outcome.

Finally, three more points remained from our briefing. They all turned out to be significant. As our research continued past the original Iraq estimate, these points became the focus of a lot of our subsequent analysis. They were:

8. What is the insurgent political concept: is it "limited developed political thought" or is it based upon a "central political idea?"
9. What is the insurgent force size: is it above 20,000 insurgents?
10. What is the influence of Force Ratios and how should they be measured

The political concept of an insurgency was a set of definitions we created to answer a specific question. The original question came from reviewing articles that were examining Al-Qaeda as an insurgent group with an overarching concept, much like the early internationalist communist revolutionaries almost 100 years ago. This raised the question, are such ideologically-motivated, overarching insurgencies particularly dangerous? The U.S. had faced communist insurgencies before (like Vietnam) and had found them particularly tough. Were these ideologically-based insurgencies, as some form of revolutionary warfare, the most dangerous insurgent foes?

The short answer is no, they are not. The most dangerous insurgencies are those fueled by good old-fashioned nationalism. We created three definitions for what we referred to as political concept. Political concept is a description of the overall political concept behind the insurgency, although not necessarily the politics of the insurgency. These were limited developed political thought, central political idea and overarching idea.

Limited developed political thought means a regional or factional insurgency. It is an insurgency that is fundamentally confined to a specific faction or region. Factional insurgencies develop as a conflict over which person, tribe, religion, or political party will rule. It is not a rebellion fueled by a revolutionary idea, and the real differences in policy between the factions are either not clear, not significantly different, or not fundamentally the basis of the insurgency.

Central political idea usually means nationalism. These are insurgencies fueled by nationalism in its various forms (for example, anti-colonialism, anti-occupation and all the diverse independence movements), other "isms" and "antis," or any other similar centrally-themed (for example, anti-Christian) movement. Other examples, not necessarily nationalistic, are broad insurrectionary manifestations of the popular will, like jacqueries of revolutionary France.

Finally, there is the overarching idea, the basis for insurgencies characterized by a well-developed body of political thought (exegesis or catechism) that constitutes the revolutionary mantra. In the cases we dealt with, this meant communism, but it could apply easily to any well-developed religiously- or politically-based movement.

What our data from the 28 cases showed was that insurgencies based upon nationalism or anti-colonialism won 75% of the time. Those that were overarching in nature won only half the time. Most of those cases had a strong component of nationalism or anti-colonialism in them (for example in Vietnam). Those insurgencies that we coded as fundamentally regional or factional did not win at all!

This appeared to be the critical dichotomy. If an insurgency was broadly based, it was dangerous. If it was not broadly based, it was much easier to defeat. This led to the following statements:

1. If the insurgency in Iraq is (and remains) a factional or regionally based rebellion, the based upon our 8 other examples, it should fail. (in bold in the original briefing).
2. If Iraq is (or becomes) a nationalist revolt against intervening powers, then based upon 15 examples, it should succeed.
3. Therefore, the critical issue here: is the U.S. facing a regionally and factionally based insurgency in Iraq or facing a widespread anti-intervention insurgency?

This was the big open question: What is the basis for the Iraqi insurgency? Was it regional or factional or was it a wide-spread nationalist or anti-interventionist insurgency? It appeared at the time to be regional or factional. The fact that it was regional or factional turned out to be part of the lever that generated the favorable results in Iraq as part of the "surge" strategy in 2007. Whether any of this came about as a result of our studies and analyses, I don't know, but I think not. Still, this was a salient point in our Iraq brief and was the one point of optimism throughout the brief. It also became a major focus of our understanding and analysis of insurgencies.[10]

The next point was asking about the size of the insurgency. At the time we were providing these briefings, the Department of Defense (DoD) was saying the strength of the insurgency in Iraq was 5,000.[11] Based upon the number of incidents, the number of U.S. troops being killed and the size of the some of the operations the insurgents were conducting, we knew that this could not be right. It did not take a sophisticated analysis to look at the number of counterinsurgents killed or the number of violent incidents that occurred in other historical insurgencies as compared to the number of insurgents they had, and determine that something was amiss with the DoD public estimate. For the Iraqis to be able to maintain that level of violence with only 5,000 insurgents meant that they were either the most motivated and competent insurgents in modern history, or there were a whole lot more of them than 5,000 of them.

We cut the data many different ways, but what the historical data showed was that insurgents rarely achieve an activity rate of more than one violent reported incident per insurgent per year! This seems very low, but is what the data shows. Of course, insurgents included full-time insurgents, part-time insurgents, support personnel and some people who are doing it very casually. Still, in insurgencies like Algeria, they were generating tens of thousands incidents a year with tens of thousands of insurgents. At their peak (1956–1958), they were killing over 2,000 French soldiers a year, and the French were reporting more than 20,000 incidents a year, and were estimating there were 20,000 to 50,000 insurgents. In 2004, as we were doing this study, the level of violence in September ballooned to 2,368 incidents in one month and 87 U.S. and coalition troops killed, including 69 U.S. and 5 coalition troops killed in combat.

Continued at this rate would generate something like 28,416 incidents a year and 1,044 U.S. and coalition killed a year. This was being done by 5,000 insurgents? Based upon historical examples, this was an absurd proposition. It is clear that we were looking at an insurgency in excess of 20,000. And, if it is in excess of 20,000, then were these really just a collection of "dead-enders?" The statements from the administration had taken on an air of comical absurdity.

We developed our estimates of insurgent strength by working backwards from the historical data of other insurgencies. We looked at the total number of blue forces killed and the number of incidents reported in these other cases as compared to their reported, sometimes estimated, insurgent strength. For example, for each of the 28 insurgencies, we looked at the number of insurgents compared to the number of counterinsurgents killed so as to end up with a rate of counterinsurgents killed per thousand insurgents. Comparing that to the number of U.S. troops being killed in Iraq produced the following estimates depending on which war was being examined:

1. From Vietnam data: 8,472 to 13,464 insurgents
2. From Malaya and Algeria data: 12,567 to 25,133 insurgents
3. From the list of 25 other insurgencies: 19,842 to 145,000
4. Based upon the average rate for the 28 insurgencies: 48,645

All these numbers are larger than 5,000. The Vietnam data is probably not the best comparison. It is clear that this data is pointing to a figure of 20,000 to 50,000 or more insurgents.

We then did the same analysis looking at number of incidents report (as reported by the counterinsurgents) compared to insurgent strength. Again working backwards and comparing it to the Iraq data, we were looking at 35,632 to 89,080 insurgents if based upon the Iraq incident data from February 2004 to January 2005. But, the Iraq insurgency had ramped up following Fallujah, so if one looked at the incident data from September 2004 to January 2005, it was 61,107 to 152,767 insurgents.

These two different estimated, based upon two different sets of data and two different comparisons, let us to conclude that the Iraq insurgency at this point was between 20,000 to 60,000. We did not, nor could not, parse the insurgents into those that were "full-time" or "core" insurgents, versus "part-time" and "support." This was data derived from multiple sources, based upon multiple definitions that were in many cases simply a good estimate. It was not precise, but it appears to be accurate.

The key point is that the insurgent force size was from 20,000 to 60,000. In all reality, we suspected at the time that it was towards the high end of that range. When we based our analysis on casualties (killed) we ended up on the lower side of the estimate. When we used the more amorphous and poorly defined incident data, we ended up with the higher estimate.

How big was the Iraq insurgency? Well, the various public official estimates have never wandered much above 20,000. Figures above that seem to make people nervous. Yet, when it came time in 2006–2007 to pay off the Sunni Awakening Councils, consisting of local militias and former insurgents, the payroll was more like 65,000 and would eventually grow to more than 100,000.[12] It is clear that we were facing more than 20,000 full-time, part-time, and supporting insurgents.

And finally we tried to address the issue of force ratios. These are now discussed in depth in Chapter Four of this book. At the time we did the estimate we did not fully understand their impact. There were certain classic counterinsurgency experts (like Bernard Fall) who said they were important, and there were others that said they were not important at all. Our first cut of the data indicated to us that force ratios *did* seem to matter, especially ratios above 25-to-1. But as our original data set was only 28 cases, we could not establish that for certain. This became the focus of some of our future work.

The key interesting effect that we found was that in the 28 cases that we examined, the events were either over in the first four years, or the insurgencies dragged on for at least seven years. This was irrespective of winning or losing. There was a gap in the data between 4.5 to 7 years. We had no cases with such durations. What data showed was that the insurgencies fell into one of four categories:

1. A short successful counterinsurgency of 1,037 days (2.8 years) in length (7 cases)

2. An extended successful counterinsurgency of 5,614 days (15.4 years) in length (7 cases)
3. An early withdrawal (unsuccessful) international of 1,555 days (4.3) in length (3 cases)
4. A typical successful insurgency of 4,256 days (11.7 years) in length (9 cases)

Therefore, for the sake of estimating the duration of an insurgency, one should determine which of these four situations apply (see briefing slide 4 in Appendix I).

This clearly was going to have an impact on our analysis. Basically, insurgencies were either over relatively quickly (less than 4.5 years in 10 of our cases), or they dragged on for an average of 12 to 15 years. Obviously, at this point, we did not consider that Iraq fit well into the quickly-to-be-resolved category. This meant that any estimate we did needed to assume a 12 to 15 year duration.

Early in this effort the U.S. reporters appeared. The contract was issued as a sole source effort, since we happened to have been the only organization that had done anything like this before (see our Bosnia Casualty Estimate, Appendix II). Before a sole source contract (meaning one issued without competitive bidding) can be awarded, it must be announced in the Commerce Business Daily. Our contract was duly listed by the government, along with considerable detail pulled directly from our proposal. At the time, of course, one of the ongoing controversies were the much, much larger sole source contracts being awarded to companies like Halliburton, which Vice President Dick Cheney used to head. With modern search engines, any sole source announcement of a contract on Iraq was going to be noticed by the press. Sure enough, our sole source announcement was spotted, and was, of course, very much out of the ordinary. So, before the contract was even awarded, we started receiving calls from *USA Today*, *Newsweek*, etc. This, of course, was not exactly welcomed in the quiet backwaters that make up the U.S. defense analytical community, although as a private contractor, *The Dupuy Institute* appreciated the free advertising. There was not much we could tell them, as we had yet to do any actual work.[13]

Being professionally persistent, various reporters continued to call us over the years, and this finally resulted in our first article addressing the subject of duration in *USA Today* that stated in May 2007 that insurgencies lasted an average of 10 years.[14] If one takes the average of the cases in the viewgraph above, one can see where such a figure would come from. The real figure was 12–15 years based upon the extended cases. In fact, we had done a little additional analysis that looked at duration by type of event that ended up serving as the basis for this figure.[15] It was a conservative figure that was not controversial, as similar figures had already been batted around in the press from multiple sources over the last two years, including a figure of 7–12 years in February 2005 by JCS Chairman Richard Myers.[16] The following month, General Petraeus, the commander in Iraq, issued out a similar figure.[17]

Getting back to the work at hand, what the above chart told us was that we were going to be in Iraq at least 10 years, and any estimate should probably be based upon that. It was also the average of all 28 cases (including the shorter cases). Good enough, ten is a nice, round, easy number to work with.

The next big question was how to forecast changes in the environment. For example, do casualty rates remain the same throughout the duration of an insurgency? Does the intensity of combat remain the same year after year? Are force levels a constant year after year?

Well, we could produce a wide range of estimates depending on the assumptions we made, but we did have some history to go by. We could go through our 28 cases and see if their casualties changed over time, and we could see if the force strengths changed over time. This effort generated the following conclusions:

1. There is a tendency for Counterinsurgency casualties to be steady or steadily increasing.
2. There is a strong tendency for Counterinsurgency force strength to be steady or steadily increasing.

The first conclusion, we simply looked at the pattern of casualties across the 28 cases. In three cases, the counterinsurgent casualties peaked early in the insurgency, in one case (the Vietnam War) they peaked much later. In four cases they remained steady over the course of the war, and in 10 cases they increased over the course of the war. We did have five cases where they steadily decreased and five cases where we had yet to collect enough data. Still with the data we had, we had 16 cases of late peak, steady or steadily increasing counterinsurgent casualties, vice 8 cases of early peak or steadily decreasing.

The case was stronger with force strength where we have only one case of an early peak,[18] one later peak (again Vietnam), 5 cases of steady state, 20 cases of increasing,

---

SALIENT POINTS

- Insurgent force strength is probably between 20,000–60,000
- This is a major insurgency
  - It is of medium intensity
- It is a regional or factionalized insurgency and **must** remain that way
- US commitment can be expected to be relatively steady throughout this insurgency and will not be quickly replaced by indigenous forces
- It will last around 10 or so years
- It may cost the U.S. 5,000 to 10,000 killed
  - It may be higher
  - This assumes no major new problems in the Shiite majority areas

and one unknown. Effectively, in almost all cases, the intervening force strength remained the same or grew larger over the course of the insurgency.

This is again significant and surprising. It is significant because it clearly showed that rarely does intervening force strength decline during an insurgency and rarely are insurgents quickly brought under control. It is surprising that no one had bothered to do this analysis before. Still, it was hard to collect all the data needed for this analysis in the brief time available, but we were certainly able to collect enough to establish a clear trend.

With only a few cases of insurgencies peaking in violence and activity early, and with each of these cases fairly easy to understand and explain, and with very few cases of significant force decline during an insurgency, then it is clear we were now on very safe ground to take the existing casualties over the last year and simply straight line them out for ten years, under the assumption of steady casualty rates and steady force strength.

This was a fairly straightforward process, soundly based upon analysis of historical data. More than anything else, the data was used to make sure that we had a good understanding of the nature of insurgencies. It was from this understanding that we were able to assemble a casualty estimate.

This resulted in the following chart (also see Appendix I):

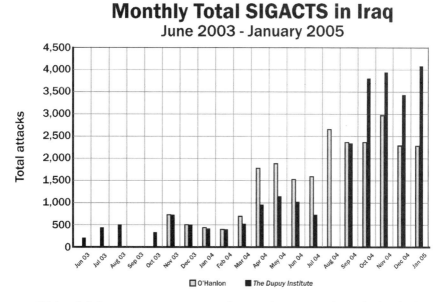

We briefed this estimate on 28 December 2004. We were then asked to look at "tipping points." The buzz inside the Pentagon was that the Iraq insurgency had reached a tipping point and that the elections in January would turn things around.[19]

At the time, the violence was soaring. It had been increasing steadily throughout the last half of 2003 and first half of 2004, and then went shooting skyward in September. That much higher level of violence continued throughout the rest of the year. Below is a chart we created at the time showing incidents up through January 2005. It records both the data we were receiving informally directly from the field and that recorded by Michael O'Hanlon of the Brookings Institution.[20] The data we were receiving informally from the field was producing higher counts than the Brookings Institution data. (See preceding chart.)

To believe that this insurgency was suddenly going to turn around because of elections seemed very Pollyanna-ish, but as the chairman was claiming it, we were asked to look into it. In the case of elections, the analysis was very simple. We just looked at the 12 cases where there were elections out of the 28 cases we had. We then determined if there were any significant changes in violence or activity soon after the elections. We did not see a single case of this. Of significance, the government of South Vietnam held several elections during the Vietnam War. In 4 of the 12 cases where elections occurred that we looked at, the insurgents won the war! So, at least in the short-term, the impact of elections seemed nil.21 Needless to say, the elections in January 2005 did not tip the insurgency towards a quick resolution.

This revised version of the briefing, as partly shown in Appendix I, was presented from January through March 2005 to various people inside the Army and the Department of Defense. As far as we know, the briefing never went to decision-making levels in the defense community.

Part of the reason this briefing did not travel higher was that many of the analysts and managers inside DoD didn't really believe the results. There were several reasons for this. In some cases, government analysts simply decided that there were too many "colonial wars of national liberation" and that this biased our results. In other cases, they assumed that the Iraq army would quickly take over the war and our losses would be considerably less than 5,000 killed. Some were concerned about publicizing the results due to official announcements having been made and this study clearly not being in line with those announcements. We disagreed with these assessments, but in the end, we were only a contractor and our task was to provide the best data and analysis we could to help and support their decision making.

As of December 2011, the U.S. had lost 4,485 troops, the UK had lost 180 troops, and our other allies have lost 139. Contractors (a mix of nationalities) had lost at least 468, and the Iraqi Army and police had lost at least 10,125. This is total of at least 15,397 among the counterinsurgent forces.[22] The U.S. part of war effectively ended mid-December 2011, after having continued for almost 105 months (8.7 years). This was well within the range of our estimates. The war still continues as of the time of this writing.

Instead of reworking and refining the estimates we had developed in January 2005, we were contracted to take the data we used and put them in a spread sheet format for the government to use. This data was later used for the much of the subsequent analysis provided in this book. Unfortunately, we were not asked to expand our effort to look at Afghanistan.

NOTES

1. The complete quote is: "Oh, CNN—come now. Look, General [John] Abizaid just gave a presentation up there to the United States Senate that was powerful—and it is that we are up against a very serious collection of enemies, terrorists, extremists, people who use terrorism as their weapon of choice, people who've cut off people's heads. And the task that the moderate people in this world who are being opposed by the extremists, the task we have is to deal with them wherever they are, and it will take time. I think anyone who pulls a number out of midair and says it'll take one year, or five years, or 10 years, must have mystical powers that most people don't have." From news transcript, U.S. Defense Department, Office of the Assistant Secretary of Defense (Public Affairs), 21 Sept. 2004.

2. These are the total losses during 19 Mar. 2003–31 Dec. 2004. We record 130 killed in the conventional phase of the war (19 Mar.–14 Apr. 2003), of which 27 were non-combat or due to illness. For our coalition allies, we record from 19 Mar. 2003–31 Dec. 2004, a total of 151 killed, of which 113 were from combat. In the conventional phase of the war, we record 31 allied troops killed, of which 27 were from combat.

3. The troop strength data is drawn from the Dupuy Insurgency Spread Sheets (DISS), a database of 109 post-World War II insurgencies, interventions and peacekeeping operations.

4. Interestingly, only limited estimates of expected losses and levels of commitment were done during the Vietnam War. Some estimates were done by the senior commanders, but nothing was soundly, analytically based. General Paul D. Harkins, the commander in Vietnam from 1962 to 1964, once predicted victory in one-and-a-half years. Once the decision was made to commit troops in 1965, General William C. Westmoreland, who replaced Harkins in June 1964, had a three-phase plan that in effect predicted victory in three to three-and-a-half years using 300,000 troops. This meant by the end of 1968. Secretary of Defense Robert McNamara in a July 1965 memorandum provided President Johnson with the following estimate: "U.S. killed-in-action might be in the vicinity of five hundred a month by the end of the year." One could extrapolate that this was an estimate of 18,000 killed for the war.

   In November of 1965, the U.S. lost 545 killed and missing from all causes, and over the course of the war, which continued for the U.S. until Jan. 1973, the U.S. lost over 58,000 killed and missing.

   McNamara's memorandum of 30 November 1965, indicated that "U.S. killed-in-action can be expected to reach 1,000 a month and the odds are even that we will be faced in early 1967 with a `no-decision' at an even higher level." This was in response to troop requests from Westmoreland that were now up to 400,000 by the end of 1966, and it was anticipated that he might ask for more than 200,000 additional troops in 1967.

   In Jan. 1966, Marine Corps General Victor Krulak did a back of the envelope calculation and determined that the current attrition strategy would require the loss of 10,000 Americans and 165,000 South Vietnamese soldiers to achieve a 20 percent reduction in the North Vietnamese and Viet Cong manpower pool. This served as part of an argument for a policy of "pacification" vice "attrition."

See Neil Sheehan, *A Bright Shining Lie: John Paul Vann and American in Vietnam* (London: Picador, 1990), 554, 568–569, 579, 613, 630.

One of the more accurate predictions at the time was made by Clark Clifford in a meeting with President Johnson at Camp David in July 1965 when he told him: "I can picture us, Mr President, going into a ground war and losing more than 50,000 troops and still not being able to win the war." Quote is from the interview with Clark Clifford for the show "Iron Curtain, Episode 2" at http://www.gwu.edu/~nsarchiv/coldwar/interviews/ episode-2/clifford3.html. We do not believe this statement was based upon any analysis.

5.   This quote is from memory and perhaps not exact, but it captures the sentiment of the moment.

6.   As late as May 2005, Vice President Cheney was referring to the insurgents as a collection of dead-enders.

7.   The Ho Chi Minh trail was the name of a series of paths through the jungle that started in North Vietnam, moved through Laos and Cambodia and ended in South Vietnam. It was a major supply conduit for the insurgents in South Vietnam, and more supply was moved down this path than had been for any insurgency in history. Toward the end of the war, the "trail" had considerable paved sections, multi-lane highways, and regular truck convoys.

8.   For example, in a Pentagon Briefing on 30 June 2003, Secretary of Defense Donald Rumsfeld stated: "*There are so many cartoons where people, press people, are saying, 'Is it Vietnam yet?' hoping it is and wondering if it is. And it isn't. It's a different time. It's a different era. It's a different place.*"

9.   For example, see *USA Today* (3 Aug. 2005), "U.S. laying groundwork for Iraq pullout," and *The Seattle Times* (Oct. 1, 2005), "Top Generals say U.S. troops' presence may fuel insurgency." This includes a quote from General George Casey, the U.S. commander in Iraq at that time, that troop reductions were required to "take away one of the elements that fuels the insurgency, that of the coalition forces as an occupying force."

10.   For which, see Chapter Six.

11.   The original estimate of 5,000 insurgents was provided in Nov. 2003 by General John Abizaid, the U.S. senior commander in the Middle East at that time. He confirmed in Apr. 2004, that this estimate was still good. This estimate remained unchanged, even though it was being questioned in July 2004. It was revised to 13,000–17,000 insurgents in Feb. 2005. See *Los Angeles Times* (Nov. 14, 2003), "U.S. commander: Coalition 'in control',"; *USA Today* (12 Apr. 2004), "U.S. needs help of former senior Iraqi military, commanders say"; *Associated Press* (9 July 2004), "Iraq insurgency larger than once thought: Anti-U.S. forces may be as large as 20,000, U.S. officials say," (although the article does not quote any official by name); and Barbara Starr, "Official: 13,000–17,000 insurgents in Iraq," *CCN.com* (9 Feb. 2005).

12.   See Chapter Twenty-Two for a more detailed discussion of these figures.

13.   The articles specifically referencing our contracts at that time included Mark Thompson, "How Long a War? Let's Ask," *Time Magazine* (16 Aug. 2004) and Jim Michaels and Charles Crain, "Insurgents showing no sign of letting up," *USA Today* (22 Aug. 2004).

14.   Jim Michaels, "Study: Insurgencies like Iraq's usually fail in 10 years," *USA Today* (May 9, 2007).

15.   See Chapter Sixteen for discussion of duration by type of event.

16.   "Top U.S. general sees lasting Iraq insurgency," *Reuters* (26 Feb. 2005), stating: "Air Force General Richard Myers say that in the past century, insurgencies around the world have

lasted anywhere from seven to 12 years, making a quick fix to the problem in Iraq unlikely."

17. See Mark Kukis, "Can Counter-insurgency Succeed?" *Time Magazine* (18 June 2007)
and "US Iraq chief warns of long war" *BBC News* (9 July 2007). Petraeus's quotes were:
"In fact, typically, I think historically, counter-insurgency operations have gone at least
nine or 10 years;" and, "I don't know whether this will be decades, but the average counterinsurgency is somewhere around a nine or a 10-year endeavor."

18. This was Malaya and this conclusion was probably not a good representation of the situation. There was an early peak from various militia and home defense forces being temporarily enlisted, but the core regular UK, allied and Malaysian troops remained relatively
constant in strength though most of the war.

19. For example, in early Feb. 2005, SecDef Rumsfeld was quoted as saying, " . . . [T]he
voting may have marked a 'tipping point' at which Iraqis who had been intimidated by
the insurgents decide to step forward and join the army or other security force or provide
useful information to U.S. forces." See "Rumsfeld: Election may embolden Iraqis to fight
insurgents," *USA Today* (3 Feb. 2005).

20. This discrepancy in the various counts of incidents was later noted in the Iraq Study
Group Report. The report notes that: "In addition, there is significant underreporting
of the violence in Iraq. The standard for recording attacks acts as filter to keep events
out of reports and databases. A murder of an Iraqi is not necessarily counted as an attack.
If we cannot determine the source of a sectarian attack, that assault does not make it into
the database. A roadside bomb or a rocket or mortar attack that doesn't hurt U.S. personnel doesn't count. For example, on one day in July 2006 there were 93 attacks or significant acts of violence reported. Yet a careful review of the reports for that single day
brought to light 1,100 acts of violence. Good policy is difficult to make when information
is systematically collected in a way that minimizes its discrepancy with policy goals. . . .
*Recommendation 78: The Director of National Intelligence and the Secretary of Defense should
also institute immediate changes in the collection of data about violence and the sources of violence in Iraq to provide a more accurate picture of events on the ground."* From James A.
Baker, III, et al., *The Iraq Study Group Report: The Way Forward—A New Approach* (New
York: Vintage Books, 2006), 94–95.

21. See Appendix I for our concluding slide on tipping points

22. Data drawn from our charts and from the Iraq Coalition Casualty Count at icasulaties.
org. Our figures for UK losses are one higher, a non-battle casualty, than icasualties.org
counts.

CHAPTER 2

The Art and Science of Counterinsurgency Warfare[1]

As I have shown, I was unfortunately as much in command of the campaign as I pleased, and was untrained. In military theory I was tolerably read, my Oxford curiosity having taken me past Napoleon to Clausewitz and his school, to Caemmerer and Moltke, and the recent Frenchmen. They had all seemed to be one-sided; and after looking at Jomini and Willisen, I had found broader principles in Saxe and Guibert and the eighteenth century. However, Clausewitz was intellectually so much the master of them, and his book so logical and fascinating, that unconsciously I accepted his finality, until a comparison of Kuhne and Foch disgusted me with soldiers, wearied me of their officious glory, making me critical of all their light. In any case, my interest had been abstract, concerned with the theory and philosophy of warfare especially from the metaphysical side.

—T. E. Lawrence in *Seven Pillars of Wisdom*[2]

The modern study of conventional military art in the west almost seems to have started with Clausewitz. Since it was published in 1832, after the Napoleonic Wars, we have a complete cohesive universally read body of work of the art and science of ground warfare. While it is not the first such attempt to understand the nature of war,[3] it is now the common point where almost all military theorists start their analysis from.

It is from that point that people either agree or diverge or further develop ideas. Still, there is not a Clausewitz school and an anti-Clausewitz school. There is no anti-Clausewitz school. This almost 200-year old work is accepted as it is and from that point, many other theoretical works have developed including J.F.C. Fuller, Liddell Hart, and Trevor N. Dupuy. Even the most recent works developing the ideas of a revolution in military affairs begin with Clausewitz. This is convenient, because in the case of conventional war, it at least provides a basis with which to frame the theoretical debate.

No such universally accepted work exists for counterinsurgent warfare or for guerilla warfare. While guerilla warfare is a very old concept, discussing the art and strategy behind it is not. In all reality, the starting point for such literature has been Colonel C. E. Callwell's Small Wars: Their Principles & Practice, first published in 1896.

EARLY INSURGENCY THEORISTS

Clausewitz and his contemporary, Antoine-Henri Baron de Jomini, were the first modern theorists to view insurgency and counterinsurgency as a natural consequence of rising nationalism, the growing industrialism of the western world, and the "nation at arms" created by the French Revolution. They did so at the end of the Napoleonic Wars, which witnessed extensive insurgent and partisan warfare, from the peasants of the French counterrevolutionary Vendée and Chouans, to the Tyrolean irregulars of Andreas Hofer, the *ordenanzas* of Portugal, and the Cossacks of Russia, and of course the eponymous guerillas of Spain.

Clausewitz approached the question of insurgency and counterinsurgency from a purely military point of view; they were only an adjunct to conventional operations and were simply a phenomena of the "nation at arms" and *levee en masse* that had characterized Napoleonic warfare, rather than a separate and unique form of warfare, distinct from conventional warfare.

> *To be realistic, one must therefore think of a general insurrection within the framework of a war conducted by the regular army, and coordinated in one all-encompassing plan . . . [Insurgent forces] are not supposed to pulverize the core but to nibble at the shell and around the edges.*[4]

Clausewitz also delineated a set of five conditions he believed were required to enable an insurgency to be effective.

> *The war must be fought in the interior of the country.*
> *It must not be decided by a single stroke.*
> *The theater of operations must be fairly large.*
> *The national character must be suited to that type of war.*
> *The country must be rough and inaccessible, because of mountains, or forests, marshes or the local methods of cultivation.*[5]

And he further commented that, "Without . . . regular troops to provide encouragement, the local inhabitants will usually lack the confidence and initiative to take to arms."[6] On the other hand, Clausewitz apparently gave little thought to counterinsurgency operations, remarking only that the,

. . . only answer to militia actions is the sending out of frequent escorts as protection for his convoys, and as guards on all his stopping places, bridges defiles, and the rest.[7]

Clearly Clausewitz's theory envisioned insurgency as only a sub-set and adjunct to conventional warfare, rather than as a unique form of warfare. Jomini, his contemporary, on the other hand, was less interested in theory and more interested in practical military applications. In fact, in his opening chapter he addressed one of the fundamentals of counterinsurgency and small wars in general, the "war of intervention."

. . . . When a state intervenes with only a small contingent, in obedience to treaty stipulations, it is simply an accessory, and has but little voice in the main operations; but when it intervenes as a principal party, and with an imposing force, the case is quite different.[8]

Then he categorized a second type of war, the "war of opinion."

. . . . Wars of opinion between two states belong also to the class of wars of intervention; for they result either from doctrines which one party desires to propagate among its neighbors, or from dogmas which it desires to crush, - in both cases leading to intervention. [9]

And, most interestingly, he remarked on "national wars," that he thought, "are the most formidable of all."

. . . . This name can only be applied to such as are waged against a united people, or a great majority of them, filled with a noble ardor and determined to sustain their independence; then every step is disputed, the army holds only its camp ground, its supplies can only be obtained at the point of the sword, and its convoys are everywhere threatened or captured.[10]

Jomini then, like Clausewitz, went on to discuss the effects of terrain and the advantages to the insurgent of operating in forests or mountains, and the necessity of supporting guerillas with regular troops.

Both Clausewitz and Jomini seemed more interested in describing the phenomena of guerilla war in terms of defining what it was rather than how it came about and why it was. Then for some 60 years after Jomini was first published western military nations were more occupied in actually fighting guerillas than in theorizing about fighting guerillas. Two of the largest conflicts of that period, the American Civil War (1861–1865) and the Franco-Prussian War (1870–1871) were characterized by large-scale guerilla and counter-guerilla operations and many western nations were also heavily engaged in colonial wars that would today be called counterinsurgencies (the French in North Africa, the British in India, the Indian Wars in North America, the Spanish in Cuba, and the British in South Africa, to name a few).

CHARLES CALLWELL'S SMALL WARS

The aftermath of these large and small wars was a spate of new campaign histories, but also – and most significant for our purposes—one new theoretical treatise on the art and science of warfare, the eponymous *Small Wars* by a young British Army major, Charles Callwell.[11] Most importantly, Callwell appears to have been the first modern author to devote his entire work to insurgent and counterinsurgent strategy and tactics, as well as some of the conditions that could give rise to insurgent movements. He first very succinctly defined what his "small wars" were.

> *Practically it may be said to include all campaigns other than those where opposing sides consist of regular troops. It comprises the expeditions against savages and semi-civilized races by disciplined soldiers, campaigns undertaken to suppress rebellions and guerilla warfare in all parts of the world.… Small wars are a heritage of extended empire, a certain epilogue to encroachments into lands beyond the confines of existing civilizations, and this has been so from early ages to the present time,*

Then, just as succinctly, he defined the three general classes that small war operations could fall into.

> *. . . . campaigns of conquest or annexation, campaigns for the suppression of insurrections or lawlessness or for the settlement of conquered or annexed territory, and campaigns undertaken to wipe out an insult, to avenge a wrong, or to overthrow a dangerous enemy.*

Callwell then systematically defined each and every aspect of the small wars campaign, giving specific and concrete historical examples to illustrate each of his points. His subjects included general examinations of the roles of intelligence, supply, initiative, broad strategy and tactics, and communications in small wars, as well as very specific examinations of the effects and responses to different types of terrain and the uses and limitations of specific kinds of troops.

Even more intriguingly, Callwell treated one form of small war to a very special examination, guerilla war. In his view guerilla war was the single most difficult form of warfare that a regular army could encounter.

> *. . . . guerilla warfare is a form of operations above all things to be avoided. The whole spirit of the art of conducting small wars is to strive for the attainment of decisive methods, the very essence of partisan warfare from the point of view of the enemy being to avoid decisive engagements.*

> *. . . . Guerilla warfare is what the regular armies always have to dread, and when this is directed by a leader with a genius for war, an effective campaign becomes well-nigh impossible . . .*

Although very much a product of its time and society, and now more than somewhat anachronistic in many of its chapters, Callwell's work was the first study of small wars that was more than a simple history of campaigns directed at "savages" or "peasants." However, it never achieved a significant degree of acceptance in military circles. Just three years after the first edition was published in 1896, the British were mired in the Boer War, where they repeatedly made the same mistakes highlighted in his work. And, just eleven years after the publication of his second edition incorporating the lessons of the Boer War, the world was plunged into the first of the great wars between the industrialized European nations in the twentieth century, the First World War. This war, although the largest conventional war in history at that time, generated two of the most famous guerilla or irregular troop leaders.

THOMAS E. LAWRENCE AND PAUL VON LETTOW-VORBECK

Although primarily a war "between regular troops", the First World War also witnessed two significant unconventional campaigns; that of the British Thomas E. Lawrence in Palestine and that of the German Paul von Lettow-Vorbeck in East Africa. Both men wrote postwar memoirs of their experience, of which Lawrence's became much more famous. Lawrence's elaborate memoirs were originally released in very limited publication as *Seven Pillars of Wisdom* in 1922, with a limited publication abridged version in 1926. A further abridged *Revolt in the Desert* was released for general publication in 1927 and the 1926 version was finally released to the general public after his tragic death in 1935. Lawrence's work was much more a personal, political, philosophical, and ethnological treatise than it was a study of insurgent or counterinsurgent warfare.[12] It was not a definitive work on guerilla warfare or counterinsurgency theory. However, even given those limitations, Lawrence's insightful comments and practical understanding of his subject resulted in a work of some significance.

Lettow-Vorbeck's less romantic memoir on the other hand has been nearly forgotten. It has apparently only been reprinted three times in English, in its initial English-language release in 1920, then in a later, undated second edition by the same publisher, and most recently in a 1990 facsimile reprint. Lettow-Vorbeck's campaign is not what is now defined as a "classic guerilla war," even though there were elements of such, but was a conventional operation in the face of overwhelming force. Still, this isolated conventional force made much use of guerilla tactics in his fight against overwhelming odds. He managed, despite being almost entirely cut off from outside support, to maintain an army in the field for four years, with a strength that never exceeded 14,000 men and that averaged only about 3,000, against an enemy that always heavily outnumbered him and that eventually fielded more than 160,000 men against him.

THE UNITED STATES MARINE CORPS AND THE *SMALL WARS MANUAL*

It wasn't until after the First World War that the first officially sanctioned study of small wars began in the United States when the U.S. Marine Corps began analyzing the extensive, practical experience it was receiving in the so-called "Banana Wars" in the Caribbean, Central America and Mexico during the late nineteenth and early twentieth centuries. By 1921 the *Marine Corps Gazette* was regularly publishing articles on Marine experience in counter-guerilla operations and interventions, some of which today would be termed peacekeeping operations; between 1918 and 1926 a total of 17 articles in the Gazette and the Naval Institute *Proceedings* were published on topics related to civil and military operations in Haiti and the Dominican Republic.[13]

In 1921, Major Earl H. Ellis wrote a study of the strategy and tactics then being used to combat rebels in those countries. Ellis summarized the responses utilized by conventional forces when confronted by unconventional tactics as,

- *Killing or wounding the insurgents and destroying their property;*
- *Destroying the property of aiders and abettors—that is, people felt to have helped the insurgency in some manner;*
- *Laying waste to entire areas inhabited by those friendly to rebels—the Sherman approach; and*
- *Removing and dispersing the women and children from the area of unrest, resettling them elsewhere, and then waging a campaign against the males remaining at large.*[14]

Ellis concluded that the first tactic was the most effective and that the best way to implement it was to seize the seaports by encirclement, trapping potential insurgent bands in those cities and towns, then establish fortified bases in the interior of the country that secured agricultural areas and rural market towns, and then finally by sending small mobile columns into the interior to destroy the remaining bands. This rather simplistic scenario ignored the simple fact that the first step—the encirclement of the seaports—didn't actually apply to Haiti, where the insurgent Cacos were entirely rural, and that it had little applicability to anything other than operations on Caribbean islands. Shortly after publication Ellis returned to his role as an intelligence officer and set out on his clandestine tour of the Japanese positions in Micronesia where he met a mysterious death on 12 May 1923.

In that same year Major Samuel M. Harrington published a report entitled *The Strategy and Tactics of Small Wars*. Harrington's work basically described an intervention, based upon his recent experience in the Dominican Republic. The first third was a treatise on amphibious landing operations in which cities and villages were secured, followed by a second phase in which counterinsurgency operations eliminated terrorist and outlaw bands. Harrington envisaged six steps that were required to suppress an insurgency. In the first and second steps coastal cities and towns would be secured, followed by all the major interior cities, towns and villages. In the third step the occupied country would be divided into military districts, centered on vital economic centers, such as agricultural, manufacturing, or mining areas. The fourth step was to initiate continuous, localized operations against the insurgents from the safety of the secure cities, towns and villages.

In 1923, Major C. J. Miller also wrote a detailed report on the Marine Corps experience in the Dominican Republic entitled *Diplomacy and Spurs in the Dominican Republic*. Originally considered for publication in the *Marine Corps Gazette*, it never appeared, although it was distributed throughout the Marine Corps Schools system along with Harrington's work. Miller focused on the importance of disarming the general populace, limited martial law, and censorship, analyzed the failings of the intelligence system used, and the failures in planning and coordinating operations against insurgents.

The final impetus to the production of an officially-sanctioned doctrinal work on small wars was the publication by Lt. Colonel Harold Utley of *Tactics and Technique of Small Wars*, which was serialized in the *Gazette* in 1931 and 1933. Utley synthesized much of the previous published work of Callwell, Ellis, Harrington, Miller, and also incorporated some of the views other Marine officers, including Merrit A. Edson and Evans Carlson, and borrowed liberally from some U.S. Army work, including parts of a nine-page study titled *Small Wars and Punitive Expeditions*, that was part of the U.S. Army Infantry School Curriculum for 1925–1926.[15] In 1935 the first edition of the *Marine Corps Small Wars Manual* was published under Utley's general supervision. In many ways it closely resembled Callwell's work in organization and layout and followed his practice of reinforcing points with historical vignettes.

However, Marine Corps Headquarters was not completely satisfied with the 1935 edition and in addition there was a growing dispute over the future role of the Marine Corps that was coming to a head in the late 1930s. During the 1920s and 1930s there had been an undercurrent of conflict within the Marine Corps between those who saw the Marines primary doctrinal role as being a intervention force fighting classic small wars and those who saw its role in terms of possible future major wars, where it would seize and secure bases for use by the Navy against conventional opponents. Curiously, it was the late Earl Ellis who had started the discussion of small wars in 1921 that had also become the early apostle for a Marine Corps designed for conventional amphibious operations.

In May 1939, Merritt Edson, who had just returned to Marine Corps Headquarters after a stint as operations officer with the 4th Marines in Shanghai, was directed to chair a board to review and rewrite the *Small Wars Manual*. That task was completed by early 1940 when the new edition was published, but the review and publication was overshadowed by the outbreak of war in Europe in 1939 and the continued tensions with Japan over their ongoing war in China.[16] As a result all classes on small wars subjects in the Marine Corps Schools system were cancelled in 1939 and the emphasis in the curricula increasingly turned to the attack and defense of bases and the requirements of amphibious operations. The result was that the study of small wars in the U.S. Marine Corps languished for over 20 years.

MAO TSE-TUNG'S *ON GUERILLA WARFARE*

Between the publications of the two editions of the USMC *Small Wars Manual*, another significant work on insurgency was produced, Mao Tse-Tung's *On Guerilla Warfare*, written by Mao and an unnamed set of "collaborators," as an instructional and propaganda pamphlet in 1937. Cheaply produced it was widely distributed in China and was first translated into English by a U.S. Marine Corps captain, Samuel B. Griffith, in 1940. That translation is still widely available, most recently by Dover Publications in 2005.[17] Oddly enough, one of the Marine Corps officers consulted by Utley in the publication of the 1935 edition of the *Small Wars Manual* and a colleague of Merritt Edson, who supervised publication of the 1940 edition, was Capt. Evans F. Carlson. And Carlson was actually in China as an official liaison and observer with the Communist Eighth Route Army and was well acquainted with Mao, Mao's early biographer Edgar Snow, and all the senior Chinese Communist hierarchy including Zhou Enlai and Deng Xiaopeng. However, the amount of doctrinal "cross-pollination" between the U.S. Marine Corps and the Chinese People's Liberation Army may only be speculated.

Of course from 1939 to 1945 most military theorists were preoccupied with the practical aspects of insurgency and counterinsurgency operations in the context of the Second World War. However, in 1944 and 1945 the U.S. Army did publish a number of informational articles and pamphlets on counterinsurgency operations as part of contingency planning in the event that the Germans had attempted to transition from conventional to guerilla warfare at the end of the war. And the basis for those was translations of the German counterinsurgency doctrinal manuals that had been in use during the war.

THE FIRST U.S. ARMY DOCTRINAL MANUALS
FM 31-20 AND *FM 31-21*

Then in 1949 the U.S. Army assigned Lieutenant Colonel Russell W. Volckmann, who had commanded guerilla forces in the Philippines during the war, to complete the first Army-sanctioned doctrinal document solely devoted to counterinsurgency warfare, FM 31-20.[18] Volckmann utilized his own experience, the German doctrinal work, and recent experience gained by U.S. Army advisors in Greece during its civil war (where Greek doctrine also heavily drew on German operations during the war), completing the work in September 1950 when the manuscript was rushed to Korea where the Army was encountering significant problems with Communist guerillas while conducting a conventional campaign against North Korean aggression. In February 1951, it was formally published as FM 31-20 *Operations Against Guerilla Forces*. Volckmann followed with FM 31-21 *Organization and Conduct of Guerilla Warfare* as a companion piece in October 1951.

MODERN INSURGENCY AND
COUNTERINSURGENCY THEORISTS

These three works, Mao's *On Guerilla Warfare*, FM 31-20, and FM 31-21, essentially defined doctrinal understanding on the subject of counterinsurgency and insurgency warfare until well into the 1960s in western military circles (the *Small Wars Manual* was essentially forgotten until reprinted by the U.S. Navy in 1961), although Callwell and Lawrence remained popular, especially in Britain and the Commonwealth and practical experience ruled in France. However, what quickly followed in the 1960s was a spate of theoretical studies of insurgencies that came about as a consequence of France and Britain becoming embroiled in various guerilla wars with mixed success. These include works by Trinquier, Galula, Fall, and Clutterbuck and are the true beginning of modern counterinsurgency studies.[19] However, these were often contradictory and none have achieved the broad level of acceptance gained by Clausewitz's theories on conventional war over the last 200 years. Their writing not only served as the starting point for the study of all insurgency and counterinsurgency doctrine since the start of the Vietnam War (the last forty years), but also served as a road map for the study of the tactics and strategy utilized by the U.S. Army in Vietnam. Still, the U.S. approach towards the Vietnamese insurgency has only nominally built from these works, as the basic American approach appeared to be developed on the fly by conventional warfare trained commanders and by U.S. politicians.

But as the Vietnam War, the bloodiest guerilla war in history, dragged on and wound down, interest in theoretical studies slowly dried up and during the 1970s only Kitson's (1971) and Asprey's (1975) works were notable. Similarly, although the U.S. Army conducted a large number of studies on guerilla warfare in the 1960s, many through the Special Operations Research Office (SORO), by the 1970s funding for studies evaporated, SORO was shut down, and the Army turned its back on unconventional warfare and instead emphasized the rebuilding of the Army based on conventional threats from the Soviet Union. The U.S. Army never did produce an extensive set of practical or theoretical work based upon their experiences. It would appear that there was no intellectual desire to do so as everyone choose to leave the lesson of the Vietnam to be later discovered.[20] The 1976 revision to the Army's "keystone warfighting manual" *Operations* (FM 100-5) did not mention counterinsurgency.[21] The lack of interest continued into the 1980s and 1990s with the only prominent work being a BDM report (1984) by Douglas S. Blaufarb and Dr. George K. Tanham, O'Neill (1990), and Joes (1992). In many cases, much of what was offered was an intelligent discussion of the previous authors, some additional historical analysis and a set of conclusions that often appeared to be a synthesis of previous work. Regardless, they were not universally accepted. They are sometimes contradictory. In all reality, these works are a direct extension of the thinking on the subject as of 1964. Therefore, for all practical purpose, the development of strategic and tactical thought on counterinsurgent warfare is fundamentally at the same intellectual crossroads as is was 40 years ago.

However, the new millennium has seen a flood of new and updates and reprints of the older works on insurgency and counterinsurgency, much of it propelled by the events of 11 September 2001 and the subsequent U.S. led wars in Afghanistan and Iraq. They include reprints of Trinquier, Galula, Fall, Clutterbuck, Kitson, and Taber; renewed interest in Lawrence, Guevara, and Mao; new work by Manwaring, updates by O'Neill and Joes, a new edition of FM 3-24 *Counterinsurgency*, and new works by Nagl (2002) and others; and a constant barrage of opinions from pundits and counterinsurgency "experts," in newspapers, magazines, and television.

SCHOOLS OF THOUGHT

It is possible to crudely lump all the theorists into ten rough "schools" of thought regarding counterinsurgency studies:

1. Small Wars (Calwell, U.S. Marine Corps Small Wars Manual)
2. Influenced by the 1950s and 1960s Communist movements (Mao Tse-Tung, Guevara, Bard E. O'Neill, the BDM report)
3. Influenced by the English experience (Richard L. Clutterbuck, Frank Kitson, Robert Thompson, John Nagl)
4. Influenced by the French Experience (David Galula, Roger Trinquier, Bernard Fall, current version FM 3-24)
5. Quantitative Analysis of Causes of Political Violence (Ted Gurr, Ivo and Rosalind Feierabend)
6. Influenced by the U.S. Experience (Colonel Harry Summers, General Bruce Palmer, Anthony James Joes, Max. G. Manwaring, Bard O'Neill, the BDM report and John Nagl)
7. Questioning the limitations of the rules of war (Edward Luttwak, Ralph Peters and to some extent Roger Trinquier)
8. Other independent analysts (T. E. Lawrence, Bernard Fall)
9. Influenced by recent events
10. Quantitative analysis of insurgencies (*The Dupuy Institute*, Dr. Andrew Hossack)

While this classification does a disservice to the depth of thought behind each individual's work, it does provide some sense of the basic nature, structure, confusion and contradictions of counterinsurgency theory. Each school tends to have a slightly different focus. Not only do the theorists disagree within each school, but the various schools sometimes talk past each other.

The first, which we could call the Small Wars School, are those authors that focused on addressing "Small Wars," or the various European and U.S. interventions and guerilla wars from the Napoleonic Wars through the 1930s. While these books do discuss guerilla war, they also cover a range of interventions, small conventional wars, colonial wars, etc.

The second, or Communist Movement School, are those authors that are heavily influenced by the communist movements of the 1950s and 1960s. They tend to focus on such issues as popular support, organization and propaganda. It effectively begins with the writings of Mao and other communist leaders (such as Che Guevara), but also includes Western scholars who have been heavily influenced by their writings, even though they might be anti-communist. In the case of Bard O'Neill and the BDM report, we classify them in this school as well as in the "Influenced by the U.S. Experience" school.

The third, or English School, includes British authors and those influenced by them and is focused on the lessons of the Malaya, Kenyan, Borneo, Cypriot, Levantine, Arab and Northern Irish insurgencies. They made up the core group of theorists that influenced U.S. doctrine going into Vietnam. They tend to be focused on such issues as resettlement programs, counter-guerilla tactics, intelligence gathering, small-unit operations, taking action early on, and so forth. It is the experience of a group of people who fought a series of fairly small insurgencies, mostly successfully (but not always). They had a significant influence on U.S. planning for Vietnam. One common thread among them all is that they do not believe that force ratios are important.

The fourth, or French School, like the English School, is also primarily focused on winning by the better use of tactics, although they sometimes look at the bigger picture. Their experiences were shaped by the large insurgencies in Indochina and Algeria. They focus on such issues as intelligence gathering, dividing up areas for patrolling and controlling, controlling the population, censuses, and so forth. They are effectively the French theorists of the 1960s as opposed to the English school. While not fundamentally in opposition to the "English school," the emphasis is different. They are a group of people who fought some of the largest insurgencies in history, although not successfully. The differences in emphasis between these two groups has lead to some whipsawed changes in U.S. counterinsurgency doctrine as the earlier version of FM 3-24, FMI 3-07.22 (October 1984), was influenced by the English school, while the current version, produced under direction of General David Patraeus, is clearly influenced by the French school. One notable change in FM 3-24 is the discussion force ratios, a subject not seriously addressed in the English School but important in the French School. A common thread among most of the French School is that they believe force ratios are important (only Trinquier does not address the issue). They also tend to be much more focused on the causes of the insurgency (primarily Galula and Fall).

The fifth, or Analysis of Political Violence School, in this roughly chronological listing is primarily represented by two teams of quantitative social scientists in the 1960s who conducted a broad cross-national quantitative analysis on causes of political violence. This is Ted Gurr, author of *Why Men Rebel* and the far less widely known husband and wife team of Ivo and Rosalind Feierabend. Their work, methodology, and results parallel each other. Their work was focused on the basic causes of political violence, and as such was not focused on counterinsurgent warfare. There had been other similar efforts since then but nothing as comprehensive as these initial explorations. Still, they have had considerable influence, with Ted Gurr clearly influencing Bard O'Neill and the work of Feierabend & Feierabend influencing some of the work at *The Dupuy Institute*. This group of academic researchers has been primarily U.S.-based, although not always U.S. born.

The sixth, or American School, are primarily American theorists who to some extent are trying to address why the U.S. lost in Vietnam. Unfortunately, some of them are a little too close to the subject. In some cases, they have made the argument that the U.S. actually won the guerilla war in Vietnam but lost the conventional war. *The Dupuy Institute* thinks this argument misses the point of the war entirely. The French school does not argue that they won Algeria, although their military successes there were certainly greater than what the U.S. achieved in Vietnam. The American School theorists tend to focus on the importance of outside support, and this appears to be universal among them all. There is also a tendency among some of them to focus or favor tightly organized guerilla structures (Manwaring and O'Neill). This is certainly the Vietnam influence since the English and French schools do not discuss guerilla organization. There is also a tendency to try to view the guerilla warfare in terms of applying J.F.C. Fuller's principles of war (Summers, Manwaring and O'Neill). In some cases, they remain very closely tied to the British school of thought (Nagl).

The seventh, or Questioning Rules of War School, is a single issue-focused group that basically questions the efficacy of the current rules of war in a counterinsurgency effort. Among them, only Trinquier, is a more general theorist, while the others tend to be issue specific.

The eighth, or Independent School, includes those independent thinkers who have a definite thrust that separates them from the other categories. They certainly includes Bernard Fall, for while he is clearly a member of the French school in many respects, his focus on the much bigger picture in an insurgency makes him stand out even though he was a journalist, not a military theorist. It is in effect a focus on the salient issues of an insurgency (including force ratios and cause) as opposed to worrying about the details of tactics. By default, T. E. Lawrence also falls into this category. They tend to write personalized memoirs and accounts as opposed to detached analytical works.

The ninth, or Current Events School, of analysts includes those heavily influenced by recent events over the last decade or so. They are not a very cohesive group. While watching a major guerilla war unfold before them, we have seen their viewpoints sometimes migrate over time. One could derisively refer to them as "finger-in-the-wind," "just-in-time" or the "church-of-what's-happening-now" analysts. More to the point, it is the natural outgrowth of not having a clear counterinsurgency doctrine in the U.S. for 40+ years, and then getting into the type of war the U.S. did not expect or plan for. In many cases, they are conventional war theorists or generalists who have had to convert themselves into counterinsurgency experts for the sake of providing public comments. To some extent, that is driven by the need to have group of experts available to comment in the press and academic journals on the events related to the Iraq insurgency. Still, this constant drumbeat of forming and sometimes changing opinions does not add much clarity to the understanding of the subject.

Only very recently has there been any systematic attempt to analyze insurgencies, creating a tenth school, the Analytical School. This includes the analytical efforts of Andrew Hossack of the UK Ministry of Defence. The analytical efforts of *The Dupuy Institute* also fall into this category, if we do not fall into the previous category. Still, our earliest such efforts include the analysis used for the Bosnia casualty estimate in 1995 and the research and databases assembled around mid-1985. This work by *The Dupuy Institute* would include *Casualty Estimates in Contingency Operations* (1985), the *Bosnia Casualty Estimate* (1995), The *Modern Contingency Operations Data Base* (MCODB—1995), various studies on the effects of banning land mines (1996 & 2001), the *Warfare, Armed Conflict, and Contingency Operations Data Base* (WCCO—1997), the *Small Scale Contingency Operations Database* (SSCO—2000), the SSCO analysis in the Enemy Prisoner of War Study (2001), the SSCO analysis in the Medium Weight Armor Study (2001), followed by the *Iraq Casualty Study* (2005), and the ongoing *Modern Insurgency Spreadsheet Database* (MISS—2005–present). There are some other such efforts developing now. Some of the work done by others based upon the Correlates of War (COW) data base fall into this category.

Finally there are those that are not a member of any particular school, in the sense that they are more interested in recording what happened as opposed to providing a theory of what to do. That category certainly includes the very useful work recently completed by Dr. Andrew J. Birtle of the U.S. Army Center of Military History on *U.S. Army Counterinsurgency and Contingency Operations Doctrine*. It also effectively includes John Nagl, as the focus of his writing in not on insurgency theory, but whether the U.S. Army is a learning institution. It also includes such general subject authors as Max Boot (although he has also provided commentary on strategy in Iraq), Robert Asprey, and others.

NOTES

1. I was helped considerably by Richard C. Anderson in this task. Parts of this chapter were effectively written by him.

2. Lawrence, T. E., *Seven Pillars of Wisdom, A Triumph* (Garden City, NY: Doubleday, Doran & Co, 1935), Chapter XXXIII.

3. The theoretical study of conventional military art in the west has a long and complex history before Carl von Clausewitz's *Vom Kriege* (*On War*). Of course in fact theoretical studies of warfare date well into antiquity and are not confined to the western world. From Sun Tzu in China, through the Roman and Byzantine writers Vegetius, Tacitus, Maurice, Leo, and Nikephoros Phokas, to the early moderns such as Machiavelli, Turenne, Saxe, Frederick the Great, and Napoleon, the theoretical structure of conventional warfare were well understood prior to the publication of Clausewitz's synthesis. And many, if not all of them, wrote of their practical experience in dealing with tribal insurrections, wars of ambushes, and how to defeat the hit-and-run tactics of nomadic horsemen.

4. Carl von Clausewitz, *On War* (Princeton: Princeton University Press, 1976), Chapter 26, pages 480–481.

5. *Ibid.*

6. *Ibid.*

7. *Ibid.*

8. Baron de Jomini, *The Art of War.*

9. *Ibid.*

10. *Ibid.*

11. Callwell, C. E. *Small Wars Their Principles and Practice* (Lincoln: University of Nebraska Press, 3rd ed. 1996 [1896, 1906]). The genesis of Callwell's work was an essay he wrote in 1885 for publication in the journal of the Royal United Services Institution while he was a 26-year old captain attending the British Army Staff College at Camberley. He then expanded it and published it in book form in 1896 and after his service in the Boer War republished it in a new edition in 1906.

12. Lettow-Vorbeck, Paul von. *My Reminiscences of East Africa* (London: Hurst and Blackett, 1920). Lawrence, T. E. *Revolt in the Desert* (New York: George H. Doran Co, 1927) and *Seven Pillars of Wisdom, A Triumph* (Garden City, NY: Doubleday, Doran & Co, 1935). There is no relation between T. E. Lawrence and the author of this book.

13. An excellent précis of the Marine Corps doctrinal development in this period may be found in Keith B. Bickel. *Mars Learning: The Marine Corps Development of Small Wars Doctrine, 1915–1940* (Boulder, Colo: Westview Press, 2001).

14. Ibid., 131.

15. In a similar way the 1940 edition of the *Small Wars Manual* borrowed parts of a 30-page chapter in the 1937 edition of *Infantry School Special Text 13, Infantry in Special Operations.*

16. United States. *Small Wars Manual U.S. Marine Corps, 1940* (Washington, D.C.: U.S. G.P.O., 1940).

17. Mao, Zedong. *On Guerrilla Warfare.* (Mineola, N.Y.: Dover Publications, 2005). At least seven English editions have appeared, two in 1961, one in 1978, one in 1989, one in 1992, one in 2000, and one in 2005.

18. For U.S. Army counterinsurgency doctrinal development see Andrew J. Birtle, *U.S. Army Counterinsurgency and Contingency Operations Doctrine, 1860–1941* (Washington, D.C.:

U.S. Army Center of Military History, 1998) and *U.S. Army Counterinsurgency and Contingency Operations Doctrine, 1942–1976* (Washington, D.C.: U.S. Army Center of Military History, 2006). Prior to the publication of FM 31-20 Army counterinsurgency doctrine was contained in a three-page section first found in the *Field Service Regulations—Special Operations* of 1922 and then in the *Field Service Regulations* (FM 100-5) of 1939 and 1941.

19. Noted works by recent theorists include Richard L. Clutterbuck, *The Long, Long War: Counterinsurgency in Malaya and Vietnam* (New York: Praeger, 1966); Bernard Fall, *Last Reflections on a War* (Mechanicsburg, PA.: Stackpole Books, 2000) and *Street Without Joy* (Harrisburg, PA.: Stackpole Co., 1964); David Galula, *Counterinsurgency Warfare* (Westport Ct., and London: Praeger Security International, 2006 [1964]); Anthony James Joes, "Recapturing the Essentials of Counterinsurgency Warfare" (Philadelphia: Foreign Policy Research Institute, W. W. Keen Butcher Lecture Series on Military Affairs, 24 Mar. 2006); Frank Kitson, *Low Intensity Operations: Subversion, Insurgency, Peace-Keeping* (Mechanicsburg, PA.: Archon Books 1989 [1971]); Max G. Manwaring, *Internal Wars: Rethinking Problem and Response* (Carlisle, PA.: Strategic Studies Institute, September 2001); Bard E. O'Neill, *Insurgency & Terrorism: From Revolution to Apocalypse*, 2nd ed., rev. (Washington, D.C.: Potomac Books, Inc., 2005 [1990, 2001]); Roger Trinquier, *Modern Warfare: A French View of Counterinsurgency* (New York: Praeger, 1964); BDM Corporation. *Fourteen Points: A Framework for the Analysis of Insurgency* (McLean, VA.: The BDM Corporation, 31 July 1984).

20. There was, of course, no shortage of books on the War in Vietnam, of which one of the more theoretical is Harry G. Summers' *On Strategy: A Critical Analysis of the Vietnam War* (New York: Ballantine Books, 1995 [1982]). Summers attempted to explain the U.S. failure in Vietnam based upon a model built on Clausewitz and J.F.C. Fuller's principles of war.

21. John A. Nagl, *Learning to Eat Soup with a Knife* (Chicago & London: University of London Press, 2005 [2002]), 206.

CHAPTER 3

The Acid Test: Predicting the Present

It is unknowable how long that conflict [the war in Iraq]
will last. It could last six days, six weeks. I doubt six months.

—Secretary of Defense Donald Rumsfeld, February 7, 2003[1]

Most of the major pre-1980 counterinsurgent theorists were either French or English, or people who were heavily influenced by them. Therefore, one either had to take the advice of people who lost big wars or the advice of people who won small wars. Neither set of experiences may be applicable to winning big wars. This is significant as there were very few big wars that were won. In the 62 cases of insurgency in the MISS database, there were 36 cases where a significant outside intervening force was involved. Of those, only 8 to 13 were big wars, depending on how size is measured.

INSURGENCIES WITH FOREIGN INTERVENTION

CIRCUMSTANCES	NUMBER OF CASES	PERCENT BLUE VICTORY
Indigenous Population > 9 million	10	20[2]
Intervening Force Commitment > 100,000	8	0
Peak Insurgent Force Size > 30,000	13	23

As can be seen, the track record for winning large counterinsurgency wars with outside intervening force is not very good.[3] Yet some of the theorists attempted to make predictions about the situation then facing them, which at the time was either the very large American involvement in the Vietnam War or the very much smaller insurgency in Northern Ireland. Manwaring, the authors of the BDM report, Joes, O'Neill, and Trinquier made no predictions that can now be tested against what actually occurred. But the more adventurous Galula, Fall and Clutterbuck did provide comments or predictions on Vietnam and Kitson did the same for Northern Ireland and possibly Vietnam. Let us look at these specific examples and see what they tell us.

GALULA

David Galula did not make any predictions regarding Vietnam but claimed in a description of the Viet Cong in 1963 that,

> The insurgent has really no cause at all; he is exploiting the counterinsurgent's weaknesses and mistakes. Such seems to be the situation in South Vietnam today. The Vietcong cannot clamor for land, which is plentiful to South Vietnam; nor raise the banner of anticolonialism, for South Vietnam is no longer a colony; nor offer Communism, which does not appear to be very popular with the North Vietnamese population. The insurgent's program is simply: "Throw the rascals out." If the "rascals" (whoever is in power in Saigon) amend their ways, the insurgent would lose his cause.[4]

We think it somewhat suspect that what was then already developing into the bloodiest insurgency in history and where 50,000 or more insurgents were in the field was supposedly based upon "no real cause." This was a war that eventually resulted in over 2 million deaths and an insurgent force in excess of 300,000. As it is, one could infer from Galula's statement that he felt that the insurgency could be easily defeated since it was based upon "no real cause." We believe that this view has been proven incorrect by historical events.

CLUTTERBUCK

Richard Clutterbuck bravely made a prediction about Vietnam in his book published in March 1966,

> By 1965, this had reached a situation beyond the power of the South Vietnamese Army to restore, and led to massive intervention of U.S. combat units. By escalating into the kind of war in which the U.S. can inevitably outbid them the Viet Cong have probably signed their own death warrant.[5]

In hindsight, this prediction was obviously in error, unless one wishes to argue that the Viet Cong were indeed defeated in 1968–1969 and the United States was instead defeated by the North Vietnamese. In Clutterbuck's defense though, he does note later in his book that,

> The patience and power of the U.S. have given the South Vietnamese Government a second chance; but this chance, too, will be thrown away unless the foundations are laid for stable and effective government in the villages, both to win the war and to maintain the peace.[6]

FALL

Bernard Fall, writing in *Street Without Joy* in 1964, clearly indicated that he did not consider that the war would end in that decade,

> *The later part of the "grand design" in Viet-Nam would involve the gradual clearing of whole key areas in which the population had been regrouped into Strategic Hamlets; while highly mobile anti-guerilla forces seek out the enemy hard-core units and destroy them. In a final phase, now hardly expected to come about before the late 1960's, the remaining hostile guerillas will either be pushed back across the border or sealed off to starve and die out in the most inaccessible pats of the Vietnamese jungle. That, at least, is the theory. The reality, as will be seen, is somewhat different.[7]*

Bernard Fall in *Last Reflections on a War* stated the following:

> *When Hanson Baldwin, the New York Times' noted military commentator, suggested last spring [1966?] that one million Americans might be required in Viet-Nam he was greeted with general derision and disbelief. Now we can say that one million American troops is a quite possible figure, although it might be reduced if other nations send in troops. The United States is constantly on the search for allies.*

> *If one accepts the 10-to-1 ratio of "stabilizing" troops to guerillas, then at least 1.5 million men would be required in Viet-Nam. The South Vietnamese army now has 600,000 men with all para-military forces included, but has low morale and efficiency, and a high desertion rate—and is having a very hard time finding more men. Anyway, it is quite pointless in one sense to project a "stabilization" period in terms of years—the British had a 55-to-1 superiority in Malaya and it took them 13 years to win.[8]*

Also, earlier in the same book,

> *In South Viet-Nam, after being stopped at Chu-Lai, Plei-Me and the Ia-Drang, the Communist regulars lost enough of their momentum for the time being not to be able to bring about the military and political collapse of the Saigon government late in 1965—a situation which would have altogether closed out the American "option" of the conflict. But just as at the Marne 52 years ago, or before Moscow a quarter-century ago, nothing had been decided as yet. Years—perhaps a decade—of hard fighting could still be ahead. And the political collapse of the government in Saigon is still a distinct possibility. It is, however, important to assess in detail the military and political elements on which this precarious balance rests and what real possibilities for maneuver*

(as against wishful thinking on one side or party rhetoric on the other) exist at present in the Viet-Nam situation.[9]

It is clear that by 1966, Fall believed that the U.S. was going to need more troops and a lot more time to be successful in Vietnam. Certainly, he was seeing a war that he expected would extend well into the 1970s (the U.S. withdrawal began in 1969), which also appears to have been his view in 1964.

KITSON

Frank Kitson made predictions on both Vietnam and Northern Ireland in 1971. In the case of Northern Ireland, he had served there the previous year and was responsible (and somewhat infamous) for helping establish British Army Special Operations in Northern Ireland in the early 1970s.

> *... at the time of writing both the British and United States army are heavily engaged in these activities in Northern Ireland and Viet Nam respectively. But it can be argued that the recent past has been exceptional, that Northern Ireland and Viet Nam will both be settled within five years, and that with the proposed withdrawal of all but a small remnant of the British Army into Europe, the requirement to fight insurgents or to take part in peace-keeping operations will cease.[10]*

Later though he did indicate that by 1971 he felt that the Northern Irish insurgency was nearly over:

> *In practice the fact that the army is so heavily engaged in Ireland now makes it unlikely that it will be involved in exactly this task between 1975 and 1980 because it is reasonable to hope that the present emergency will be resolved within five years.[11]*

In retrospect, it is clear that prediction was dead wrong. The insurgency in Northern Ireland continued for almost 30 years, if counting it as ending in 1998, and in fact some violence occurred and a British Army presence remained after that.

In the case of Vietnam, he was correct in that it was over in five years. But it is not mentioned in the book whether or not he had believed that the end would result in a U.S. withdrawal and the subsequent collapse of the South Vietnamese Army and Government, or that the Paris Peace Accords would not bring "peace with honor". But, considering the very positive statements he made about U.S. counterinsurgency operations in Vietnam it was probably some form of U.S. victory that he expected.[12]

In the end, one could argue that Galula, Clutterbuck and Kitson all failed to properly appreciate and predict the outcomes of the single insurgency they were examining at the time and that only Fall got it right. Still, one right or wrong prediction does not make or break the value of a theorist. But there does seems to be an inverse correlation between the expertise of the insurgency theorist and his predictive ability, given that Galula, Clutterbuck and Kitson were all professional military men and yet were unable to properly predict what was going to happen in Vietnam or Northern Ireland, while Bernard Fall, a civilian journalist (although no stranger to warfare) was eerily prescient in his understanding of the situation in Vietnam.

THE DUPUY INSTITUTE

The Dupuy Institute has made formal published predictions for three U.S. operations over a 15 year period. These were for the 1991 Gulf War, the 1995 Bosnia Peacekeeping operation, and in 2004–2005 for the current Iraq insurgency. A review of these is in order in light of us taking other theorists to task about the accuracy of their published predictions.

GULF WAR

On 13 December 1990, Trevor N. Dupuy, President of TNDA (Trevor N. Dupuy & Associates) provided testimony to the U.S. House of Representatives on the U.S. losses if UN forces intervened to expel Iraqi forces from Kuwait. This estimate was privately developed by TNDA using their combat model, the TNDM (Tactical Numerical Deterministic Model). TNDA's estimate at the House testimony was that U.S. casualties would probably not exceed 2,000 total U.S. casualties with less than 500 dead assuming a successful air campaign (e.g. Iraq withdraws from Kuwait). TNDA created multiple estimates to allow for different contingencies. TNDA's highest estimate was 3,000 dead and 20,000 total casualties; the lowest estimate was 300 dead and 1,800 total casualties. Assuming that a ground campaign was going to be necessary to expel Iraqi forces from Kuwait TNDA estimated 1,280 battle deaths and 8,000 total casualties.[13]

TNDA also stated that ground combat would likely not exceed 10 days (it lasted a mere 100 hours), and would certainly be less than 40, even if U.S. forces go to Baghdad (incidentally, when U.S. forces drove to Baghdad in 2003 it took approximately 20 days from the start of the operations on 20 March to the formal occupation of Baghdad on 9 April).[14]

TNDA's estimate was then expanded into a book, *If War Comes: How to Defeat Saddam Hussein*, which mapped out multiple operational and strategic options, provided casualty estimates and provided a final estimate roughly in line with the House testimony. The book's estimates revised and expanded on those provided in the House testimony and ran from a low of 190 dead and 380 total casualties for a nine-day air campaign to a high of 2,149 dead and 11,700 total casualties (allowing for 50% underestimation).[15] *If War Comes: How to Defeat Saddam Hussein* was published on 13 January 1991, four days before the Gulf War air campaign began.

Throughout the period of deployment called Operation Desert Storm (7 August

1990 to 17 January 1991) Trevor Dupuy had the lowest public estimate of U.S. casualties. Many public and private sources estimated between 10,000 and 30,000 U.S. killed. General Swarzkopf's prewar estimates ranged from 10,000 to 20,000 casualties.[16] Prior to the Gulf War, the U.S. military shipped more than 20,000 body bags to the Persian Gulf.[17] Sen. Sam Nunn, Chairman of the Senate Armed Services Committee, claims the potential cost and length of the war influenced him to oppose the war and push for sanctions.[18] The accuracy of the TNDM prediction has been noted in a number of sources.[19]

The war actually consisted of a 38-day air campaign followed by a 4-day ground campaign. In the days before the ground campaign, Trevor Dupuy stated on national news that in fact his estimate was too high, and it was going to be much lower than that.[20] Actual U.S. casualties in the Gulf War were 382 killed from all causes, with 511 non-U.S. coalition killed from all causes.[21] Total U.S. battle deaths were 147.[22]

BOSNIA

On 1 November 1995, *The Dupuy Institute* was issued a contract to provide a casualty estimate to the JCS for a potential U.S. deployment in Bosnia. The first draft of the casualty estimate was provided to JCS on 28 November 1995, although the original estimate was completed within 10 days. It estimated that there was a 50% chance that U.S. killed from all causes in Bosnia in the first year would be below 17 (12 combat deaths and 5 non-combat fatalities) and a 90% chance U.S. killed would be below 25.[23] Actual U.S. casualties from all causes in the first year in Bosnia were 6 and there were no combat deaths.

JCS Chairman General John Shalikashvili had the draft executive summary of the Bosnia casualty estimate with him in the meeting with President Clinton where the decision was made as to whether to commit the U.S. forces to the peace mission.[24]

IRAQ

On 21 April 2004, *The Dupuy Institute* provided an unsolicited proposal to CAA (Center for Army Analysis) to prepare a casualty estimate for Iraq. A contract was awarded 23 August 2004 and the draft estimate was provided to CAA on December 2004, with the final briefing presented in January 2005.

In making the casualty estimate we compared Iraq with 28 historical insurgencies (14 Insurgent or Red Wins and 14 Counterinsurgent or Blue wins). This effort included considerable analysis on the nature of insurgencies. Below is a summary of the predictions that came from that analysis:

As can be seen, the estimation effort involved not only an estimation of casualties, but also of duration, intensity, force strength, insurgent force size of the insurgency, and also analysis on the nature of insurgencies and how those relate to casualties and outcome. As events have shown over the last four years, all of these conclusions were on-target or close to on-target.

SALIENT POINTS

- Insurgent force strength is probably between 20,000–60,000
- This is a major insurgency
  - It is of medium intensity
- It is a regional or factionalized insurgency and **must** remain that way
- U.S. commitment can be expected to be relatively steady throughout this insurgency and will not be quickly replaced by indigenous forces
- It will last around 10 or so years
- It may cost the U.S. 5,000 to 10,000 killed
  - It may be higher
  - This assumes no major new problems in the Shiite majority areas

UNLESS THERE IS A SUDDEN CHANGE ON THE GROUND IN THE NEXT MONTH

- U.S. losses are **not** likely to be **less than** 3,000 killed
  - It is already half of that
- May well be in the 5,000 to 10,000 range
- May be higher
- Duration is likely to be around 10 years
  - Lets say 63% chance between 7 to 13 years
  - Lets say 37% chance of being 15 years or longer
- U.S. & Allied force size is likely to be a constant (for the estimate)
  - U.S. Force Size is likely to remain fairly high
  - Iraqi government force size is growing

NOTES

1. Susan Page, "Confronting Iraq," *USA Today* (1 April 2003).
2. This includes the ongoing U.S. insurgencies in Afghanistan and Iraq. The two blue wins are Mozambique Civil War (1976–1992) and Tanzania in Uganda (1978–1980), the overthrow of Idi Amin. In the case of Peak Insurgent Force Size, the three cases of blue wins are Yemen (1962–1970), Angola Civil War (1975–1988) and UN Peacekeeping in Angola (1988–1999).

3. It is much better when the counterinsurgency forces are primarily indigenous (little or no outside intervening forces).

Insurgencies without Foreign Intervention

CIRCUMSTANCES	NUMBER OF CASES	PERCENT BLUE VICTORY
Indigenous Population > 9 million	12	50
Counterinsurgent Force Commitment > 100,000	9	67
Peak Insurgent Force Size > 30,000	4	50

4. Galula, 71.
5. Clutterbuck, 50.
6. Clutterbuck, 75.
7. Fall, *Street Without Joy*, 348.
8. Idem, *Last Reflections on a War*, 235.
9. Idem, *Last Reflections*, 173.
10 Kitson, op. cit., 13.
11. Ibid., 24.
12. Ibid., 52, 58–59, 70.
13. House Armed Services Committee. *Testimony of Col. T. N. Dupuy, USA, Ret.* (Washington D.C.: 13 Dec. 1990).
14. *Ibid.*
15. Trevor N. Dupuy, *If War Comes, How to Defeat Saddam Hussein.* (McLean, VA.: HERO Books, 1991).
16. John P. Jumper (Lt. Gen.) "In Gulf War, Precision Air Weapons Paid Off," *New York Times* (14 July 1996) http://query.nytimes.com/gst/fullpage.html?res=9803EEDB1E39F937 A25754C0A960958260. The actual statement in the article is: "The coalition air assault on Iraq forces in Kuwait results in fewer than 400 casualties versus Gen. H. Norman Schwarzkof's prewar estimate of 10,000 to 20,000." The author was the Deputy Chief of Staff, Plans and Operations, U.S. Air Force in 1996.
17. Brad Knickerbocker, "Pentagon's Quietest Calculation: The Casualty Count," *The Christian Scientist Monitor* (28 Jan. 2003). http://www.csmonitor.com/2003/0128/p01s02-woiq.html
18. Michael R. Gordon, "Cracking the Whip," *The New York Times* (27 Jan. 1991). http://query.nytimes.com/gst/fullpage.html?res=9D0CEED8163EF934A15752C0A967958260
19. For example, the Wikipedia article on the Gulf War discusses Trevor Dupuy's estimate compared to the others.
20. Interview with Ted Koppel on the evening news, Mar. 1991.
21. U.S. Casualties from http://www1.va.gov/opa/fact/amwars.asp other casualties from Clodfelter
22. U.S. Department of Veterans Affairs. *Fact Sheet: America's Wars* (July 2007). http://www1.va.gov/opa/fact/amwars.asp
23. *Peacekeeping in Bosnia Fatality Estimates* (McLean, VA.: The Dupuy Institute, 1995).
24. As relayed by General John Shalikashvili in private conversations with Nicholas Krawciw (MG, USA, ret), who was, at the time, president of *The Dupuy Institute*.

CHAPTER 4

Force Ratios Really Do Matter

You can kill ten of my men for every one I kill of yours,
but even at those odds, you will lose and I will win.

—Ho Chi Minh to the French, late 1940s[1]

A lot of time and effort has been spent by writers trying to claim that force ratios do not matter. The starting point of this conclusion appears to be a statement by Richard Clutterbuck in his 1966 book *The Long, Long War*:

Much nonsense is heard on the subject of tie-down ratios in guerrilla warfare—that 10 to 12 government troops are needed to tie down a single guerrilla, for instance. This is a dangerous illusion, arising from a disregard of the facts.[2]

The interesting thing is that the people who state that force ratios really do not matter have not presented any analysis of them or any data that clearly establishes their point. So, while Brigadier Clutterbuck states that it is a dangerous illusion arising from a disregard of the facts, he does not provide any facts or data to prove the point or to establish the opposite theme. It appears to be a declaration based upon superior expertise. Unfortunately, this has also led to the failure of U.S doctrine to address this issue of force ratios.

But there is no need to really argue these points. Instead we just laid out all 83 of the cases we have in our MISS database starting with the lowest force ratio first, and then up to the highest. This table is presented in Appendix IV. The two columns to pay attention to are the second column (force ratio) and the fifth column(winner).

What this table shows is that the lower the force ratio the better chances the insurgency has of winning, while the higher the force ratio, the better chances the intervening force has of winning. There is clearly a correlation between force ratios and outcome. The most salient observation with this data is that there are no red wins at force ratios above 13-to-1 and only one red win out of 18 cases at force ratios above 10.3-to-1. Therefore, we have a basis for concluding:

While high force ratios are not required to win an insurgency, intervention or peacekeeping operation, force ratios above 10-to-1 pretty much guarantee a counterinsurgent victory.

In the table below, the data in Appendix IV was divided into four categories, very low force ratios (0.38 to 0.75 counterinsurgents per insurgent), low force ratios (1.07 – 4.89), medium force ratios (5.67 – 10.28) and high force ratios (10.47 to 162.73). We then compared that to whether the counterinsurgents or intervening force won (a blue win), whether the insurgents won (a red win) or whether there was a result that could not be clearly identified as a blue or red win (a gray result). This was done for the 83 cases that were insurgencies, interventions and peacekeeping operations, although we only had good force ratio data for 78 of them. The data shows:[3]

FORCE RATIO	CASES	BLUE WINS	GRAY RESULTS	RED WINS
0.38 – 0.75	4	1	0	3
1.07 – 4.89	38	18	2	18
5.67 – 10.28	18	10	2	6
10.47 – 162.73	18	13	4	1
Total	78	42	8	28

Or to put in another format:

	PERCENT BLUE WINS	PERCENT RED WINS
Very low force ratio cases	25	75
Low force ratio cases	47	47
Medium force ratio cases	56	33
High force ratio cases	76	6

In many of these cases (like peacekeeping) the blue and the red side are not always in clear opposition, and a number of cases are conventional operations. If one just scales this dataset back to the 59 cases that are clearly insurgencies, then one has a more pure case where the ratio of blue to red is more uniformly meaningful.

The most salient observation from previous larger data collection remains in that there are no red wins at force ratios above 13-to-1 and only one red win out of 15 cases at force ratios above 10.3-to-1. Therefore, we have a basis for concluding:

While high force ratios are not required to win an insurgency, force ratios above 10-to-1 pretty much guarantee a counterinsurgent victory.

Now that the data has been boiled down to only insurgencies, we also see that the opposite is true. We have no blue force wins at force ratios below 1-to-1 and only four blue wins out of 14 cases at forces ratios below 2.3-to-1. There we have a basis for concluding:

While low force ratios do not preclude a win for the counterinsurgency, force ratios below 2-to-1 greatly favor an insurgent victory.

The actual data for just the insurgencies as divided into four force ratio categories:[4]

FORCE RATIO	CASES	BLUE WINS	GRAY RESULTS	RED WINS
0.38 – 0.75	3	0	0	3
1.07 – 4.89	26	9	1	16
5.67 – 10.28	15	9	1	5
10.47 – 162.73	15	11	3	1
Total	59	29	5	25

Or to put in another format:

	PERCENT BLUE WINS	PERCENT RED WINS
Very low force ratio cases	0	100
Low force ratio cases	35	55
Medium force ratio cases	60	33
High force ratio cases	73	7

Here the pattern is very clear, higher force ratios help win an insurgency. It may be the single most important variable.

We then divided this into insurgencies against foreign forces (coded as INS/C & INS/I or INS/F) as opposed to insurgencies against primarily domestic forces (coded as INS/NI). In this case, INS/C means those insurgencies against colonial powers, a category created specifically for the purposed of addressing those "colonial wars of national liberation". INS/I are insurgencies that involve a significant presence from an outside intervening power. INS/F is a catch all term that includes all INS/C and INS/I. It means insurgencies against foreign powers or foreign interventions. INS/NI is the other side of the coin, is it insurgencies with no significant outside interventions. Basically, it is an exclusively domestic civil war.

The actual data for insurgencies opposing outside intervening forces (INS/C & INS/I) as divided into four force ratio categories:[5]

FORCE RATIO	CASES	BLUE WINS	GRAY RESULTS	RED WINS
0.38 – 0.75	2	0	0	2
1.07 – 4.89	21	8	1	12
5.67 – 10.28	8	4	0	4
10.47 – 162.73	5	4	1	0
Total	36	16	2	18

Or to put in another format:

	PERCENT BLUE WINS	PERCENT RED WINS
Very low force ratio cases	0	100
Low force ratio cases	38	57
Medium force ratio cases	50	50
High force ratio cases	80	0

Nothing here changes the conclusion based upon the large data set of 59 insurgencies.

The actual data for insurgencies with little outside intervening forces (INS/NI) was also examined:[6]

FORCE RATIO	CASES	BLUE WINS	GRAY RESULTS	RED WINS
0.38 – 0.75	1	0	0	1
1.07 – 4.89	5	1	0	4
5.67 – 10.28	7	5	1	1
10.47 – 162.73	10	7	2	1
Total	23	13	3	7

Or to put in another format:

	PERCENT BLUE WINS	PERCENT RED WINS
Very low force ratio cases	0	100
Low force ratio cases	2	80
Medium force ratio cases	71	14
High force ratio cases	70	10

Nothing here changes the conclusion based upon the large data set of 59 insurgencies.

Clearly force ratios are important. They are important whether looking at the entire data set, with its mix of insurgencies, interventions and peace keeping operations; whether looking at insurgencies only; or whether looking at outside interventions as compared to primarily domestic insurgencies. That is what the data tells us.[7]

But, combating insurgencies is not just a simple matter of superior forces ratios; the nature of the insurgency also matters as will be discussed in the next chapter.

NOTES

1. Original source not identified.
2. Richard L. Clutterbuck, *The Long Long War* (New York: Frederick A. Praeger, 1966), 42.
3. We conducted various Fisher's exact tests about the (null) hypothesis of association between outcome and each of the five variables that describe the nature of insurgencies. Smaller p-values are indicative of a possible association between the outcome and the levels of the respective variable. Fisher's exact test two-sided p-value: 0.0142, meaning statistically there is about a 1% chance that this relationship is due to chance.
4. Fisher's exact test two-sided p-value: 0.0021.
5. Fisher's exact test two-sided p-value: 0.1158.
6. Fisher's exact test two-sided p-value: 0.0575
7. The data used is provided in Appendix IV. Also, an analysis of the data using slightly different definitions of the four categories was done, with each category having an equal number of cases. It resulted in cases that were very similar in size being in different categories. This does not happen when we divide the categories where there are gaps in the data. Regardless, it made no difference in the results.

CHAPTER 5

Cause Really is Important

The Revolution was effected before the War commenced. The Revolution was in the minds and hearts of the people; a change in their religious sentiments of their duties and obligations . . . This radical change in the principles, opinions, sentiments, and affections of the people, was the real American Revolution.

—John Adams, 1818[1]

T*he Dupuy Institute* obtained very clear results from looking at the political concept of an insurgency (limited, central or overarching). One can relate this to "cause" or whether the insurgency is broadly-based or not. This was, of course, one of the factors examined as part of our original Iraq Casualty Estimate.[2]

These categories were the closest thing we had to measuring the impact of "cause" on the effectiveness of an insurgency. At the time, we did not have a category for "cause," and if we did create one, we were uncertain how we would code it. We also tried to categorize by "type of insurgency" definitions provided by Bard O'Neill, but we did not get as clear results from that effort.[3] So instead, we built our analysis from our original coding of the political concept of an insurgency.

We then decided to conduct a simple statistical comparison of each of them to the entire database (all 83 cases, including 21 interventions and peacekeeping operations), then to just the 62 insurgencies, and then to just the 36 insurgencies against foreigners (insurgencies with significant intervening powers or against colonial powers). This parallels what we did in the previous chapter on force ratios.

THE 83 CASE DATASET

The table below is the data from all 83 cases, presented by outcome (blue, gray and red) as compared to the political concept of the insurgency.[4]

OUTCOME BY TYPE OF POLITICAL CONCEPT

OUTCOME	LIMITED	CENTRAL	OVERARCHING	NOT APPLICABLE	TOTAL
Blue	24	8	8	2	42
Gray	7	2	2	0	11
Red	9	18	3	0	30
Total	40	28	13	2	83

As can be seen here, there is a clear correlation between the political concept underlying the insurgency and its outcome. In the cases that are based upon a limited political concept[5], the counterinsurgents won 60% of the time while the insurgents won 23% of the time. In the cases that were based upon a central political idea, the counterinsurgents won only 29% of the time while the insurgents won 64% of the time. In the cases that were based upon an overarching idea (communism), the counterinsurgents won 62% of the time while the insurgents won only 23% of the time. There is clearly a difference here with those cases based upon a central political idea.

THE 62 CASE DATASET

The same pattern clearly shows itself when we look at the 62 cases that we coded as insurgencies.[6]

OUTCOME BY TYPE OF POLITICAL CONCEPT

OUTCOME	LIMITED	CENTRAL	OVERARCHING	TOTAL
Blue	15	7	7	29
Gray	3	1	2	6
Red	7	17	3	27
Total	25	25	12	62

Again, for just the insurgencies, there is a clear correlation between the political concept underlying the insurgency and its outcome. In the cases that are based upon a limited political concept, the counterinsurgents won 60% of the time while the insurgents won 28% of the time. In the cases that were based upon a central political idea, the counterinsurgents won only 28% of the time while the insurgents won 68% of the time. In the cases that were based upon an overarching idea (communism), the counterinsurgents won 58% of the time while the insurgents won only 25% of the time. This is pretty much the same pattern as shown above.

THE 36 CASE DATASET

For the 36 cases that we coded as insurgencies against a foreign power or with significant foreign support, the pattern is even more pronounced.[7]

OUTCOME BY TYPE OF POLITICAL CONCEPT

OUTCOME	LIMITED	CENTRAL	OVERARCHING	TOTAL
Blue	10	4	2	16
Gray	2	0	0	2
Red	2	14	2	18
Total	14	18	4	36

In the cases that are based upon a limited political concept, the counterinsurgents won 71% of the time while the insurgents won 14% of the time. In the cases that were based upon a central political idea, the counterinsurgents won only 22% of the time while the insurgents won 78% of the time. In the cases that were based upon an overarching idea (communism), the counterinsurgents won 50% of the time while the insurgents won 50% of the time. This is pretty much the same pattern as shown above. **There is a clear correlation between the political concept underlying the insurgency and its outcome.**

This point is clearest in the 36 case dataset, which is much smaller than the rest, but all three datasets showed a clear correlation between the political concept underlying the insurgency and its outcome. In the case of the type of the insurgency, nationalistic movements work best and every other type is not nearly as successful.

NOTES

1. From letter of H. Niles, 13 February, 1818.
2. *Casualty Estimate for the Insurgency in Iraq* (Annandale, VA.: The Dupuy Institute, 28 February 2005).
3. Bard O'Neill listed nine types of insurgencies, of which only six types show up in our 83 cases: commercialist, egalitarian, pluralists, reformists, secessionist and traditionalist. We had no examples of anarchist, apocalyptic-utopian or preservationist
4. We conducted various Fisher's exact tests about the (null) hypothesis of association between outcome and each of the five variables that describe the nature of insurgencies. Smaller p-values are indicative of a possible association between the outcome and the levels of the respective variable.
   Two-sided p-value from Fisher's exact test excluding the not applicable cases: 0.0077. Two-sided p-value Fisher's exact test excluding the not applicable and gray cases: 0.0031
5. This is the same as the term "limited developed political thought" that we used earlier.
6. Two-sided p-value from Fisher's exact test: 0.0230. Two-sided p-value from Fisher's exact test excluding the gray group: 0.0163
7. Two-sided p-value from Fisher's exact test: 0.0014. Two-sided p-value from Fisher's exact test excluding the gray group: 0.0019.

CHAPTER 6

The Two Together Seem Really Important

It's hard to conceive that it would take more forces to provide stability in post-Saddam Iraq than it would take to conduct the war itself and to secure the surrender of Saddam's security forces and his army. Hard to imagine.

—Deputy Defense Secretary Paul Wolfowitz, testifying before the House Budget Committee, February 27, 2003[1]

T he previous two chapters clearly identify both force ratios and "political concept" as important factors influencing the outcome of insurgencies. We first identified force ratios and cause as important factors in our Iraq estimate in 2004. We then further examined both in depth in our studies in 2006. But, it was not until late in 2006 that we finally decided to test the two together.

The simplest first step was to separate the data into three groups based upon political concept (limited, central and overarching). We then just lined them up in each category by force ratio, and the data pretty much came out of the charts and slapped us in the face. This data is provided in Appendix V.

When one looks at the 36 cases where the counterinsurgent or intervening force are facing insurgences, interventions or peacekeeping operations that based upon a limited political concept, the one notes that the counterinsurgent or intervening force won 24 out of 33 times (73%) as long as they had a favorable force ratio. If they did not have a favorable force ratio (the other 3 cases), then they did not win. If we look at just the 10 cases among those 36 that are classic insurgencies, we find that the intervening force won 79% of time where they had a favorable force ratio. Clearly, if there is a regional or factional insurgency, the odds are in the counterinsurgent forces favor as long as they have sufficient force.

The situation is very different when facing an insurgency based upon a central political idea like nationalism or anti-colonialism. In those 27 cases the force ratios mattered. In the 12 or 14 cases where these were less than a 5-to-1 force ratio, the counterinsurgents lost in every case![2] In those seven to nine cases where the force ratio was between 6-to-1 and 10-to-1 (actually 5.71 to 10.28-to-1), the counterinsurgents won only 43 or 44% of the time.[3] Interesting enough, the old rule-of-thumb that you needed to a 10-to-1 force ratio to defeat an insurgency does seem to be at play here, although we do not know how that rule-of-thumb was ever established. Yet, when a force is facing an insurgency based upon a central idea at a force ratio of greater than 10-to-1 (actually greater than 10.67-to-1), the counterinsurgents defeat the insurgency 67% of the time. This is based upon only 6 cases though. Still, all this does seems to validate the old 10-to-1 rule-of-thumb.

We have 13 cases of insurgencies based upon an overarching idea, in all cases being communism. The counterinsurgent or intervening force won 62% of those cases regardless of the force ratio.[4] One cannot rule out that the force ratios when facing overarching insurgencies are following the exact same rules as for insurgencies based upon a central idea (below 5-to-1 insurgent victory, between 5-to-1 and 10-to-1 it could go either way, above 10-to-1 mostly counterinsurgent victory).

If we combine those insurgencies based upon either a central or overarching idea, then we have 40 cases to work with. In this expanded data set, if they do not have at least a 5-to-1 force ratio, the counterinsurgent force lost the insurgency in every case based upon 14 cases. This is pretty significant. In the 6-to-1 to 10-to-1 range, the counterinsurgent force wins only half the time. This is based upon 12 cases. Above a force ratio of 10-to-1, the counterinsurgents win 73% of the time based upon 11 cases.

The bigger picture from this data is clear:

1. **Force ratios, within reason, are not an issue when facing regional or factional insurgencies.**
2. **When facing insurgencies that have a broad base of support, one needs at least 5-to-1 force ratio and preferably 10-to-1 force ratio.**
3. **It appears that the two most important factors in determining the outcome of an insurgency are the force ratio and the nature of the cause of the insurgency.**

If we distinguish between three major types of political concept (limited, a central idea or an overarching idea), the relationship between the probability of blue side success and force ratios, by the type of political concept, can be graphically depicted as on the following page. The curves are estimated based on a logistic regression.

The force ratios positively affect the probability of blue side success across all three types of political concept. Larger force ratios lead to a higher probability of blue side victory. However, at force ratios below 30-to-1, the probability of blue side success will be lower when the political concept is based upon a central idea then when the political concept is limited. So, a larger force ratio will be needed to suppress an insurgency where the political concept is based on a central idea (like nationalism) than where the political concept is limited. The insurgencies where the political concept is an overarching idea are somewhere in between, meaning that to suppress such insur-

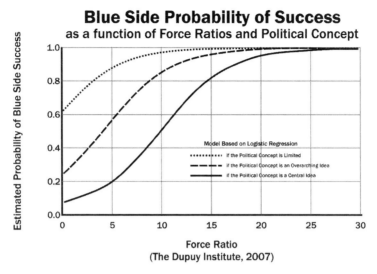

Blue Side Probability of Success
as a function of Force Ratios and Political Concept

Estimated Probability of Blue Side Success

Model Based on Logistic Regression
•••••••• If the Political Concept is Limited
– – – – If the Political Concept is an Overarching Idea
——— If the Political Concept is a Central Idea

Force Ratio
(The Dupuy Institute, 2007)

gencies the force ratios should be larger than when the political concept was limited, but less than when the political concept was based on a central idea.[5]

The actual formula for this logistic regression is:

$$\log\left(\frac{\pi_i}{1-\pi_i}\right) = -1.36 + 0.29(\textit{Force Ratios}) + 1.74(\textit{Limited}) - 1.76(\textit{Central})$$

| s. errors | (1.06) | (0.11) | (1.04) | (1.00) |
| p-values | (0.1999) | (0.0068) | (0.0936) | (0.0797) |

Roughly speaking, if the probability of blue side success in an insurgency with a central idea and a force ratio of 5-to-1 for a particular situation was 16%, then had the political concept been limited (instead of a central idea) but the force ratio maintained at 5-to-1, the probability of blue side success would have been 86%. So, a 5-to-1 force ratio would be sufficient to defeat a regional or factional insurgency but be entirely inadequate if facing a more broadly based insurgency.

We then tested this model back to the 68 cases we used. This model predicted correctly the insurgency outcome in 53 out of 68 cases used (overall, 77.9% of the cases were correctly predicted). Namely, 34 out of 40 blue victories were correctly predicted (85.0% of the blue cases were correctly predicted) and 19 out of 28 red victories were correctly predicted (67.9% of the red cases were correctly predicted). The specific examples are shown in Appendix VI.

Now this simple two-variable model incorrectly predicted 15 out of the 68 cases used. Four of these cases are the ones where the force ratios were less than one-to-one. As we noted earlier in our discussion, it appears, based upon three of these cases, that at least even force ratios are required (there is one exception). In all of these three cases, the model predicted a blue win and the outcome was a red win (and in the one exception, the model predicted a red win when the outcome was a blue win, but this was a peacekeeping operation vice an insurgency).

Still, one notices that there are no errors in prediction for insurgencies based upon a central idea with force ratios below 5-to-1 and no errors in predictions regardless of Political Concept behind the insurgency in cases of 13-to-1 or better. This is probably two significant observations, leaving much of the modeling confusion with the limited political concept cases and the cases between 5-to-1 and 13-to-1.

This model could be improved by adding a rule: Insurgencies conducted at a force ratio of less than 1-to-1 result in insurgent victory. That would certainly correct three of the incorrect 15 cases. Note that this rule applies only to insurgencies, not interventions or peacekeeping operations.

The other 12 cases come in two categories, those that can be explained easily and those that are difficult to explain. Four of these cases are easy to explain, although it does require addressing more factors than just force ratio and cause. They are:

CASE	RESULT	PREDICTED RESULT	CLASSIFICATION
Polisario (1973–1991)	Blue	Red	INS/I
Mau Mau Revolt (1952–1956)	Blue	Red	became INS/C
Puerto Rico (1950–1954)	Blue	Red	became INS/NI
First Intifada (1987–1993)	Red	Blue	INS/NI

In the case of Polisario, the insurgent strength is probably overestimated. The terrain could not be more hostile to an insurgency. The insurgents were mostly in camps outside of the country and could not easily infiltrate back in. There were certainly were not that many active and very few operating in country in the occupied southern Sahara. It is also a case where a barrier system actually may have helped win the counterinsurgency (unlike Vietnam and Algeria).

In the case of the Mau Mau Revolt in Kenya, the country became independent in 1963, seven years after the nationalist revolt was suppressed. Even though this was a nationalistic revolt, it was still fundamentally regionally and tribally based, primarily built around the Kikuyu tribe. The British also initiated the action with suppression, which certainly proved useful for getting the situation under control in the short run, even though it did not seem to make much difference in the long run. One of the people they arrested in 1952 was Jomo Kenyatta, the first president of the future independent Kenya. So this is a case where we code this one as a blue win because the insurgency was brought under control in 1956, but by 1963, the leaders of the independence movement were given control of the country. So, after the insurgency was successfully suppressed, it became a "red result" (insurgent victory).

Puerto Rico probably should not be in the data set. It hardly amounted to anything like an insurgency. It was effectively two entirely separate incidents four years apart. It was a truly minor affair with only a very small number of people involved in the "insurgency."

In the case of the First Intifada in Palestine, this needs to be placed in the larger context of continuous pro-Palestinian violence since 1967. The cost of this political violence over the decades certainly added up to make this one particularly effective. Subsequent efforts have not been as effective.

In each of these four cases, it is relatively easy to see why a simple two-variable model did not correctly predict the outcome. The other eight cases more difficult to explain and are probably not entirely explainable by a simple two-variable model. They are:

| | | PREDICTED | |
CASE	RESULT	RESULT	CLASSIFICATION
Peacekeeping in Cambodia (1991–1993)	Blue	Red	PEACE
Colombian Civil War (1964–present)	Blue	Red	INS/NI
Hungary (1956)	Blue	Red	SUP
UN Mission to Somalia (1992–1995)	Red	Blue	VIOLENCE
Chad Civil War (1965–1969)	Red	Blue	INS/NI
Peacekeeping Rwanda (1993–1996)	Red	Blue	PEACE
Uganda Civil War (1979–1986)	Red	Blue	INS/NI
Cuban Revolution (1956–1959)	Red	Blue	INS/NI

Peacekeeping in Cambodia was a brief and successful U.N. peacekeeping mission with widespread internal support. It is the one case of a mission occurring at below 1-to-1 strength and resulting in a blue win. This one is a unique case of a low odds win. It, along with the other seven cases above are hard to otherwise explain unless there is a third or a forth or more factors in play.

Now, we have dismissed three of the "errors" away because the two-variable model did not address well those cases with forces ratios below 1-to-1. While we may be able to explain or rationalize four of the other errors, there are still 8 cases that cannot be easily explained. Therefore, the focus of our search became to see if we could find an obvious third single factor that could be added to our model that could address these remaining 12 cases.

We did not find a clear third variable to add to this model that would explain a significant potion of the remaining twelve cases. We looked at such factors as terrain and intensity of combat, but could see no clear pattern.

For example, in the cases below the actual result was blue while the predicted result was red.

CASE	FORCE RATIO	GENERAL LEVEL OF BRUTALITY	TERRAIN
PK in Cambodia (1991–1993)	0.70	1.47[6]	Covered
Polisario (1973–1991)	5.71	Low?	Uncovered
Mau Mau Revolt (1952–1956)	5.97	4.59	Covered
Colombian Civil War (1964–present)	8.03	0.94	Covered
Hungary (1956)	8.90	17.48[7]	Covered
Puerto Rico (1950–1954)	10.67	0.09	Covered

The general level of brutality is low in all but one of the blue wins where the model predicted it would be red. This could indicate that general level of brutality could be the third factor in this model.

But we do not see the same indication in those cases where the actual result was red but the predicted result was blue.

CASE	FORCE RATIO	GENERAL LEVEL OF BRUTALITY	TERRAIN
UN Mission to Somalia (1992–1995)	1.09		Covered
Chad Civil War (1965–1969)	1.60		Uncovered
Peacekeeping Rwanda (1993–1996)	2.37	1,616.86[8]	Covered
Uganda Civil War (1979–1986)	3.73		Covered
Cuban Revolution (1956–1959)	10.00	Low	Uncovered
First Intifada (1987–1993)	12.95	2.88	Covered

Looking at the figures, if "Level of Brutality" was added as a third variable, it might explain 6 of the remaining 12 cases, but other cases that were previously explained may now be incorrectly predicted because of this new variable. Still, this would have been worth pursuing except we only have civilian loss rate data for 40 of the insurgencies. Therefore, we could not test the entire data set using this variable. We were not comfortable testing only half the data set, especially as we had already broken it into three categories of political concept. We will have to wait on this test until such time as we can research more civilian loss rate data.

In the case of terrain, it does not appear that adding this to the model will improve the fidelity of the model. In least in this case, we do have data for all 83 cases. But this researcher is wary of adding variable to a regression analysis model just to get a fit. Add enough variables, if you will eventually succeed, but there is some question about the value of what you are saying.

But the focus of our search, and a significant part of the rest of this book, became an examination of those other factors that may be influencing the outcome of the insurgencies besides force ratio and cause. In that regard, our work now began to parallel and address the same issues as other counterinsurgent and insurgent theorists do.

NOTES

1. Secretary of Defense Donald Rumsfeld's quote from that same day is even more direct: "What is, I think reasonably certain, is the idea that it would take several hundred thousand U.S. forces, I think, is far from the mark." These statements by the Secretary of Defense and his deputy were made in direct contradiction to Generals Shinseki's statements two days earlier. Shinseki stated, in part: "I would say that what's been mobilized to this point, something on the order of several hundred thousand soldiers, are probably, you know, a figure that would be required. We're talking about post-hostilities control over a piece of geography that's fairly significant with the kinds of ethnic tensions that could lead to other problems."

2. We could never decided if the cases of Vietnam II or the Vietnam War should be counted as based upon nationalism or communism. If they are counted as based upon nationalism then we have 14 cases.

3. Nine cases if all insurgencies, interventions and peacekeeping operations from the data are used, seven cases if only the insurgencies are counted.

4. If one takes out the Vietnam cases, which were heavily influenced by nationalism, then they win in 73% of the cases.

5. According to this model, at any given force ratio, the odds of blue side success in insurgencies with a limited political concept may be about 33.1 times higher than the odds of blue side success in insurgencies where the political concept is based on a central idea and 5.7 times higher than when the political concept is based an overarching idea (the 90% Wald confidence interval for these odds ratio estimates are (1.65, 664.64) and (1.03, 31.46), respectively).

6. Calculated from reported data in MISS database. Brutality is measured as the average number of civilians killed per 100,000 population per year.

7. Calculated from total Hungarian killed over 4 months in the MISS database. This certainly includes people who are insurgents as well as many civilians. Calculation is based on one year even though there were only losses for four months. Figure could be considered to be three times higher if annualized. This figure is not currently in the MISS.

8. Calculated based upon the official figure of 937,000 from the Rwandan genocide and the population in 1994. Used as an annual figure. This figure is not currently in the MISS.

CHAPTER 7

Other Similar Work

Copy from one, it's plagiarism; copy from two, it's research.
—Wilson Mizner[1]

The above analysis was the first clear comparison of force ratios to outcome that we had seen. It was the only such comparison we were aware of at the time. Still, there have been a few other pieces of work on the subject worth noting. Most of these are not widely published.

QUINLIVAN

First is Dr. James T. Quinlivan at RAND. His thesis was not on force ratios but on troops required for stability operations. He specifically stated that successful nation-building usually requires 20 troops per thousand population.[2] Now, this is something fundamentally different than force ratios, as it is not based upon the size of the insurgency, but the size of the population. It is also based upon the forces needed for successful nation-building.

This would be apples as compared to oranges to our work above, if Quinlivan's work was not being used to address insurgencies. Even though his data was primarily drawn from recent peacekeeping operations, vice insurgencies, suddenly this rule migrated over to insurgencies. This was done by Quinlivan himself with the following statement in 2003: "The population of Iraq is nearly 25 million. That population would require 500,000 foreign troops on the ground to meet a standard of 20 troops per thousand residents." This widely quoted statement has been repeated in numerous articles, pieces of analysis, and other papers.[3] Unfortunately, it is based upon a very thin reed.

We find ourselves in the odd situation where we entirely disagree with his analysis, even though we fundamentally agree with his conclusions. In our original Iraq casualty estimate, we did take a look at Quinlivan's work. We took our 28 cases and calculated the number of counterinsurgency troops per thousand population. We then compared them to whether they won and lost. The pattern was:

COUNTERINSURGENTS PER THOUSAND POPULATION	PERCENT OF CASES WHERE THE INSURGENTS WON	NUMBER OF CASES	AVERAGE DURATION
1.0 to 4.4	60%	5	3.9 years
7.4 to 7.8	33%	3	5.0
15.1 to 31.1	38%	13	10.5
44.6 to 88.4	71%	7	10.6

Quinliven used only 13 points of data to establish his theme. Five were in the 0.5 to 4.6 range, three were in the 5.7 to 6.6 range and five were in the 20.0 to 23.7 range.[4] None were higher than that. These higher density insurgencies include significant cases like the Vietnam War. On the other hand the original purpose of this estimate was the look at "stability operations", not necessarily insurgencies. It was the expansion of this hypothesized relationship into insurgencies, based upon little analysis of the data, that we take issue with.[5]

As can be seen from the table above, there is simply no correlation between the troops per thousand population and the outcome of the insurgency. We see lower rates with blue wins, and we see very high rates with red wins. Our highest number of troops per thousand population is the Vietnam War.

We never did any further analysis of Quinlivan's theme, as we think our initial examination of it pretty much discredited it in our eyes as a relationship that can be used analytically for predictive purposes for an insurgency. Still it is published, widely distributed and still being used by some people. Unless Dr. Quinlivan can establish the validity of this by further research and hard data, or at least carefully define what it does apply to and what it does not apply to, then we have to say that this work should have no particular weight.

ANDREW HOSSACK'S WORK

Independent of *The Dupuy Institute's* effort was a parallel effort being done by Dr. Andrew Hossack at the Ministry of Defence in the United Kingdom. He started some work along this line in 2003, but began serious analytical effort, very similar to what we have done, in the following year. His broader work on analysis of insurgencies based upon historical data started in August 2004, the same month we started our Iraq estimate, and he effectively completed his work in September 2006. This was first publicly briefed at the Cornwallis Group meeting in Halifax, Nova Scotia in March 2005 (referred to as Cornwallis X).

It was as a result of that briefing, which was forwarded to us, that we first became aware of his work and he first became aware of our work, even though Dr. Hossack and I were already acquainted.

Therefore, we have a unique situation in which two separate teams of researchers, using two different sets of data, with two different sets of researchers, in two different countries, and slightly different methodologies, working at the same time, produced very similar results. His work is summarized in a paper he prepared in 2007 along with several briefings.[6]

Dr. Hossack's data set in 2005 consisted of only 18 cases. It grew to 44 cases, of which 34 were resolved and used for all of his analysis. Many of his cases were the same as ours. His research tended to be more top-level and primarily drawn from secondary sources. They also tended to have a bias towards British cases, and they dated back as early as post-World War I (that is, after 1918).

Dr. Hossack's work on force ratios clearly paralleled ours in conclusions, although it was based upon only 34 completed cases. One of his graphs shows:

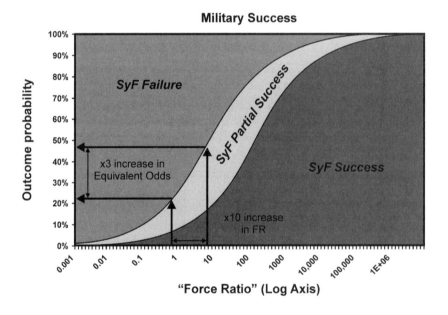

We will not go into detail on his paper as it is publically available, but he also independently developed a force ratio model. The model states that at 10-to-1 odds the counterinsurgents have around a 47% chance of success or partial success. While this does not match our conclusions in detail, it does reinforce what we are doing. In the case of our model, at 10-to-1 odds, there is a 96% chance of counterinsurgent victory if the insurgency is based upon a limited political concept and a 45% chance if the insurgency is based upon a central idea. Dr. Hossack's model is an interesting complementary effort, and we greatly respect the work that he has done. We do not think he was operating with the same resources as we were, and that affected the depth and extent of his research. Still, this is clearly in line with our analysis.

THE CAA WORK

Finally, in 2009, the Center for Army Analysis (CAA) also did some analysis of force ratios based upon the data base we provided them. It also demonstrated that force ratios do matter.

They identified 34 variables that they tested for significance compared to the winner (what we call outcome), and then the 11 significant ones were used to create a model. Six of those 11 were dropped, and they created a model based upon five variables in the data base. They were "Number of Red Factions," "Insurgent Population (Average)," "Counterinsurgent per Insurgent Ratio (Peak)," "Counterinsurgent Developed Nation," and "Political Concept." Note that two of the five factors are force ratio and political concept. These are the same two variables we use in our model. This effort was done independently and without consultation with us.

They then dropped "insurgent population (average)" from their model, giving them four variables, of which the model was driven primarily by political concept and force ratio. This four-variable model was built off the expanded database of 102 cases (vice the 83 cases we used). Of those 102 cases, it was build from 74 of them. It predicted 6 outcomes incorrectly, predicted 44 correctly, with 24 being uncertain. This is 88% accuracy if comparing just correct versus incorrect outcomes.

The accuracy of the model is certainly helped by having two more variables. Adding variables to a regression model always improves its statistical accuracy. If you add enough, it becomes a nice little mathematical curve-fitting exercise. The question is whether those added variables have any real explanatory value.

The use of the variable "number of factions" is interesting. In our original research, we did not systematically and rigorously establish a count of factions for each insurgency. What was listed in our spread sheets was based upon the data we had gathered in whatever manner it was reported. As we had never considered using that as an independent variable, we did not make sure this was assembled and counted in any systematic manner. It should not have been used as a variable without further research. Our work was the only source for their data.

What we did use was "structure of insurgency." Multi-faction insurgencies get incorporated under that. Just to demonstrate:

OUTCOME BY TYPE OF STRUCTURE

OUTCOME	DISORDERLY	DIRECTED	ORDERLY	NOT APPLICABLE	TOTAL
Blue	25	8	7	2	42
Gray	8	2	1	0	11
Red	17	9	4	0	30
Total	51	19	11	2	83

Two-sided p-value from Fisher's exact test excluding the not applicable cases: 0.8527
Two-sided p-value Fisher's exact test excluding the not applicable and Gray cases: 0.6624

Now, this shows that there is not a clear correlation here. My fear is that this variable ("number of factions") worked in their regression model because it was helping to shape the curve even though there is not a clear cause-and-effect relationship here.

Also, because of the methodology they choose, which was establishing variables based upon statistical significance, as opposed to there being a solid theoretical basis for it, then I believe statistically there should be around two "false" correlations among those 11 variables. If they tested 34 variables to the 5% level, then I gather this means that on the average 1.7 of those variables (34 x 0.05) are actually not real variables, they just happened to accidentally correlate with outcome (spurious correlation).

We are also concerned about the six variables they threw out because they did not add to the regression model. We have found reason to suspect that some of these do have some influence on the outcome, in particular: rules of engagement, type of insurgency, and indigenous force government type.

The one variable of the five that they originally kept, but then threw out, "Insurgent population (average)," we suspect may very well be a factor. We ended up examining this subject in depth in one of our reports for CAA and concluded:

> *Our analysis from Appendix V again indicates some form of relationship between population and outcome for those 34 cases of insurgencies against foreigners (colonial or intervening powers) where we had a clear outcome. . . .*
>
> **It appears that there is the some correlation between population and outcome from this sample of 34 cases (excluding the two ongoing examples), especially above 9,500,000 population.**
>
> *This relationship was established at the 20% significance level. It could be a spurious correlation driven by the dozen anti-colonial insurgencies with over an 80% success rate, but we suspect it is a weak, but real, correlation. As with area, this was a relationship we first saw in our Phase I effort.[7]*

My suspicion is that the actual cause-and-effect correlation is not between population size and outcome, but the levels of commitment and outcome. As large indigenous populations lead to large counterinsurgent commitments, there appears to be weak correlation between these two factors.

We suspect that the variable "counterinsurgent developed nation" is not a direct cause-and-effect correlation. I have not looked at it in depth, but instinctually feel that there are other factors at play here, including rules of engagement and "degrees of brutality." In their model, a developed nation had no impact on winning the insurgency, while an undeveloped nation has some positive impact and a partly-developed nation had considerable. We think this is counterintuitive and probably incorrect.

My natural tendency as a modeler was to make sure I had clearly identified cause-and-effect relationships before I moved forward. That is why my approach starts simply (two variables) and moves forward from there. It is also why I independently examined each possible variable in some depth. In addition, I reviewed and examined a range of theorists before proceeding (see Chapter Seventeen). I have had the experience of dumping lots of variables into a regression model, and lo-and-behold, something fits. It is important to make sure you have clearly established cause-and-effect.

On a further note, all of the work to date has been focused on examining already developed insurgencies. At the point most military organizations start collecting data on insurgencies, they already have a major problem. What has not been addressed are the early stages of insurgencies, a period of time where it is much easier and less costly to correct or suppress. This probably cannot be addressed with the data collection we currently have.

Still it is not surprising that we achieved very similar results, considering that the methodology was similar to what we did and the data was almost the same. In this case, they used 74 of the 102 cases we had provided, which included the 83 cases used in our analysis above. Still, it provides further confirmation that there is a clear relationship between force ratio and outcome. This work at CAA was primarily the effort of Justine Blaho and Lisa Kaiser.[8] We were not involved in it.

This was a useful effort. It is a third demonstration that force ratios do matter. As far as I know, CAA has done nothing further on this.

BOOTS ON THE GROUND

I think the above chapters have clearly established that force ratios are important. I think that those who pooh-pooh its significance need to provide some evidence to establish their counterargument. Still, there is a phrase that has become very popular inside the Defense Department which is sort of related to force ratios, but is not quite force ratios. This is "boots on the ground."

The problem is that we don't know precisely what "boots on the ground" means. Is it force ratios or is it something else? I have been in meetings where I am talking force ratios and the other analysts are talking "boots on the ground," and I don't know if we agree or disagree. Is "boots on the ground" a fuzzier way of expressing force ratios or a more sophisticated way of addressing the forces needed? I fear that it is still a phrase still influenced by Clutterbuck. As he said:

> *Much nonsense is heard on the subject of tie-down ratios in guerrilla warfare—that 10 to 12 government troops are needed to tie down a single guerrilla, for instance. This is a dangerous illusion, arising from a disregard of the facts. It is quite true that, against the armed guerillas in any such war, the difference is large. This does not, however, represent the difference in the jungle, for three*

reasons: first, because a large part of the army consists of "overheads"—men, concerned with command, control, supply support, and road and air movement, who wear uniforms but never go into the jungle; second, because, though some of these overheads may be luxuries, others (such as command and supply) are provided for the guerillas as well, not by uniformed men but by the Party organization and the supporter in the village, who are numbered not in thousands but in hundreds of thousands, and third, because the protection and control of these villages ties up large numbers of policemen who, like so many of the soldiers, do not go into the jungle but are necessary all the same.[9]

If one ignores for the moment that this paragraph can be read to be support force ratios, even though Clutterbuck calls them a "dangerous illusion," it does lead to an extended discussion on the "jungle strength" of the army. For example: "By the turning point of the war (1952), the effective jungle strength of the army and police together probably reached a 2-to-1 superiority over the guerillas; but it was never anywhere near the 10- or 12-to-1 ratio so often quoted by commanders."[10]

"Boots on the ground" is an undefined slang phase that has been around for at least 30 years. Now, any deployed armed force is going to have support troops. There are a certain percent of troops that are primarily combat (infantry, armor) and another group that are primarily, but not exclusively, support. The lines get blurred in a guerilla war. Obviously, "boots on the ground" refers to adding more combat troops. While having a better tooth-to-tail ratio (ratio of combat troops to support troops) is always a good thing, within reason, adding any more combat troops to a theater invariably requires you to add support troops. It is hard to add "boots" without additional support. Therefore, increasing the number of "boots on the ground" means increasing the overall force size, unless one is specifically talking about significantly changing the tooth-to-tail ratio. Otherwise, "boots on the ground" does appear to be synonymous with changing the force ratio.

NOTES

1. Quote is given as "If you steal from one author it's plagiarism, if you steal from many it's research" in Alva Johnson, *The Legendary Mizners* (New York: Farrar, Straus & Young, 2003), page 66.

2. For example, see James T. Quinlivan, "Burden of Victory: The Painful Arithmetic of Stability Operations" (RAND, Summer 2003), and "Force Requirements in Stability Operations," *Parameters* (Winter 1995).

3. For example, see Stephen Budiansky, "A Proven Formula for How Many Troops We Need," *The Washington Post* (May 9, 2004); Fred Kaplan, "The Army, Faced With its Limits," The New York Times (Jan. 1, 2006); Carlos L. Yordan, Ph.D., "Are More Troops Needed in Iraq?" Small Wars Journal (Feb. 2006); Paul Krugman, "The Arithmetic of Failure," *The New York Times* (Oct. 27, 2006) and many others. None of those who quote Quinliven seem to note that his conclusions are based upon only 11 cases, of which 4

are insurgencies, and that he then applies this formula for "nation-building" to insurgencies. Considering how short the original two papers are (9 and 3 pages respectively), it is surprising that this is not noted with some concern.

4. His data from various sources includes a U.S. figure of 2.3 sworn officers per thousand population or 3.1 per thousand if one includes the civilian support apparatus of police departments (Quinlivan 1995), 0.5 per thousand for Afghanistan in 2002 (Quinlivan, 2003), 2.2 for Germany after October 1945 (Quinlivan 1995), 3.5 for Haiti in 1994 (Quinlivan 2003), 4.6 for Somalia in 1993 (Quinlivan 2003), 5.7 for Punjab (Quinlivan 1995), 6.1 for Iraq in 2003 (Quinlivan 2003), 6.6 for Dominican Republic in 1965 (Quinlivan 1995), 20 or more for in Malaya (Quinlivan 1995), steadily around 20 per thousand in Northern Ireland (Quinlivan 1995), more than 20 per thousand for Bosnia in 1995 and after five years, fell below 10 per thousand (Quinlivan 2003), 22.6 for Bosnia in 1996 (Quinlivan 2003) and 23.7 for Kosovo in 1999 (Quinlivan 2003).

5. We are also bothered by the fact that he has established such a theme based on only 13 points of data (effectively only 11 as 2 of them are recently-developing wars). Furthermore, he had no cases in the database with more than 23.7 troops per thousand population, even though we had 14 cases higher than his highest ratio, which included 8 counterinsurgent wins and 6 insurgent wins. With two of his 13 cases being ongoing operations for which don't know the outcome (Iraq and Afghanistan), this left us with 11 cases, and only 4 of them are insurgencies. Therefore, he is extending this rule over to insurgencies based upon four cases in which there was only one insurgent victory. This is hardly a statistically significant sample, let alone one that is unbiased or representative of the population as a whole. Considering the resources available to RAND and also that Dr. Quinlivan is the head of its Arroyo Center, this paucity of data is surprising.

6. Andrew Hossack, Ph.D., "Security Force & Insurgent Success Factors in Counter-Insurgency Campaigns," presented in spring 2007 at Cornwallis XII.

7. See *Examination of Factors Influencing the Conduct of Operations in Guerilla Wars: Task 12: Examining the Geographic Aspects of an Insurgency* (Annandale, VA.: The Dupuy Institute, 4 February 2008), section G, 30–32.

8. "A Predictive Model for Irregular Wars based on a Structured Historical Database" presented at the 48th Annual AORS Symposium, 14–15 October 2009.

9. Richard L. Clutterbuck, *The Long, Long War* (New York: Praeger, 1966), 42.

10. *Ibid.*

CHAPTER 8

Outside Support and Structure of Insurgencies

You just don't understand. There is no need for special orders anymore. The mujahideen are just doing what they are responsible for doing. To kill and attack Germans is the goal and that is clear to everyone. The entire chain and network is responsible.

We are unaware of any shuras located outside of Afghanistan. Every local commander is responsible for his own areas. The area commander is account-able to the district commander who is in turn accountable to the provincial governor. The governor is then accountable to the provincial executive coun-cil, which deal with Taliban military shura.

—Qari Bashir Haqqani, Taliban military commander in Kunduz and head of the radical Islamist executive council for Kunduz, 21 May 2008[1]

In addition to looking at political concept of an insurgency, we also looked at type of outside support (primarily indigenous, some or considerable) and the structure of the insurgency (disorderly, directed and overarching). In effect, we were re-peating the analysis that we did for the Iraq Casualty Estimate but using 83 cases in-stead of 28.

We conducted a simple statistical comparison of each of them to the entire data-base (all 83 cases, including 21 interventions and peacekeeping operations), to just the 62 insurgencies, and to just the 36 insurgencies against foreigners (insurgencies with significant intervening powers or against colonial powers).

THE 83 CASE DATASET

An examination of outcome (blue, gray or red result) compared to type of outside support produced no discernable pattern. The counterinsurgents or intervening force tended to win more often then not, no matter what the degree of outside sup-port was for the insurgency. Our statistical test indicated that there was no correla-tion here.[2]

OUTCOME BY TYPE OF OUTSIDE SUPPORT

OUTCOME	PRIMARILY INDIGENOUS	SOME	CONSIDERABLE	NOT APPLICABLE	TOTAL
Blue	11	20	9	2	42
Gray	5	6	0	0	11
Red	7	18	5	0	30
Total	23	44	14	2	83

The same was the case with structure of the insurgency. The degree of organization of the insurgents did not seem to have much impact on the outcome of the insurgencies.[3]

OUTCOME BY TYPE OF STRUCTURE

OUTCOME	DISORDERLY	DIRECTED	ORDERLY	NOT APPLICABLE	TOTAL
Blue	25	8	7	2	42
Gray	8	2	1	0	11
Red	17	9	4	0	30
Total	50	19	12	2	83

THE 62 CASE DATASET

When we stripped the data down to only the 62 cases that are clearly insurgencies, we again found no pattern when comparing type of outside support to the outcome.[4]

OUTCOME BY TYPE OF OUTSIDE SUPPORT

OUTCOME	PRIMARILY INDIGENOUS	SOME	CONSIDERABLE	TOTAL
Blue	8	15	6	29
Gray	2	2	0	6
Red	6	16	5	27
Total	16	33	11	62

The same was the case with type of structure of the insurgency.[5]

OUTCOME BY TYPE OF STRUCTURE

OUTCOME	DISORDERLY	DIRECTED	ORDERLY	TOTAL
Blue	17	7	5	29
Gray	5	1	0	6
Red	16	9	2	27
Total	38	17	7	62

THE 36 CASE DATASET

As we stripped the data down to only those 36 cases where the insurgencies were facing intervening outside forces, there were still no indications of any patterns or fits.[6]

OUTCOME BY TYPE OF OUTSIDE SUPPORT

OUTCOME	PRIMARILY INDIGENOUS	SOME	CONSIDERABLE	TOTAL
Blue	2	9	5	16
Gray	0	2	0	2
Red	3	11	4	18
Total	5	22	9	36

This was also the case for type of structure of the insurgency compared to outcome.[7]

OUTCOME BY TYPE OF STRUCTURE

OUTCOME	DISORDERLY	DIRECTED	ORDERLY	TOTAL
Blue	12	3	1	16
Gray	2	0	0	2
Red	11	5	2	18
Total	25	8	3	36

What led us to look at these particular issues of outside support and structure of insurgency was the emphasis on these points from the "American school" of counterinsurgent theorists, like Joes and O'Neill. The consistent null results no matter how we looked at the data, indicate that perhaps other factors may be playing a much more important part in determining the outcome of an insurgency that the size of the supply trails and how disciplined and tightly controlled the organization is that runs the insurgency.

The conclusions we drew from this analysis was:

1. A lack of outside support does not necessarily doom an insurgency.
2. Considerable outside support does not mean an insurgency will win.
3. There appears to be little correlation between the degree of outside support for an insurgency and the outcome of the insurgency.
4. A disorderly insurgency is not necessarily a doomed insurgency.
5. An orderly insurgency is not necessarily a successful insurgency.
6. There appears to be little correlation between the structure of an insurgency and the outcome of an insurgency.

The first point, on lack of outside support, is reinforced by all the data sets. For those 83 cases where there was little outside support, the insurgents still won 30% of the time. For those 62 insurgencies where there was little outside support, the insurgents still won 38% of the time. For those 36 insurgencies against foreigners where there was little outside support (whereas the counter insurgency has considerable outside support), the insurgents still won 50% of the time. For the 29 cases of primarily domestic insurgencies, the insurgents still won 33% of the time.

The second point, on considerable outside support, is also reinforced by all the data sets. For those 83 cases where there was considerable outside support, the insurgents still won 36% of the time. For those 62 insurgencies where there was considerable outside support, the insurgents still won 45% of the time. For those 36 insurgencies against foreigners where there was considerable outside support (and the counter insurgency also has considerable outside support), the insurgents still won 50% of the time. For the 29 cases of primarily domestic insurgencies, the insurgents still won 40% of the time. Note that these numbers and the pattern of the numbers parallel those in the second point, above.

This leads to our third point: If there is little correlation between the amount of outside support and the outcome of the insurgency, then insurgencies succeed or fail for entirely different reasons. This would lead one to wonder whether control of borders, as is so often discussed by various theorists, is that important other than helping to kill off an already doomed insurgency (as in the case of Greece) and even when done effectively (as in the case of Algeria), it might not kill off an insurgency that is otherwise soundly based? It is clear when the data is sectioned out into the 62 insurgencies or the 36 cases of insurgencies against foreign powers, the percent of insurgent wins is pretty much the same (roughly 40–50%) in all categories of support.

The fourth point, on disorderly insurgencies, is reinforced by all the data sets. For those 83 cases where the insurgency was "disorderly", the insurgents still won 33% of the time. For those 62 insurgencies where the insurgency was "disorderly", the insurgents still won 42% of the time. For those 36 insurgencies against foreigners where the insurgency was "disorderly" (whereas the counterinsurgency was usually "orderly"), the insurgents still won 43% of the time. For the 29 cases of primarily domestic insurgencies, the insurgents still won 40% of the time. This indicates that there is no clear cause and effect between the structure of an insurgency and the outcome. Note that 61% of all the insurgencies examined were disorderly as were 70% of those against foreign powers.

The fifth point, on orderly insurgencies, is reinforced by all the datasets. For those 83 cases where the insurgency was "orderly", the insurgents won 36% of the time. For those 62 insurgencies where the insurgency was "orderly", the insurgents won 29% of the time. For those 36 insurgencies against foreigners where the insurgency was "orderly" (whereas the counterinsurgency was usually "orderly"), the insurgents won 50% of the time. For the 29 cases of primarily domestic insurgencies, we recorded no insurgent wins. Still, "orderly" insurgencies only make up 11% of the cases and they did not result in insurgent wins as often as the disorderly ones did (29% versus 42%).

The sixth point, about there being little correlation between structure and outcome, follows naturally from the preceding ones and the very poor fits found in the Fischer's Exact Test. One should not assume that means that direction, unified command and better control are not desirable for the insurgency, it means that the underlying reason for insurgent success appears to be caused by other and more important factors.

This leads us to the factors that we think are important to determine the outcome.

NOTES

1. Susanne Koelbl and Sami Yousafzi. "Interview with a Taliban Commander: What's Important is to Kill the Germans." Spiegel Online International (21 May 2008).
2. Two-sided p-value from Fisher's exact test excluding the not applicable cases: 0.4003. Two-sided p-value Fisher's exact test excluding the not applicable and gray cases: 0.6862.
3. Two-sided p-value from Fisher's exact test excluding the not applicable cases: 0.8527. Two-sided p-value Fisher's exact test excluding the not applicable and gray cases: 0.6624.
4. Two-sided p-value from Fisher's exact test: 0.8240. Two-sided p-value from Fisher's exact test excluding the gray group: 0.8785
5. Two-sided p-value from Fisher's exact test: 0.6522 Two-sided p-value from Fisher's exact test excluding the gray group: 0.5121.
6. Two-sided p-value from Fisher's exact test: greater than 0.9. Two-sided p-value from Fisher's exact test excluding the gray group: greater than 0.9
7. Two-sided p-value from Fisher's exact test: 0.9. Two-sided p-value from Fisher's exact test excluding the gray group: 0.8

CHAPTER 9

Rules of Engagement and Measurements of Brutality

We're not running out of targets, Afghanistan is!

—Secretary of Defense Donald Rumsfeld, 9 October 2001[1]

Next, our analysis attempted to look at more operational issues, vice the bigger picture strategic issues of the previous chapters. In particular we attempted to find some way of addressing rules of engagement, the use of firepower and measuring the results of the general level of brutality of these wars. In our examination of this complex subject, we attempted to explore four distinct issues.

1. The actual rules of engagement used,
2. The value, or lack thereof, of the use of torture,
3. The controlled or indiscriminate use of firepower, and
4. The effect of a brutal counterinsurgent effort or a brutal insurgency.

These are four completely different measures, even though they fundamentally overlap in concept. It is unusual to find a war in which the counterinsurgent force used strict rules of engagement and yet regularly used torture; nor does one often find a war in which counterinsurgents subjected villages to indiscriminant use of firepower and yet followed strict prohibitions on the abuse of prisoners. Still, they remain four different subjects, although it is easy to envision that rules of engagement and overall civilian losses are fundamentally linked.

A. RULES OF ENGAGEMENT

Rules of engagement are described in the MISS database as strictly defensive, polite, strict, restricted, unrestricted, and brutal.[2] Of the 83 cases recorded, the distribution is:

RULES OF ENGAGEMENT	ALL CASES	INSURGENCIES ONLY	INSURGENCIES VERSUS FOREIGNERS	PRIMARILY DOMESTIC INSURGENCIES
Strictly Defensive	0	0	0	0
Polite	5	0	0	0
Strict	15	6	5	1
Restricted	24	21	13	8
Unrestricted	34	31	15	16
Brutal	2	4	3	1
Total Cases	83	62	36	26

Clearly the rules of engagement are often a function of the type of situation one is facing. One would expect that the rules of engagement for a force in a peacekeeping mission would be much more restricted than those for someone fighting an insurgency. Just to look at the data for a moment:

TYPE OF SITUATION	RULES OF ENGAGEMENT					PERCENT POLITE OR STRICT
	POLITE	STRICT	RESTRICTED	UNRESTRICTED	BRUTAL	
Peace	4	6	0	0	0	100
Conventional	1	2	0	0	0	100
VIOLENCE	0	1	0	2	0	33
CONV/INS	0	1	2	3	0	17
INS/I	0	3	7	7	2	16
INS/C	0	1	4	6	0	9
INS/NI	0	1	7	14	1	4
SUP/INS	0	0	1	1	1	0
GUERINV	0	0	3	1	0	0
SUP	0	0	0	0	1	0

For example, it would be expected that the rules of engagement for a force in a peacekeeping mission would be much more restricted than those fighting an insurgency and a force fighting a full-scale, conventional civil war would be expected to follow rules of engagement that were much less restrictive.

There seems to be a clear correlation between the rules of engagement and the outcome. This is shown in the following four charts, three of them which measure a subset of the overall data set:

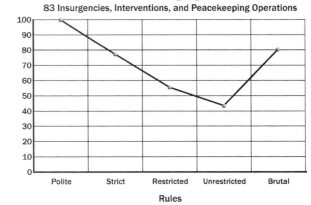

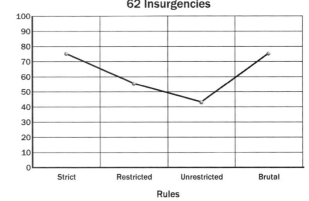

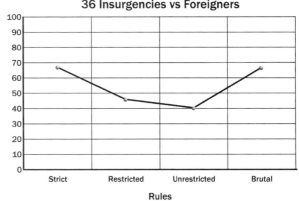

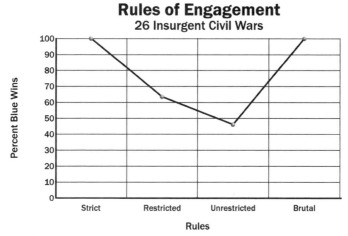

Rules of Engagement
26 Insurgent Civil Wars

There also seems to be a clear correlation between the rules of engagement and the outcome, but this does not establish cause and effect; for example, perhaps the reason less strict rules of engagement were used was because one insurgency was particularly difficult or less tractable than the other. On the other hand, it is clear that the rules of engagement are sometimes a function of the type of insurgency being fought. It is hard not to notice the difference between primarily domestic insurgencies (where 64% are unrestricted or brutal) compared to insurgencies versus foreigners (where 53% are unrestricted or brutal).

This results in a clear, consistent pattern which in the face of no other data on the subject (and we are not aware of any other data collection that addresses this subject) produces a powerful argument that there is some correlation between rules of engagement and outcome, and that there might be a cause-and-effect relationship between rules of engagement and outcome.

Statistical Testing of the Above Relationships
All Insurgencies, Interventions and Peacekeeping Operations (72 cases)

RULES OF ENGAGEMENT

OUTCOME	POLITE	STRICT	RESTRICTED	UNRESTRICTED	BRUTAL	TOTAL
Blue wins	4	10	12	12	4	42
Blue losses	0	3	10	16	1	30
Total	4	13	22	28	5	72

We tested the hypothesis that the success of the counterinsurgents is independent of the rules of engagement employed to combat the insurgency. The result was somewhat ambiguous in that at the 10 percent confidence level (p-value of 0.0783) following Fisher's exact test that hypothesis was rejected (implying that it may be a false assumption and that counterinsurgent success **was** dependent on the rules of engagement), while at the 5 percent confidence level the test accepted the hypothesis (implying that it may be a true assumption and that counterinsurgent success **wasn't** dependent on the rules of engagement). This table and the next three tables exclude all the cases that were draws or ongoing. However, when we narrowed the selection to a more strict definition of insurgencies only (56 cases), insurgencies against foreigners (34 cases), and primarily domestic insurgencies (22 cases), we found that the null was consistently rejected, implying that in those cases the assumption that counterinsurgent success **was** dependent on the rules of engagement **was** correct.

Insurgencies only (56 cases)

RULES OF ENGAGEMENTS

OUTCOME	POLITE	STRICT	RESTRICTED	UNRESTRICTED	BRUTAL	TOTAL
Blue wins	0	3	11	12	3	29
Blue losses	0	1	9	16	1	27
Total	0	4	20	28	4	56

Fisher's exact test two-sided p-value is 0.4587—no reason to reject the null hypothesis.

Insurgencies versus Foreigners (INS/C and INS/I) only (34 cases)

RULES OF ENGAGEMENTS

OUTCOME	POLITE	STRICT	RESTRICTED	UNRESTRICTED	BRUTAL	TOTAL
Blue wins	0	2	6	6	2	16
Blue losses	0	1	7	9	1	18
Total	0	3	13	15	3	34

Fisher's exact test two-sided p-value is 0.8196—no reason to reject the null hypothesis.

Primarily Domestic Insurgencies (INS/NI) only (22 cases)

RULES OF ENGAGEMENT

OUTCOME	POLITE	STRICT	RESTRICTED	UNRESTRICTED	BRUTAL	TOTAL
Blue wins	0	1	5	6	1	13
Blue losses	0	0	2	7	0	9
Total	0	1	7	13	1	22

Fisher's exact test two-sided p-value is 0.6076—no reason to reject the null hypothesis.

B. USE OF TORTURE

We did not analyze, code, or otherwise specifically examine the use of torture in the 83 cases we studied. That was primarily due to time constraints in researching and assigning a consistent, measurable data point to such a factor and the difficulty in determining a pattern from such variable and inconsistent data for each of the 83 cases. On the other hand, we consider that torture exists in the context of the rules of engagement, use of firepower and the general level of brutality found in a counterinsurgency. Thus, if the counterinsurgent rules of engagement are brutal, then most likely torture is being used to some extent, and may often be extensively used. Or, if the counterinsurgent's rules of engagement are strict, then most likely torture is only being used only to a very limited extent. While there may be some fine difference between the extent and nature of the torture practiced in those cases where there are "restricted" rules of engagement, we suspect there is no objective way to make a determination between "small," "medium," and "large" in this context, nor is there any realistic measure that can distinguish between the effect of psychological degradation and heinous acts of physical abuse that we can easily construct. Therefore, we relied on our analysis of the rules of engagement, the extent of firepower used and the general level of brutality as surrogates for this important question.

C. USE OF FIREPOWER

The easiest metric we could determine for measuring the use of firepower was the number of civilians killed divided by the number of insurgents killed. Still, this was a difficult figure to assemble. At the conclusion of our studies we had found civilian casualty data for only some 35 insurgencies. Thus, a simple comparison between civilian and insurgent deaths is possible in those 35 or so cases, except that we have so far only been able to measure civilian deaths as the number killed by all actors in the insurgency—intervening forces, government forces, militias and death squads, insurgents—and by factional violence, and to all causes, including deliberate acts of aggression and accidental acts of "collateral damage." Still, the pattern is clear: Because of their firepower superiority, the majority of civilians in almost all insurgencies are killed by intervening or indigenous government counterinsurgency forces. We have found that in some Latin American insurgencies the militia and death squads, which are often allied to a wing of the government, also made a significant contribution to the body count. Of course, the insurgents are not innocent and frequently kill large numbers of civilians, but it appears that they are rarely directly responsible for more than perhaps 30 percent of the civilian deaths (possibly because they lack the capability to do more), although there are some notable exceptions. So this metric can be used so long as it is understood that while it is valid in the majority of cases, it always overmeasures, and is invalid in a few cases.

A more precise measure would be to determine the actual number of civilians killed by counterinsurgent forces and compare those to the number of insurgents killed. However, this more precise and correct measure is only possible in a few of the better documented insurgencies. At this point, even with the extensive research we have already completed, we have only been able to find this in about ten cases. Therefore, we used both measures and compared and contrasted them.

Looking at the more complete data first, the number of civilians killed by counterinsurgent forces compared to the number of insurgents killed by counterinsurgent forces, we found:

NAME	WINNER	RULES	CIVILIANS KILLED BY CI/INS KILLED	CIVILIANS KILLED/INSURGENTS KILLED	TOTAL CIVILIANS KILLED/100,000 POPULATION
Hamas (2006)	Gray	R	0.48	0.56	9.98
Hezbollah War (2006)	Red	R	0.49	1.43	16.62
First Intifada (1987–1993)	Red	R	2.32	2.53	18.74
Algerian War (1954–1962)	Red	U	0.69	1.09	214.37
Shining Path in Peru (1980–1999)	Blue	R	1.07	1.92	108.94
El Salvador (1979–1992)	Blue	U	1.23	2.11	791.07
Second Intifada (2000–2005)	Gray	R	2.40	2.88	69.19
U.S. Invasion of Panama (1989)	Blue	S	4.62[3]	4.62	12.66
Northern Ireland (1968–1998)	Blue	S	See Below	See Below	123.93

The ratio of civilians killed by counterinsurgents to those killed by insurgents varied from 0.48 to 4.62, while the ratio of civilians killed to insurgents killed varied from 0.56 to 4.62, and the ratio of civilians killed to 100,000 population varied from 9.98 to 791.07. It should be realized that a "low" figure such as 0.48 for Hamas meant that even with their restricted rules of engagement the counterinsurgents were responsible for killing nearly 5 civilians for every 10 insurgents they killed. For Hamas, Hezbollah and First Intifada the number means that one civilian was killed for every two insurgents. Furthermore, the values that are greater than 1.0 indicate that the counterinsurgent forces killed more civilians than they did insurgents, which appears to be as common as not.

Northern Ireland was a special case that highlights some of the problems with this line of analysis. It was a Blue win with strict rules of engagement, but with three distinct parties inflicting civilian deaths; IRA insurgents, British and Irish national government counterinsurgents and Irish Loyalist militias, who might be considered either as insurgents or counterinsurgents, depending on the circumstances.

FACTION SUFFERING DEATHS	FACTION CAUSING DEATHS BRITISH/IRISH CI	IRA INS	LOYALIST CI/INS
Civilian Deaths	190	738	873
IRA Deaths	150	185	42
Loyalist Deaths	14	45	91
British/Irish CI Deaths	13	1,088	14

From our analysis we can say that the ratio of civilians killed by CI (190) to the number of IRA insurgents killed by CI (150) was 1.27 but 1.16 if the Loyalist deaths are included as insurgents. Similarly, the ratio of total civilians killed (1,801) to IRA insurgents killed (377) was 4.78, but the total of civilians killed to IRA and Loyalist insurgents killed was 3.42. However, it is perhaps more significant to the eventual outcome of this insurgency that the ratio of civilian deaths caused by the IRA to those caused by British/Irish CI was 3.88, while that of civilian deaths caused by Loyalists to those caused by the British/Irish CI was 4.59 and the combined IRA/Loyalist ratio as a cause for civilian deaths to those by the British/Irish CI was 8.48.

The comparison of the total number of civilians killed to the total number insurgents killed is much simpler, with the data falling into three basic categories. Those are, less than one civilian killed per insurgent, 1-to-10 civilians killed per insurgent and more than 10 civilians killed per insurgent.

NAME	WINNER	RULES	CIVILIANS KILLED/ INSURGENTS KILLED	TOTAL CIVILIANS KILLED/100,000 POPULATION
Rhodesia I (1966–1972)	Blue	U	0.02	0.11
Borneo (1963–1966)	Blue	R	0.06	0.16
Mozambique (1964–1974)4	Red	U	0.11	11.37
Aden (1963–1967)	Red	R	0.14	7.54
Tamil Insurgency (1983–2002)	Blue	U	0.14	14.50
Mau Mau Revolt (1952–1956)	Blue	U	0.15	22.94
Indonesia (1945–1949)5	Red	U	0.24	8.91
Ukraine (1944–1954)	Blue	B	0.25	104.76
U.S. Invasion of Grenada(1983)	Blue	S	0.34	26.97
Vietnam War (1965–1973)	Red	R	0.50	2,471.27
Rhodesia II (1972–1979)	Red	U	0.52	75.76
Hamas War (2006)	Gray	R	0.56	9.98
Puerto Rico (1950–1954)	Blue	R	0.59	0.45

Kashmir (1988–present)	Blue	R	0.70	143.85
Colombian Civil War (1964–present)	Blue	U	0.88	40.61
Algerian War (1954–1962)	Red	U	1.09	1,644.20
UK in Palestine (1944–1948)	Red	S	1.13	60.96
Operation Tacaud (1978–1980)	Red	R	1.23	70.75
Hezbollah War (2006)	Red	R	1.43	16.62
PK in Sierra Leone (1997–2005)	Blue	R	1.77	226.52
Shining Path in Peru (1980–1999)	Blue	R	1.92	108.94
El Salvador (1979–1992)	Blue	U	1.99	791.07
UN PK in Congo (2000–present)	Blue	S	2.20	25.53
First Intifada (1987–1993)	Red	R	2.69	18.74
Malaya (1948–1960)	Blue	R	2.71	11.34
Cyprus (1955–1959)	Blue	R	2.82	57.37
Second Intifada (2000–2005)	Gray	R	2.88	69.19
U.S. Invasion of Panama (1989)	Blue	S	4.62	12.66
Northern Ireland (1968–1998)	Blue	S	5.22	123.93
Iraq (2003–present)	Gray	S	6.44	136.03
Cameroun (1955–1960)	Red	U	7.33	114.80
Indonesia in Timor (1975–1999)	Red	B	8.74	15,615.14
Guatemala (1960–1996)	Blue	U	19.34	550.49
UN PK in Angola (1988–1999)	Blue	S	31.90	5,785.87
Vietnam II (1961–1964)	Red	R	51.99	42.66

This data is far from perfect, since it is incomplete, but the real issue is with the cases where the data is so flawed that it may place the case in the wrong category. For example, in the 15 cases in the lowest category (less than one civilian killed per insurgent), there are at least 4 where further research will probably result in a significant change in that ratio. We are nearly certain that will be the case for Ukraine, the Mau Mau Revolt, the Tamil Insurgency, and Indonesia.

We are relatively more comfortable with the data in the 17 cases that make up the middle tier. The decision to include the U.S. Invasion of Panama in the middle tier is based primarily on the assumption that the data is accurate and is certainly not much higher than what we currently show (that is, it will not exceed 5.00). Furthermore, Panama was a small conventional operation with a low overall loss rate, so we would not expect the overall losses to increase. On the other hand, the data for UK in Palestine, Iraq and Indonesia in Timor may change, and that change may increase their numbers. We suspect that there is a reasonable chance that with additional research some of these three cases may increase to between 5.00 and 10.00 may well exceed 10.00.

The dividing point for the upper tier may actually be driven by the size of the gap between 8.74 and 19.34, rather than anything else. On the other hand additional research may result in a notable increase in the three values that fall at 5.22 and 8.74 now.

However, based upon the current division of the three categories, into three unequal groups, a comparison shows that:

- Low Civilian Loss Rates (less than 1.00 civilians killed per insurgent killed) results in 33% Red Wins (15 cases)
- Medium Civilian Loss Rates (1.09 – 8.74) results in 41% Red Wins (17 cases)
- High Civilian Loss Rates (19.34 – 103.16) results in 33% Red Wins (3 cases)

Or, to look at it from the other viewpoint:

- Low Civilian Loss Rates (less than 1.00) results in 60% Blue Wins (15 cases)
- Medium Civilian Loss Rates (1.23 – 8.74) results in 47% Blue Wins (17 cases)
- High Civilian Loss Rates (19.34 – 103.16) results in 66% Blue Wins (3 cases)

For the total of 35 cases, 37% result in Red Wins, 9% in Gray outcomes (only one ongoing), and 54% in Blue Wins. Or, to put it into a matrix:

	BLUE	GRAY	RED	TOTAL
Low	9	1	5	15
Medium	8	2	7	17
High	2	0	1	3
Total	19	3	13	35

The Fisher's exact test two-sided p-value for the above is greater than 0.9. If we remove the "gray" results, then the two-side p-value is greater than 0.8, indicating that there is probably no correlation here.

In general, there does seem to be a pattern where insurgencies win more often if the number of civilians killed compared to the number of insurgents killed is greater than ten, but it there is no statistical support for such an assumption.

D. GENERAL LEVEL OF BRUTALITY

Finally, there is the general level of brutality of the war, which can be measured as the number of civilians killed per 100,000 in the population. We have found this data for 40 cases and can certainly add to and improve this dataset given additional research.

The insurgencies we have found relatively complete civilian casualty data for include:

NAME	WINNER	RULES	CIVILIANS KILLED PER 100,000 POPULATION	
			YEARLY AVERAGE	TOTAL
Rhodesia I (1966–1972)	Blue	U	0.02	0.11
Borneo (1963–1966)	Blue	R	0.03	0.16
Puerto Rico (1950–1954)	Blue	R	0.09[6]	0.45
Tamil Insurgency (1983–2002)	Blue	U	0.72	14.50
Malaya (1948–1960)	Blue	R	0.87	11.34
Colombian Civil War (1964–present)	Blue	U	0.94	40.61
Aden (1963–1967)	Red	R	1.51	7.54

Argentina (1969–1983)	Gray	U	2.22	33.36
First Intifada (1987–1993)	Red	R	2.88	18.74
UN PK in Congo (2000–present)	Blue	S	3.19	25.53
Northern Ireland (1968–1998)	Blue	S	4.00	123.93
Mau Mau Revolt (1952–1956)	Blue	U	4.59	22.94
Shining Path in Peru (1980–1999)	Blue	R	5.45	108.94
Kashmir (1988– present)	Blue	R	7.99	143.85
Indonesia (1945–1949)	Red	U	8.91[7]	N/A
Ukraine (1944–1954)	Blue	B	9.52	104.76
Hamas War (2006)	Gray	R	9.98	9.98
Vietnam II (1961–1964)	Red	R	10.67	42.66
Mozambique (1964–1974)	Red	U	11.37[8]	N/A
Cyprus (1955–1959)	Blue	R	11.47	57.37
Second Intifada (2000–2005)	Gray	R	11.53	69.19
UK in Palestine (1944–1948)	Red	S	12.19	60.96
Rhodesia (1972–1979)	Red	U	12.63	75.76
U.S. Invasion of Panama (1989)	Blue	S	12.66[9]	12.66
La Menos Violencia (1958–1964)	Gray	U	14.86	103.99
Guatemala (1960–1996)	Blue	U	14.88	550.49
Hezbollah War (2006)	Red	R	16.62	16.62
Cameroun (1955–1960)	Red	U	22.96	114.8
Operation Tacaud (1978–1980)	Red	R	23.58	70.75
Yemen (1962–1970)	Blue	U	25.00[10]	N/A
PK in Sierra Leone (1997–2005)	Blue	R	25.17[11]	226.52
U.S. Invasion of Grenada (1983)	Blue	S	26.97	26.97
Iraq (2003– present)	Gray	S	34.01	136.03
Lebanon (1975–1990)	Blue	U	38.93	622.89
El Salvador (1979–1992)	Blue	U	56.50	791.07
Colombia La Violencia (1948–1958)	Gray	U	115.14	1,266.57
Algerian War (1954–1962)	Red	U	182.69	1,644.20
Vietnam War (1965–1973)	Red	R	274.59	2,471.27
UN PK in Angola (1988–1999)	Blue	S	482.16	5,785.87
Indonesia in Timor (1975–1999)	Red	B	624.16	15,615.14

In three cases, we only had data for one year, but used it anyway, noting it as such. The decision was then made to divide the data for analysis somewhere between the value of 5.00 and 10.00, driven in part by the knowledge that additional research in the cases falling in that area would not result in significant changes to the figures. In the six cases where the value falls between 2.00 and 5.45, five were very complete, with accurate and detailed data. As a result, we believe that those figures in the table closely mirror reality, with the slight possibility that only the data for the Mau Mau Revolt may have actually been higher than 5.00. On the other hand, of the five cases ranging from 7.99 to 10.67, in two of them at the upper range (Indonesia and Vietnam II) we believe that the numbers found are too low and that further research may well produce higher ones. This gave us confidence to assume that there was indeed a gap in the data between 5.00 and 10.00 and that it should be split somewhere around 5.00 or 8.00. And, inasmuch as we do not think that further research will result in an increase in the value of 7.99 for Kashmir, we chose to split the data at that point. Note that there was also a gap between 16.62 and 22.96, and between 56.50 and 115.14, but those are rather more nebulous ones, since there are many fewer data points falling in those ranges. Nevertheless, we chose to select the later gap as our 'High' range, since it seemed greater and in the case of El Salvador we again have considerable confidence in the accuracy of that figure, so know that the actual number (or perhaps more accurately a number derived from additional research) would not be much higher.

Having divided the data into these three unequal groups, a comparison shows:

- Low Civilian Loss Rates (less than 8.00 killed) results in 14% Red Wins (14 cases)
- Medium Civilian Loss Rates (8.91 – 56.54) results in 38% Red Wins (21 cases)
- High Civilian Loss Rates (115.54 – 624.16) results in 60% Red Wins (5 cases)

Or, to look at it from the other viewpoint:

- Low Civilian Loss Rates (less than 8.00 killed) results in 79% Blue Wins (14 cases)
- Medium Civilian Loss Rates (8.91 – 56.54) results in 43% Blue Wins (21 cases)
- High Civilian Loss Rates (115.54 – 624.16) results in 20% Blue Wins (5 cases)

For the total of 40 cases 33% result in Red Wins, 15% in "Gray" outcome (only one ongoing), and 52% in Blue Wins. Or, to put it into a matrix:

	BLUE	GRAY	RED	TOTAL
Low	11	1	2	14
Medium	9	4	8	21
High	1	1	3	5
Total	21	6	13	40

The Fisher's exact test two-sided p-value for the above is 0.1135. If we remove the "Gray" results, then the two-side p-value is 0.0576, giving a strong indication (more than 90 percent) that there may be a statistically significant correlation here.

Therefore, we tentatively conclude that increased levels of brutality favor the insurgency when the number of civilians killed each year averages more than 8 per 100,000 in the population.

The inverse is that it is to the long-term advantage of counterinsurgent forces to limit damage to civilian populations, whether caused by their own or by insurgent actions. This means tightly controlling rules of engagement and probably requires a strictly limited use of artillery and airpower. It also means properly protecting the host population, which would probably require the deployment of significant security forces as part of the total counterinsurgent force.

This last point leads us back to the consideration of force ratios, or some form of population control ratio, being a key to the counterinsurgency problem. Of course, the analysis assumes that there is some cause-and-effect relationship between levels of brutality and the outcome of an insurgency. There probably is some relationship, but there is also probably a third variable affecting both of those, which may be force ratio. Also, it cannot be ruled out that as the insurgency begins to win, the level of brutality may be increased by one or both sides, which would mean that the supposed **dependent** variable is influencing the supposed **independent** variable. Welcome to the complexities of quantitative social science.

In Northern Ireland, the British lost three troops for every insurgent killed. This is the only insurgency we are aware of where the counterinsurgent troops lost more than the insurgents did. Is this a reasonable cost to pay for a chance to win an insurgency? Is there a trade-off between force protection and the larger strategic picture? In the long run, are you better off as the counterinsurgent to accept additional casualties because of strict rules of engagements in exchange for reducing the potential number of insurgents and problems you will have?

These are all questions which have not been answered. While I do not have the answer to them, the weight of the evidence appears to be that you need to tightly control and restrain firepower. The exception is if one goes to the other extreme and brutally suppresses insurgencies. For all practical purposes, that last choice is not an option for the United States. Many of our own citizens are not going to accept that this is how a war should be fought, as we are a democracy.

Therefore, it appears that we are left with one practical option, and that is to restrict the use of firepower, rules of engagement, the use of airpower, etc., to the absolute extreme of what is practical. In the long run, that appears to give a better result, even if there are short term disadvantages to such restrictions.

NOTES

1. Transcript of 9 October 2001 press conference provided by the *Washington Post* at: http://www.washingtonpost.com/wp-srv/nation/specials/attacked/ transcripts/rumsfeld_100901.html

2. See *Users' Guide for the Modern Insurgency Spread Sheets (MISS), Phases I-IV* (Annandale, VA.: The Dupuy Institute, 30 Sept. 2007) for the definitions of these terms.

3. Note that in the case of the U.S. Invasion of Panama virtually all of the known civilian deaths were caused by collateral damage associated with the American invasion.

4. 1972 only.

5. 1945 only.

6. The annual rate for 1950 was 0.45 or possibly higher, but was insignificant thereafter.

7. Losses are known only for 1945.

8. Losses are only for 1972.

9. The annualized rate for this 42-day operation is calculated as 12.70, rather than 6.35, since it occurred over the course of the New Year.

10. Losses are for 1970 only.

11. The peak yearly rate was 108.58 in 1999.

CHAPTER 10

Sanctuaries, Border Barriers and Population Resettlement[1]

Here was a pompous, professorial beginning. My wits, hostile to the abstract, took refuge in Arabia again. Translated into Arabic, the algebraic factor would first take practical account of the area we wished to deliver, and I began idly to calculate how many square miles: sixty: eighty: one hundred: perhaps one hundred and forty thousand square miles. And how would the Turks defend all that? No doubt by a trench line across the bottom, if we came like an army with banners; but suppose we were (as we might be) an influence, an idea, a thing intangible, invulnerable, without front or back, drifting about like a gas? Armies were like plants, immobile, firm-rooted, nourished through long stems to the head. We might be a vapour, blowing where we listed. Our kingdoms lay in each man's mind; and as we wanted nothing material to live on, so we might offer nothing material to the killing. It seemed a regular soldier might be helpless without a target, owning only what he sat on, and subjugating only what, by order, he could poke his rifle at.

—T. E. Lawrence in Seven Pillars of Wisdom[2]

A. SANCTUARIES AND BORDER BARRIERS

Oddly enough, although all students of insurgencies are aware of the issues related to sanctuaries, border barriers and population relocation, we could not find a very clear correlation between them and outcome. First of all, we could not find a clear correlation between degree of outside support and outcome. Just to repeat a chart we previously presented in Chapter Eight:[3]

OUTCOME BY TYPE OF OUTSIDE SUPPORT

OUTCOME	PRIMARILY INDIGENOUS	SOME	CONSIDERABLE	NOT APPLICABLE	TOTAL
Blue	11	20	9	2	42
Gray	5	6	0	0	11
Red	7	18	5	0	30
Total	23	44	14	2	83

Sanctuaries are obviously a significant form of outside support and border barriers are specifically oriented towards preventing people from providing outside support across that border, or from their sanctuaries. So, these issues are interrelated. But if there is no clear correlation between degree of outside support and outcome, then what would one expect when they examine sanctuaries and border barriers.

1. SANCTUARY

A sanctuary is the existence of safe, or relatively safe, areas that provide a place of refuge and sustenance in various forms to the insurgency. Such safe havens were defined by Bernard Fall as: "[A] territory contiguous to a rebellious area which, though ostensibly not involved in the conflict, provides the rebel side with shelter, training facilities, equipment, and—if it can get away with it—troops."[4]

Although Fall recognized the existence of historic sanctuaries for insurgencies (explicitly the role of Bourbon France [and Spain] in the American Revolution), he stressed that such sanctuaries were more a result of the bi-polar world post-1945:

> The active sanctuary came into being as a result of the "Cold War," for the simply reason that the nations providing such services to a rebellion could always count upon one (or even both) of the super-powers to protect them from the direct reprisals that would have been their fate at almost any other moment of history.

> In brutal fact, the success or failure of all rebellions since World War II depended entirely on whether the active sanctuary was willing and able to perform its expected role.[5]

There is any number of examples of the putative importance of sanctuaries in modern insurgencies, but the representation of sanctuaries in the MISS is just 21 in the 83 cases—approximately one-fourth and a rather small number when considered against the relative importance analysts have assigned to sanctuaries. The MISS cases in which sanctuaries were present and relatively instrumental in the outcome of the insurgency are:

1. Greek Civil War (1946–1949)
2. Indochina War (1946–1954)
3. Algerian War (1954–1962)
4. Vietnam II (1961–1964)
5. Yemen (1962–1970)
6. Borneo (1963–1966)
7. Mozambique (1964–1974)
8. Vietnam War (1965–1973)
9. Dhofar Rebellion (1965–1976)
10. Chad Civil War (1965–1969)
11. Rhodesia I (1966–1972)
12. Namibia (1966–1989)
13. Rhodesia II (1972–1979)
14. Polisario Rebellion (1973–1991)
15. Angola Civil War (1975–1988)
16. Cambodia (1978–1989)
17. USSR in Afghanistan (1979–1989)
18. Contras in Nicaragua (1981–1990)
19. Kashmir (1988–present)
20. U.S. in Afghanistan (2001–present)
21. Hezbollah War (2006)

This list omits two cases involving "soft" sanctuaries, that is, relatively small-scale or insignificant safe havens. These last refer to Malaya, where there was an insignificant sanctuary on the Thai frontier, and the Tibetan Revolt and Insurgency, in which there was a pseudo-insurgent enclave in Nepal (Mustang district). We further ruled-out apparent sanctuaries *within* states experiencing insurgency, such as "no-go areas," the government-sanctioned Revolutionary Armed Forces of Colombia (FARC) enclave in present-day Colombia, and the Shining Path base area in highland Peru. Additional problems of definition were posed by insurgents moving easily across international borders that were not secured defensively by the nations involved. Examples in this instance include Chechen rebels and certain insurgent groups in sub-Saharan Africa, such as those in the Economic Community of West African States (ECOWAS) region, for example Ivory Coast, Liberia and Sierra Leone. In these cases, we did not include the (again) apparent sanctuaries that others might be tempted to include, because of the relative permeability, if not irrelevance, of the borders involved and the transitory nature of any such "safe havens" that might seemingly be found in the record.

Sanctuaries, where they have not been altogether negated, as in the case of Algeria, have generally been of great assistance to insurgents. In the case of the long Namibian insurgency (1966–89), for example, South African General Jannie Geldenhuys, noted that: "Many military observers consider 27 March 1976 to be the date on which the

[SWAPO] insurgency war really started in all seriousness....For the first time they obtained what is more or less a prerequisite for successful insurgent campaigning, namely a border that provided safe refuge."[6] However, obtaining sanctuary in Angola, although it allowed SWAPO to expand greatly, came with a price. SWAPO had to contribute a significant portion of its strength to the host MPLA's fight against UNITA and became subject to devastating cross-border incursions against its camps by the South Africans.

STATISTICAL ANALYSIS OF SANCTUARY

We conducted a statistical analysis of the relationship between outcome and the presence or absence of sanctuary among the 83-case MISS dataset using Fisher's exact test (see below).

OUTCOME BY PRESENCE/ABSENCE OF SANCTUARY

OUTCOME	YES	NO	TOTAL
Blue	9	33	42
Gray	1	10	11
Red	11	19	30
Total	21	62	83

When we test the hypothesis about a nonrandom relationship between insurgency outcome and the presence or absence of a sanctuary in the two-by-three table above using Fisher's exact test, the p-value is 0.1739. Based on this result, the data do not provide strong evidence that there may be some association between the two factors.

We also tested the more specific hypothesis that the odds of a Blue outcome are higher in the absence than in the presence of a sanctuary by ignoring the gray observations in the testing procedure. The p-value from the Fisher's exact test is 0.1241 in this case, which is a little high to be considered very strong evidence in support of this hypothesis.

Based on these tests, we did not find strong evidence between the presence of sanctuaries and outcome. Nonetheless, insurgents won 52% of the time when sanctuaries were present vice 31% when sanctuaries were not present.

This does indicate that sanctuaries are of importance, but we do wonder if their importance is overrated. Still, many theorists have regarded external support, or the lack thereof, as a major factor affecting the course and outcome of insurgencies. For example, the RAND Corporation's experts have identified "the amount of" external support as one of the three "most important" factors in defeating an insurgency. According to a RAND analyst:

The ability of insurgent groups to gain external support is highly correlated with insurgent success. Research by the RAND Corporation, which examined 91 insurgencies since 1945, suggests that insurgencies that have gained and main-

tained state support have won more than half the time. Those with support from
non-state actors and diaspora groups (but not state support) won a third of the
time, and those with no external support at all won only 17% of the time.[7]

Note, that this really does not agree with our results. Another student of insurgencies posits that external support is the "the most significant component" in insurgent success and "correlates more consistently with insurgent success than any other factor."[8]

These statements are broadly consistent with those of other counterinsurgency theorists (such as Anthony James Joes) who consider denial of external support to be one of the most important factors in counterinsurgent success.[9] So, let us look at some of the efforts made in the past to deny of support to the insurgents.

2. BORDER CONTROLS

The use of border controls is surprisingly not very common in fighting insurgencies. The principal types of border controls included various kinds of border fences and barrier systems and population controls, typically relocation and regroupment.

BARRIER SYSTEMS

The earliest border barriers typically were stone walls and wooden palisades with ditches, berms, watchtowers, forts and fortified military camps, such as the famous Roman *limes* (frontier) system which marked the borders of the Roman Empire.[10] Over time, these defenses were breached repeatedly by the barbarians they were meant to keep out of the empire, and the central power was replaced by regional and local politico-military organizations that did not require border barriers. In our 83 examples there were 13 in which the counterinsurgency force utilized border barriers. Thus, barriers were present in approximately 16% of our cases.

1. Indochina War (1946–1954)
2. Algerian War (1954–1962)
3. Vietnam II (1961–1964)
4. Vietnam War (1965–1973)
5. Namibia (1966–1989)
6. Rhodesia II (1972–1979)
7. Polisario Rebellion (1973–1991)
8. Cambodia (1978–1989)
9. USSR in Afghanistan (1979–1989)
10. Kashmir (1988–present)
11. Second Intifada (2000–2005)
12. Hamas War (2006)
13. Hezbollah War (2006)

The earliest examples of barriers in the MISS were those constructed by the French in their wars against insurgents in Indochina and in the Maghreb. In Indochina, the French attempted to isolate the population and infrastructure of the vital Red River Delta area from the Vietminh rebels by constructing the De Lattre Line, a 378-km-long barrier of 1,200 concrete blockhouses arranged in groups of 3-6 in 250 strong points, which were linked by belts of barbed-wire and other obstacles and backed-up by concentrations of artillery and quick-reaction forces.[11] The line initially fulfilled its purpose, since the Vietminh, using conventional warfare techniques, attacked it frontally in several major operations during January-June 1951. However, against guerilla warfare techniques, utilizing cover, camouflage, concealment, dispersion, hit-and-run attacks and infiltration, it "never had more retaining power than a sieve" (in Fall's oft-quoted phrase). Moreover, it tied down 82,000 French troops that might have been more useful in offensive operations, all the while providing the illusion of effectiveness. The Vietminh moved freely through it, and by October 1952, effectively controlled the Tonkin region *within* the line.

The U.S. during the Vietnam War managed to emulate the French De Lattre Line with the so-called McNamara Line, constructed at immense cost during 1967–1968. The McNamara Line never fulfilled the expectations of its architects.[12] Note the comments of Bernard Fall in his classic, *Street Without Joy*, on the impossibility and irrelevance of border control measures in the Vietnam War.

> *Not that total jugulation of the South Vietnamese border area would by now guarantee eventual victory any more than the successful closing of the Algero-Tunisian border brought French victory in the Algerian war: the hard fact is that, save for a few specialized antiaircraft and antitank weapons and cadre personnel not exceeding perhaps 3,000 to 4,000 a year or less, the VC [Viet Cong] operations inside South Viet-Nam has become self-sustaining. In fact, the worst guerilla areas are not even abutting on any of Viet-Nam's foreign borders.*
>
> *And while the complete closing of the South Vietnamese border to infiltrators certainly remains a worthwhile objective, to achieve it along 700 miles of jungle-covered mountains and swamp would just about absorb the totality of South Viet-Nam's 1964 forces of 250,000 regulars and 250,000 paramilitary troops of various kinds.[13]*

By contrast to their effort in Indochina, the French had relative success with their barrier systems in Algeria, the Morice-Challe lines, or simply, the barrages. The purposes of the barrages were two-fold: 1) To prevent the passage of recruits outbound from Algeria to rebel bases in Morocco and Tunisia; and (2) To prevent the passage of trained fighters and war materiel from the exterior into the *wilayas* (as the rebels' six politico-administrative areas were defined) in Algeria. The plan, essentially, was to isolate the insurgent Armée de Libération Nationale (ALN, or National Liberation Army) in the wilayas from the exterior ALN, starving it of men and weapons, and then to destroy it systematically in search-and-destroy type military operations called *ratissages* (rat hunts).

Construction of the Morice Line, named after the French minister of defense André Morice, began in August 1956, and was essentially complete in 1959, although work continued until 1960. In its final form, perfected under the aegis of French commander-in-chief in Algeria General Maurice Challe—hence the Morice-Challe Line—the construction consisted of extensive barrier systems on the Tunisian frontier in the east and the Moroccan frontier in the west. Figures on the finished product vary, but the line was about 460 km long on the Moroccan border and 700 km long on the Tunisian frontier. The total length of the fortifications, however, was 2,700 km, since the barrage on the Algeria-Tunisia frontier was in effect a double line, with an immense no-man's land not only between the lines but also before and behind, and there were two significant double-line sections on the Moroccan border. The sea frontier was patrolled by the French Navy.

In cross-section, the line consisted of extensive barbed-wire obstacles and mine-fields, supplemented by electrified fences, and ground-surveillance radars coupled to automatic radar cannon. It was patrolled by military vehicles and trains, using pro-tected roadways and rail lines and had an average depth of 1-5 km, although in places the depth of the *zone interdite* between double lines was 60 km. The removal of the entire civilian population from the areas along the barrages and significant parts of the interior (see the discussion below of the French regroupment program) allowed the forces of order to operate freely against anyone observed in the free-fire zones.

The ALN began the war in November 1954, with fewer than 400 weapons, most of which were hand firearms, many of those sporting weapons. It was vital to their ef-fort to pass weapons, generally obtained in Arab and socialist countries, from the ex-terior into Algeria. One of the first directives of the External Coordinating Committee (CEC) in the summer of 1957 stated that "the battle of the armaments is virtually won." The remaining big problem of the ALN was the distribution of the weapons. "The CEC will devote all its efforts to forward the weapons in the wilayas."

So, it is apparent that at first, the rebels encountered few impediments to move-ment. Krim Belkacem, one of the six "historic leaders" of the rebellion, and Mah-moud Cherif, commander in Wilaya 1, writing in *El Moudjahid*, the journal of the FLN, on May 5, 1958, insisted that "the electric fence has not created serious diffi-culties for the ALN."

However, just two months later, on July 8, Colonel Omar Ouamarane, the Di-rector General of Armament and Resupply (DARG) of the ALN, stated in *El Moud-jahid* that it had become "very difficult" to pass arms and supplies into the interior "because of the closure of the frontier."[14]

The effectiveness of the barrages in interdicting the flow of weapons from the exterior is shown in the table below:

DATA ON THE BARRAGES: WEAPONS INTERDICTION

YEAR	EST.WPNS SMUGGLED INTO ALGERIA/MO (HIGH)	EST.WPNS SMUGGLED INTO ALGERIA/MO (LOW)	TOTAL WPNS (HIGH)	TOTAL WPNS (LOW)
1957	1,200	1,000	14,400	12,000
1958	400		4,800	
1959	200		2,400	
1960	60		720	

Note: Infiltration into the *wilayas* from the exterior took from two to three months.
Source: Vernet, Jacques, Les barrages pendant la guerre d'Algerie, p. 266

As can be seen, the high estimate of the number of weapons smuggled through the barrages dropped precipitously over time, so that the average number per month in 1960 was just 5 percent what it had been four years earlier in 1957.

The table below gives partial data on the arms the rebels lost through interdiction at the barrages. Unfortunately, data is available only for selected six-month periods during 1958–1962 and is wholly lacking for a two-year period—the 2d semester 1958 through the 1st semester 1960. Nonetheless, it provides a useful snapshot of the diminution of rebel attempts to actually pass the barrages as reflected by the corresponding diminution of weapons' captures.

WEAPONS CAPTURED ON THE BARRAGES

YEAR	SMALL ARMS	CREW-SERVED	MORTARS	BAZOOKAS	TOTAL
1st semester 1958	2,950	350	0	0	3,300
2nd semester 1958					
1st semester 1960	n.d.	n.d.	n.d.	n.d.	n.d.
2nd semester 1960	347	5	2	3	357
1st semester 1961	579	19	5	9	612
2nd semester 1961	104	1	2	2	109
1st semester 1962	0	0	0	0	17
1st semester 1961	3,980	375	9	14	4,378

Source: Failure, L'ALN exterieure, p. 124

It should be noted that during the period September 1957–May 1958, there was heavy fighting along the barriers, especially on the Tunisian frontier ("the Battle of the Barrages"). In these battles, according to French sources, the ALN lost 6,000 men and 4,300 weapons. This indicates that 1,000 weapons were lost on the barrages during the last quarter of 1957 (not reported on the table).[15]

There is no doubt that the barrages were effective from a strictly military standpoint. We have the testimony of both sides on this point and the agreement of historians. For the historian Guy Pervillé, the construction of the barrages, "was a turning [point] in the war of considerable consequences." The ALN gravely underestimated the consequences of the mammoth constructions and did little to interrupt the French in their progress. Algerian workers conscripted by the French to work on the lines were undisturbed by the guerillas as long as they contributed a portion of their pay to the coffers of the revolution. When the barrages were finally tested in the Battle of the Frontiers in 1958, the ALN discovered that the lines could not be breached and sustained such heavy losses of men and material that it created "a very grave crisis of moral in the ALN, on the exterior and in the interior."[16]

The barriers drastically reduced the flow of trained men, weapons, and other military materiel into Algeria from the exterior and materially assisted in the asphyxiation of the insurgency, as the French had intended. They were a major factor too in isolating and marginalizing the armed forces of the exterior ALN. Between 1959 and 1960, the ALN in Tunisia and Morocco increased dramatically from 11,500 to 21,500; yet, in the words of one analyst, "these forces had little military significance" due to the effectiveness of the barriers.[17] In the following year, the exterior ALN increased to 29,700, representing some 50% of the total strength of the ALN and a force effectively isolated from its comrades of the interior.

Moreover, by checking the approximately two-thirds of the enemy's force on the exterior (1962 figures) with the approximately 12% of its own operational battalions manning the barrages (as of December 31, 1961), the French were able to generate enormous force ratio preponderances against the rebellion in the interior (see table below).

DEPLOYMENT OF FORCES OF ORDER IN ALGERIA

(number of battalions)			
DATE	BARRAGES	URBAN	RESERVES	QUADRILLAGE
1 Nov 1960	47	3	51	209
31 Dec 1961	30	72	50	90

Source: Jean Paul Bencil, "Chronologie de la guerre of Algerai," La Nef, 12–13(Oct. 1962 Jan 16963) p.10

At the same time, the barrier system allowed an economy of force in the interior that enabled the French to fight the insurgency and deal simultaneously with the gravely disabling effects of the army mutiny, settler uprising ("Week of the Barricades," 24–31 January 1960), and the white terror of the Secret Army Organization (note the augmentation of battalions in the urban sectors between 1960 and 1961).

During the Polisario [Popular Liberation Front for Western Sahara] rebellion against Morocco the Moroccans erected a massive, layered barrier system called simply "The Berm" in the Western Sahara during 1980–1987. It was approximately 2,500 km. in length (figures vary among sources) and consisted primarily of a three-meter-high sand and earth berm, supplemented by stone walls, wire fences and extensive minefields (reportedly, over one million land mines were laid). There were six "walls" altogether, proceeding generally southward from the inland northeast near the Algerian border to the Atlantic coast in the southwest near the Mauritanian border, and each encompassing an additional area of the Western Sahara that was annexed to Morocco. Moroccan garrisons were posted in forts and observation posts every 5 km.., and surveillance was carried out by aircraft, motorized patrols, electronic sensors, and radars. The construction of this security barrier is said to have turned the tide in the long war against the Polisario in Morocco's favor. The morale of Moroccan troops improved, counterinsurgent casualties fell, and the Moroccans gradually gained the upper hand military.[18] This is one of two insurgencies in which a border barrier was present that resulted in a Blue win (Kashmir being the other). It is likely that in this case the open, starkly forbidding nature of the desert terrain itself acted as a barrier and inhibited guerrilla operations, while the extensive man-made barrier allowed COIN forces to detect, track, fix, and engage successfully insurgent forces moving in the free-fire zones.

Contemporaneous with the Moroccan berm, the Soviets in Afghanistan appear to have constructed a barrier system on the Afghan-Pakistan frontier (USSR in Afghanistan, 1979–1989). There is some reference to this in publications of the time, but we have been unable to establish facts of the nature, extent or efficacy of the Soviet effort.[19] According to the source cited:

[T]he rugged mountains along the Afghanistan-Pakistan border have hindered guerrilla operations and allowed the Soviets to use border barriers with a minimum of manpower along a border of almost 1200 miles in length.

In this regard, it has been reported that barriers erected by Soviet forces within the mountain passes of the Afghanistan-Pakistan border have limited Afghan rebel resupply across that border to less than twenty percent of the total supplies received. As a result, the rebels have been denied most of the United States aid that originates in Pakistan, and have instead had to rely heavily upon internal support.[20]

Interestingly, there was recently an attempted revival of this idea. The U.S. and Pakistan explored the feasibility of "selective fencing" on the Afghanistan-Pakistan border in 2005, but it is not clear that much if anything was actually done on it, although the project reportedly had U.S. backing.[21]

Several of the border barriers we examined fall into the category of tripwires, and some of them were more or less passive obstacles, not entirely covered by fire or even an active defense during much of their extent. The extensive Cambodian fence (Cambodia, 1978–1989) and the barriers erected during the Rhodesian and Namibian insurgencies fall into this category.

The barrier on the Namibia-Angolan border followed the old 1,000-km.-long "cut line," a 100-meter-wide strip cleared through the brush. Fenced, mined, and patrolled from garrisons by police and reservists, it was easily and frequently breached, because it simply could not be adequately monitored by the forces available due to its length. Moreover, short-term reservists patrolling in the open strip of the cut line, and unused to the cover and concealment requirements of the bush war, were often targets of insurgents concealed in the brush on the Angolan side.[22]

The Rhodesians, in constructing their "Corsan" (so named since it was designed by a Cordon Sanitaire Committee) faced difficult physical and environmental obstacles which were never completely overcome. Essentially, a no-go zone consisting of minefields of varying depth and density fenced with barbed wire and thorn bushes and monitored on its western front by radars, the Corsan, Mod-Corsan (an extension), and "Border Minefield" (an extensive unfenced eastern portion on the Mozambique border) were constructed during 1974–1979, and eventually covered about one-third of Rhodesia's 3,000-km.-long frontier with Mozambique and Zambia. In addition, the Rhodesians removed and resettled the indigenous population of the frontier areas, creating an enormous, ruthlessly enforced free-fire zone. Curiously, the Rhodesian barriers proved ineffective from an early stage of their development. The great dependency on mines was vitiated by the fact that the minefields were not observed due to the extent of the barrier and the small numbers of COIN forces available. Moreover, the insurgents were adept at breaching the minefields. Finally, the minefields were frequently washed away during the rainy seasons or were detonated by elephants and other wild animals that stumbled into them.[23]

The Israelis have employed security barriers in three recent insurgencies involving the Palestinians (Second Intifada [2000–2005], Hamas War [2006]) and Hezbollah (Hezbollah War [2006]). These security barriers are meant generally to protect the population from terrorist attacks. The first of these barriers, the Gaza Barrier, was begun in 1994 and was continuously improved through 2005. The imposing Separation Barrier, enclosing the West Bank, was begun in 2002; work continues on it to this day. Finally, there is a border barrier with Lebanon, constructed since the final Israeli withdrawal from southern Lebanon in May 2000. This serves more or less as tripwire against Hezbollah infiltration from Lebanon. In essence, it is a technologically-superior version of the older (early 1960s) double cyclone fence so easily and routinely penetrated by the Palestinian *fedayeen* of that day. Characteristics of the Israeli security barriers are given in Appendix VII.

According to official statistics, the Israeli security barriers have been successful in countering terrorist infiltration and attacks. In late 2004, one analyst noted: "[T]here is little doubt that the security barriers work. Suicide attacks in Israel declined 75 percent in the first six months of 2004 compared to an equivalent period in 2003."[24] This assessment was reinforced but qualified recently by a reporter profiling the Separation Barrier:

[Prime Minister Ariel] Sharon's security cabinet approved the barrier's first three segments in June 2002, a year when the number of Palestinian suicide attacks peaked at 60.

Last year [2006], according to Israel's Foreign Ministry, there were 5. But some Israeli military officials say factors besides the barrier—including stepped-up army operations in the West Bank and a two-year-old decision by most armed Palestinian factions to refrain from such attacks—better explain the sharp decline.[25]

On the Israel-Lebanon border, the security fence represents perhaps the most complex manifestation of the integration of the time-tested physical barrier and 21st-century technological means, including motion detectors, area surveillance through a CCTV system, and continuous monitoring of the barrier's approaches by various reconnaissance means. The technological potential of the barrier system was such that Israeli chief of staff General Dan Halutz was able to boast that Israel had achieved "full situational awareness through intelligence superiority" on its northern border, allowing it "to choose the time, place and conditions when it will act."[26] Nonetheless, the Hezbollah War began with a Hezbollah incursion that involved the disabling of a TV camera, infiltration through "dead space," and the ambush of a rapid-reaction force that was sent to investigate. The ambush resulted in eight IDF reservists dead and two captured by Hezbollah, in addition to one Merkava tank destroyed.

STATISTICAL ANALYSIS OF BORDER BARRIERS

We conducted a statistical analysis of the relationship between outcome and the presence or absence of border barriers among the 83-case MISS dataset using Fisher's exact test (see below).

OUTCOME BY PRESENCE/ABSENCE OF BORDER BARRIERS

OUTCOME	YES	NO	TOTAL
Blue	2	40	42
Gray	2	9	1
Red	9	21	30
Total	13	70	83

When we test the hypothesis about a nonrandom relationship between insurgency outcome and the border barriers factor in the two-by-three table above using Fisher's exact test, the p-value is 0.0090. The data suggest strong evidence that the two factors may be associated.

We also tested the more specific hypothesis that the odds of a Blue outcome are different in the absence vs. the presence of border barriers by ignoring the gray observations in the testing procedure. The p-value from the Fisher's exact test is 0.0045 in this case, which can be considered strong evidence in support of this hypothesis.

Thus, it appears that the tests confirm that border barriers have not been significant in combating insurgencies, based on the outcome. This is not unexpected, although it could perhaps be considered counterintuitive. Overall, the insurgents won 69% of the time when there was a border barrier vice 30% of the time when there was not one. We suspect that there is another factor in play here (for example: border barriers are usually built in response to large, intractable insurgencies).

B. POPULATION RELOCATION AND REGROUPMENT

Border controls very often included population controls. These were any and all means used to prevent and control the interaction of the indigenous population—a source of manpower, supplies, and shelter—with the insurgents. Typically, such means included removal of the population from border areas (or other militarily-sensitive areas) and resettlement, usually in large camps. Once the indigenous population ("friendlies") was concentrated in resettlement camps, the COIN forces logically could conclude that anyone outside the camps was hostile. Certain areas, then, could be designated as "free-fire zones," and anti-insurgent military operations in those areas could be conducted freely, without fear of harming innocent civilians. That at least was the ideal.

Below is a list of the MISS cases with those that incorporated some form of population resettlement. Of the total of 83 cases, population resettlement was a factor in 10, or just 12%. In one case, UN Peacekeeping in Burundi, there had been a policy of regroupment (aimed specifically at the Hutu population), but it had been terminated prior to deployment of UN peacekeepers. Therefore, it is not considered among the 10 cases in the MISS. The cases considered are:

1. Malaya (1948–1960)
2. Algerian War (1954–1962)
3. Vietnam I (1957–1960)
4. Vietnam II (1961–1964)
5. Angola (1961–1974)
6. Portuguese Guinea (1963–1974)
7. Mozambique (1964–1974)
8. Vietnam War (1965–1973)
9. Rhodesia II (1972–1979)
10. Mozambique Civil War (1976–1992)

Modern, insurgency-related population control efforts were first used by the Spanish in Cuba under General Valeriano Weyler (anti-guerilla operations, 1896–1897). Weyler established fortified villages called *reconcentrados* for the rural population, so as to separate it from the insurgency. It is likely that the English-language term "concentration camp" is based on the Spanish *reconcentrado*, and the pejorative meaning associated with the term in the modern consciousness certainly dates to Weyler's time in Cuba, when disease and starvation killed an estimated 155,000–175,000 people, about 10% of the Cuban population, in a relatively brief period.[27]

The Spanish example was adopted by the British during the Second Anglo-Boer War (1899–1902), who instituted a policy of regroupment for the Boer and African civilian population in the war zone. About 154,000 Boer women and children and blacks were herded into camps after the countryside had been ravaged by a "scorched earth" policy instituted by the military in 1899. Approximately 27,000 Boers (of whom 22,000 were children) and 12,000 blacks died in the filthy, disease-ridden camps, many from starvation. Reports on conditions in the camps provoked outrage in Britain, particularly in the "political culture," which was scandalized.[28]

Moving forward into our period of inquiry, the regroupment policy of the French during the Algerian War provides possibly the most ambitious and far-reaching example of population controls in modern counterinsurgency warfare. The statistics of the effort are remarkable:[29]

- Initially (1 November 1956), there were 382 camps (called centers), of which 246 were permanent
- In June 1957, there were 237,231 people in the camps
- In April 1961, there were nearly 2,400 camps; these housed nearly 1.5 million people
- In the end, there were 1.9 million (French data)—2.5 million (FLN estimate) in the camps
- This was 20–26% of the Muslim population of Algeria (~9,545,000)

Beyond this, there were synergistic demographic effects that were severely destructive of the rural social, economic and political structures and folkways of the population and whose traumatic effects continue to this day. The number of displaced persons (DPs) was larger than the statistics above suggest. For example:

- An additional 600,000 emigrated to the towns and cities from rural areas during 1954–59
- 260,000 were refugees in Morocco and Tunisia
- The grand total displaced was 2.76-3.53M (29–35% of the Muslim population; or, an estimated 50% of the rural population)

But, for all this, the regroupment policy was a colossal failure: An "absolutely utopian" program that, in the words of French General André Beaufre, "more often than not, turned against us."[30] The FLN for its part echoed Beaufre's evaluation. One insurgent remarked that the policy, "Turned all the inhabitants against the French and facilitated the propaganda of the ALN."[31] The French press likened the regroupment centers to Nazi death camps, and the French public, as well as world popular opinion, condemned the resettlement program as yet another aspect of the "dirty war" (together with reprisals, collective punishment, and torture) that made France "the second-most-hated country in the world, after South Africa, in the United Nations."[32]

In fact, of the ten cases of population resettlement in the MISS, in one case only—Malaya—was the policy found to have made a net positive contribution to the COIN effort. However, in that case, the 423,000 ethnic Chinese "squatters" that were removed from their marginal existence in jungle areas to "new villages" in a more or less humane fashion and given the land and implements to make a better life themselves and their families actually were better off in the new environment.[33]

STATISTICAL ANALYSIS OF POPULATION CONTROLS

We conducted a statistical analysis of the relationship between outcome and the presence or absence of population controls in the 83-case MISS dataset using Fisher's exact test (see below).

OUTCOME BY PRESENCE/ABSENCE OF POPULATION CONTROLS

OUTCOME	YES	NO	TOTAL
Blue	2	40	42
Gray	0	11	11
Red	8	22	30
Total	10	73	83

When we test the hypothesis about a nonrandom relationship between the insurgency outcome and the population controls factor in the two-by-three table above using the Fisher's exact test, the p-value is 0.0163. The data suggest strong evidence that the two factors may be associated.

We also tested the more specific hypothesis that the odds of a Blue outcome are different in the absence versus the presence of population controls by ignoring the Gray observations in the testing procedure. The p-value from the two-sided Fisher's exact test is 0.0133 in this case, which can be considered strong evidence in support of this hypothesis. This difference is due to larger estimated odds of a Blue outcome in the absence of population controls (1.8) than in the presence of population controls (0.3). This indicates that a Blue outcome is about 6 (or approximately 1.8/0.3) times as likely to occur in the absence of population controls as in the presence of population controls which is, to us, counterintuitive but consistent with the results obtained for the border barriers factor.

In this case, the insurgents won 80% of the time when population controls were present vice 30% of the time when they were not. Again, we suspect that there is another factor at work here.

C. CONCLUSIONS REGARDING DEGREE OF OUTSIDE SUPPORT, SANCTUARIES, BORDER BARRIERS, AND POPULATION CONTROLS

The following observations, drawn from analysis of the datasets on outside support and border controls, are relevant:

1. **A lack of outside support does not necessarily doom an insurgency.**
2. **Considerable outside support does not mean an insurgency will win.**
3. **There appears to be little correlation between the degree of outside support of an insurgency and the outcome of the insurgency.**
4. **Border controls (to include population controls), although apparently effective counterinsurgency measures, are in fact strongly correlated with insurgent success.**

The first observation is reinforced by all the data sets. Looking at the overall 83 case dataset, for the 23 cases in which there was little outside support, the insurgents still won 30% of the time. In the 62 case dataset of insurgencies, there were 16 cases that were primarily indigenous (little outside support), yet the insurgents still won 38% of the time. In the 36 insurgencies against foreigners dataset, there were 5 cases in which there was little outside support (and the counterinsurgency inevitably had considerable outside support), the insurgents still won 60% of the time. Finally, in the 26 case dataset of insurgent civil wars, there were 11 cases that were primarily indigenous, and the insurgents won 3 of them, or 27% of the time.

The second point is also reinforced by all the data sets. In the overall 83 case dataset, for the 14 cases in which there was considerable outside support, the insurgents won 36% of the time. In the 62 case dataset of insurgencies, of the 11 cases in which there was considerable outside support, the insurgents won 5, or 45%. In the dataset of 36 insurgencies against foreigners, there were 9 cases in which there was considerable outside support, and the insurgents won in 4 instances, or 44% of the time. Finally, in the 26 case dataset of insurgent civil wars, there were two cases characterized by considerable outside support, and the insurgents won one of them, or 50%. Note that these numbers, and the pattern of the numbers, correspond generally with those in the first point, above.

This leads to our third point. If there is little correlation between the amount of outside support and the outcome of an insurgency, this means that *insurgencies succeed or fail for entirely different reasons*. This would lead one to question whether control of borders, as so often discussed by various theorists, is that important, other than in helping to kill off an already doomed insurgency (as in the case of Greece), and even when done effectively (as in the case of Algeria), it might not kill off an insurgency that is otherwise soundly based? It is clear when the data is viewed in the datasets of the 62 insurgencies or the 36 cases of insurgencies against foreign powers, the percent of insurgent wins is pretty much the same (roughly 40–50%) in all categories of support.

This is reinforced by our fourth point, since the data clearly indicate that investment of major resources in border barriers and population controls (such as was the case in Algeria), although perhaps deceptively reassuring for Blue planners from a strictly military standpoint ("shaping the battlefield" comes to mind), has rarely positively affected Blue success and in fact is strongly correlated with Red success.

Thus, the statistics on the importance and efficacy of external support as a major factor influencing the outcome of insurgencies are in general counterintuitive and contrary to the assertions of many contemporary analysts of insurgencies.

This is interesting, because in general border controls and particularly border barriers *appear* to be effective in combating insurgency. On the other hand, we are not aware of any modern (post-1945) case in which border controls actually defeated an insurgency that had become established or "gained traction."

NOTES

1. I was helped considerably by C. Curtiss Johnson in this task. The chapter was effectively coauthored by him.
2. Lawrence, T. E., *Seven Pillars of Wisdom, A Triumph* (Garden City, NY: Doubleday, Doran & Co, 1935), Chapter XXXIII.
3. Two-sided p-value from Fisher's exact test, excluding the not applicable cases: 0.4003. Two-sided p-value Fisher's exact test, excluding the not applicable and gray cases: 0.6862.
4. Bernard B. Fall, *Street Without Joy* (Mechanicsburg, PA.: Stackpole, 1994 [1961]), 375. Actually, Fall used the term "active sanctuary."
5. *Ibid.*, 375– 376. Historian Howard H. Peckham assessed French assistance to the Americans in the Revolutionary War as "of immense and even decisive significance" but pronounced the question of whether the Americans could have won without it "one of history's imponderables." In his view, the war in that event would have become an "endurance contest," with the Americans likely winning because of intangibles: "ideals, faith, self-sacrifice, and determination." See *The War of Independence: A Military History* (Chicago: Univ. of Chicago Press, 1958), 202.
6. Gen. Jannie Geldenhuys, *A General's Story* (Johannesburg: Johnathan Ball, 1995), 58– 59.
7. Seth G. Jones, "Pakistan's Dangerous Game." *Survival*, 49:1 (Spring 2007), 16, referencing John Gordon, et al., *The Challenge of Insurgency*, draft document, RAND, 2006.
8. See Jeffrey Record, *Beating Goliath: Why Insurgencies Win* (Washington, D.C.: Potomac Books, 2007), chap. 2: "The Role of External Assistance" and *ibid.*, "External Assistance: Enabler of Insurgent Success," *Parameters* (Autumn 2006), 36– 49. Curiously, in his *Parameters* article, 36, Record stipulates that "[v]ictorious insurgencies are exceptional because the strong usually beat the weak."
9. Anthony James Joes, "E-Notes: Recapturing the Essentials of Counterinsurgency," based on the W. W. Keen Butcher Lecture on Military Affairs (March 24, 2006), Foreign Policy

Research Institute (May 30, 2006) http://www.fpri.org/enotes/20060530.military.
joes.counterinsurgency.html. Joes discusses this under the heading "isolating the combat
area," as one of three elements in "shaping the strategic environment in counterinsurgency."

10. Vestiges and reconstructions of the *limes* may be seen today in Britain (the 118-km long
Hadrian's Wall) and in Germany, where the frontier walls stretched for approximately
550 km from the Rhine River in the northwest to the Danube in the southeast.

11. The line was named after General Jean de Lattre de Tassigny, the French commander in
Indochina in 1951. De Lattre has been profiled in Lt. Col. Michel Goya and Lt. Col.
Philippe François, "The Man Who Bent Events: `King John' in Indochina," *Military Re-
view* (Sept.–Oct. 2007), 52– 61. The line is aptly described and analyzed in Martin
Windrow, I (Cambridge, MA.: Da Capo Press, 2004), esp. 116, 118, and 213, and
Bernard B. Fall, Street *Without Joy* (Repr., Mechanicsburg, PA.: Stackpole Books, 1994),
180.

12. The McNamara Line is fully described and its efficacy analyzed in Peter Brush, "The
Story Behind the McNamara Line," *Vietnam* (Feb. 1996), 18– 24. The Brush article is
available on the web at http://chss.montclair.edu/english/furr/pbmcnamara.html.

13. Fall, *op. cit.*, 347– 348.

14. See the discussion in Gen. Maurice Faivre, "L'ALN extérieure face aux barrages frontaliers." *Revue internationale d'histoire militaire*, 76 (1997) http://www.stratisc.org/parte-
naires /cfhm/rihm/76/rihm_76_faivrewps.html.

15. Casualties and losses reported in Alistair Horne, *A Savage War of Peace: Algeria,
1954–1962* (Repr. New York: New York Review of Books, 2006), 266.

16. See Guy Pervillé, "La ligne Morice en Algérie, 1956–1962." Online version of "Des murs
et des hommes." *Panoramiques*, 67 (2ème trimestre 2004), found at: http://guy.perville.
free.fr/spip/article.php3?id_article=95.

17. Gil Merom, *How Democracies Lose Small Wars: State, Society, and the Failures of France in
Algeria, Israel in Lebanon, and the United States in Vietnam* (Cambridge, UK: Cambridge
University Press, 2003), 87n14.

18. There is a discussion of the military effectiveness of The Berm in Akbarali Thobhani's
*Western Sahara since 1975 under Moroccan Administration: Social, Economic, and Political
Transformation* (Lewiston, N.Y.: The Edwin Mellen Press, 2002), 61– 64.

19. See, for example: Defeating Insurgency on the Border, CSC 1985 SUBJECT AREA Na-
tional Military Strategy, Executive Summary, TITLE: DEFEATING INSURGENCY
ON THE BORDER at http://www.globalsecurity.org/military/library/report/1985/
HJR.htm.

20. *Ibid.*

21. Reported in the *Guardian Unlimited*, 53 (Sept. 14, 2005) at
http://www.guardian.co.uk/pakistan/Story/0,2763,1569495,00.html.

22. Aspects of the bush war along the cut line are described in Edward George McGill
Alexander's M.A. thesis, *The Cassinga Raid* (Cape Town: Univ. of South Africa, 2003).

23. The Corsan is described in Alex Vines' *Still Killing: Land Mines in Southern Africa* (New
York: Human Rights Watch, 1997) and J. K. Cilliers, *Counter-Insurgency in Rhodesia*
(London: Croom Helm, 1985).

24. Ben Thein, "Is Israel's Security Barrier Unique?" *Middle East Quarterly* (Fall 2004),
http://www.meforum.or/article/652.

25. Scott Wilson, "Touring Israel's Barrier with Its Main Designer," *The Washington Post* (August 7, 2007), A9.

26. Quoted in Barbara Opall-Rome, "Raid Reveals Hole in Israeli Net," *Defense News* (July 17, 2006) http://www.defensenews.com.

27. See John Leonard Tone, *War and Genocide in Cuba, 1895–1898* (Chapel Hill, N.C.: Univ. of North Carolina Press, 2006), 212, 222– 23. Tone argues that the generally accepted figure of 300,000 deaths in Weyler's camps is too large.

28. For the British camps, see S. B. Spies, *Methods of Barbarism? Roberts and Kitchener and Civilians in the Boer Republics, January 1900– May 1902.* (Cape Town: Human & Rousseau, 1977). The argument that the British had not adopted a deliberately genocidal policy in South Africa is made cogently by Isabel V. Hull in *Absolute Destruction: Military Culture and the Practices of War in Imperial Germany* (Ithaca, N.Y.: Cornell Univ. Press, 2005).

29. Statistics of the Algerian regroupment program are derived from: Charles-Robert Ageron, "Une dimension de la guerre d'Algérie: les `regroupments' de populations," in *Militaires et guerilla dans la guerre d'Algérie*, 327– 62. Edited by Jean-Charles Jauffret and Maurice Vaisse (Brussels: Editions Complexe, 2001); Robin Cohen, ed. *The Cambridge Survey of World Migration* (New York: Cambridge Univ. Press, 1995); and Keith Sutton, "Population Resettlement—Traumatic Upheavals and the Algerian Experience," J. Afr. Stud., 15:2 (June 1977), 279– 300.

30. General André Beufre quoted in Michel Veuthey, *Guérilla et droit humanitaire* (Geneva: Comité international de la Croix-Rouge, 1983), 284.

31. Quoted in Ageron, *op. cit.*, 356n28.

32. Remarks of Bernard B. Fall in "The Theory and Practice of Insurgency and Counterinsurgency," Naval *War College Review* (April 1965), accessible at http://www.au.af.mil/au /awc/awcgate/navy/art5-w98.htm.

33. See Brig. Richard L. Clutterbuck, *The Long, Long War: Counterinsurgency in Malaya and Vietnam* (New York: Praeger, 1966), chap. 7: "The Briggs Plan," 55ff.

CHAPTER 11

Estimating Insurgent Force Size

I am not going to give you a number for it because
it's not my business to do intelligent work.

—Secretary of Defense Donald Rumsfeld, asked to estimate the number
of Iraqi insurgents while testifying before Congress, February 16, 2005[1]

The two major problems with the force ratio model are that: 1) you have to be able to estimate insurgent force size; and 2) you have to be able to determine what the political concept behind the insurgency is. On this latter point, we are of little help as we never had the time to explore that concept completely. In the case of estimating insurgent force size, we have attempted to do that in several ways using different data sets.

In our original Iraq estimate, we used both incidents and blue side killed for the estimate. We believe that this two track approach is the best. While we have not examined blue side killed compared to insurgent strength in more depth since then, we have looked at incidents compared to insurgent strength in more depth. In this case, our customer wanted us to create an estimate of insurgent strengths based upon incident data, based upon the type of incident, the number of insurgents required to conduct such an incident and build it all up to an overall estimate of insurgent strength. We believed this was a dead-end approach, but did attempt such an effort anyway. It will not be discussed in depth here as we were not satisfied with the results.

What we felt was more productive was to do a top-down approach similar to what was done of the Iraq casualty estimate, which was base our estimate on the number of overall violent incidents compared to the overall number of insurgents (incidents per 1,000 insurgents) in other historical cases and develop our estimate from there. We believe this, combined with a parallel estimate based upon troop deaths per 1,000 insurgents, would at least give a reasonable range to develop an estimate from.

We have unfortunately seen how other estimates of the insurgent force size have worked. Up through most of 2005, the U.S. Department of Defense was claiming that there were only 5,000 insurgents in Iraq. They then increased that estimate to 20,000 but no higher. It was the same for Afghanistan, where the estimated insurgent strength mysteriously never exceeds 20,000, even as they spread across the country infiltrating and occupying even more area. It almost seems that 20,000 is a magic threshold that estimators are not supposed to cross. Most of our estimates, based on comparison to other insurgencies, come up with higher figures for both Iraq and Afghanistan. In the case of Iraq, it has been established that these higher estimates were correct.

A. THE TOP-DOWN APPROACH

The general estimating parameter we use for estimating insurgency force size is 500 incidents per 1,000 insurgents on the average and maybe 1,000 incidents per 1,000 insurgents during an active year. To use Iraq as an example, the most complete incident data we have is the 2005 SOC-SMG reports which gives 42,551 incidents a year (based upon data covering 69% of that year). Now, let us assume this is an average year, which would then produce an estimated insurgent strength of 85,102 full-time, part-time and casual insurgents.

The Brooking Institute also reported incidents, but their data set for 2005 was incorrect as they were underreporting the number of incidents. They did appear to correct that in the middle of 2006, possibly as a result of the Iraq Study Group identifying this issue. At *The Dupuy Institute*, we were aware of the reporting discrepancies much earlier than that. The total incidents they report from September through November 2006 are 16,230. Assuming this three-month period is representative of the entire year, this produces 64,920 incidents for the year (about 50% more than what we were showing in 2005). Assuming this is a peak year with 1,000 incidents per 1,000 insurgents, then we are still looking at 64,920 full-time, part-time and active casual insurgents. One notes that the number of "Sons-of-Iraq" (armed Sunnis now on U.S. payroll) was around 100,000.

Basically, all we are really doing with these calculations is multiplying the number of incidents by two to get the insurgent strength. Still, there is a sound basis for doing so, and it is based on a systematic analysis of the incidents from 40 insurgencies.

The two tables below are based upon the same data. They compare the number of incidents in the peak year to the peak strength of the insurgents for the 35 cases in which we had good incident data. The first table looks at the accuracy of an estimate if one uses a figure of 1,000 incidents per 1,000 insurgents. The next table looks at the accuracy of an estimate if one uses a figure of 500 incidents per 1,000 insurgents.

Based on Peak Strength Data

NUMBER OF INCIDENTS PER 1000 INSURGENTS	NUMBER OF CASES	PERCENT
0 – 500	22	63%
500 – 666	2	6%
666 – 1500	6	17%
1500 – 2000	1	3%
2000+	4	11%

One should use the peak strength data estimating parameters with considerable caution. Assuming this historical data is a randomly selected and correct representation of reality, then, if one is using an estimating parameter of 1,000 incidents per 1,000 insurgents, one would be within plus or minus 50% of actual only 17% of the time (the 666-1500 incident line above). The person using this estimating parameter would overestimate enemy strength 14% of the time and would underestimate enemy strength 69% of the time.

Changing the estimating parameter to 500 incidents per 1,000 insurgents produces no better accuracy (see table below). In this case one would be within plus or minus 50% of actual only 20% of the time. The person using this estimating parameter would overestimate enemy strength 23% of the time and would underestimate enemy strength 57% of the time.

Based on Peak Strength Data

NUMBER OF INCIDENTS PER 1000 INSURGENTS	NUMBER OF CASES	PERCENT
0 – 250	19	54%
250 – 333	1	3%
333 – 750	7	20%
750 – 1000	1	3%
1000+	7	20%

One can also look at average number of incidents per year compared to average insurgent strength. This is a more complicated calculation and because of incomplete data gives us only 33 data points.

Using the average data does not produce a much better fit. Here one would be within plus or minus 50% of actual only 21% of the time. The person using this estimating parameter would overestimate enemy strength 18% of the time and would underestimate enemy strength 61% of the time.

Based upon Average Strength Data

NUMBER OF INCIDENTS PER 1000 INSURGENTS	NUMBER OF CASES	PERCENT
0 – 250	18	55%
250 – 333	2	6%
333 – 750	7	21%
750 – 1000	0	0
1000+	6	18%

The fundamental problem is that the data tends to be tri-modal in that there is a collection of data around the average or center point of the data and a lot of data much lower than that average and a lot of data much higher than that average. The majority of insurgencies tend to be much lower placed than the number indicated by the estimating parameter or their strength has been overestimated or not very carefully defined.

Estimating the degree of uncertainly of a bottom-up approach is more difficult and probably provides even greater variability. We have examined this in some depth, and found it even less satisfactory that what was done above.

If these estimating parameters have a bias, it is to underestimate insurgent force strength. Still, these estimating parameters contain a considerable amount of uncertainty and should not be used without some knowledge of the actual conditions of the insurgency compared to the historical insurgencies the estimating parameters are drawn from.

B. FACTORS FOR ADDRESSING MIX OF FULL-TIME VERSUS PART-TIME INSURGENTS

There is some basis for estimating the number of full-time versus part-time insurgents versus casual insurgents. For the moment we will leave these terms undefined. We did have some estimates from the Cabanas Insurgency in Mexico (a very small insurgency). It provided the following data:

Cabanas Data

YEAR	PERMANENT MEMBERS	INDIGENOUS INSURGENT FORCE	RATIO	PERCENT FULL-TIME	PART-TIME
1973	92	259	2.82	26.21	73.79
1974	57	243	4.26	19.00	81.00

We also had data from Vietnam. We can consider People Army of Vietnam

(PAVN) Main Force forces to be "full-time" guerillas, the PAVN Provincial and District Forces to be "part-time" guerillas, and the PAVN Village Defense Forces to be "casual" guerillas.

The Peoples Liberation Army (PLA) Militia column should be considered Provincial and District Forces plus Village Defense Forces

Vietnam War Data

YEAR	MAIN FORCE	MAIN FORCE & PROVINCIAL	PROVINCIAL & DISTRICT FORCES	PLA MILITIA	VILLAGE DEFENSE FORCES	TOTAL GUERILLAS
1958	800		8,650		10,000	
1959	3,034		12,500		10,000	
1960		20,017			55,000	
1961		24,500			100,000	
1962		40,000			118,500	
1963		70,000			137,000	
1964		106,210			155,500	
1965				174,000		212,000
1966	67,000			170,351		237,351
1967						181,600
1968						200,000
1969						
1970						113,800
1971	140,000					97,700
1972						103,000
1973	200,000					200,000

To try to summarize this mixed reporting into some form of more consistent comparison:

PERCENT YEAR	FULL-TIME	PART-TIME	CASUAL	RATIO PART-TIME/ FULL-TIME	CASUAL/ FULL-TIME
1958	4.11	44.47	51.41	10.81	12.50
1959	11.88	48.95	39.16	4.12	3.30
1960	see part-time	26.68	73.32		
1961	see part-time	19.68	80.32		
1962	see part-time	25.24	74.76		
1963	see part-time	33.82	66.18		
1964	see part-time	40.58	59.42		
1965	17.92	see casual	82.08		
1966	28.23	see casual	71.77		

We also have data from 1990 for the Shining Path insurgency in Peru. There is a report of 816 principal forces, 4,674 local forces and 17,940 base forces. Principal forces were primarily concerned with complex and important missions, while local forces primarily conducted mundane missions and acted as support. Base forces were not invested with much responsibility and represented primarily untrained peasants.[2]

This one year snap-shot again shows that what might be considered full-time insurgents (assumed to be principal forces) made up 3.48% of insurgent strength, while the part-time (assumed to be local forces) made up 19.95% for insurgent strength and the large mass of casual insurgents (assumed to be base forces) made up 76.57% of the insurgent strength.

Now, throughout the insurgency most people considered insurgent strength to be 6,000 or less. The casual insurgents were simply not counted. In the case of the Shining Path, the base forces were probably particularly inactive.

Based upon just this data, some rules of thumb can be created for determining the mix of insurgents:

1. Full-time insurgents make up 10 to 20% of the force.
2. Full-time and part-time insurgents are 20 to 50% of the force.
3. Casual insurgents are 40 to 80% of the force.
4. If one had to pick percentage figure for full-time/part-time/casual it would be: 15.5%, 23.1% and 61.4%.
5. If one had to pick a ratio of full-time to part-time to casual it would be 1 to 1.5-to-4.[3]

We feel it is possible to estimate insurgent strength based upon blue casualties and number of incidents. It may be possible to do something more sophisticated than that, but our worked stopped at this point. As it was, our estimates of insurgent strength have to date proved more reliable that those publically released.

NOTES

1. He certainly meant "intelligence work" in his statement. Ari Berman, "The Real Story of the Insurgency," *The Nation*, 3 Mar. 2005.
2. Carlos Tapia, *Las Fuerzas Armadas y Sendero Luminoso: Dos Estrategias y Un Final* (Lima: IEP Ediciones, 1997), page 110.
3. This figure for the full-time cases has been estimated by taking the average of the four full-time cases (15.535). The figure for the part-time cases has been estimated by taking the average of the seven part-time cases less the average of the full-time cases for those five cases in which no full-time cases are distinctly reported (23.133). The average figure for the casual cases is estimated by taking the average of the first seven cases and the next two cases less the average figure for the part-time cases (61.350). These three averages = 100.018

CHAPTER 12

The Value of Elections

On January 30th in Iraq, the world witnessed . . .
*a **major turning point.***

—Secretary of Defense Donald Rumsfeld, commenting
 on the elections in Iraq on 30 January, 2005.[1]

We took a serious look at the value of elections, both in our original Iraq estimate and in our later work. In the case of the original Iraq estimate, we simply looked at those 12 cases in which we had elections during the insurgency and then looked to see if there was any immediate, measurable result. There was none.

In our later work, we got a little more sophisticated. In our database we have three fields that address government types and elections: These are: Indigenous Government Type, Intervening Force Government Type and Elections. We then compared these to both the Outcome and Duration of insurgencies to see if there were any patterns.

A. INDIGENOUS GOVERNMENT TYPE

First, we evaluated Indigenous Government Type by Outcome, the goal being to determine how government type affects the outcome of insurgencies. We have five government types: Democracy, Dictatorship, Troubled Democracy, Warlord and Theocracy. The 83-case MISS database contains multiple examples of Democracy (9 cases), Dictatorship (53 cases), and Troubled Democracy (19 cases), but only one example each of Warlord (UN Humanitarian Mission to Somalia) and Theocracy (Tibetan Revolt and Insurgency). Thus, while the Warlord and Theocracy cases have been included, the presence of just one example of each means no clear patterns or conclusions could be drawn from these. In Appendix VIII a listing of all 83 cases by Indigenous Government Type, the Presence of Elections, Duration, Winner and Type of Insurgency:

We started by looking at the indigenous government type during each insurgency for all 83 cases: [2]

GOVERNMENT TYPE	BLUE WINS	RED WINS	GRAY RESULTS
Democracy	4	2	3
Dictatorship	25	24	4
Troubled Dem.	12	3	4
Warlord	0	1	0
Theocracy	1	0	0

Looking at the data another way:

GOVERNMENT TYPE	BLUE WINS	RED WINS	GRAY RESULTS	AVG. DURATION
Democracy	44%	22%	33%	8.49 years
Dictatorship	47%	45%	8%	7.99 years
Troubled Dem.	63%	16%	21%	10.19 years
Warlord	0%	100%	0%	2.47 years
Theocracy	100%	0%	0%	18.59 years

The results of the Fisher's exact test are strong for the full dataset and the dataset excluding the Gray cases, and indicate that the results are most likely not random. When looking at all cases Democracies win twice as much as they lose, although one third of Democratic cases had Gray results. Additionally, the sample of Democracies was relatively small numbering only 9 cases. Dictatorships composed the largest sample, with 53 total cases, split evenly between Red and Blue wins. Troubled Democracies win more often (63% of cases) than not (21% of cases) but still produce sizable Gray (21% of cases) results.

One could easily lump the democracies and troubled democracies together compared to the dictatorships, theocracies and warlords. That pattern here is quite clear.

GOVERNMENT TYPE	BLUE WINS	RED WINS	GRAY RESULTS
Democracy/Troubled Democracy	16	5	7
Dictatorship/Warlord/Theocracy	26	25	4

The durations for Troubled Democracies were slightly longer than for the Dictatorships or the Democracies. However, the closeness of all three durations indicates that there are no strong conclusions to be drawn from any differences in length. The Warlord case is the Humanitarian Intervention in Somalia, and in that example the duration represents only the length of that intervention. Somalia has not had a real government since. The sole Theocracy case, the Tibetan insurgency against the Chinese, lasted a long time but at a very low intensity for the majority of its duration. As we have only one example of each, no clear conclusions can be drawn from either case.

Next we looked Indigenous Government Type by Outcome looking at just the insurgencies (62 cases):[3]

GOVERNMENT TYPE	BLUE WIN	RED WINS	GRAY RESULTS
Democracy	4	1	2
Dictatorship	15	23	2
Troubled Dem.	9	3	2
Theocracy	1	0	0

Looking at the data another way:

GOVERNMENT TYPE	BLUE WINS	RED WINS	GRAY RESULTS	AVG. DURATION
Democracy	57%	14%	29%	10.84 years
Dictatorship	38%	58%	5%	9.17 years
Troubled Dem.	64%	21%	14%	11.61 years
Theocracy	100%	0%	0%	18.59 years

Again, the Fisher's exact test results are strong, indicating a strong chance that these results are not random. Democracies clearly produced more wins than loses, although, again the sample is relatively small (7 cases). Dictatorships with a much larger sample (40 cases) produced more Red wins (58%), than Blue wins (38%), and few Gray results. The win percentages for Dictatorships changed significantly depending on whether we were looking at all cases or just insurgencies. Troubled Democracies won 64% of the time and lost only 21% of the time.

The durations for all three major categories (discounting the Theocracy) are very similar throughout the insurgent cases so there seems to be no firm conclusions to be drawn from duration from the 62 insurgency cases.

What is telling, though, is when the 62 insurgencies are divided into the 36 cases with significant outside intervention and the 26 cases without significant outside intervention.

Indigenous Government Type by Outcome (36 cases with significant outside intervention):[4]

GOVERNMENT TYPE	BLUE WINS	RED WINS	GRAY RESULTS
Dictatorship	12	16	0
Troubled Dem.	3	2	2
Theocracy	1	0	0

Looking at the data another way:

GOVERNMENT TYPE	BLUE WINS	RED WINS	GRAY RESULTS	AVG. DURATION
Dictatorship	43%	57%	0%	9.14 years
Troubled Dem.	43%	29%	29%	7.20 years
Theocracy	100%	0%	0%	18.50 years

The Fisher's exact test result for the whole dataset was strong, but when the Gray cases are excluded it becomes weak. The breaks in the win percentages combined with the weak Fisher's exact test result seem to indicate there are no strong patterns here. In Dictatorships the Red side won more often than not (57%). The average durations were similar to the previously examined durations, discounting the sole Theocracy.

Indigenous Government Type by Outcome (26 cases without significant outside intervention):[5]

GOVERNMENT TYPE	BLUE WINS	RED WINS	GRAY RESULTS
Democracy	4	1	2
Dictatorship	3	7	2
Troubled Dem. 6	1	0	

Looking at the data another way:

GOVERNMENT TYPE	BLUE WINS	RED WINS	GRAY RESULTS	AVG. DURATION
Democracy	57%	14%	29%	10.84 years
Dictatorship	25%	58%	17%	9.27 years
Troubled Dem.	86%	14%	0%	16.01 yearse

Both of these Fisher's exact test results are strong, indicating a low probability that these results came about from random chance. Our examination of government types for insurgencies without an intervening force shows a pattern. The Democracies won more often than not (57% of the time), with the insurgents losing most of the time (14%). Dictatorships lost more often (58%) than they won (25%). The Troubled Democracies win most of the time (86%) and only lost 14% of the time, like the Democracies. There is clearly a pattern here: The Democracies and Troubled Democracies won most of their insurgencies, and the Dictatorships lost most of theirs.

The durations for Democracies and Dictatorships were very similar, indicating no pattern. Both ran about 10 years on average. The Troubled Democracies insurgencies' durations were significantly longer, running on average 16.01 years.

There are no significant patterns related to indigenous government type for insurgencies with significant outside intervention (against foreigners), while there is a statistically significant trend (0.0431) for those cases where there is no significant out-side intervention (primarily domestic insurgencies).

Democracies and Troubled Democracies won more often than not in three of our four datasets (83, 62 and 26 cases). Dictatorships lost more often than not in three of our four data sets (62, 36 and 26 cases). The results were statistically significant.

In the case of primarily domestic insurgencies, a democracy or troubled democracy wins over two-thirds of the time, while a dictatorship wins only one-fourth of the time. This is a statistically significant difference. In the case of insurgencies against foreigners, there is no clear pattern.

The different government types produced patterns in the duration of their insurgencies compared to each other. Insurgencies in Democracies and Troubled Democracies countries tended to last longer than insurgencies in Dictatorships.

B. INTERVENING GOVERNMENT TYPE

Next, we examined the effect intervening government type had on the outcome and duration of insurgencies. We looked at the 36 examples we have of insurgencies with intervening powers (see Appendix VIII):

Looking first at all cases (36 cases):[6]

GOVERNMENT TYPE	BLUE WINS	RED WINS	GRAY RESULTS
Democracy	7	10	2
Dictatorship	8	8	0
Troubled Dem. 1	0	0	

Looking at the data another way:

GOVERNMENT TYPE	BLUE WINS	RED WINS	GRAY RESULTS	AVG. DURATION
Democracy	37%	53%	10%	6.48 years
Dictatorship	50%	50%	0%	12.07 years
Troubled Dem.	100%	0%	0%	8.61 years

The Fisher's exact test results were weak with this dataset indicating at least a 52% and 60% chance respectively that the data could have come about by random chance.

Democracies did not fare well in foreign interventions and lost more often than not. Dictatorships split evenly between wins and losses. There was only one example of a Troubled Democracy in a foreign intervention (Peacekeeping in Sierra Leone), so no clear conclusions can be drawn. There seems to be no clear pattern for wins and losses except that democracies tend to lose more often than they win.

Concerning duration, the Democracies had an average duration of 6.48 years, which is relatively short compared to previous examinations of government type and duration. The Dictatorships average 12.07 years, which is in keeping with our general findings. The data seems to indicate that Dictatorships are capable of winning more often and lasting longer than Democracies in insurgencies in foreign countries. But, there is no statistical support for this.

To allow for the fact that the number of colonial wars, or wars of liberation may be driving results, we looked at the data without the INS/Cs and only the INS/Is. Looking at the non-colonial cases (24 cases):[7]

GOVERNMENT TYPE	BLUE WINS	RED WINS	GRAY RESULTS
Democracy	5	4	2
Dictatorship	8	4	0
Troubled Dem.	1	0	0

Looking at the data another way:

GOVERNMENT TYPE	BLUE WINS	RED WINS	GRAY RESULTS	AVG. DURATION
Democracy	45%	36%	18%	5.91 years
Dictatorship	67%	33%	0%	12.87 years
Troubled Dem.	100%	0%	0%	8.61 years

The Fisher's exact test results for these cases were even weaker than those above, indicating a high probability that these results came about through random chance. The results for Democracies have clearly changed, though now there is no clear pattern. Dictatorships on the other hand win in two-thirds of cases. Interestingly, the durations have not changed significantly.

In conclusion, our examination of intervening government type showed that Democracies win slightly over a third of the time and lose more than half the time. Dictatorships win half the time and lose half the time. The duration for Democracies was about half the duration for Dictatorships. There is no statistical support for this.

It does not appear that intervening government type is important for determining the outcome of an insurgency.

C. ELECTIONS

Looking at election results by outcome we looked at all 83 total cases, 62 insurgencies, 36 insurgencies against foreigners and finally the 26 insurgencies without interventions. First the full data set of 83 cases:[8]

ELECTIONS	BLUE WINS	RED WINS	GRAY RESULTS
Yes	31	13	10
No	11	17	0
Undetermined	0	0	1

Looking at the data another way:

ELECTIONS	BLUE WINS	RED WINS	GRAY RESULTS	AVG. DURATION
Yes	57%	24%	19%	9.41 years
No	39%	60%	0%	7.25 years
Undetermined	0%	0%	100%	3.06 years

The Fisher's exact test results for the above data were strong, indicating a correlation between elections and winning.

In these cases there seems to be a pattern between Blue wins in cases with elections and Red wins in cases without elections. This would seem to indicate that the presence of elections is good for the Blue side. It is important to bear in mind that the Blue side might be reluctant, or might not, to hold elections, if they knew that elections would result in an insurgent win. We only have one undetermined case (Chechen Disorder), so there can be no patterns or conclusions drawn from that case. Interestingly, those cases with no elections produced no Gray results, while those with elections produced ten Gray results. Thus, the Blue side won in 57% of cases with elections and 39% without; the Red won in 24% of cases with elections and 60% without elections. **Therefore, the presence of elections seems to seriously hamper the Red side's chance of winning.**

Concerning Duration, insurgencies with elections last about two years longer than those without elections (9.41 years and 7.25 years respectively). Looking at the cases of insurgency only (the 62 cases) produces similar results:[9]

ELECTIONS	BLUE WINS	RED WINS	GRAY RESULTS
Yes	21	11	6
No	8	16	0

Or, to put it another way:

ELECTIONS	BLUE WINS	RED WINS	GRAY RESULTS	AVG. DURATION
Yes	55%	29%	16%	11.24 years
No	33%	67%	0%	8.19 years

Once again, the Fisher's exact test results are strong, indicating a correlation between elections and winning in insurgencies.

The results for just the insurgencies are similar to the results for all 83 cases. The Blue side wins in 55% of cases with elections and 33% of cases without elections. The Red side won 29% of cases with elections and 67% of cases without. Gray results occurred in 16% of insurgencies with elections and none in insurgencies without elections.

For both insurgencies with elections and those without, the average duration for insurgencies was longer than for all 83 cases combined. Those cases with elections averaged 11.24 years and those without 8.19. There seems to be a pattern with cases with elections lasting longer than those without.

Next, we looked at cases of insurgencies with an outside intervening power (36 cases):[10]

ELECTIONS	BLUE WINS	RED WINS	GRAY RESULTS
Yes	8	8	2
No	8	10	0

Looking at it another way:

ELECTIONS	BLUE WINS	RED WINS	GRAY RESULTS	AVG. DURATION
Yes	44%	44%	11%	9.03 years
No	44%	55%	0%	9.02 years

The Fisher's exact test results are weak indicating little or not correlation between elections and winning for insurgencies with a foreign power. This is an interesting case as there were an equal number of cases on each side (18 with elections and 18 without).

It is clear the results are very close, as is the duration. **This would seem to indicate the elections do not really affect the outcome of an insurgency with an outside intervening force.** The only pattern continued here is that the Red side wins more often in the absence of elections. The pattern noticed in durations earlier is not present here with both cases with elections and those without averaging about 9 years each.

Looking at insurgencies with no significant outside intervening forces (primarily domestic insurgencies) (26 cases):[11]

ELECTIONS	BLUE WINS	RED WINS	GRAY RESULTS
Yes	13	3	4
No	0	6	0

Looking at it another way:

ELECTIONS	BLUE WINS	RED WINS	GRAY RESULTS	AVG. DURATION
Yes	65%	15%	20%	13.25 years
No	0%	100%	0%	5.69 years

The Fisher's exact test result was strong, indicating a correlation between elections and winning in primarily domestic insurgencies. The number of cases with elections was more than double the amount without.

The Blue side wins in 65% of cases with elections and 0% without. Clearly, elections are important for the Blue side. The Red side wins in 15% of cases with elections and 100% of cases without. In the case of primarily domestic insurgencies, the presence or absence of elections appears to be critical.

The pattern for durations continues here with cases with elections lasting longer (13.25 years) and resulting in more Blue side wins, and cases with no elections being shorter (5.69 years) and generally resulting in Red wins.

In conclusion, the presence of elections tends to result in more Blue side wins. This pattern is observed for almost all of the datasets, with the exception of insurgencies against foreigners. Elections had a major effect on the primarily domestic insurgencies, which was also the smallest of the datasets with only 26 cases. This result is statistically significant.

In terms of duration, insurgencies with elections tend to last longer than insurgencies without, once again, this pattern held for all datasets with the exception of insurgencies with intervening powers. As noted in the above paragraph, this pattern was most pronounced in the cases of primarily domestic insurgencies.

CONCLUSION

We noted two significant trends across this data. For those insurgencies with significant outside interventions (insurgencies against foreigners), we note that: 1) Indigenous government type has no significantly measurable influence, in fact, in all but five cases the indigenous government is a dictatorship, 2) intervening government type does not seem to matter, and 3) elections do not seem to matter.

On the other hand, for those insurgencies without significant outside intervening forces (primarily domestic insurgencies): 1) having the indigenous government as a Democracy or Troubled Democracy clearly favors the Blue side. This result is statistically significant and 2) having elections favors the Blue side. This result is statistically significant.

One wonders if the process of intervening undercuts the benefits of democracy.

NOTES

1. From the *Secretary of Defense Message to the Armed Forces on the Iraqi Elections*, February 2, 2005 provided by American Forces Press Service.
2. Two-sided p-value from Fisher's exact test using all data: 0.0572. Two-sided p-value from Fisher's exact test excluding the Gray cases: 0.1317.
3. Two-sided p-value from Fisher's exact test using all data: 0.0299. Two-sided p-value from Fisher's exact test excluding the Gray cases: 0.0427.

4   Two-sided p-value from Fisher's exact test using all data: 0.0420. Two-sided p-value from Fisher's exact test excluding the Gray cases: 0.4782.

5   Two-sided p-value from Fisher's exact test using all data: 0.0664. Two-sided p-value from Fisher's exact test excluding the Gray cases: 0.0431

6   Two-sided p-value from Fisher's exact test using all data: 0.5202. Two-sided p-value from Fisher's exact test excluding the Gray cases: 0.6057.

7   Two-sided p-value from Fisher's exact test using all data: 0.5055. Two-sided p-value from Fisher's exact test excluding the Gray cases: 0.7920.

8   Two-sided p-value from Fisher's exact test using all data: 0.0004. Two-sided p-value from Fisher's exact test excluding the Gray cases: 0.0139.

9   Two-sided p-value from Fisher's exact test using all data: 0.0061. Two-sided p-value from Fisher's exact test excluding the Gray cases: 0.0298.

10   Two-sided p-value from Fisher's exact test using all data: 0.6415. Two-sided p-value from Fisher's exact test excluding the Gray cases: >0.9.

11   Two-sided p-value from Fisher's exact test using all data: 0.0009. Two-sided p-value from Fisher's exact test excluding the Gray cases: 0.0011.

CHAPTER 13

The Influence of Terrain on Insurgencies[1]

Man gazes at the stars, but his feet are in the mud.

—Lucius Annaeus Seneca, Roman Stoic
   philosopher, before 65 A.D. [2]

It is natural to assume that terrain plays an important role in insurgencies, as terrain plays an important rule in all military operations. In the case of insurgencies, its significance has been hard to evaluate.

The strategic impact of terrain on insurgencies is probably less than many suspect. Interestingly, we have found only two widely-read counterinsurgent theorists, David Galula and Bard O'Neill, who have bothered to address terrain issues in any depth. Galula spent two pages on them,[3] while O'Neill dedicates an entire chapter to "the environment,"[4] which covers many aspects of terrain. He spent eight pages on terrain in his manuscript and also addressed climate. Many other widely-read theorists have ignored or greatly downplayed the importance of terrain.

Terrain has certainly been of focus in the United States because of the experience in Vietnam. "Jungle warfare" was a term that seemed almost synonymous with counterinsurgency in the 1960s and 1970s. Many students of counterinsurgency in the U.S. spent an immoderate amount of time studying the Malayan insurgency because it was also fought in jungles, like Vietnam, while seemingly ignoring or downplaying all the other hundreds of examples of insurgencies fought in different terrain. This was a dangerous over emphasis on a limited number of cases because of surface similarities and convenience that the counterinsurgents wrote and spoke English. As Bernard Fall pointed out: "The only thing that Viet-Nam had which resembles Malaya, is the climate."[5]

Our attempt to address terrain focused on examining terrain types, percent urban population, area, population, population density, border length and arable land. We found some clear correlations when we looked at major terrain types and percent urban population.

GENERAL SUMMARY AND ANALYSIS
OF MAJOR TERRAIN TYPE DATA

Major terrain type was based upon 12 categories created by *The Dupuy Institute*. In creating the 12 categories, we were concerned with identifying rough and not-so-rough terrain in addition to identifying forested (or jungle) and non-forested. This basically led to terrain being classified as level, rough or mountainous and covered and uncovered. This resulted in six categories. We ended up with two types of level terrain (desert and plains) and an additional type of covered terrain (jungle). We also ended up with a mixed terrain type and mixed terrain and coverage. Finally, we added "primarily urban" and "marsh," giving us a total of 12 terrain types. These can be boiled down to six categories as:

	LEVEL	ROUGH	MOUNTAINOUS
Uncovered	Desert	Mixed	Mountains
	Plains	Rough	
Covered	Forested	Foliated Mixed	Foliated Mountains
	Jungle	Foliated Rough	
	Marsh	Urban	

The assignment of major terrain types to countries was based on analysts' judgment. It was actually an informal, Delphic process in that a half-dozen Institute staff sat down at a table and made a judgment call after a brief discussion of each case. In the end, there was only serious debate over a couple of cases.[6]

This variable represents the primary terrain type of a country, with a bias toward the primary terrain type where the insurgency occurred. Still, many larger countries by default were mixed terrain. For example, 8 out of 18 countries over 1,000,000 square miles were mixed or foliated mixed, and these made up one-third of the "mixed" cases.

Looking at individual terrain types produced no significant results. For example, there were no Red wins in level uncovered terrain, although we only had 2 cases of this. This was also the case for the other end of the spectrum, covered mountains, where we had 4 Blue wins and no red wins. Both cases cannot be correct, unless terrain is not a primary factor in the success or failure of these insurgencies. Still, it is hard not to notice the large number of cases of rough covered terrain and the high percent of wins for the insurgents in that terrain.

Statistical testing indicates a strong association between outcome and terrain type, if one classifies terrain as "rough covered" (foliated mixed, foliated rough and urban) versus all other terrain types. In the 83 case data set, the Blue side won only 36% of the time in "rough covered" terrain as opposed to 64% of the time in other terrain.

TERRAIN	BLUE	RED	GRAY	TOTAL
Rough Covered	14	18	7	39
Not Rough Covered	28	12	4	44
Total	42	30	11	83

Using Fisher's exact test on the contingency table above to test the hypothesis of no association between rough terrain and outcome the p-value (two-sided) is 0.0417. This is strong evidence that the outcome may depend on the terrain type, when terrain is classified as rough covered versus not rough covered.

The evidence is stronger, when we leave aside the 11 "Gray" outcome insurgencies. In this case, the Fisher's exact test one-sided p-value is 0.0223, which reflects the probability of seeing an outcome as extreme or even more extreme as the one observed in the table below when we assume no link between terrain and insurgency outcome.

If we limit ourselves to the 62 cases that are insurgencies, or became insurgencies after a conventional war or suppression, then we obtain the following contingency table, with the Blue side winning only 31% of the time in "rough covered" terrain, while winning 57% of the time in other terrain.

TERRAIN	BLUE	RED	GRAY	TOTAL
Rough Covered	9	16	4	29
Not Rough Covered	20	11	2	35
Total	29	27	6	62

The Fisher's exact test p-value (two-sided) is 0.0707, which is a weaker result than when using the set of 83 cases. Leaving the Gray cases out of the set of 62 cases, and conducting Fisher's exact test on this table gives a one-sided p-value of 0.0314, which is strong evidence that there may be an association between terrain type and outcome. Namely, there is strong evidence that the odds of winning on rough covered terrain for the Red side are higher than for the Blue side.

There is a concern with the categorization of the data. The 39 cases (or 29 insurgency cases) of rough covered terrain include 13 cases (or 9 insurgency cases) of urban terrain. Still, in the 13 cases of urban terrain, we have 4 Blue wins, 4 Red wins and 5 Gray results (or for the insurgencies only: 2 Blue wins, 3 Red wins and 4 Gray results). Clearly, this alone is not driving the results, and the values for Fisher's exact test would be lower (more favorable to establishing a relationship) if these cases were left out.

Even though the statistics are not conclusive, it is clear that the Red side is winning more often in rough covered terrain than other terrain, and this does not appear to be by accident.

This data also shows another pattern with insurgencies in covered terrain being more successful than insurgencies in uncovered terrain. Just to compare:

TERRAIN TYPE	CASES	PERCENT RED WINS	AVERAGE DURATION
Uncovered	24	33%	8.0
Covered	38	50%	11.3

Note this difference in duration also exists for "rough covered" versus "not rough covered," although not as sharp, although the percent of red wins is similar.[7]

A simple comparison of covered terrain versus uncovered terrain shows a similar relationship, although not as strong.

	INSURGENCY OUTCOME			TOTAL
TERRAIN	BLUE	GRAY	RED	
Covered	15	4	19	38
Uncovered	14	2	8	24
Total	29	6	27	62

Based on Fisher's exact test, the outcome appears to be independent of the terrain type. The p-value of this test was 0.3827 (two-sided), indicating that this pattern could occur 38% of the time even though there was no relationship between terrain (covered versus uncovered) and outcome.

Still, for a number of reasons, including a hypothetical link here between cause and effect and the completeness of the data set (over one-third to one-half of all significant post-World War II insurgencies are included in this data), there is still some basis for accepting that the relationship exists.

Therefore, we tentatively conclude that there is some relationship between terrain and outcome and that this is demonstrated by the higher rate of wins in covered terrain compared to uncovered terrain. There also appears to be some relationship between terrain and duration, which would not be surprising if there was some relationship between terrain and outcome.

Still, there is another problem with this data in that the broad category of insurgencies includes three subcategories that have very different outcomes. For example, INS/C (insurgencies against colonial powers) cases and cases that become INS/C resulted in Red wins in 10 out 12 cases (83%). The INS/I (insurgencies versus an intervening power) cases or cases that become INS/I resulted in Red wins in only 8 out of 24 cases (33%), while INS/NI (insurgencies with no intervening power) cases or cases that become INS/NI resulted in Red wins in 9 out of 26 cases (35%). These subcategories were not distributed evenly by type across the terrain features.

	UNCOVERED	COVERED
INS/C	2	10
INS/I	9	15
INS/NI	11	15

Therefore, the INS/C (over 80% Red wins) is going to help drive the statistics for covered terrain wins. But looking at the data in different way provides a comparison were can analyze:

		UNCOVERED	COVERED
INS/C	- Blue	1	1
	- Red	1	9
INS/I	- Blue	7	7
	- Gray	1	1
	- Red	2	6
INS/NI	- Blue	6	7
	- Gray	1	3
	- Red	5	4

Now, we are looking at very few data points per case, but at least there is a pattern emerging.

	UNCOVERED	COVERED
INS/C Red wins	50%	90%
INS/I Red wins	20%	43%
INS/NI Red wins	42%	29%

This pattern clearly shows some help from covered terrain. It is not statistically supported. Significantly, it shows covered terrain mattering for the INS/C and INS/I cases, the insurgencies against foreigners, but not for the INS/NI cases, the domestic insurgencies. This is discussed in more depth below.

Another concern is whether we should focus on "rough covered" terrain because the results were more significant than just being "rough" or "covered?" One of our problems is that the original categorization of rough covered in insurgencies included foliated mixed (18 cases), foliated rough (2 cases), and urban (9 cases). The first problem is that, by default, foliated mixed terrain includes many of our insurgencies in larger countries. So, does this category measure the effect of foliated mixed terrain or the effect of country size? The next problem is that urban terrain is by nature very different than foliated rough. While it shares overhead cover in common, it does not share the same sense of isolation. Urban terrain is relatively easy to get in and out of, certainly more so than the highlands of Vietnam. Therefore, "rough covered" serves more as a measure of openness of fields of fire than it does a measurement of isolation. As other researchers have focused on the importance of isolation, this may be an important issue.[8]

Still there are some tentative conclusions we can draw from this:

1. Covered terrain appears to favor the insurgents. This is supported statistically in the majority but not all of the various tests that we conducted.
2. Our data set probably includes more than a third of all significant insurgencies since World War II and almost all insurgencies against outside forces, including all major cases. As such, the failure to obtain a tight statistical result does not mean we should assume a null hypothesis (there is no relationship) is correct if a visible pattern exists.
3. Rough covered terrain or, simply, covered terrain appears to increase the chances of the Red side winning.
4. Covered terrain appears to increase the duration of insurgencies.
5. The value of covered terrain may be related to airpower. This needs to be examined further.
6. Terrain may be a more significant factor for insurgencies against outside powers than for primarily domestic insurgencies.
7. Otherwise, there is no strong indication that there are any differences between level terrain, rough terrain and mountainous terrain, or urban or any other significant terrain type as far as their strategic effect on determining outcome.
8. There is no indication that accessibility of the terrain is an issue here (isolated versus not isolated).

THE VALUE OF COVERED TERRAIN

The value of covered terrain may be closely related to its value in obscuring and protecting the guerilla from counterinsurgent airpower. This is a case where airpower and air supremacy is something that almost all counterinsurgent forces possess, and the insurgents have absolutely none.[8] Counterinsurgent air supremacy provides air recon, air support and mobility. Air recon may be the most significant as it can identify moving enemy forces and vector in reaction forces. It also has a defensive value in that it can identify major moving groups and allow time for reaction forces to respond. Obviously, there is a real tactical combat value in direct air support. It is also possible to conduct harassing and interdiction missions against visible insurgent forces. Finally, there is air mobility, which gives the counterinsurgent forces considerable capability to maneuver, envelop and surprise. Each of these is a significant advantage that the insurgents do not have. Each of these capabilities is clearly degraded by overhead cover.

The difference between rough uncovered terrain (38% Red victories) and rough covered (55% Red victories) is the overhead cover. In the case of level uncovered terrain (0% Red victories) and jungle and marshy terrain (50% Red victories), there are also accessibility and isolation issues .[10] Still, the statistics point to cover being significant to some degree, and show more significance than roughness or isolating terrain. Therefore, the difference must be in some strategic advantage derived from overhead coverage. This may be explained in part, or mostly, on the degradation of the effects of counterinsurgent air power.

This could be tested by collecting a comparable dataset of pre-World War I insurgencies and comparing their results in uncovered and covered terrain compared to the post-World War II cases. This is recommended for further exploration of this issue.

Interestingly enough, many of the theorists of counterinsurgency warfare barely address the effects of air power. Most don't discuss it at all, and some dismiss it as overrated. Clutterbuck seems to recognize that there is some value to air power if the terrain is open. He states: "In open country, such as in Algeria or parts of Vietnam, air power can be decisive if used wisely, both as an offensive weapon and for transport. Used unwisely, however, it can do real harm, both in telegraphing our punches and in alienating the local population."[11]

On the other hand, O'Neill clearly addresses this issue: "Unlike areas with heavy foliage, open spaces (e.g., deserts) are normally unfavorable for guerillas; air surveillance and attack make insurgents susceptible to detection and destruction."[12]

Another writer, Arthur Campbell, states: "Open plains are obstacles to guerillas because they have to concede mastery of the air to their opponents. Before the onset of air power, Lawrence and his Arabs were able to retreat at will in the Arabian Desert, but the FLN in Algeria, opposed by a powerful French air force, were denied access to the vast reaches of the Sahara. . . ."[13]

WHY TERRAIN SIGNIFICANCE MAY DIFFER FOR INTERVENTIONS VERSUS PRIMARILY DOMESTIC INSURGENCIES

There is clearly a difference in results for the influence of covered terrain in colonial wars and interventions (INS/I) as opposed to insurgencies with no significant outside interventions (INS/NI). This difference may be a statistical anomaly or it may be explainable by the nature of the forces involved. We suspect the latter is the case. In most cases, the intervening or colonial force is an advanced first world European-type power. These militaries have modern air forces, good communications, good mobility and many other advantages. This is true of some, but not the majority of cases of INS/NI, where the government forces often have very limited air capability and mobility. As such, in many cases, the terrain affects both sides in an INS/NI equally, while counterinsurgent forces with significant air power are more adversely affected by covered terrain.

THE VALUE OF ISOLATING TERRAIN

An article by Fearon and Laitin clearly asserts that isolating terrain is an advantage.

Still, there is not a sense that this is considered important by many counterinsurgency theorists. While theorists like Clutterbuck and Kitson talk extensively about the need for action in the early stages of an insurgency, they do not specifically address the issue of isolating terrain, as is the case with most other theorists. Instead, many of the theorists like Galula and Joes talk about the importance of isolating the guerillas.

One must also consider that isolating terrain might only be an advantage in the early stages of an insurgency. In the long run, insurgents need to move away from distant refuges and contest with the government for control of the population. Therefore, while isolating terrain may be of importance early in an insurgency, for the insurgents to be victorious, they must leave that isolation. An example of this is shown below in a map comparing traffic patterns (vehicles per day) in Colombia with areas of insurgent activity. It is clear that the insurgents are operating in areas of considerable traffic activity--certainly the opposite of isolation.

Therefore, for a developed insurgency, we suspect that the isolating effect of terrain is not the significant value of terrain.

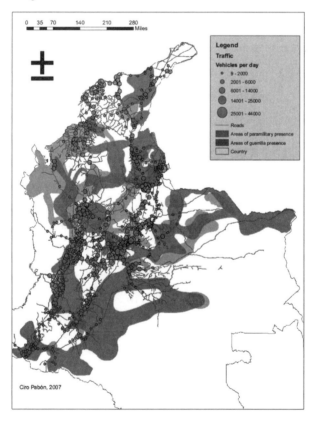

THE CONCLUSIONS OF FEARON AND LAITIN

One of the studies that covered the same ground as this effort was the article by Fearon and Laitin on "Ethnicity, Insurgency and Civil War," which also reached conclusions on terrain. They state that: "On the rebel side, insurgency is favored by rough terrain, rebels with local knowledge of the population superior to the government's, and a large population."[14] This last point (large population) was first addressed in our Iraq study and is addressed again later in Chapter Fifteen.

Their actual hypothesis is: "The presence of (a) rough terrain, poorly served by roads, at a distance from the centers of state power, should favor insurgency and civil war. So should the availability of (b) foreign, cross-border sanctuaries and (c) a local population that can be induced not to denounce the insurgents to government agents."[15] These are, of course, three completely unrelated points.

They then add a fourth element of this hypothesis (which they label as H8d): "Having a *rural base* should greatly favor insurgency. In the city, anonymous denunciation is easier to get away with, giving the government an advantage in its counterinsurgent efforts." [16] This will be examined further below.

They then define rough terrain: "As for measures, for 'rough terrain' we use the proportion of the country that is 'mountainous' according to the coding of geographer A. J. Gerard" (page 81).

We have three problems with this measurement. First, we believe foliation and covered terrain are important and may be more important than the lay of the land. Second, we suspect arable land is a better measurement, as it reflects all the land that can be used by insurgents (including urban terrain), not just the mountainous terrain in a country. Finally, their approach does not address urban warfare, which makes up a significant number of cases. Of course, Fearon and Laitin acknowledge the weakness of the measure and indicate that is was the best they could do at the time. Further on in this section we address the issue of urban warfare and later, we inconclusively address arable land.

Their conclusions were:

> **"Mountains and Noncontiguous Territory.** Mountainous terrain is significantly related to higher rates of civil war. A country that is about half 'mountainous' (ninetieth percentile) and otherwise at the median has an estimated 13.2% chance of civil war over the course of a decade. A similar country that is not mountainous at all (tenth percentile) has a 6.5% risk . . ."[17]

Of course, they are measuring the likelihood of a country having a civil war, vice the effectiveness of the insurgency. So, isolation, which may be important in the early stages of an insurgency, but not later on, might show up in the factors of the likelihood of having an insurgency. Therefore, their results do not necessarily disagree with our results and vice versa.

URBAN VERSUS RURAL INSURGENCIES

Urban insurgencies are coded two ways in our data base. First, they are coded as a type of insurgency according to O'Neill's definition of Strategic Approach. His four types of Strategic Approach were conspiratorial, military-focus, protracted popular war and urban warfare, of which only the last three categories show up among our 83 cases. Our primary concern with O'Neill's Strategic Approach taxonomy is that we fear that urban warfare is a terrain type and the actual insurgency type should be either military-focus or protracted popular war. There were ten insurgencies coded as "urban warfare" in accordance with O'Neill's definition.

We also coded the insurgencies by terrain type. We coded the terrain as "urban" in 13 cases. There are ten cases (nine were insurgencies) whose Strategic Approach is Urban Warfare and three other cases (none were insurgencies) that were not "urban warfare" in terms of Strategic Approach but which were fought in urban terrain. The cases are:

NAME		PERCENT POPULATION URBAN	POPULATION DENSITY
1.	UK in Palestine	48.47	68.38
2.	Puerto Rico Independence Movement	40.60	160.31
3.	Soviet Intervention in Hungary	41.24	105.61
4.	Tupamaro Insurgency in Uruguay	80.86	14.71
5.	Aden	10.24	2.24
6.	Northern Ireland	77.52	106.22
7.	Argentina & the Dirty War	78.40	8.53
8.	First Intifada	64.74	223.78
9.	Second Intifada	70.00	336.51
10.	Iraq War	68.56	61.53

According to our coding of terrain types, the urban cases are:

1.	UK in Palestine	48.47	68.38
2.	Puerto Rico Independence Movement	40.60	160.31
3.	Soviet Intervention in Hungary	41.24	105.61
4.	Tupamaro Insurgency in Uruguay	80.86	14.71
5.	Aden	10.24	2.24
6.	Northern Ireland	77.52	108.57
7.	Argentina & the Dirty War	78.40	8.53
8.	First Intifada	64.74	223.78
9.	US Invasion of Panama (N/A)	53.38	30.31
10.	UN Mission to Somalia (Military-focus)	30.08	10.22
11.	Second Intifada	70.00	336.51
12.	Iraq War	68.56	61.53
13.	Hamas (Military-focus)	90.00	406.96

This is 13 of our 83 cases in urban terrain or 16% of the cases. In those six cases where the percent of population living in urban terrain is greater than 75%, 50% of these are urban warfare, and two-thirds are considered to be in urban terrain. It does raise the question whether at some point urban warfare is an option or if it becomes the only choice available.

Case in point:

PERCENT URBAN	NUMBER OF CASES	PERCENT URBAN WARFARE	PERCENT IN URBAN TERRAIN
0 to 25%	41	2.4	2.4
25% to 50%	21	14.3	19.0
50% to 75%	15	20.0	26.7
75% to 100%	6	50.0	66.7

Looking at just the 62 insurgencies:

PERCENT URBAN	NUMBER OF CASES	PERCENT URBAN WARFARE
0 to 25%	34	2.9
25% to 50%	13	15.4
50% to 75%	12	25.0
75% to 100%	3	100.0

The breakpoint in the data seems to be around 65% urban population. Below that level, we have three insurgencies that are urban warfare in nature. The other six urban warfare insurgencies are above that level. More to the point is that we still have some insurgencies that are fundamentally rurally based in countries that 50% to 60% urban. The insurgencies in this range are:

INSURGENCY	PERCENT URBAN
Contras in Nicaragua	50.86
Colombian Civil War	51.98
Cuban Revolution	52.66
Cabanas Insurgency	56.54

These are all insurgencies with a strong rural element to them. The cases where the percent urban was in the 65% to 80% range (there is nothing between 56.54 and 64.60) are:

INSURGENCY	PERCENT URBAN
Shining Path in Peru	64.60
First Intifada	64.74
Lebanon (1975–1990)	67.00
Polisario Rebellion	67.52

Iraq (2003–present)	68.56
Second Intifada	70.00
First Chechen War	73.40
Second Chechen War	73.40
Northern Ireland	**77.52**
Argentina	**78.40**
Tupamaro Insurgency	**80.86**

Of these 11 cases, the 6 in bold are coded by us as urban warfare. The Shining Path was a rural guerilla movement that moved into the city, and Lebanon has a significant urban element. Still, the two Chechen cases, while sometimes centered on Grozny, were fundamentally rural, as was the Polisario Rebellion.

Not surprisingly, it seems that once the percent of urban population gets above 65%, insurgencies tend (more often than not) to be urban, and this may be absolute above 75%.

This may useful to understand and appreciate for the sake of predicting the nature of future events and future military requirements. We did not see any relationships generated by population density.

CONCLUSIONS REGARDING PERCENT URBAN POPULATION

It does looks like insurgencies are more successful in rural countries. We tested this across the entire collection of data and were able to establish a weak linear relationship between duration and percent urban population.

If we define a country as rural if the percent urban population is 50% or less, we can test the hypothesis that the odds of winning for the red group is higher in rural than in urban countries. To test this hypothesis, we ran Fisher's exact test on the contingency table below:

GROUP	PERCENT URBAN IS 50% OR LESS	PERCENT URBAN ABOVE 50%	TOTAL
Blue	33	9	42
Red	26	4	30
Total	59	13	72

Using Fisher's exact test on the table, the p-value from the one-sided test is 0.2879, which is quite high and which indicates that it is quite likely that the state of events described in the table are due to chance.

If we test the hypothesis that the odds of winning for the Red group are higher when the percent urban population is 20% or less than when the urban population is 20% and above, this is equivalent to saying that we test the hypothesis of independence between the percent urban and the outcome. We ran Fisher's exact test on the contingency table below:

GROUP	PERCENT URBAN IS 20% OR LESS	PERCENT URBAN ABOVE 20%	TOTAL
Blue	13	29	42
Red	19	11	30
Total	32	40	72

The one-sided Fisher's exact test p-value is 0.0063, which is strong evidence that the there is an association between the percent urban at the 20% cutoff and outcome.

We conducted this test again on the subset of 62 variables, except that we dropped the six cases in the Gray group, to be left with 56 Red and Blue cases. We ran Fisher's exact test on the contingency table below:

GROUP	PERCENT URBAN LESS THAN 20%	PERCENT URBAN ABOVE 20%	TOTAL
Blue	10	19	29
Red	18	9	27
Total	28	28	56

The one-sided Fisher's exact test p-value is 0.0157, which is strong evidence again that the there is an association between the percent urban at the 20% cutoff and outcome.

Now, this picture is confused by the large number of INS/C in the data, which tend to be mostly in rural areas and mostly Red wins, but our other examination of this subject indicates that there is some relationship. Therefore, our conclusions are:

One cannot rule out, from this examination, that a rural environment (low percent urban population) favors the insurgents.

This appears to be the case for up to around 20% urban population, and the effect appears to exist even though it is being influenced by other factors. Above 20%, it does not appear to be a significant factor.

If one looks at the average duration of our 13 urban insurgencies, they are 6.4 years in length compared to the database average of 8.6 years for 83 cases, and for the 9 that are insurgencies, they are 8.9 years in length compared to the database average of 10.4 years for 62 insurgencies. Still, our urban insurgencies include our third-longest case (Northern Ireland).

Added to that is the interesting comparison we did that showed that the duration of Blue wins is longer for urban terrain that for non urban terrain. This does not include most of the INS/C, indicating that this is not influencing the relationship.[18]

Beyond the hint that rural insurgencies are more successful and that insurgencies in more urban terrain may take longer to defeat, there is little here that is definite.

CONCLUSIONS

There were a few other conclusions from our examination of the effect of terrain in our studies. Our analysis eventually expanded to creating a regression model to try to predict the outcome of insurgencies based upon terrain. It was based upon these independent variables:

1. Population size
2. If the insurgency is fought in rough-covered terrain
3. If the urban population is below 20%

That model was able to correctly predict the outcome 68% of the time. It correctly predicted the victor in 72% of the cases where the counterinsurgents won, and in 63% of the cases where the insurgents won. The errors in this model appeared to be scattered fairly evenly across the dataset.

This was not as good of a predictor as we would like, and eventually our focus led us to the force ratio-political concept model that is discussed in this book. But, we did input the data from Iraq (2003) into this model to generate the probability of insurgent success. **According to this model, the probability of insurgent success in Iraq is roughly estimated to be 0.512.** This would be a prediction of a Red win although it is on the cusp.

Still, what one ought to take from this analysis is the non-negligible effect the type of terrain and level of urbanization may have on the probability of insurgent success. Although we used the population variable in order to graphically illustrate the aforementioned significant effects, the seemingly positive effect of population size on the probability of insurgent success may be statistically insignificant. This was unexpected. The analysis could be expanded to look beyond these two factors with an expansion of the data set.

It appears the terrain and percent urban population can be used to help explain the outcome insurgencies, and these should probably be considered for any modeling effort on the subject.

We also did some analysis using classification trees that reinforced some of these conclusions. Still, this all clearly shows that terrain matters to some extent. This is in three areas: rough covered terrain favors an insurgency, high populations favor an insurgency and a low percentage of urbanization favors an insurgency. These are preconditions that exist that must be understood as being a factor before one commits troops. They are not conditions that can be easily changed during an insurgency.

How important is terrain relative to other factors is harder to determine, and we need to eventually explore this further. Still, this analysis indicates that any model, intellectual or mathematical, is fundamentally missing an important element if it does not address terrain. These conclusions should not come as a surprise to any serious student of history.

The remaining conclusions from our report on terrain are included below:[19]

1. There does not appear to be much correlation between area and outcome,

except possibly for the insurgencies against foreign forces.

2. It appears that there is the some correlation between population and outcome from this sample of 34 cases (excluding the two ongoing examples), especially above 9,500,000 population. Otherwise, we saw no correlations between population size and outcome.

3. We are left to conclude that there is probably no direct correlation between density of population, the duration and the outcome of an insurgency.

4. Basically, we see no clear correlation between border length and outcome, other than that which might be generated by a correlation between area of the country and outcome.

5. There appears to be no correlation between the start date of the insurgency and outcome that is not explainable by the nature and type of the insurgency.

6. The mean duration of insurgencies won by the red side is 7.8 years, while the mean duration of insurgencies won by the blue side is 12.6 years. **Thus, it may take the blue side longer to achieve success.**

7. The main conclusion we can draw from the classification trees is that it again shows the percent urban population (less than 20%) appears to be significant as does terrain type, regardless of how terrain is coded. Still, no single variable could be ruled out as completely unimportant.

8. It appears the terrain can be used to explain the outcome of almost half the insurgencies.

9. It appears that there is some relationship between population size and outcome when outside intervening forces are involved. This may be because of the burden larger insurgencies impose on the intervening country.

NOTES

1. I was helped considerably by Dr. Victoria Plamedeala-Johnson in this task.

2. Quoted in William K. Klingaman, *The First Century: Emperors, Gods, and Everyman* (New York: Harper Perennial, 1991), 269.

3. David Galula, *Counterinsurgency Warfare: Theory and Practice* (Westport, Ct.: Praeger Security International, 2006 [1964]), 23–25. Galula also includes population as part of his discussion of "Geographic Conditions."

4. Bard E. O'Neill, *Insurgency and Terrorism: From Revolution to Apocalypse.* (draft, Washington, D.C., 2005). A final version was released July 2005, and is an update of his *Insurgency and Terrorism, Inside Modern Revolutionary Warfare*, which was first published in 1990 and again in 2001. Ch. 4, 11.

5. The entire quote is: "We always hang on for dear life to the Malayan example, which, of course, is totally unworkable. The only thing that Viet-Nam had which resembles Malaya, is the climate. We don't give the Communists credit for making mistakes, yet Malaya was one of their big mistakes. They actually decided to take on the British in a straightforward military operation and, predictably, failed." See Bernard B. Fall, *Last Reflections*

on a War: Bernard B. Fall's Last Comments on Vietnam (repr. Mechanicsburg, Pa.: Stackpole Books, 2000 [1967]).

6. Argentina and Cameroun.

7. Duration of "not rough covered" was 9.5 years average across the 33 cases compared to 10.6 years for the 29 cases of "rough covered". The percent Red wins for "not rough covered is 33% compared to 55% for "rough covered."

8. For example: James D. Fearon and David D. Laitin, "Ethnicity, Insurgency, and Civil War," *The American Political Science Review*, 97: 1 (Feb. 2003), 75–90.

9. There are few reports of insurgent use of airpower: A handful of incidents in South Vietnam during the Vietnam War, a couple of recent incidents in Sri Lanka, some from supporting South African troops in the Angola Civil War ,and of course, the U.S. supporting the Northern Alliance in Afghanistan, and that is about it.

10. For the 62 cases of insurgencies, there were 13 cases of rough uncovered terrain, 29 cases of rough uncovered terrain, two cases of level uncovered terrain and six cases of jungle and marshy terrain (level covered).

11. Clutterbuck, *op. cit.*, 164.

12. O'Neill, *op. cit.*, Chapter 4, 3.

13. Arthur Campbell, *Guerillas* (New York: The John Day Company, 1968), 283.

14. Fearon and Laitin, *op. cit.*, 76.

15. *Ibid*, 80.

16. *Ibid*.

17. *Ibid.*, 85.

18. For more details see *Examination of Factors Influencing the Conduct of Operations in Guerilla Wars: Task 12: Examining the Geographic Aspects of an Insurgency* (Annandale, VA.: The Dupuy Institute, 4 Feb. 2008).

19. See *Examination of Factors Influencing the Conduct of Operations in Guerilla Wars: Task 12: Examining the Geographic Aspects of an Insurgency* (Annandale, VA.: The Dupuy Institute, 4 Feb. 2008).

CHAPTER 14

Other Issues

Civic action is not the construction of privies or the distribution of anti-malaria sprays. One can't fight an ideology; one can't fight a militant doctrine with better privies. Yet this is done constantly. One side says, "Land reform," and the other side says, "Better culverts." One side says, "We are going to kill all of those nasty village chiefs and landlords." The other side says, "Yes, but look, we want to give you prize pigs to improve your strain." These arguments just do not match. Simple but adequate appeals will have to be found sooner or later.

—Bernard Fall, 1967[1]

A. DURATION OF INSURGENCIES BY TYPE OF INSURGENCY

In 2007, *The Dupuy Institute* did a little analysis of duration for an interview we did with *USA Today*. At the time, our database still had 83 cases. Of those, we categorized 62 as insurgencies, 10 as peacekeeping operations (those peacekeeping operations that had not turned into insurgencies), and 11 as "other." Of the 62 insurgencies, there were 12 that were insurgencies against colonial powers (INS/C), 24 that were insurgencies against intervening powers (INS/I) and 26 that were insurgencies with no significant outside intervening power (INS/NI). Of the 62 insurgencies, 7 started as conventional wars and then mutated into insurgencies (7 CONV/INS became 5 INS/I and 2 INS/NI) and 2 started as suppressions that mutated into insurgencies (2 SUP/INS became 1 INS/C and 1 INS/NI). The 11 "other" cases consisted of 1 suppression (SUP), 3 conventional operations (CONV), 4 guerilla invasions (GUERINV) and 3 that were coded as factional violence (VIOLENCE). We then calculated durations based upon the type of event:

Average Duration (all 83 cases):	8.6 years
Average Duration of Blue wins (42 cases):	9.9 years
Average Duration of Red Wins (30 cases):	7.2 years
Average Duration of Draws (7 cases):	6.9 years
Average Duration of ongoing cases (4 cases):	9.1 years *

Note six ongoing cases had been adjudicated as Blue wins (for example, Colombia).

To list their duration by type of event (as we coded them):

BY CATEGORY:	CASES:	AVERAGE DURATION:
CONV	3	0.5 years
CONV/INS	7	8.6 years
GUERINV	4	1.7 years
INS/C	11	8.5 years
INS/I	19	9.4 years
INS/NI	23	12.4 years
SUP	1	0.1 years
SUP/INS	2	3.4 years
PEACE	10	6.4 years
VIOLENCE	3	6.2 years
Total	83	8.6 years

These average duration figures include those cases where the conflict was resolved in around four years or less. As our original work established, the cases tended to fall into being either short insurgencies (four-and-a-half years or less) or insurgencies that lasted seven years or longer. There were no cases between 4½ and 7 years in our original data collection of 28 cases and almost none in the larger 83 case database. So we decided to look at average duration of only those cases that lasted longer than five years. As can be seen, the average duration of an insurgency looks to be something like 12 or more years.

BY CATEGORY:	AVERAGE CASES:	DURATION:
CONV	0	0
CONV/INS	4	12.9 years
GUERINV	0	0
INS/C	6	12.1 years
INS/I	15	11.2 years
INS/NI	17	15.8 years
SUP	0	0
SUP/INS	0	0
PEACE	2	13.6 years
VIOLENCE	2	8.1 years
Total	47	13.1 years

This is probably a better representation of the reality of a significant insurgency. The 10 year figure thrown out to the press was a nice round figure a little shy of what the average really should have been.

Finally we clustered the data together, which of course reinforces the 12-year figure for insurgencies.

CATEGORY	CASES	AVERAGE DURATION
Civil Wars	26	12.4 years
versus Intervening Forces	24	9.5 years
versus Foreign Forces (INS/C & INS/I)	36	9.0 years
All Insurgencies	62	10.4 years

Or to take out all the cases below five years in length:

CATEGORY	CASES	AVERAGE DURATION
Civil Wars	18	15.3 years
versus Intervening Forces	18	11.7 years
versus Foreign Forces (INS/C & INS/I)	24	11.8 years
All Insurgencies	42	13.3 years

This drives home the point clearly. If you are facing an insurgency with any form of real traction (meaning it can't be suppressed in four years), then you should prepare to gird your loins and plan on staying there for a least a dozen years.

These figures represent the data as of August 2007. There were ten ongoing cases in this dataset, so five years later, the data would be slightly different. The assumed end date for ongoing insurgencies was 31 December 2007 in these cases.

B. OUTCOME OF INSURGENCIES BY TYPE OF INSURGENCY

In general, it is worthwhile to look at the outcome of these 83 cases by type of operation. This is touched upon to some extent in Chapter Nine in the discussion of Rules of Engagement. But, just to display the data in a slightly different format:

TYPE	CASES	BLUE WIN	GRAY RESULT*	RED WIN
SUP	1	1		
CONV	3	3		
SUP/INS	2	2		
CONV/INS	7	2	2	3
INS/C	11	1		10
INS/I	19	12	1	6
INS/NI	23	12	3	8
GUERINV	4	1	2	1
PEACE	10	8	1	1

VIOLENCE	3		2	1
	—	—	—	—
Totals	83	42	11	30

*Ongoing or a draw

Or to put it into percents:

TYPE	BLUE WIN	RED WIN
SUP	100%	
CONV	100	
SUP/INS	100	
CONV/INS	29	43%
INS/C	9	91
INS/I	63	32
INS/NI	52	35
GUERINV	25	25
PEACE	80	10
VIOLENCE		33
Totals	51%	36%

If one adds the nine cases where suppression or a conventional invasion mutated into an insurgency (INS/C, INS/I or INS/NI), then you end up with the following statistics for insurgencies:[2]

TYPE	BLUE WIN	RED WIN
INS/C	17	83
INS/I	58	33
INS/NI	50	35
Totals	47	44

Now, these 83 cases are not the complete database of post-World War II cases, which may be well over 300 cases, if all peacekeeping and interventions are included. Mankind has certainly not deprived us of a shortage of cases of warfare to study. Nor is it a representative sample of the master sample of unknown size. It does represent most important and major cases, and many better known smaller cases. As such, it can be used make some basic observations. Just to state a few obvious ones:

1. Counterinsurgencies win 50 to 60 percent of the time (excluding INS/C). If one takes out the INS/C cases and all the ongoing cases (down to 47 cases), the figure is 57%, with the insurgents winning 36% of the time.
2. Insurgents win about one-third of the time (excluding INS/C).

3. Peacekeeping operations are usually successful. Now in four cases, there were peacekeeping operations coded as insurgencies (for example UK in Palestine (1944–1948), UN Peacekeeping in Angola (1988–1999), Peacekeeeping in Liberia (1990–1997), Peacekeeping in Sierra Leone (1997–2005). In these four cases the counterinsurgents won twice and the insurgents won twice. Still, this is a limited selection of the data of the more than 50 peacekeeping missions since World War II, but in general peacekeeping missions have a track record of being successful in the long run.

C. WINNING HEARTS AND MINDS?

The quote at the start of this chapter from Bernard Fall summarizes the problem succinctly: "One can't fight an ideology; one can't fight a militant doctrine with better privies." In one of our contracts, we were directed to review the writings of eight major theorists of counterinsurgency warfare (including Fall). What was surprising after review is that we still did not know what it took to win hearts and minds. None of the theorists really discussed it. We had tasks to look at those factors that increase or decrease insurgent recruitment, and had tasks to look at government reforms.[3] Yet, we could not find anything among the various counterinsurgent theorists that actually addressed how to decrease insurgent recruitment or what reforms to make that may reduce support for the insurgency. It simply is a subject that is only discussed in the most general sense.

We have some idea of what does not work. We are pretty certain that in the short term elections do not have any immediate impact. They may have a long-term impact, especially in countries that are facing insurgencies without significant outside foreign support (see Chapter Twelve). We are pretty certain that having looser rules of engagement works against the intervening power, unless they emulate the Genghis Khan approach. Beyond that, it is simply speculation.

As much as people talk about winning hearts and minds (a Vietnam-era phrase, which of course, was not entirely successful), there is no program, theory, agenda or list that tells the counterinsurgent what he must do to achieve this. So, lacking any other basis, are we reduced to building privies?

In the long run, there needs to be a focused analytical effort that looks at what efforts in other insurgencies have actually worked in the long run to gain support from the population, and what efforts in other insurgencies have not made that much of an impact. Considering the large amount of money being spent on these efforts, it is surprising that nothing systematic has been developed on this.

D. DECAPITATING INSURGENCIES

The U.S. military is very focused on decapitating, or killing the leadership, the lower levels of command, headquarters, and staff of an insurgency. This is fundamentally a carry over from the current U.S. conventional warfare doctrine (popularly known as "shock and awe") and the capabililty to do so have already been developed. It is a capability now being further expanded upon, in particular with the development of more armed drones.

This is both a new capability and an old strategy. It was tried by us in Vietnam with the Operation Phoenix program, which ended up targeting and executing 26,369 suspected Viet Cong leaders and disloyal Vietnamese from 1967 to 1972.[4] As far as guerilla leaders killed among the 83 cases we have examined, it is not common. Some of the more famous cases included Amilcar Cabral in Portuguese Guinea; General Dzhokhar Dudayev, Maskhadov, Basayev and other insurgent leaders in Chechnya; Abimael Guzman and other leaders of the Shining Path; and Abu Musab al-Zarqawi, the leader of "Al Qaeda in Iraq." The head of the Tamil insurgency and many of his immediate entourage were killed in 2009, in the period after we cease tracking the insurgency (which we code as a blue or counterinsurgent win).

Still, with only dozen or so examples of this, there is not much to go on as far as actually measuring the success of decapitation. In the four cases we examined, the insurgents still won in every case.[5] In the case of Iraq, the killing of Zarqawi did not result in any immediate short-term benefit.

The interesting aspect of this is that in our review of 16 practitioners and theorists (see chapters Seventeen and Eighteen), we don't recall any one of them focusing on this approach as major successful tactic. It certainly was done in other insurgencies. There is no doubt that there is clearly a disruptive effect from killing the leadership, or even forcing them to constantly take protective measures. That said, historically it has not been that successful, that significant, or that effective when it did succeed. In some cases, it has served to have a positive or inspirational effect on the insurgency.

First, we need to consider it relative to the structure of an insurgency. If the insurgency consists of multiple factions with no or limited central command (what we label a disorderly insurgency), as is the case in 61% of our examples, then decapitating any part of the insurgency will have, at best, a local or tactical effect, not strategic. For those insurgencies that have a central leadership but the units are very much local raise and led, then decapitating the leadership of the insurgency will probably have limited influence on the field. Those highly structured insurgencies (what we label orderly) do actually have a more traditional command structure that can be gutted. This has value, but unless much of it is gotten at one time, being a structured insurgency, the leadership will be replaced by the lower levels after a brief moment of disruption. If the leadership is highly charismatic, like for example, Amilcar Cabral, then removing that charismatic leader may have some effect, although it did not in this particular case. Amilcar Cabral was still considered the inspirational leader of the insurgency in Guinea, even though he was dead when they won.

Finally, there seems to be an assumption that killing the leadership is removing the insurgency of capable people. This may be the case if a large number of leaders are killed (for example, as occurred with the Viet Cong as a result of the Tet Offensive, even though this was nominally self-inflicted). On the other hand, there is no basis to assume that removing any single leader will result worse or weaker leadership. It is probably fifty-fifty that the person taking over will be better or worse than the person he replaced.

A systematic attrition of leadership may indeed result in the insurgency command becoming weaker. From the start of the Malayan Insurgency, Chin Peng did not provide central command to the individual cells, in part due to a lack of means to do so and in part due to British pressure. As such, an insurgency that was nominally "orderly" was in fact centrally directed but locally raised and run. Heavy pressure on the leadership of any insurgency will certainly force it to take a less centralized command role. This is probably a good thing, but as shown in Chapter Eight, it is clearly not the end of an insurgency.

Also the importance of decapitation may change during the course of an insurgency. If the counterinsurgents are trying to resolve the insurgency by negotiation (which is a common way to end an insurgency), then decapitating the leadership at that point and time may well work against that.

Now this is not to say we should not go after insurgent leadership when we have the chance. We obviously should. But, it is to stress that you should be careful about giving "decapitation" too much importance as a strategic answer to your counterinsurgent problems.

Still, if you have the means to try decapitation, it is important to do so in such a way that you do not kill civilians or give them propaganda tools that they can use. In the end, if you are losing the propaganda war while you are trying to decapitate, then you are working against yourself.

E. EARLY SUPPRESSION OF INSURGENCIES

In two of our cases, the insurgency began with the wholesale arrest of a large number of the insurgency leadership. This is effectively decapitating an insurgency before it begins. This was done by the British in both Malaya and Kenya and both were tactically very successful operations.

In Malaya, with the help of their paid informant, who was head of the communist party, the British were able to arrest most of the senior leadership. This left the communist party under command of the 23-year old Chin Peng. As the party did have an existing military command structure with soldiers and local commanders already in the field, it was able to begin operations even though the party had been decapitated. It would eventually lose after a 12-year fight.

In the case of the Mau Mau revolt, the Mau Mau had only just begun setting up training camps and training people when the British arrested the leaders of the independence movement. This left a leaderless movement gathering in the jungles to try to organize itself. It was not very effective and within four years had collapsed. Still, even with their suppression, in the long-term the UK was not able to hold onto Kenya, and many of the people they arrested took over the reigns of government in 1963.

In both of these cases the British actually initiated the insurgency by their suppression before the insurgency properly developed. This is probably the most effective "decapitation" of insurgencies we have seen. They were both very effective in that they gutted the command on the insurgencies. The Mau Mau revolt never really got going, and the Malayan insurgency never had an effective central command.

These are both case studies worth exploring, especially as the surviving insurgent commanders have left accounts (Chin Peng and General China). These accounts give a very different view of the insurgency than the traditional British histories.

F. WOUNDED TO KILLED RATIOS

One unique feature of Iraq (and Afghanistan) is that the wounded-to-killed ratios are much lower than previous wars. This ratio consists of the total number of wounded as compared to the total killed. For example, in the U.S. Civil War the wounded-to-killed ratio was 4.55-to-1. For World War I, it was 5.96-to-1, or 4.20-to-1 without gas casualties included. For World War II, it was 3.57-to-1, or 4.25-to-1 if U.S. Army Air Forces losses are not included (air losses tended to have a much higher percentage of fatalities among the total casualties). For the Korean War, it was 4.02-to-1. Roughly, for conventional wars, a figure of four wounded soldiers for every soldier killed may be expected.

We have the data for two U.S. counterinsurgent efforts. In the Philippine insurgency (1899 to 1905), it was 3.81-to-1. This is in contrast to the figures for the Spanish-American War (1898) of 5.88-to-1. And then there is Vietnam, which is 4.45-to-1. All this data is drawn from past studies done by Trevor Dupuy.[6]

In the case of Iraq, as of 31 December 2009, we have 3,380 U.S. servicemen killed in combat and 31,616 U.S. servicemen wounded.[7] This produces a wounded-to-killed ratio of 9.35-to-1. This is very different that what has gone before. Of course, the U.S. medical community certainly played a part of this difference over time, but while they have been doing a good job, this is far from the whole story.

First, the way we report wounded has changed. The U.S. Army has always defined wounded as those who spent the night in a hospital. If you were wounded, received treatment, but did not stay in the hospital than you were not counted as wounded, or counted as wounded but "carded for the record" only. You could still receive a purple heart, even though you were not officially counted among the wounded. The U.S. Army in World War II had 123,836 wounded "carded for the record only."

The U.S. Marine Corps, at least in Vietnam, actually counted a higher percent of all their wounded as wounded. Therefore, they effectively counted 30% more wounded than the Army would, given the same number of killed or hospitalized casualties. For example, in Vietnam the army counted 30,915 battle deaths versus 96,802 wounded. This is a 3.13-to-1 wounded-to-killed ratio. The Marines counted 13,082 battle deaths killed versus 51,392 wounded. This is a 3.93-to-1 wounded-to-killed ratio. The primary cause of this difference is counting methodology, vice better medical care, use of armor, quicker evacuation, better first aid, tougher Marines, etc. We have actually studied this issue![8]

In the case of Iraq, both forces (U.S. Army and U.S. Marines, seeing how the U.S. has two distinct, separate and parallel armies), are now counting all wounded as wounded, regardless of how much of a draw they make on medical resources. If I include all "carded for the record only," "wounded in action, not evacuated (WIANE)," etc., from Vietnam into the wounded-to killed ratio, then we get a figure for the U.S. Army and Marine Corps of 6.71-to-1 for Vietnam.[9] This is much closer to our Iraq wounded-to-killed ratio of 9.34-to-1. Still, this is an improvement.

But there are some other factors that are driving this figure. First, is the mix of munitions we are facing. Direct fire weapons (like rifles and machineguns) have a much higher fatality rate per hit than indirect fire weapons (like mortars) or various demolitions (like mines, booby traps, claymore mines, or IEDs—improvised explosive devices). As such, if the majority of your casualties are being caused by IEDs, then your wounded-to-killed ratio will be higher (more wounded per person killed). For example, lethality of small arms in Vietnam is given as 0.39, which would produce a 2.56-to-1 wounded-to-kill ratio, while lethality of grenades, mortars and mines are, respectively, 0.13, 0.12 and 0.11 or a wounded-to-kill ratio between 7.69-to-1 to 9.09-to-1.[10] So, wounded to killed ratios are heavily influenced by the mix of weapons types that are causing the casualties. Vietnam was a very different war than Iraq, with an estimated 204 "maneuver battalions" deployed by the communists in Vietnam as of 19 June 1968.[11] It was extremely rare for the U.S. to encounter an opposing force "maneuver battalion" in Iraq.

The second reason is that U.S. soldiers are now wearing considerable body armor, armored vest, helmets, etc. As such, explosives that in the past would have been fatal, are indeed ameliorated, and therefore, more soldiers are saved (wounded vice killed).

After these two effects are accounted for, then what is left is the improvement caused by better medical care. While this is not inconsiderable and always desirable, its impact is much less than appears based upon a casual observance of the issue.

But, there is one other big impact of the changing wounded-to-killed ratios. All of our analysis was based upon historical data. Most of our analysis was based on the number killed, as that was what was regularly reported and had a clear definition. As already seen, the definition of who is wounded is different for different parts of the U.S. Armed Forces, at least through Vietnam. There is also wide variability between other countries.

Therefore if, because of armor, weapon mix and better medical care, the wounded-to-killed ratio has changed, then this affects our estimates. In the case of the Iraq estimate, we actually mathematically calculated the range of U.S. deaths based upon our data to be from 6,000 to 12,000. We then lowered our estimate to 5,000 to 10,000, in part to address the changing dynamics. Because of use of body armor, the weapons mixes we were facing and the better medical care, this estimate should have probably been lower.

G. EXCHANGE RATES

One of the most seductive things about being a counterinsurgent is that you over-match your opponent militarily. The counterinsurgents are usually professional, trained military forces with all the advantages of modern technology. The insurgents are often not very professional. For example, the leader of the Malayan Insurgency was a 23-year-old kid.[12] Many of the insurgents have limited formal military training and often only as enlisted.[13] Many of them are ad-hoc organizations. Most of the in-surgents are not doing this full time. They are doing whatever their regular business or job is, and the insurgency is a part-time occupation, unlike the full-time profes-sional soldiers that they are facing.

Therefore, it should not come as a surprise that in virtually every insurgency we examined the counterinsurgents killed at least three insurgents per counterinsurgent killed. In some cases, the exchange ratios are reported as high as 20 to 1. While some of this may be biased due to our extensive use of counterinsurgent sources for our re-search (as most insurgencies keep limited records and access to them has been diffi-cult), it still is clear that the counterinsurgents almost invariably have the impression that they are causing many more casualties than they are receiving, and that they have the edge militarily.

This is in almost every case. This military superiority is seductive. It gives the counterinsurgents the sense that they are always winning, even if indeed they really do not have control of the situation. Still it is difficult, but not impossible, to bleed an insurgency to death. Attrition does work against the insurgents and makes it harder for them to achieve their goals. It does contribute to their defeat. Still, the norm is that the counterinsurgents will always kill many more insurgents than they loose, and that pattern is true for almost all insurgencies, whether the insurgents won or lost in the end. The only notable exception we have found to this rule is Northern Ireland, where the British lost more troops than they killed IRA. Not only that, the IRA killed more IRA than the British Army did![14] That was an insurgency the counterinsurgents won.

H. BLEEDING AN INSURGENCY TO DEATH

Bleeding an insurgency to death is possible, but rare. Let's just look at a graph from the Greek Civil War:

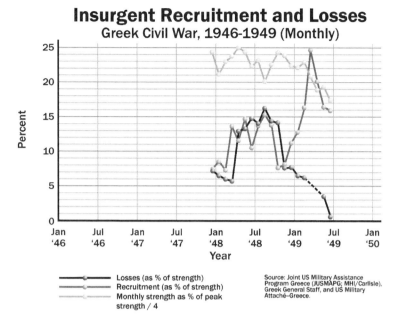

Insurgent Recruitment and Losses
Greek Civil War, 1946-1949 (Monthly)

Legend:
— Losses (as % of strength)
— Recruitment (as % of strength)
— Monthly strength as % of peak strength / 4

Source: Joint US Military Assistance Program Greece (JUSMAPG; MHI/Carlisle), Greek General Staff, and US Military Attaché–Greece.

This dramatic graph was created from a number of sources, all combined onto the same chart. The scale for monthly strength was divided by four fit them all together (meaning a figure of 25% for Monthly strength is actually 100% of strength). At the time, when I put the graph together, I intended it to illustrate the process where one could bleed an insurgency to death, by interrelating loss rates, exchange rates, recruitment, force strength, etc. When I presented this in a meeting in December 2004, I was then asked to look at tipping points.

It is difficult to bleed an insurgency to death. The problem is that only a small portion of the insurgents you are facing are active, full-time insurgents. So, mostly you are attriting the spearpoint. The part-time and casual insurgents tend to be active when they have a reason to, and tend to become inactive (and otherwise invisible) when the environment becomes too hot. As such, "search-and-destroy" missions and other such efforts tend to focus on the active people.

The problem is, as long as the rate of casualties among them is moderate, they can recruit and pull in new people. There is a base of support for insurgencies, and that base is a source of recruits. Unless one has shut down the recruiting source, then they can quickly replace the losses.

For example, let us say you have 10,000 insurgents, of which 2,000 are "full-time." They are operating in a country with a population of one million. So we have the insurgency making up 1% of the population of the country. That is not out of line with historical cases. Let us say that 30% of the population favors the insurgency or are in areas under control of the insurgency.

Now, out of a population base of 300,000 civilians, one would expect to see about 3,000 new insurgents to come of age each year.[15] This means that the insurgents potentially have a new population of 3,000 coming-of-age boys each year to draw upon. Therefore, the counterinsurgents must grind through probably around 2,000 or more insurgents a year to actually be able to reduce insurgent strength from year to year. Otherwise, they get replaced as fast as they are being lost.

Expand this example to a country with 30,000 insurgents and 24 million population, like is potentially the case for Afghanistan and Iraq, and it is clear that bleeding the insurgency to death becomes almost an impossible proposition, no matter how long you stay.

Still, it was done in the case of the Greek Civil War. This was caused in part by a decision by the insurgents to increase the tempo of operations and go almost conventional. The result is that the insurgents conveniently choose to help the counterinsurgents bleed the insurgency to death. As can be seen, this quickly broke the back of the insurgency, and this occurred before Yugoslavia cut off support and bases for the insurgents. Basically, the insurgency was losing by fighting a traditional insurgency, so they changed their approach to increase the tempo of operations, and this simply sped up their eventual and inevitable defeat.

To some extent, the same thing happened in Vietnam with the Tet Offensive. Military, the offensive gutted the Viet Cong, and left them permanently weakened and less effective for the rest of the war. If the only force the U.S. was facing in Vietnam was the VC (Viet Cong), then this would have potentially led to a U.S. victory. The presence of a continued flow of forces from North Vietnam, including fully-armed combat regiments, compensated for the heavy losses the VC suffered.

Beyond those two cases, we do not have examples of insurgencies being bleed to death. The mathematics does not favor such an approach, although people invariably try it. One could describe General Westmoreland's strategy in as Vietnam heavily oriented towards an attrition approach.

I. FOCUS ON POPULATION

The focus on population is both a theoretical construct and a set of buzzwords. In a briefing I was giving in 2008 at an intelligence agency a couple of their analysts seemed to say that the focus needed to be on the population every time I mentioned force ratios.

First, they are not the same thing. Focus on population or on the people is a strategy or approach used to combat the insurgency. We never tested this or many other strategies in our original effort. Partly, this was because we had not gotten around to it; partly because we were not sure how to measure all these strategies; partly because I avoided going into depth about a lot of strategies on the first phase of our analysis;

and partly because I noticed that most counterinsurgent forces try most approaches to a lesser or greater extent during of a long insurgency.

It does need to be explored further, both as to effectiveness and how it affects duration. In this case, I am not sure what the contrary case would be (a strategy that ignores the population, either refusing to protect them or refusing to try to win them over?). I can't think of any extended insurgency where the counterinsurgents choose not to try to protect, control or influence the local population. I was therefore concerned that if we tried to test it, we would have almost no cases of something else to test it to. Focusing on the population is sort of a mom and apple pie statement. It is hard to argue against.

That said, to be able to focus on the population, you need troops! You need troops to protect them, you need troops to protect your building projects (like privies), you need troops to flush out the insurgents from the population, you need troops to work with the population and bring them around to your side, etc. To focus on the population, you need troops. I suspect that if there are any cases in our database where the counterinsurgents did not focus on the population, it was because there were not enough troops.

So, I suspect we are back to discussing force ratios. Still, some form of detailed study on the effects of different "focus on population" approaches would be very useful.

NOTES

1. Fall, *op. cit.*, 222.

2. One SUP/INS became an INS/C and one became an INS/NI. Both were Blue wins. Of the 7 CONV/INS, 5 became INS/I (2 Blue wins, 1 ongoing and 2 Red wins), and 2 become INS/NI (one ongoing and one Red win). The two cases of Conventional invasions becoming INS/NI are the First and Second Chechen wars.

3. For example, see *Examination of Factors Influencing the Conduct of Operations in Guerilla Wars, Task 4: Factors That Increase and Decrease Insurgent Recruitment & Task 7: Examination of Government Reforms* (Annandale, VA.: The Dupuy Institute, 24 Oct. 2007).

4. Micheal Clodfelter, *Vietnam in Military Statistics: A History of Indochina Wars, 1772–1991* (Jefferson, N.C.: McFarland & Company, Inc. 1995), 236. Of the people killed, Clodfelter states, "many . . . were probably only marginally involved in the insurrectionary movement (less that half were Communist Party members)." Another 33,358 VC suspects were captured, and 22,013 surrendered.

5. These were Farhat Achad (1952) with the Tunisian Independence insurgency, Eduardo Mondlane (1969) with the Mozambique insurgency, Amilcar Cabral (1973) in Portuguese Guinea insurgency and Herbert Chitepo (1975) in the Rhodesian Insurgency. In our test data base on this subject, we rated three of these cases as having a "positive" or inspirational effect on the rebellion.

   There were two leaders killed after we record the insurgency as over. These were Felix

Moumie (1960) with the Cameroun insurgency and Jonas Savimbi with Angola's Third War. Only the last one was a "Blue win."

There were a number of cases we have not examined yet, including Sylvanus Olympio (Togo Coup 1963), Mehdi Ben Armka (Morocco—abducted in 1965 in Paris and killed in 1966), Mohammed Murtala (Nigerian Coup 1976), Dulcie September (South Africa 1988—killed in Paris), Guzman (Peru—captured 1992) and the Shining Path in Peru, Dudayev (Chechnya 1996), Maskhadov (Chechnya 2005), Basayev (Chechnya 2006), Zarqawi (Iraq 2006) and Veluillai Prabhakaran (Sri Lanka 2009). These include one counterinsurgent win, one insurgent win and two ongoing cases among the 83 cases we have examined.

It would be worthwhile doing a complete examination of this subject and clearly in some cases, decapitation has an effect.

6. Trevor N. Dupuy, *Attrition: Forecasting Battle Casualties and Equipment Losses in Modern War* (Fairfax, VA.: HERO Books, 1990), page 49.

7. The wounded figure is from the Iraq Coalition Casualty Count (www.icasualty.org).

8. Ronald F. Bellamy, MD, and Christopher A. Lawrence, Combat Mortality: Why is Marine *Combat Mortality Less Than That of the Army* (Gray and Associates, 1998).

9. The statistics from Vol. II, Fig. 9 of the *Combat Mortality* study are Army: 25,342 killed, 3,520 died of wounds, 96,811 nonfatal wounds, hospital care required, 104,725 nonfatal wounds, hospital care not required, 1,781 died while missing. This comes out to a wounded-to-killed ratio of 6.58 to 1. For the Marines it is 11,097 killed, 1,454 died of wounds, 51,399 nonfatal wounds, hospital care required, 37,234 nonfatal wounds, hospital care not required, 55 died while missing. This gives a wounded-to-killed ratio of 7.03 to 1. Data is derived from Table 1051, DoD, OASD [Comptroller] Directorate for Information, Operations and Control (15 Jan. 1976).

10. From Fig. 18 of the *Combat Mortality* study. This data is drawn from Wound Data Munitions Effectiveness Team (WDMET) Data Base. Also see Figs. 52–56, 60–63, 68, 73–74, 78, 81–86, 89–91A, 93, 94, 97-98, and 112–114.

11. *Combat Mortality*, Fig. 40.

12. See Chin Peng, *My Side of History: As Told to Ian Ward and Norm Miraflor* (Singapore: Media Masters, 2003), 29–30.

13. For example, the leader of the Mau Mau revolt, General China, was formerly a sergeant in the British Army. See Waruhiu Itote (General China), *"Mau Mau" General* (Nairobi, Kenya: East African Publishing House, 1967). The appendices are particularly interesting.

14. See Chapter Eleven for the details of this.

15. 300,000 divided by an average 50-year life span, divided by two to account for only males.

CHAPTER 15

The Burden of War

We were succeeding. When you looked at specifics, this became a war of attrition. We were winning.

—General William Westmoreland, Commander of the
    Military Assistance Command, Vietnam 1964–1968[1]

We had already noted a relationship between population size, total burden and average commitment, although it was nothing that was statistically significant.[2] So we wanted to find some way to test the cost of these insurgencies on the forces deployed and the nations that deployed them. This led us down the path of trying to measure the burden of these wars. In this case, we were contracted to do a study on measuring popular support for these wars. The customer envisioned that it would be based upon polling data. We did collect that data and examined it, but found no meaningful consistency in the polling data across different countries in different wars. So after writing up those findings, we proceeded to establish some mathematical definitions of burden and tested them.[3]

The Dupuy Institute ended up measuring the burden of war in two ways: commitment and intensity. Commitment measures personnel committed per 100,000 population in a given insurgency. Intensity measures killed per 100,000 population. Both commitment and intensity track the cost or burden of an insurgency or counterinsurgency effort. Trying to track the actual monetary cost of a counterinsurgency effort would also be worthwhile, but would be a major research effort. Certainly commitment is a good ersatz measurement for this.

We then ended up testing commitment to the data set. This were four different elements of commitment: intervening force, government force, insurgent force, and total commitment. This was tested against the four different data sets, all 83 cases, the 62 insurgencies, the 36 cases of insurgencies with outside intervening forces and the 26 cases of primarily domestic counterinsurgencies. We did the same for intensity, comparing intervening forces killed, government forces killed, insurgent forces killed and civilians killed against all four data sets.

What this produced was a fairly consistent trend across all the data that was sometimes statistically significant, but in many cases was not. Still, the trend across the data was very clear. Therefore, it is important to go through it step-by-step. We will detail out our first test, but then will try to summarize the results for each subsequent step except where necessary for further elucidation.

A. COMMITMENT
1. INTERVENING FORCE COMMITMENT

We started this effort by looking at intervening force commitment. Intervening force commitment is defined as the number of intervening forces committed (deployed abroad against an insurgency) per 100,000 home population. So for example, a value of 21 means 21 troops committed per 100,000 home population. Committing 1% of your population to the war would be a value of 1,000. We had intervening force commitment data for 58 of 83 total cases, 41 of 62 insurgencies and all 36 of insurgencies against foreigners. Intervening force commitment data for all cases (58 cases) falls into three groups:

- Low Intervening Force Commitment (0-21) results in 28% Red Wins 32 cases)
- Medium Intervening Force Commitment (29-81) results in 36% Red Wins (11 cases)
- High Intervening Force Commitment (141-791) results in 67% Red Wins (15 cases)

Or, to put it another way:

- Low Intervening Force Commitment (0-21) results in 69% Blue Wins (32 cases)
- Medium Intervening Force Commitment (29-81) results in 55% Blue Wins (11 cases)
- High Intervening Force Commitment (141-791) results in 27% Blue Wins (15 cases)

It appears that when the average level of commitment exceeds more than 0.1% of the population of the intervening country (more than 141 per 100,000 home population in our data set), then the counterinsurgency, intervention or peacekeeping operation fails in two-thirds of the cases. This gave us our first finding and it was statistically significant.[4]

When we limited our examination to the cases that we code as insurgencies against foreign interventions (36 cases), we see:

- Low Intervening Force Commitment (0-21) results in 40% Red Wins (15 cases)

- Medium Intervening Force Commitment (34-77) results in 38% Red Wins (8 cases)
- High Intervening Force Commitment (141-791) results in 69% Red Wins (13 cases)

Or, to put it another way:

- Low Intervening Force Commitment (0-21) results in 53% Blue Wins (15 cases)
- Medium Intervening Force Commitment (34-77) results in 50% Blue Wins (8 cases)
- High Intervening Force Commitment (141-791) results in 31% Blue Wins (13 cases)

It appears that when the average level of commitment by an outside power exceeds more the 0.1% of the population of the intervening country (more than 141 per 100,000 home population in our data set), the insurgency wins in two-thirds of the cases.

The two-sided p-value from Fisher's exact test was 0.3944, indicating that there is a high probability (around 40%) that this relationship is because of chance. However, we have reasons for not believing this is the case due to the tendencies seen in all tests we have developed. For example, the first test we did using all the data produced a p-value of close to 5%. The number of cases in the category above 141 per 100,000 in this data set was only two less than in the previous data set. Part of the reason the previous test had a good p-value was that it was built from 58 cases instead of only 36 cases.

There are four cases of Blue wins in the high intervening force commitment cases. Three of the four cases are relatively unique cases. In two cases they were dictatorships involved directly in an action right next door, so it was something that was in the immediate national interest. In one case it is coded as a Blue win because the government won the war, although the outside intervening forces, which were withdrawing Cuban forces and UN peacekeepers, were not really a factor. The fourth case was the Cuban intervention in the Angola Civil War. This clearly stands out as an exception among the insurgent cases where commitment exceeded 0.1% of the population. Still, in this particular case, Cuba was being heavily subsidized by the Soviet Union (including economic support back in Cuba) to maintain this mission. It is an unusual case. In the nine other cases, which fundamentally represent a dictatorship or a democracy intervening in a foreign land (including the French in Algeria, the USSR in Afghanistan or Vietnam in Cambodia), the insurgency always won.

Another major issue affecting intervening force commitment for all cases is the numerous peacekeeping operations for which the commitment is not practically measurable, for example, those cases with small contingents from large countries (a few thousand soldiers from India or Pakistan). Eleven out of 32 total cases from our Low Intervening Force Commitment category (0-21) are peacekeeping operations. This does not heavily affect the insurgencies though, with only three peacekeeping missions coded by us as insurgencies. Peacekeeping in Liberia and Peacekeeping in Sierra Leone both had commitment below 1 per 100,000 population; only UN Peacekeeping in Angola, discussed in the above paragraph, had significant commitment, 291 per 100,000 population.

2. GOVERNMENT FORCE COMMITMENT

We did a similar test for government forces, except this time we were able to do it across all four data sets. Government force commitment measures the number of government forces committed to an insurgency per 100,000 population. We examined government intervening forces for all cases for which we have data (70), all insurgencies (56 cases), insurgencies with intervening forces (32 cases) and insurgencies without intervening forces (24 cases). As with intervening force commitment, we divided Government force commitment data into three categories, with the Government force commitment data showing (70 cases):

- Low Government Force Commitment (20-499) results in 33% Red Wins (45 cases)
- Medium Government Force Commitment (500-999) results in 23% Red Wins (13 cases)
- High Government Commitment (1,000-7,224) results in 50% Red Wins (12 cases)

Or, to put it another way:

- Low Government Force Commitment (20-499) results in 51% Blue Wins (45 cases)
- Medium Government Force Commitment (500-999) results in 77% Blue Wins (13 cases)
- High Government Commitment (1,000-7,224) results in 33% Blue Wins (12 cases)

It appears that when the average level of commitment by the indigenous government exceeds more than 1% of the population of the indigenous country, then the counterinsurgency, intervention or peacekeeping operation fails in about half the cases. The two-sided p-value from Fisher's exact test was 0.2245, which is not as good a statistic as we would prefer. Also, no particular pattern appears here except at the high end of the data. This is a similar pattern to what we saw with intervening forces, although the values are much higher. Whether this is random or indicative is hard to determine, but in light of the previous patterns, one is left to suspect that there is a pattern here also.

Our test with insurgencies only (56 cases) produced a similar comparison but again without significant statistics.[5] Still it appears that when the average level of commitment by the indigenous government exceeds more than 1% of the population of the indigenous country, then the insurgency succeeds in almost two-thirds of the cases.

A look at the cases involving insurgencies against intervening forces (32 cases) produced a similar pattern and was almost statistically significant:[6]

- Low Government Force Commitment (20-499) results in 44% Red Wins (18 cases)
- Medium Government Force Commitment (500-999) results in 33% Red Wins (9 cases)
- High Government Commitment (1,067-7,224) results in 100% Red Wins (5 cases)

Or, to put it another way:

- Low Government Force Commitment (20-499) results in 44% Blue Wins (18 cases)
- Medium Government Force Commitment (500-999) results in 67% Blue Wins (9 cases)
- High Government Commitment (1,067–7,224) results in 0% Blue Wins (5 cases)

It appears that when the average level of commitment by an indigenous government supported by an outside government exceeds more the 1% of the population of the indigenous country, then the insurgency succeeded in all five cases that fit this description.

Those 24 cases of insurgencies that do not involve significant outside intervening forces did not display any particular pattern and were not statistically significant.[7] Still, one is tempted to accept that there is such a pattern here due to the patterns seen in our other related tests.

The most interesting aspect when looking at these last two data sets is that we have 5 cases where the government forces committed more than 1% of it population as armed forces against the insurgency and it lost in every case where they were supported by outside intervening forces. Yet, we have 5 cases of commitment above 1% where there are no outside intervening forces, and the insurgency only won once.

These last two comparisons argue that if an insurgency becomes large enough that 1% or more of the population is committed to fighting it, then it can either be controlled or resolved by domestic forces, or it cannot be defeated, regardless of the number of outside forces. Still, this is only based on ten cases.

In general, indigenous governments seem capable of supporting a higher burden than intervening countries. This pattern held true for all types of operation as well as just insurgencies.

3. INSURGENT FORCE COMMITMENT

Next, we measured insurgent force commitment. Insurgent force commitment represents the number of insurgents involved in an insurgency per 100,000 home population. We have insurgent force commitment data for 76 of 83 cases, 57 of 62 insurgencies, all 36 insurgencies with an intervening force and 21 of 26 insurgencies without an outside intervening force. High levels of force commitment might indicate a high level of popular support, or willingness to bear the costs of the insurgency.

All the datasets exhibited the same pattern, which is that insurgencies won 28% to 60% of the time with low and medium levels of commitment, and won 67% to 75% of the time with higher levels of commitment. But, none of these were statistically significant.

Still, it appears that when the average level of commitment by the insurgents exceeds more than 1% of the population of the indigenous country, then the counterinsurgency, intervention or peacekeeping operation fails in two-thirds of the cases.[8]

This is similar to what we saw with Government forces per 100,000 population in that there is no particular pattern except at one end of the data. This is not surprising as it would be expected that these two data sets would display similar patterns.

Our case with the highest level of commitment, the Polisario rebellion, has an exceptionally high insurgent force commitment (8,196 per 100,000 population). This is because of the nature of the data. Polisario force strength may be grossly overestimated. Many of these "insurgents" were in camps outside of the area of the insurgency and not otherwise actively engaged. Additionally, the Sahrawi population from which the insurgent force was drawing, had largely moved outside the territory of Western Sahara, and was based in these refugee camps in neighboring Algeria. The next highest case of insurgent force commitment is the Vietnam War (with 1,671 per 100,000 population).

Our look at just the insurgencies produced similar results based on 57 cases. Again, it was not statistically significant but clearly was a good fit.[9] It appears that when the average level of commitment by the insurgents exceeds more than 0.5% of the population of the indigenous country, then the insurgency succeeds in more than two-thirds of the cases.

A further division into insurgencies with intervening forces and insurgencies without intervening forces produced similar results and again, poor statistics. In the case of outside intervening forces (36 cases), it appears that when the average level of commitment by the insurgents facing an indigenous government supported by an outside government exceeds more than 1% of the population of the indigenous country, then the insurgency succeeds in more than two-thirds of the cases.[10]

Still, because of the sum total of data, we have a bias towards accepting this conclusion as the same pattern is occurring in outside intervening forces and government forces also. Furthermore, we note that no insurgencies that are not facing an outside intervening force ever exceed 1% (highest was 755 out of 100,000) of the population in the insurgencies without significant outside intervention, compared to 9 cases in those insurgencies against foreigners.

Looking at those insurgencies that do not involve significant outside intervening forces (21 cases) produced results that forced us to reconsider our categorization.[11] The level of commitment here is much lower than those that faced outside intervening forces. The average commitment of the 36 INS/Cs and INS/Is is 664 insurgents per 100,000 population, while the average commitment for the 21 INS/NIs that we have commitment data for is 94 insurgents per 100,000 population. Therefore, insurgencies that are not facing outside intervening forces are much smaller relative to their population than those facing outside intervening forces.

The very low levels of insurgent commitment seem to demonstrate a pattern. Below an average of 40 insurgents per 100,000 population there is a shortage of insurgent wins. This was the case with the entire dataset where very low insurgent force commitment (0.26-36) resulted in only 15% Red wins and 70% Blue wins in 20 cases, while the low insurgent force commitment (41-499) resulted in 38% Red wins and 51% Blue wins in 37 cases. It appears that when the average level of commitment by the insurgents is less than 0.04% (less than 40 per 100,000 population) of the population of the indigenous country, then the counterinsurgency, intervention or peacekeeping operation succeeds in more than two-thirds of the cases. The two-sided p-value from Fisher's exact test was 0.2247, which is not very strong but it still fits into the pattern that we are seeing across the other data.

Narrowing down the data and looking only at insurgencies (57 cases) we see the same pattern where the very low insurgent force commitment (0.26-36) results in 19% Red wins and 75% Blue wins in 16 cases while the low insurgent force commitment (41-499) results in 40% Red wins and 48% Blue wins in 27 cases. It appears that when the average level of commitment by the insurgents is less than 0.04% (less than 40 per 100,000 population) of the population of the indigenous country, then the insurgency fails in more than two-thirds of the cases. The two-sided p-value from Fisher's exact test was 0.2250, which is also weak, but still indicates that there is a basis for assuming a trend.

A further division into insurgencies with intervening forces and insurgencies without intervening forces was not useful. There were only two really small insurgencies against intervening foreign countries in our database, and too few to draw any real conclusions. In both cases the counterinsurgents won. This does not really tell us much except to emphasize that there are few really small insurgencies against foreign powers (at least in our database).

In those cases of insurgencies that do not involve significant outside intervening forces (21 cases), there was a difference at the lower levels, with very low insurgent force commitment (0.25-36) resulting in 14% Red wins or 71% Blue wins in 14 cases, while low insurgent force commitment (41-499) resulted in 33% Red wins or 50% Blue wins in 6 cases. There was only one case above 500 insurgents per 100,000 population in the insurgencies without significant outside intervention, compared to 14 cases in those insurgencies against foreigners.

The above data shows that most insurgencies that do not involve a foreign country tend to remain small, and once they achieve a certain size, they tend to win as often as not. It raises the question of whether the fundamental difference between the percent win of the 36 INS/C and INS/I (50% insurgent wins) compared to the 26 INS/NI (35% insurgent wins) is entirely due to differences in the relative size of the insurgent forces.

4. TOTAL COMMITMENT

Total commitment is an aggregate of government forces commitment and insurgent force commitment and represents the total commitment of the country (forces per 100,000 population) in which the insurgency is located (as such, intervening force commitment is not included). As with government commitment and insurgent commitment, there are no clear breaks in this dataset. We again divided the data into three groupings (76 cases), but it was hard to discern any clear pattern from this data.[12]

The 14 high commitment cases show roughly an even split between blue and red wins. At the upper end of that split the outcomes become very red. Basically, at above 2% commitment nationally (government and insurgencies), the insurgents win in 6 out of 8 cases.[13]

Looking at the insurgencies only showed some pattern in that when the average level of commitment by the government and insurgents exceeds more than 0.5% of the population of the indigenous country, then the insurgency succeeds in about half of the cases.[14]

Looking at Insurgencies involving outside intervening forces (36 cases) show almost 2/3rd Red wins at levels of commitment above 0.5% of the nation's population, and less than 30% wins below that point. The statistical tests were not particularly strong.[15]

Looking at insurgencies that did not involved outside intervening forces showed no pattern.[16]

B. INTENSITY

With intensity, we did the exact same measurements, except based upon the number killed per 100,000 home population. The analysis them proceed exactly as we did with commitment. But it was our first test, intervening forces killed, that presented us with our most significant results.

1. INTERVENING FORCES KILLED

Intervening force intensity measures the costs in killed that an intervening country is willing to support. The average intervening forces killed (intervening forces killed per 100,000 home population) falls into three groups (49 cases):

- Low Intervening Intensity cases (0) result in 11% Red Wins (18 cases)
- Medium Intervening Intensity cases (0.01-0.09) result in 47% Red Wins (17 cases)
- High Intervening Intensity cases (0.12-4.08) result in 71% Red Wins (14 cases)

Or, to put it another way:

- Low Intervening Intensity cases (0) result in 89% Blue Wins (18 cases)
- Medium Intervening Intensity cases (0.01-0.09) result in 41% Blue Wins (17 cases)
- High Intervening Intensity cases (0.12-4.08) result in 21% Blue Wins (14 cases)

It appears that when the average intervening forces killed exceeds more than 0.00001% of the population of the intervening country (more than 0.12 per 100,000 home population), then the counterinsurgency, intervention or peacekeeping operation fails in over two-thirds of the cases.

Furthermore, it appears that if the average intervening forces killed exceeds more than 0.00001% of the population of the intervening country (more than 0.01 per 100,000 home population) that the chances of failure rises to around 50%. The two-sided p-value from Fisher's exact test was 0.0006, which clearly indicates a correlation. This is whole lot better than any figure we obtained on commitment, leading us down the path of considering whether losses is a more critical burden in fighting an insurgency that level of commitment.

The same trend is the case if the data is coded by total intervening forces killed (the sum of the average over the duration). This is an attempt to measure the overall burden of losses, as opposed to an annual rate of losses. The total intervening forces killed data basically falls into three groupings (49 cases):

- Low Intervening Intensity cases (0-0.02) result in 12% Red Wins (17 cases)
- Medium Intervening Intensity cases (0.03-0.92) result in 41% Red Wins (17 cases)
- High Intervening Intensity cases (1.02-32.60) result in 73% Red Wins (15 cases)

Or, to put it another way:

- Low Intervening Intensity cases (0-0.02) result in 88% Blue Wins (17 cases)
- Medium Intervening Intensity cases (0.03-0.92) result in 47% Blue Wins (17 cases)

- High Intervening Intensity cases (1.02-32.60) result in 20% Blue Wins (15 cases)

It appears that when the total intervening forces killed exceeds more than 0.001% of the population of the intervening country that the insurgents win more than two-thirds of the time. The two sided p-value from Fisher's exact test was 0.0007, which again clearly indicates a correlation.

Average intervening forces killed for insurgencies against outside intervening forces (31 cases):

- Low Intervening Intensity cases (0) result in 17% Red Wins (6 cases)
- Medium Intervening Intensity cases (0.01-0.09) result in 64% Red Wins (11 cases)
- High Intervening Intensity cases (0.12-4.08) result in 71% Red Wins (14 cases)

Or, to put it another way:

- Low Intervening Intensity cases (0) result in 83% Blue Wins (6 cases)
- Medium Intervening Intensity cases (0.01-0.09) result in 27% Blue Wins (11 cases)
- High Intervening Intensity cases (0.12-4.08) result in 21% Blue Wins (14 cases)

It appears that when the average intervening forces killed facing an insurgency exceeds more than 0.00001% of the population of the intervening country (more than 0.01 per 100,000 home population), then the insurgency succeeds in over two-thirds of the cases. The two-sided p-value from Fisher's exact test was 0.0889, which indicates a correlation.

The same trend is the case if the data is coded by total intervening forces killed (the sum of the average over the duration). The total intervening forces killed data versus insurgencies basically falls into three groupings (31 cases):

- Low Intervening Intensity cases (0-0.01) result in 25% Red Wins (4 cases)
- Medium Intervening Intensity cases (0.03-0.92) result in 46% Red Wins (13 cases)
- High Intervening Intensity cases (1.02-32.60) result in 79% Red Wins (14 cases)

Or, to put it another way:

- Low Intervening Intensity cases (0-0.01) result in 75% Blue Wins (4 cases)
- Medium Intervening Intensity cases (0.01-0.09) result in 27% Blue Wins (11 cases)
- High Intervening Intensity cases (0.12-4.08) result in 21% Blue Wins (14 cases)

The two sided p-value from Fisher's exact test was 0.1125.

There seems to be a very high degree of correlation for the intervening force intensity.

These correlations all turned out to be stronger than any we had seen for commitment, and clearly made the point that intervening loss rates and total casualties were a clear factor is determining insurgent success. Furthermore, as it was based upon 14 to 15 cases in the highest category, it was clearly not driven by one nation's willingness or unwillingness to accept casualties.

2. GOVERNMENT FORCES KILLED

We then assessed government forces killed per 100,000 indigenous population. Unlike the above analysis of intervening force intensity, there was little correlation and very poor statistics no matter what we examined. This was the case when we looked at the average and total government forces killed.[17] This data does not give us a particular line of thought other than perhaps reinforcing a trend previously observed by *The Dupuy Institute* that a more extended insurgency tends to favor the counterinsurgent.

We could also not achieve any pattern for those cases that we coded as insurgencies.[18] It is clear from this data that government forces facing an insurgency are not as casualty sensitive as intervening forces facing an insurgency. The casualty sensitivity of intervening forces is clearly supported by statistics, while that of government forces is not.

3. INSURGENT FORCES KILLED

We then examined how insurgent intensity (insurgents killed per 100,000 indigenous population) affects outcome. Again, there was not a very clear trend in the data when looking at the entire data set.[19]

If we limited ourselves to looking at only those cases coded as insurgencies, we produced similar results.[20] This data does not give us a particular line of thought other than perhaps reinforcing a trend previously observed by *The Dupuy Institute* that a more intense insurgency tends to favor the insurgents.

4. CIVILIANS KILLED

Finally we examined civilian intensity, or the number of civilians killed per 100,000 indigenous population. This also did not produce significant results. For example an examination of civilian loss rates across all the cases shows a weak correlation.[21] Certainly our statistics would have been helped if we had more than 39 cases we were able to collect civilian loss data on. This data does not give us a particular line of thought other than perhaps reinforcing a trend previously observed by *The Dupuy Institute* that a more intense insurgency tends to favor the insurgents.

The same was the case if we limited our examination to the cases that we coded as insurgencies, except now the number of cases with civilian data is down to only 28, wreaking havoc with our statistical tests.[22]

Now, we did have total number of indigenous people killed for 70 of our 83 total cases and for 58 of our 62 insurgency cases. In those cases, we could calculate average total indigenous people killed. Even with those much large number of cases, we could not get a significant fit.[23] Again, this examination of the data over time does not generate a clear pattern except to possibly reinforce the idea that extended durations favor the counterinsurgent.

C. FINDINGS AND CONCLUSIONS ON
COMMITMENT AND INTENSITY

Just to highlight the main points from above first we found that when an intervening force is involved, and when intervening force commitment exceeds more than 0.1% of population of the intervening country, the insurgents win in about two-thirds of cases, although this could be because of chance.

Second our numbers for government force commitment indicate that once an insurgency becomes large enough that 1% or more of the population is involved, then it can either be controlled or resolved by domestic forces, or it cannot be defeated, regardless of the number of outside forces. There is some statistical support for this conclusion, but it is based on only ten cases.

Insurgent force commitment seemed to break down into two groups based on whether or not an intervening force was present. The average insurgent commitment for insurgencies facing an intervention is six times higher than the average insurgent commitment for an insurgency with no intervening force. For example, the average commitment for an insurgency against foreigners is 664 per 100,000 population compared to 94 per 100,000 population for insurgencies without an intervening force. This raises the question of whether the win percentage of insurgencies against foreigners (50% insurgent wins) and insurgencies with no outside interventions (35% insurgent wins) is affected by the relative size of insurgent forces.

Third, concerning intervening force intensity, we found that when intervening forces killed exceeds more than 0.00001% of the population of the intervening country, the counterinsurgency, intervention, or peacekeeping operation fails in over two-thirds of all cases. Furthermore, it appears that if the average intervening forces killed exceeds more than 0.00001% of the population of the intervening country, the chances of failure rise to around 50%. There is a very high degree of correlation for the intervening force intensity—higher than the other categories.

In summation, low commitment and intensity tends to lead to blue side wins;

high commitment and intensity tends to lead toward red side wins. Indigenous governments are able to support a higher level of commitment and intensity than intervening nations. Once the insurgents reach a certain threshold of commitment, they tend to be difficult to defeat.

D. CHEESE EATING SURRENDER MONKEYS, WIMPY DEMOCRACIES, AND OTHER MODERN MYTHS

In May 1940, the Germans invaded France and occupied Paris the following month. The French surrendered shortly thereafter and formed up a government allied with Nazi Germany. This appears to have started the contemptuous view, widely held in the U.S., that the French are somehow not very good at war. This is regardless of the fact that the French stuck it out through World War I even after the Russian Empire had collapsed and withdrew from the war. This ignores the geographic reality of Paris being only 190 miles (310 kilometers) from the German border. The Germans took Paris 35 days after the campaign started in 1940. When the Germans invaded the Soviet Union the following year, they advanced 330 miles (540 kilometers) in the first 25 days and took Smolensk. They then went another 210 miles (340 kilometers) to go all the way to Moscow. London certainly would have been in danger of being taken by the Germans if there was no English Channel. The graphic below shows a clear comparison of the amount and degree of fighting the French have done over the last 400 years compared to the neighboring English, well protected by the English Channel.

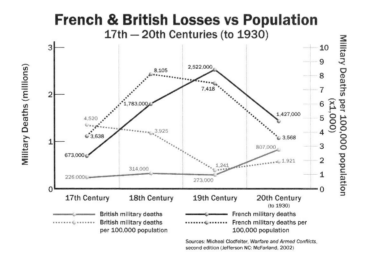

In the post World War II period, the French have lost more troops relative to their population fighting insurgencies than any other country. From 1946 through 1962 they were continuously involved in repeated bloody insurgencies. Most prominent are the Indochina War from 1946 to 1954 following immediately by the Algerian War from 1954 to 1962. It also included Madagascar (1947–1948), Tunisia (1952–1956), Morocco (1953–1956), Cameroun (1955–1960) and others. This was 17 years of continued warfare, in all but one of those years, the French lost from 1 to 8 French soldiers per 100,000 French.[24]

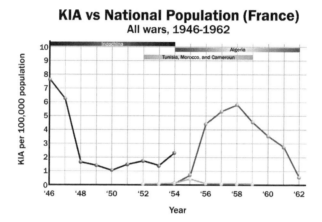

This is higher relative losses than any other counterinsurgency effort since World War II. The U.S. in Vietnam, the bloodiest insurgency since World War II, had one year that was as bloody as what the French dealt with. This was 1968, during the Tet offensive when the U.S. lost 7.07 killed per 100,000 Americans. The years on either side of this, 1967 and 1969, were 4.59 and 4.50, respectively. The years before and after that, 1966 and 1970, were 2.47 and 1.99 respectively. The rest of the time, the figures were lower than one.[25] The U.S. in Vietnam had five years of a counterinsurgency effort that was of similar intensity to what the French had dealt with for 16 years!

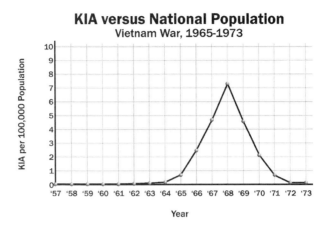

Yet, it is the French that have a reputation among some people in the U.S. of being "wimpy" or being "cheese-eating surrender monkeys."[26] This flies in the face of the historical record, or more to point, if the French armed forces are somehow or other wimpy, then the Russian, British and U.S. are even much more so, relatively speaking. To show a few more modified charts from our briefings:[27]

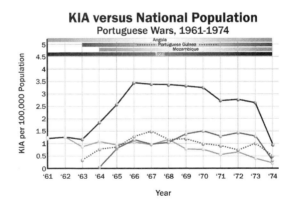

Comparative casualties over time carried across multiple countries addresses a few other issues. First, there appears to be nothing that indicates that democracies are wimpier or less determined during a guerilla war. We did some statistical tests on the subject in Chapter Twelve. But, to look at the individual cases, we note that the French suffered more than 1 to 8 killed per 100,000 people for 16 years. France, of course, was a democracy during that period. We note that the Portuguese suffered 1 to 3.5 killed per 100,000 Portuguese for 14 years fighting three insurgencies in Africa. This included nine years at rates between 2.5 and 3.5.[28] It was a dictatorship. They also lost, and it played a part in the dictatorship being overthrown. The U.S. suffered losses of 1 to 7 per 100,000 Americans in Vietnam but only for five years. We are of course a democracy but not as determined as our fellow democratic French or the dictatorial Portuguese.

Almost everyone else is noticeably less determined than those three cases. For example, the Soviet Union, with its fearsome reputation, was only losing less than one people per 100,000 Soviet population a year in Afghanistan over the course of around nine years. There values were between 0.22 and 0.75 from 1980 through 1988. Their total killed in the war was reported as 14,751.[29] The U.S. lost more than 58,000 in Vietnam. The Soviet Union withdrew and their dictatorial communist government collapsed in less than two years after that. So much for the dangerous Soviet bear.

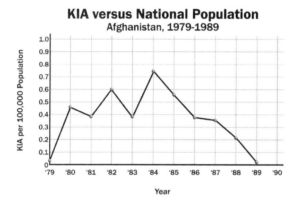

KIA versus National Population
Afghanistan, 1979-1989

The United Kingdom, which has developed a reputation in some circles as counterinsurgency experts, has never had a particularly big fight since World War II, although they have fought multiple insurgencies at the same time. In the case of Malaya (1948–60), the losses never got above 0.09 British killed per 100,000 during its 13 years. Northern Ireland (1968–1998) never got above 0.19 British soldiers killed per 100,000 during its 31 years and for 20 of those years was below 0.025 per 100,000. The British also lost several insurgencies during this time, including their withdrawal from Palestine in 1948 and Aden in 1967. The relatively bloodiest year fighting insurgencies by the U.K. since World War II was 1948 in Palestine, where the loss rate peaked at 0.28.[30] That was the year they withdrew, and they were not there for half the year. One can argue whether they should really be considered victorious in Cyprus, where the head of the insurgency became the defense minister for the new independent Cypriot government, or Kenya, where seven years after the insurgency ended, the head of the independence movement there took over as prime minister of the newly-independent country and a year later became president. Even Malaya is not that clear cut, as the British gave them independence during the time they were defeating the communist insurgency.

KIA vs National Population (UK)
All British Interventions, 1945-1967

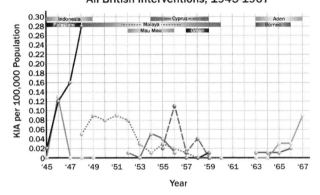

A comparison of this British chart to the French chart show above really drives home the point about the nature of the different insurgencies they were facing. The French are regularly running figures like 1 to 8 killed per 100,000 population, while the British figures never rise above 0.28 killed per 100,000 population.

When one reviews a theme like developed in Nagl's book about the British being a learning army in Malaya vice the U.S. in Vietnam, one must ask why he did not extend the theme to address all of the UK insurgencies, including those that they lost and those that were seriously compromised by their own strategic incompetence (for example Cyprus). Again, one can overstress the importance of the one case study of Malaya.[31] One cannot help but notice that the British insurgencies were simply much smaller than anything the French or the U.S. faced.

There are a number of other countries are up there among the toughest and most determined counterinsurgent fighters, as represented by the French, Portuguese and the U.S. This certainly includes the Soviet Union versus the Ukrainian Independence Movement (1944–1954), the Dutch in Indonesia (1945–1949), the Egyptians in Yemen, Mauritania in Western Sahara, Cuba in Africa, Israel and Syria in Lebanon, Vietnam in Cambodia, among others. It is also the case that the levels of losses in civil war, like the Greek Civil War, tend to be higher, and in many cases much higher, than for interventions. None of these cases obviate the argument made above.

For comparison, the U.S. loss rate in Iraq for 2009 was 0.02 per 100,000 and in 2010 was 0.01. Its worse year was 2007, when it was 0.25. The U.S. loss rate in Afghanistan for 2009 was 0.09 and for 2010 was 0.17.

NOTES

1. Original source not identified.
2. See *Examination of Factors Influencing the Conduct of Operations in Guerilla Wars, Task 12: Examining the Geographic Aspects of an Insurgency* (Annandale, VA.: The Dupuy In-

stitute, 4 Feb. 2008), Section N, 62–68.

3. *Examination of Factors Influencing the Conduct of Operations in Guerilla Wars, Task 11: Examine Measurement of Popular Support* (Annandale, VA.: The Dupuy Institute, 25 Feb. 2008).

4. The two-sided p-value from Fisher's exact text was 0.0532.

5. Low Government Force Commitment (20-499) results in 40% Red Wins (35 cases). Medium Government Force Commitment (500-999) results in 27% Red Wins (11 cases). High Government Commitment (1,034-7,224) results in 60% Red Wins (10 cases).

   Low Government Force Commitment (20-499) results in 46% Blue Wins (35 cases). Medium Government Force Commitment (500-999) results in 73% Blue Wins (11 cases). High Government Commitment (1,034-7,224) results in 30% Blue Wins (10 cases).

   The two-sided p-value from Fisher's exact test was 0.3253. Again, this is not a statistic that gives one confidence in this particular case, but there is a fairly consistent pattern throughout this data.

6. The two-sided p-value from Fisher's exact test was 0.1129, which is close to an acceptable confidence range.

7. Low Government Force Commitment (20-499) results in 35% Red Wins (17 cases). Medium Government Force Commitment (500-999) results in 0% Red Wins (2 cases). High Government Commitment (1,055-2,378) results in 20% Red Wins (5 cases).

   Low Government Force Commitment (20-499) results in 47% Blue Wins (17 cases). Medium Government Force Commitment (500-999) results in 100% Blue Wins (2 cases). High Government Commitment (1,055-2,378) results in 60% Blue Wins (5 cases).

   The two-sided p-value from Fisher's exact test was 0.9339. Basically, this means that the odds of getting such a distribution by random luck are much higher than this indicating a pattern.

8. In all cases (76 cases) it showed: Low Insurgent Force Commitment (0.26-499) results in 28% Red Wins (57 cases), Medium Insurgent Force Commitment (500-999) results in 30% Red Wins (10 cases), High Insurgent Force Commitment (1,000-8,196) results in 67% Red Wins (9 cases).

   Low Insurgent Force Commitment (0.26-499) results in 60% Blue Wins (57 cases), Medium Insurgent Force Commitment (500-999) results in 60% Blue Wins (10 cases), High Insurgent Force Commitment (1,000-8,196) results in 33% Blue Wins (9 cases).

   The two-sided p-value from Fisher's exact test was 0.2795, which is not very strong.

9. Low Insurgent Force Commitment (0.26-499) results in 30% Red Wins (43 cases), Medium Insurgent Force Commitment (500-999) results in 50% Red Wins (6 cases), High Insurgent Force Commitment (1,000-8,196) results in 75% Red Wins (8 cases)

   Low Insurgent Force Commitment (0.26-499) results in 60% Blue Wins (43 cases), Medium Insurgent Force Commitment (500-999) results in 33% Blue Wins (6 cases), High Insurgent Force Commitment (1,000-8,196) results in 25% Blue Wins (8 cases).

   The two-sided p-value from Fisher's exact test was 0.1165, which is not statistically significant at the 10% level, but is still close.

10. Low Insurgent Force Commitment (0.26-499) results in 39% Red Wins (23 cases), Medium Insurgent Force Commitment (500-999) results in 60% Red Wins (5 cases), High Insurgent Force Commitment (1,000-8,196) results in 75% Red Wins (8 cases).

    Low Insurgent Force Commitment (0.26-499) results in 52% Blue Wins (23 cases), Medium Insurgent Force Commitment (500-999) results in 40% Blue Wins (5 cases), High Insurgent Force Commitment (1,000-8,196) results in 25% Blue Wins (8 cases).

The two sided p-value from the Fisher's exact test was 0.5081, which is not good.

11. Low Insurgent Force Commitment (0.26-499) results in 20% Red Wins (20 cases), Medium Insurgent Force Commitment (500-999) results in 0% Red Wins (1 case), High Insurgent Force Commitment (1,034-8,196) results in 0% Red Wins (0 cases).

    Low Insurgent Force Commitment (0.26-499) results in 70% Blue Wins (20 cases), Medium Insurgent Force Commitment (500-999) results in 0% Blue Wins (1 cases), High Insurgent Force Commitment (1,034-8,196) results in 0% Blue Wins (0 cases).

    The two-sided p-value from Fisher's exact test was 0.1429, which is not statistically significant at the 10% level, but is still close.

12. Low Total Commitment (23-499) results in 27% Red Wins (37 cases), Medium Total Commitment (500-999) results in 38% Red Wins (21 cases), High Total Commitment (1,000-8,430) results in 44% Red Wins (18 cases).

    Low Total Commitment (23-499) results in 54% Blue Wins (37 cases), Medium Total Commitment (500-999) results in 57% Blue Wins (21 cases), High Total Commitment (1,000-8,430) results in 50% Blue Wins (18 cases).

    The two sided p-value from Fisher's exact test was 0.4429, which is not a strong supportive statistic.

13. Or, four out of six cases, since all three consecutive Vietnam cases from 1957–1973 are in this dataset.

14. Low Total Commitment (23-499) results in 28% Red Wins (29 cases), Medium Total Commitment (500-999) results in 50% Red Wins (15 cases), High Total Commitment (1,000-8,430) results in 53% Red Wins (14 cases).

    Low Total Commitment (23-499) results in 55% Blue Wins (29 cases), Medium Total Commitment (500-999) results in 43% Blue Wins (15 cases), High Total Commitment (1,000-8,430) results in 47% Blue Wins (14 cases).

    The two-sided p-value from Fisher's exact test was 0.2653, which was not very strong.

15. Low Total Commitment (23-499) results in 29% Red Wins (14 cases), Medium Total Commitment (500-999) results in 64% Red Wins (11 cases), High Total Commitment (1,007–8,430) results in 64% Red Wins (11 cases).

    Low Total Commitment (23-499) results in 57% Blue Wins (14 cases), Medium Total Commitment (500-999) results in 36% Blue Wins (11 cases), High Total Commitment (1,007–8,430) results in 36% Blue Wins (11 cases).

    The two sided p-value from Fisher's exact testy was 0.2296, which again is not very strong but does show a trend that is in line with the other trends that we are seeing.

16. Low Total Commitment (0.25-499) results in 27% Red Wins (15 cases), Medium Total Commitment (500-999) results in 0% Red Wins (3 cases), High Total Commitment (1,034-8,196) results in 25% Red Wins (4 cases).

    Low Total Commitment (0.25-499) results in 53% Blue Wins (15 cases), Medium Total Commitment (500-999) results in 67% Blue Wins (3 cases), High Total Commitment (1,034-8,196) results in 75% Blue Wins (4 cases).

    The two-sided p-value from Fisher's exact test was 0.9425.

17. Low Government Intensity cases (0.02-0.97) result in 28% Red Wins (36 cases), Medium Government Intensity cases (1.11-8.87) result in 47% Red Wins (15 cases), High Government Intensity cases (9.95-106.53) result in 44% Red Wins (9 cases).

    Low Government Intensity cases (0.02-0.97) result in 56% Blue Wins (36 cases), Medium Government Intensity cases (1.11-8.87) result in 40% Blue Wins (15 cases), High Government Intensity cases (9.95-106.53) result in 56% Blue Wins (9 cases).

    The two-sided p-value from Fisher's exact test was 0.5658, which indicates that this result could have just as easily come from chance. The same trend is the case if the data is coded by total intervening forces killed (the sum of the average over the duration):

Very Low Government Intensity cases (0.05-0.92) result in 11% Red Wins (9 cases), Low Government Intensity cases (1.05-7.73) result in 40% Red Wins (25 cases), Medium Government Intensity cases (10.46-92.27) result in 40% Red Wins (15 cases), High Government Intensity cases (120.73-958.77) result in 33% Red Wins (9 cases).

Very Low Government Intensity cases (0.05-0.92) result in 67% Blue Wins (9 cases), Low Government Intensity cases (1.05-7.73) result in 44% Blue Wins (25 cases), Medium Government Intensity cases (10.46-92.27) result in 47% Blue Wins (15 cases), High Government Intensity cases (120.73-958.77) result in 67% Blue Wins (9 cases). The two-sided p-value from Fisher's exact test was 0.5992.

18. The two-sided p-value from Fisher's exact test fro these two tests were 0.9396 and 0.9248, which is very poor. For the actual data *see Examination of Factors Influencing the Conduct of Operations in Guerilla Wars, Task 11: Examine Measurement of Popular Support* (Annandale, VA.: The Dupuy Institute, 25 Feb. 2008).

19. Very Low Insurgent Intensity cases (0.05-0.84) result in 14% Red Wins (14 cases), Low Insurgent Intensity cases (1.01-7.93) result in 38% Red Wins (21 cases), Medium Insurgent Intensity cases (9.95-65.06) result in 44% Red Wins (25 cases), High Insurgent Intensity cases (123.61-531.02) result in 67% Red Wins (6 cases).

Very Low Insurgent Intensity cases (0.05-0.84) result in 64% Blue Wins (14 cases), Low Insurgent Intensity cases (1.09-7.73) result in 52% Blue Wins (21 cases), Medium Insurgent Intensity cases (10.46-57.86) result in 52% Blue Wins (25 cases), High Insurgent Intensity cases (120.73-958.77) result in 33% Blue Wins (6 cases).

It appears that when the average insurgent forces killed exceeds more than 0.001% of the population of the country (more than 1.01 per 100,000 home population), then the counterinsurgency, intervention or peacekeeping operation fails in around half of the cases. The two-sided p-value from Fisher's exact test was 0.2507, which was not very strong.

The same trend is the case if the data is coded by total insurgent forces killed (the sum of the average over the duration). The total insurgent forces killed data basically falls into four groupings (61 cases):

Low Insurgent Intensity cases (0.03-0.97) result in 25% Red Wins (4 cases), Medium Insurgent Intensity cases (1.85-8.14) result in 20% Red Wins (10 cases), High Insurgent Intensity cases (10.77-95.54) result in 41% Red Wins (29 cases), Very High Insurgent Intensity cases (103.13-4,779.14) result in 44% Red Wins (18 cases).

Low Insurgent Intensity cases (0.03-0.97) result in 75% Blue Wins (4 cases), Medium Insurgent Intensity cases (1.85-8.14) result in 70% Blue Wins (10 cases), High Insurgent Intensity cases (10.77-95.54) result in 48% Blue Wins (29 cases), Very High Insurgent Intensity cases (103.13-4,779.14) result in 56% Blue Wins (18 cases).

This data does not give us a particular line of thought other than perhaps reinforcing a trend previously observed by *The Dupuy Institute* that a more intense insurgency tends to favor the insurgents. The two-sided p-value from Fisher's exact test was 0.4537.

20. Looking at average insurgent intensity, the data once more falls into four groupings (50 cases):

Very Low Insurgent Intensity cases (0.05-0.84) result in 11% Red Wins (9 cases), Low Insurgent Intensity cases (1.05-8.61) result in 50% Red Wins (16 cases), Medium Insurgent Intensity cases (9.95-65.06) result in 47% Red Wins (19 cases), High Insurgent Intensity cases (123.61-531.02) result in 67% Red Wins (6 cases).

Very Low Insurgent Intensity cases (0.05-0.84) result in 67% Blue Wins (9 cases),

Low Insurgent Intensity cases (1.05-8.61) result in 38% Blue Wins (16 cases), Medium Insurgent Intensity cases (9.95-65.06) result in 53% Blue Wins (19 cases), High Insurgent Intensity cases (123.61-531.02) result in 33% Blue Wins (6 cases).

It appears that when the average insurgent forces killed exceeds more than 0.001% of the population of the country (more than 1.05 per 100,000 home population), then the insurgency succeeds in around half of the cases. The two-sided p-value from Fisher's exact test was 0.1303.

The same trend is the case if the data is coded by total insurgent forces killed (the sum of the average over the duration).

Very Low Insurgent Intensity cases (0.40-0.97) result in 25% Red Wins (4 cases), Low Insurgent Intensity cases (1.85-8.14) result in 25% Red Wins (4 cases), Medium Insurgent Intensity cases (10.77-95.54) result in 43% Red Wins (23 cases), High Insurgent Intensity cases (103.13-4,779.14) result in 47% Red Wins (17 cases).

Very Low Insurgent Intensity cases (0.40-0.97) result in 75% Blue Wins (4 cases), Low Insurgent Intensity cases (1.85-8.14) result in 50% Blue Wins (4 cases), Medium Insurgent Intensity cases (10.77-95.54) result in 43% Blue Wins (23 cases), High Insurgent Intensity cases (103.13-4,779.14) result in 53% Blue Wins (17 cases).

This data does not give us a particular line of thought other than perhaps reinforcing a previously observed trend by us that a more extended insurgency tends to favor the counterinsurgent. The two-sided p-value from Fisher's exact test was 0.5340.

21. Very Low Civilian Intensity cases (0.00-1.03) result in 20% Red Wins (10 cases), Low Civilian Intensity cases (2.74-7.99) result in 13% Red Wins (8 cases), Medium Civilian Intensity cases (10.67-56.54) result in 29% Red Wins (17 cases), High Civilian Intensity cases (115.14-624.16) result in 50% Red Wins (4 cases).

Very Low Civilian Intensity cases (0.00-1.03) result in 70% Blue Wins (10 cases), Low Civilian Intensity cases (2.74-7.99) result in 75% Blue Wins (8 cases), Medium Civilian Intensity cases (10.67-56.54) result in 47% Blue Wins (17 cases), High Civilian Intensity cases (115.14-624.16) result in 25% Blue Wins (17 cases).

The two sided p-value from Fisher's exact test was 0.6456, which would indicate that there is a better than 50% chance that this result came about randomly.

The same trend is the case if the data is coded by total civilians killed (sum of the average over the duration). The total civilians killed data basically falls into three groupings (39 cases):

Low Civilian Intensity cases (0-0.45) result in 0% Red Wins (5 cases), Medium Civilian Intensity cases (2.91-103.99) result in 36% Red Wins (22 cases), High Civilian Intensity cases (108.94-15,615.14) result in 17% Red Wins (12 cases).

Low Civilian Intensity cases (0-0.45) result in 100% Blue Wins (5 cases), Medium Civilian Intensity cases (2.91-103.99) result in 40% Blue Wins (22 cases), High Civilian Intensity cases (108.94-15,615.14) result in 67% Blue Wins (12 cases).

The two-sided p-value from Fisher's exact test was 0.2045, which is not great but is better than the previous result.

22. Very Low Civilian Intensity cases (0.02-0.94) result in 14% Red Wins (7 cases), Low Civilian Intensity cases (1.96-7.99) result in 43% Red Wins (7 cases), Medium Civilian Intensity cases (10.67-56.54) result in 36% Red Wins (11 cases), High Civilian Intensity cases (115.14-624.16) result in 67% Red Wins (3 cases).

Very Low Civilian Intensity cases (0.02-0.94) result in 71% Blue Wins (7 cases), Low Civilian Intensity cases (2.74-7.99) result in 71% Blue Wins (7 cases), Medium Civilian Intensity cases (10.67-56.54) result in 45% Blue Wins (11 cases), High Civilian Intensity cases (115.14-624.16) result in 33% Blue Wins (3 cases).

The two sided p-value from Fisher's exact test was 0.7702, which would indicate that there is a better than 50% change that this result came about randomly.

The same trend is the case if the data is coded by total civilians killed (the sum of the average over the duration). The total civilians killed data basically falls into three groupings (28 cases):

Low Civilian Intensity cases (0.11-0.45) result in 0% Red Wins (3 cases), Medium Civilian Intensity cases (2.91-75.76) result in 50% Red Wins (14 cases), High Civilian Intensity cases (108.94-15,615.14) result in 18% Red Wins (11 cases).

Low Civilian Intensity cases (0.11-0.45) result in 100% Blue Wins (3 cases), Medium Civilian Intensity cases (2.91-75.76) result in 36% Blue Wins (14 cases), High Civilian Intensity cases (108.94-15,615.14) result in 73% Blue Wins (11 cases).

This data does not give us a particular line of thought other than perhaps reinforcing a trend previously observed by *The Dupuy Institute* that a more extended insurgency tends to favor the counterinsurgent. The two-sided p-value from Fisher's exact test was 0.2282, which was not very strong.

23. For detailed statistics of this test see *Examination of Factors Influencing the Conduct of Operations in Guerilla Wars, Task 11: Examine Measurement of Popular Support* (Annandale, VA.: The Dupuy Institute, 25 Feb. 2008).

24. This does not include non-French fighting for the French, French colonial troops, and non-French troops in the French Foreign Legion. We have not collected the data for Madagascar (1947–1948).

25. This is 0.68 per 100,000 for 1965, 0.61 per 100,000 for 1971, 0.14 for 1972 and 0.11 for 1973. In the worst year of the advisory period (1964), it was 0.07

26. For example, Wikipedia has an article on "cheese-eating surrender monkeys" and another on "anti-French" sentiment in the United States. The phrase dates from an episode of *The Simpsons*, a popular satirical cartoon, which aired on 30 April 1995. It was been repeated many times since then.

27. These charts were updated from charts provided in our January 2005 briefing.

28. In 1974, the calculated loss rate is 0.96, which rounds up to one.

29. G. F. Krivosheyev, *Grif Sekretnosti Snyat: Poteri Vooryzhennnyikh Sil SSSR v Voinakh, voyevyikh Deistviyakh I voyennyikh konfliktakh* (Moscow: Voyennoye Izdatelstvo, 1993), 407. Total Soviet losses, including Interior Ministry troops, were probably higher than that figure.

30. There may have been a higher rate in 1946 in Indonesia, but we do not have UK casualties separated from the Indian casualties in this particular case. Certainly the majority of losses were from the Indian troops. The rate for all troops was 1.29 British and Indian troops compared to the UK population. It is suspected that actual British losses would have been 10% of that or less.

31. See John A. Nagl, *Learning to Eat Soup with a Knife* (Chicago & London: University of London Press, 2005 [2002]). This book is based on two case studies, Malaya and Vietnam.

CHAPTER 16

A Model of Insurgencies

The military value of a partisan's work is not measured by the amount of property destroyed, or the number of men killed or captured, but by the number [of the enemy which] he keeps watching [him].

—John Singleton Mosby, 1833–1916, Confederate cavalry leader[1]

All of the above assembles into a model of insurgencies. In the simplest of forms, it is represented as a two-variable model based upon force and cause. This is shown in the graph below:

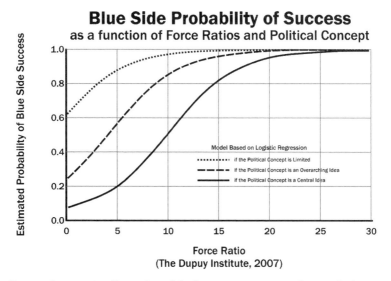

Blue Side Probability of Success
as a function of Force Ratios and Political Concept

Model Based on Logistic Regression
········· if the Political Concept is Limited
– – – – if the Political Concept is an Overarching Idea
——— if the Political Concept is a Central Idea

Estimated Probability of Blue Side Success

Force Ratio
(The Dupuy Institute, 2007)

But, we have an intellectual model of insurgency success that is a little more sophisticated than that. It is based on looking at each of the elements we examined in the chapters above, seeing which appeared to be influencing the results and which did not appear to have much influence. Therefore, we postulate that there are two factors of primary importance.

OF PRIMARY IMPORTANCE

1. Force Ratios
2. Cause

These appear to be the two most important factors in an insurgency and need to be addressed before one addresses anything else. Once these factors are addressed, then other lower order factors come into play. On the other hand, if these two factors are not addressed, then I suspect it does not matter how brilliantly one conducts all the other aspects of the war, there will be a problem.

In this case, force ratios are an element very much under the control of the counterinsurgents. They have the resources to push the force ratios up to 10 to 1 or 25 to 1. The insurgents have less flexibility over force ratios, as the nature of their business is that it is more difficult to quickly recruit, arm, train and support troops in the field.

Cause is an element very much under the control of, or pushed forward by the insurgents. The counterinsurgent may be able to undermine or compromise the cause but does not determine the cause.

ALSO OF IMPORTANCE

We feel that this elements are also of some importance, and may make up the third, fourth or fifth element in a model of insurgent success. The importance of these three elements, related to the two first listed (force ratio and cause) has not yet been analyzed or evaluated. It is clearly something that can and should be done.

1. Rules of Engagement and Rectitude
2. Terrain
3. Burden

ALSO MAY BE IMPORTANT

These two elements may have some importance, or may be important in certain situations. It does appear that they are having some impact in some insurgencies.

1. Insurgent Strategy[2]
2. Indigenous Government Types and Elections

NOT SURE OF THEIR IMPORTANCE

And then there are those elements of an insurgency that so far have not been shown to be that important. It does not mean that they are not important, it just means that their impact may be of a lower order in the overall picture than the issues discussed above. These include:

1. Structure of insurgencies
2. Specific Government Reforms
3. Degree of outside support
4. Sanctuary
5. Barrier Systems
6. Population Resettlement
7. Staying the Course

Two elements we did not get around to testing, but would like to at some point was the value of intelligence and the fracture lines in society. Most likely these will also be cases where we are unable to show that they are important, but we are not sure until such time as we have tested them.

This is a fairly simple and deterministic construct that hardly begins to show the complexities of what is actually happening on the ground. Still, in the broadest strategic levels it does provide some order as to what has to be addressed first, what has to be addressed next, and what doesn't seem really to be a major factor. It is an outline for priorities.

For example, when even considering whether to engage in fighting an insurgency, the basic issues of the insurgent cause and the nature of the insurgent cause needs to be addressed. This will give the intervener a strong indication of what is needed to fight that insurgency. They then need to make sure they have enough forces assigned to successfully pacify a country and that their country is willing to commit the time and effort it is going to take. This is where the force ratios come into play. These two subjects need to be addressed before you consider any other issues.

Once these have been addressed, then they can certainly influence the course of the insurgency by their rules of engagement and degree of rectitude. This is certainly what the U.S. is attempting to do in Afghanistan. Furthermore, the outcome of the insurgency may be influenced by presence of covered terrain. The ability of the intervening force to win may be influenced by the total burden fighting the insurgency will impose. Again, this is back to determining if their country is willing to commit the time and effort it is going to take for a successful result.

Of significance is those seven items listed that we have not gotten results for. This does not mean the counterinsurgent should not use barrier systems, or try not to restrict their use of sanctuaries, but they should not assume that this will be a war winning strategy into and of itself. For example, just "staying the course" does not guarantee counterinsurgent success. The picture is more complex than that

This does provide us through with a model or at least of hypothesis of the underlying factors driving an insurgency. It allows us to compare it to other theorists. As there have been a wide range of theoretical works on insurgencies, and most of them disagrees on certain salient points, it is worthwhile to look at nine of the more widely known or quoted theorist and see how they compare relative to this model.

NOTES

1. James Joseph Williamson, *Mosby's Rangers: A Record of the Operations of the Forty-Third Battalion Virginia Cavalry, from Its Organization to the Surrender, from the Diary of a Private, Supplemented and Verified with Official Reports of Federal Officers and Also of Mosby; with Personal Reminiscences, Sketches of Skirmishes, Battles and Bivouacs, Dashing Raids and Daring Adventures, Scenes and Incidents in the History of Mosby's Command; Muster Rolls, Occupation and Present Whereabouts of Surviving Members* (New York: R. B. Kenyon, 1896), 26.

2. This subject is briefly discussed in Chapter Seventeen under the discussion of Strategic Approach in section I.D. This was based upon a Bard O'Neill definition and he favors the category of insurgent strategy he called Protracted Popular War (PPW). Our analysis supported that. See our Task 6 & 9 report for further analysis of this: *Examination of Factors Influencing the Conduct of Operations in Guerilla Wars: Task 6: Examine Forms of Warfare & Task 9: Study the Leadership, Organization, and Political System* (Annandale, VA.: The Dupuy Institute, 22 February 2008).

CHAPTER 17

Other Theorists

It is always better to have no ideas than false ones;
to believe nothing, than to believe what is wrong.

—Thomas Jefferson, letter to Rev. James Madison, July 19, 1788[1]

I. COMPARING THE THEORISTS

T*he Dupuy Institute* has developed and tested some hypothetical constructs relating to insurgencies. This analysis has considerable overlap with the ideas put forth by the various other theorists. Therefore, the most expedient way to address some of their suggestions is to compare their theories and ideas to our existing analysis.

We compared our conclusions with those of nine established counterinsurgency experts. These are the authors we first discussed in Chapter Two and they represent a wide range of schools of thought. They are Manwaring, Trinquier, Joes, Galula, Clutterbuck, Fall, Kitson, O'Neill and a BDM report by Blaufarb and Tanham.

Clutterbuck and Kitson are both from the classic British school of thought, while Galula, Trinquier and Fall tend to be from the French school of counterinsurgent theorists. Manwaring, Joes, O'Neill and the BDM report tend to be representatives of the American school.

We had conducted our analysis independent of our review of these nine theorists. Our work was based upon only our own data and not directly influenced by their writings (although we were not entirely unaware of them). We then systematically reviewed one or more works by each of these authors and extracted from them what they believed were the factors influencing the outcome of insurgencies. We then compared their results to our relatively independently developed conclusions. This was an usual exercise where we were testing our theory to nine other developed theories.

We looked at each of them by specific subject area. For example, in the subject of area of a country, seven of the theorists never clearly stated an opinion on the subject in their works that we reviewed, but two of the other theorists clearly did. We then compared those two conclusions to our own findings to see where we agreed or disagreed.

A. TERRAIN AND GEOGRAPHIC CONSIDERATIONS

Our first broad-based examination of factors affecting insurgencies was done under contract for CAA. A report specifically written to address Task 12 of that contract examined the influence of area, population, population density, border length, percent arable land, percent urban population, terrain, and location on the duration and outcome of insurgencies. It also examined the distribution of action in an insurgency. What follows is a comparison of the terrain issues addressed by various theorists as compared to our findings on the subject.

AREA

We concluded that, "it does appear that there is not much correlation between size and outcome, except possibly for the insurgencies against foreign forces." Only two authors address this same subject. David Galula stated on page 23 of his book that "The larger the country the more difficult . . . to control it." O'Neill also noted that large areas favor the insurgency; small areas do not.

POPULATION

We concluded that, "It does appear that there is the same correlation between population and outcome from this sample of 31 cases (excluding the two ongoing examples), especially above 9,500,000 population. This relationship was established at the 20% significance level. . . . Otherwise, we saw no correlations between population size and outcome."

Again, only the same two authors addressed it, with both Galula and O'Neill stating that large populations favor the insurgency.

POPULATION DENSITY

We concluded that, "there is probably no direct correlation between density of population and the duration or the outcome of an insurgency." None of the nine other theorists we examined addressed this.

BORDER LENGTH

We concluded that, "Basically, we see no clear correlation between border length to outcome, other than that which might be generated by a correlation between area of the country and outcome."

Six of the theorist did not address this. Galula states that the length of the border favors the insurgency. Joes in his discussion regarding "Isolating the Combat Area" indicates that this is very important to him. He states that, "If it is believed impossible to cut off, or at least greatly impeded, outside help to the guerillas, the wisest course may be to decline to undertake a counter-guerilla effort." (This may best be addressed by examining degree of outside support.). Fall does not address this, although he does discuss the need for an "active sanctuary" as a very important factor.

PERCENT ARABLE LAND

The Dupuy Institute concluded that, "In the case of arable land, we have not found any comparisons that we are comfortable with." None of the nine other theorists we examined addressed this.

PERCENT URBAN POPULATION

We concluded that, "one cannot rule out from this examination that a rural environment (low percent urban population) favors the insurgents. This appears to be the case for up to around 20 percent urban population, and the effect appears to exist even though it is influenced by other factors. Above 20 percent, it does not appear to be a significant factor. . . . Beyond the hint that rural insurgencies are more successful and that insurgencies in more urban terrain may take longer to defeat, there is little definite here."

Again, Galula is the one theorist that also tended to examine the same terrain elements that we did. He stated that a high ratio of rural to urban population gives an advantage to the insurgent. In our work, we found that when the percent of rural to urban population is below about a 4 to 1 ratio, the insurgents tended to win. This was significant at the 3 percent level.[2]

O'Neill stated that inaccessible terrain favors the insurgents, while the other seven theorists we examined did not address this.

TERRAIN

We concluded that there was some correlation between covered terrain and outcome and covered terrain and duration. There might also be a correlation between rough terrain and outcome. Our tentative conclusions were:

1. *Covered terrain appears to favor the insurgents and this is supported statistically in the majority but not all of the various tests that we conducted.*
2. *As our data set probably includes more than a third of all significant insurgencies since World War II and almost all insurgencies against outside forces, including all major cases, then the failure to obtain a tight statistical result does not mean we should assume a null hypothesis (there is no relationship) is correct if there exists a visible pattern.*
3. *Rough covered terrain or simply covered terrain appears to increase the chances of the red side winning.*
4. *Covered terrain appears to increase the duration of insurgencies.*
5. *The value of covered terrain may be related to airpower. This needs to be examined further.*

6. *Terrain may be a more significant factor for insurgencies against outside powers than for civil wars.*

7. *Otherwise there is no strong indication that there are any differences between level terrain, rough terrain or mountainous terrain, urban or any other significant terrain type as far as their strategic effect is on determining outcome.*

8. *There is no indication that accessibility of the terrain is the issue here (isolated vs not isolated).*

Oddly enough, six of the theorists did not examine this issue. Again Galula is at the forefront of the terrain discussion. He stated "It helps the insurgent insofar as it is rugged and difficult, either because of mountains or swamps or because of the vegetation." O'Neill also notes that rugged terrain and covered terrain favor the insurgents.

Clutterbuck seems to recognize the value of covered terrain with the statement that, "In open country, such as in Algeria or parts of Vietnam, air power can be decisive if used wisely, both as an offensive weapon and for transport. Used unwisely, however, it can do real harm, both in telegraphing our punches and in alienating the local population."

LOCATION

Only Galula specifically addressed this point, stating that a naturally isolated country or one situated among countries that opposed the insurgency favored the counterinsurgent. In our Task 12 report we examined countries with low border areas and found that, "Out of these 15 cases, we still note 5 wins, or 33%. This is clearly not enough to claim that islands, island-like nations, or isolated nations are noticeably less successful at insurgencies than otherwise. One may be able to argue, based upon 4 cases, that small islands (less than 70,000 square kilometers) always produce blue wins."

SUMMARY

To try to boil this down is a single chart, on the left is listed the theorist and across the top is listed the subject. If the author addressed the issue as important, it is listed as "yes". If they did not address the issue, it is listed as "N/A" (not addressed). If they actually said it was not important then it is listed as "no".

As can be seen, *The Dupuy Institute's* work mostly parallels the conclusions independently reached by David Galula, and based upon a very different methodology than ours.

THEORIST	AREA	POPULATION	POPULATION DENSITY	BORDER LENGTH	PERCENT ARABLE LAND	PERCENT URBAN TERRAIN	TERRAIN	LOCA-TION
Manwaring	N/A	N/A	N/A	N/A	N/A	N/A	No	N/A
Trinquier	N/A	N/A	N/A	N/A	N/A	N/A	No	N/A
Joes	N/A	N/A	N/A	N/A	N/A	N/A	No	N/A

Galula	Yes	Yes	N/A	Yes	N/A	Yes	Yes	Yes
Clutterbuck	N/A	N/A	N/A	N/A	N/A	N/A	Yes[3]	N/A
Fall	N/A	N/A	N/A	N/A?	N/A	N/A	N/A	N/A
Kitson	N/A	N/A	N/A	N/A	N/A	N/A	N/A	N/A
O'Neill	Yes	Yes	N/A	N/A	N/A	Yes	Yes	N/A
BDM	N/A	N/A	N/A	N/A	N/A	N/A	N/A	N/A
The Dupuy Institute	Maybe	Yes	No	Maybe	No	Yes	Yes	No

B. RULES OF ENGAGEMENT AND DEGREES OF BRUTALITY

RULES OF ENGAGEMENT

The Dupuy Institute conducted an analysis of Rules of Engagement, the specific details of which are provided in Chapter Nine.

A couple of the theorists did not address rules of engagement, including Manwaring and Trinquier. Joes specifically discussed, "practicing rectitude towards civilians, prisoners and enemy defectors." Many of the authors did not discuss the issue in depth, leaving you to wonder what they mean. It appears that O'Neill favors some from of "restricted" or "strict" rules. Clutterbuck did not specifically address this subject but seems to favor strict. Fall probably favored strict rules. The BDM report seemed to prefer strict although leaning towards tightly restricted. Kitson did not specifically address the subject but seemed to favor limited rules. Pseudo gangs, which he advocates, can sometimes fall outside the laws of war. As he was the commanding officer in North Ireland in 1970, his actions there probably need to be examined in some depth

Galula, who does seem to address the same issues as us, clearly supported some form of limited rules of engagement but does support free fire zones. As he noted: "Since antagonizing the population will not help, it is imperative that hardships for it and rash actions on the part of the forces be kept to a minimum. The units participating in the operations should be thoroughly indoctrinated to that effect, the misdeeds punished severely and even publicly if this can serve to impress the population. Any damage done should be immediately compensated without red tape. . . . Areas very sparsely populated and difficult to access because of terrain may be turned into forbidden zones where trespassers can be arrested or eventually shot on sight by ground or air fire."

As all these authors seem to favor strict rules of engagement or at least tightly restricted rules of engagement, we did consult also with Luttwak and Peters for this section of rules of engagement and degrees of brutality. Luttwak did not address rules of engagements, while Peters seemed to support something akin to restricted to unrestricted.

USE OF TORTURE

The Dupuy Institute conducted an analysis of Use of Torture. The specific details are provided in Chapter Nine. Even though use of torture has also been practiced in a large number of insurgencies, it was not addressed in the writings we looked at by Manwaring, Fall, Kitson, O'Neill, or Peters.

Clutterbuck clearly objected to the use of torture. As he states: "The quickest way to get immediate information from a captured guerilla or from an arrested supporter is by torture, but this is a fatal mistake in the long run." As Joes specifically discussed "practicing rectitude towards civilians, prisoners and enemy defectors," we also suspect he objected to the use of torture. BDM repeats Clutterbuck's recommendation, but not as emphatically

The authors of the French school, except for maybe Bernard Fall, seem to support the use of torture. Trinquier felt it should be limited, immediate and tactical (actionable intelligence). Galula appears to support limited and selective use of torture, "If intelligence is still slow in coming, pressure may be applied . . . bureaucracy can be a powerful weapon in the hand of the counterinsurgent, provided it used with moderation and restraint and never against a community as a whole but only against a few individuals. In still tougher cases, visits to the inhabitants by pseudo insurgents are another way to get intelligence and to sow suspicion at the same time between the real guerrillas and the population. . . . If the counterinsurgent wishes to bring a quicker end to the war, he must discard some of the legal concepts that would be applicable in ordinary conditions. Automatic and rigid application of the law would flood the courts with minor and major cases, fill the jails and prison camps with people who could be won over, as well as with dangerous insurgents. Leniency seems in this case a good practical policy, but not blind leniency."

At the other end of the spectrum Luttwak addresses the need to "out-terrorize" the insurgents.

USE OF FIREPOWER

The Dupuy Institute conducted an analysis of use of firepower. The specific details are provided in Chapter Nine. Again, Manwaring and Trinquier did not address this.

Joes discussion of "practicing rectitude towards civilians, prisoners and enemy defectors" probably also applies to use of firepower also. A number of other authors prefer strict limits including Clutterbuck, probably Kitson and probably Fall. Clutterbuck states that: "Worse still, if bombs were dropped in or near inhabited areas, the people's means of livelihood (rubber trees or cultivation) would be destroyed, and innocent people might be killed. One aborigine woman or child killed or maimed by bombing would leave a lasting scar on hundred of "hearts and minds. . . . Inhabited villages were never shelled, strafed, or bombed in Malaya. It can be argued that such attacks are justified if troops entering the village are likely to be fire upon, or even as a punishment for harboring Communist guerillas—whether or not such 'harboring' was willing or coerced. It has even been argued that the people would, in fact, turn against the Communists for bringing it down on their heads. Fortunately, however,

Army of the Republic of Vietnam (ARVN), 2nd Armored Cavalry Regiment troops with their American-supplied M-113 Armored Personnel Carriers (APCs), IV Corps area, Vietnam, 1962. At this time the U.S. Army was only there in a training and advisory role.—*photo by Nicholas Krawciw*

Center photo: This ARVN M-113 was destroyed by a 200-pound aerial bomb, buried in the ground, rigged with a remote control wire, and command detonated, Vietnam, IV Corps area, January 1963. These mines are now called IEDs (improvised explosive devices). This was the first M-113 lost in the Vietnam War. Eight U.S. soldiers were killed in this penetrated compartment, 3 were wounded (including Lt. Krawciw).—*photo from collection of Nicholas Krawciw*

Bottom: Vietnam, IV Corps. This was the crater left by an exploded 200-pound bomb that was converted to a command detonated mine.—*photo from collection of Nicholas Krawciw*

The 128th Aviation Company operation area, December 1965.—*photo by William A. Lawrence*

Vietnam, III Corps. "007," a helicopter gun ship before the development of the Cobra, December 1965.—*photo by William A. Lawrence*

Vietnam, III Corps. The wrong side of a Huey. Photo is labeled "First Crash," November 1965.—*photo by William A. Lawrence*

Vietnam, III Corps. Winning hearts and minds, hopefully, July 1966.—*photo by William A. Lawrence*

Vietnam, III Corps. Tay Ninh, March 1966.—*photo by William A. Lawrence*

Vietnam, III Corps. The Chinook unloading troops during a demonstration, Phoi Loi, March 1966. It was rarely done this way in operations. —*photo by William A. Lawrence*

Vietnam, III Corps. Viet Cong dead from a failed night assault on a U.S. camp, July 1966. The helicopters just rose over the parapets and emptied their fire on the enemy positions, dropped down to reload and then rose back up to fire again. It is claimed that 75 Viet Cong (VC) died in that attack.—*photo by William A. Lawrence*

Vietnam, I Corps, 1969. Command post protection platoon manning the machinegun.—*photo by Nicholas Krawciw*

Major Nicholas Krawciw is receiving congratulations and a Silver Star from General Richard G. Stilwell, Vietnam, 1969. General Stillwell was the nephew of the U S. General "Vinegar Joe" Stilwell of the China-Burma-India Theater in World War II.—*photo from collection of Nicholas Krawciw*

Vietnam, I Corps, 1969. A Hughes OH-6A Cayuse Light Observation Helicopter (LOH), part of the headquarters of the cavalry squadron. —*photo by friend of Nicholas Krawciw*

Vietnam, I Corps, 1969. A U.S. Army M-113 command vehicle. —*photo by Nicholas Krawciw*

U.S. Army M-113s, 3rd Squadron, 5th Cavalry, I Corps area, Vietnam, Spring 1969, near the demilitarized zone (DMZ), which was the border area between North and South Vietnam and hardly demilitarized. Note the improvements in the armament and the gun shields now on the M-113s.—*photo by Nicholas Krawciw*

Left: A Huey from the 116th Assault Helicopter Company (Hornets) unloading American troops in Vietnam, III Corps area, 1969.—*photo by SP David R. Wood,* Hawk *magazine, October 1969*

Center: "Slicks of the 116th AHC lay down suppressive fire on insertion in the 'Mushroom'" (photo and caption by SP David R. Wood, *Hawk* magazine, October 1969). The 116th AHC is the 116th Assault Helicopter Company (Hornets). The area called the "Mushroom" has not been identified.

"An M-60 machine gun is the only armament carried on a CH-47 Chinook" (photo and caption from *Hawk* magazine, November 1969). The CH-47 was from the 242nd Assault Helicopter Company (Muleskinners), 269th Aviation Battalion, III Corps area, 1969.

Base entrance, Vietnam.
—*photo by William A. Lawrence, 1969*

"Baron's Retreat," Vietnam.
—*photo by William A. Lawrence, 1969*

Party at the 269th Combat Aviation Battalion, Vietnam.
—*photo by William A. Lawrence, 1969*

Above: A Cobra gunship, no longer operable; *below:* also non-operable, a Cayuse, Vietnam 1969.—*both photos by William A. Lawrence*

Business end of a Cobra gunship. Pilot is in rear seat while gunner occupies front seat.—*photo by friend of William A. Lawrence, probably around 1970*

Rhino Runner, used to shuttle Embassy staff from Baghdad International Airport to the Green Zone, June 2004. —*photo by Jared Jalbert*

Boeing AH-64 Apache attack helicopter landing in Basra, June 2004.—*photo by Bill Allen*

Oil pipeline bombing near Basra, May 2004.—*photo by Jared Jalbert*

British forces re-deploying near Basra, June 2004.—*photo by Jared Jalbert*

Basra: Ambassador Bremer (on left, blue shirt and tie) in Basra, 17 June 2004. Ambassador Bremer was involved in some of the controversial decisions concerning the early management of the conflict. He was the leading American figure in Iraq at that time.— *photo by Jared Jalbert*

An Iraqi Soviet-built T-72 tank in Baghdad, March 2010. —*photo by Jared Jalbert*

U.S. Army near Kunduz, Afghanistan, 5 May 2008.—*photo by William A. Lawrence II*

Soviet Hind helicopter carcass used as a monument near Kunduz, 4 May 2008.—*photo by William A. Lawrence II*

Older mothballed Soviet-made police trucks at the police provincial HQ's in Baghlan Province. The Afghans said most were broke and they could not get parts for them.—*photo by William A. Lawrence II, 15 May 2008*

New police recruits   (557 police already killed this year)

Kunduz Province: New police recruits, 28 June 2008.—photo and legend by William A. Lawrence II

Unexploded ordnance from the police station in the city of Baghlan, 30 miles south of Kunduz. —*photo by William A. Lawrence II, 1 April 2009*

Suicide bomber in Baghlan Jadid, April 2009. The bomber was walking down the road trying to set of an explosive device as the photographer passed by in a truck. The bomb failed to explode. The bomber was found later by the local Afghan police still wearing the harness, but with no explosives. They released him.—*photo by William A. Lawrence II*

The old and the new, Soviet tank park next to the Dyncorp compound near Kunduz, 4 May 2008. Note the Soviet PT-76 light amphibious tanks.—*photo by William A. Lawrence II*

Tank park of Soviet tanks near Kunduz, 4 May 2008. These were left-over ordnance from the previous war.—*photo by William A. Lawrence II*

Near Jalalabad: Incoming police students, 30 July 2010.—*photo by William A. Lawrence II*

Afghan Police
in training,
5 October 2010.
—*photo by William
A. Lawrence II*

Afghan police
in training near
Jalalabad, 15
August 2010.
—*photo by William
A. Lawrence II*

A Russian designed
NSV 12.7mm
machinegun.
—*photo by William
A. Lawrence II,
12 August 2010*

Graduation day for 500 Afghan Border Police officers. Their basic academy was six weeks long and they were trained in small unit tactics, firearms, law enforcement, and conducting mobile and dismounted patrols utilizing their police vehicles.—*photo by William A. Lawrence II, 2010*

Market in Kabul, 18 September 2006.—*photo by Nicholas Klapmeyer*

Ruins of a Soviet tank near Kabul, 18 September 2006.—*photo by Nicholas Klapmeyer*

Picture of area of the missing statue of the Buddah, destroyed by the Taliban government when they were in charge, near Bamiyan, August 2006. —*photo by Nicholas Klapmeyer*

The Dupuy Institute researcher Nicholas Klapmeyer in Kabul, 18 September 2006.—*photo by friend of Nicholas Klapmeyer*

Picture from the Egyptian street protests (and revolution) in Cairo, 26 February 2011.—*photo by Nicholas Klapmeyer*

these arguments never prevailed in Malaya; if they had, I am quite sure that any village so attacked would never have cooperated with the government again."

Kitson states: "Accidents can play an appreciable part in embittering the population, especially if the impression is allowed to become established that the government is prepared to accept them for the sake of causing casualties to the enemy. . . . It is therefore reasonable to view with some reserve the use of a weapon system which is likely to cause them in a campaign which is ultimately based on the need to regain and retain the allegiance of the people." It is hard to say if "with some reserve" means strict use of firepower.

Galula clearly supports some limitations, O'Neill favors either restricted or strict, and the BDM report favors strict although leaning towards tightly restricted.

At the other end of the spectrum, Luttwak does not address this while Peters appears to favor something more like unrestricted use of firepower.

SUMMARY

Again, in boiling this down is a single chart, it can be seen is this case that *The Dupuy Institute's* work mostly parallels the British school, some of the Americans (Joes and BDM) and Bernard Fall. It does not so closely track with the French school on this.

THEORIST	RULES OF ENGAGEMENT	USE OF TORTURE	USE OF FIREPOWER
Manwaring	N/A	N/A	N/A
Trinquier	N/A	Limited	N/A
Joes	Strict?	No	Restricted
Galula	Restricted	Limited	Restricted?
Clutterbuck	Strict?	No	Strict
Fall	Strict?	N/A	Strict?
Kitson	Restricted?	N/A	Strict?
O'Neill	Restricted?	N/A	Restricted?
BDM	Strict	No	Strict
Luttwak	N/A	Brutal?	N/A
Peters	Restricted?	N/A	Unrestricted?
The Dupuy Institute	Strict?	See Chapter Nine	Strict?

C. FORCE RATIOS

The Dupuy Institute conducted an analysis of Force Ratios, the specific details of which are in Chapter Four. This emphasis on force ratios is perhaps the most controversial element of our work.

Surprising for such a central and critical issue, it is not address by Manwaring, Trinquier or the BDM report.

It is clear important to Bernard Fall and he mentions the 10-to-1 rule. Joes specifically recommends committing sufficient forces, but it is uncertain if he means something akin to 10-to-1 ratio. Galula states: "Because the counterinsurgent cannot escape the responsibility for maintaining order, the ratio of expenses between him and the insurgent is high. It may be ten or twenty to one, or higher."

It is the British school seems to think it is not important. Clutterbuck (quoted in Chapter Four) clearly states that is it not. Kitson does not specifically address force ratios, but he appears to oppose to the idea that they are important. O'Neill goes as far as to say ". . . implicitly in the often-misleading rule of thumb that government needs a favorable ten-to-one ratio of military forces to subdue guerillas"

Fundamentally, Fall, Galula and Joes come down heavily on the 10-to-1 to 20-to-1 rule for force ratios. Manwaring, Trinquier, and Kitson do not address it, and Clutterbuck and O'Neill claim it is not the important point and, by implication, so does Kitson. This last point is a position that has also been adopted by RAND and in FMI 3-07.22 (October 1984). However, the current revision of that U.S. counter insurgency manual, FM 3-24, stresses the need for sufficient forces.

SUMMARY

Again, this single issue, boiled down to a single chart, shows the comparison. In this case *The Dupuy Institute's* work mostly parallels the French school, and Joes. We appears to be opposite to the ideas of the British school, although as we have always noted before, they usually had favorable, and in many cases, overwhelming force ratios, in the insurgencies that they fought.

THEORIST	FORCE RATIOS
Manwaring	N/A
Trinquier	N/A
Joes	Yes
Galula	Yes
Clutterbuck	No!
Fall	Yes
Kitson	No?
O'Neill	No
BDM	N/A
The Dupuy Institute	Yes

D. NATURE OF INSURGENCIES

The Dupuy Institute conducted an analysis of five factors that it considered to be part of the basic nature of insurgencies. These are Degree of Outside Support, Political Concept of the Insurgency, Structure of the Insurgency, Strategic Approach (using the definitions established by Bard O'Neill) and Type of Insurgency (using the definitions established by Bard O'Neill). The first three categories are *The Dupuy Institute* creations. The last two were taken from Bard O'Neill at the request of CAA and applied to the insurgency in general, even though he usually applied it only to specific insurgent groups.

DEGREE OF OUTSIDE SUPPORT

This issue was not addressed by Trinquier, Clutterbuck, Kitson or the BDM report. It was probably not addressed by the members of the British school because it was not a major issue during their various insurgencies.

Galula is a little ambivalent on this, stating: ". . . outside support in the middle and later stages of an insurgency. . . . is a help that may become a necessity"

On the other hand, the American school usually picks up on this as a major factor, as our experience was Vietnam. Manwaring states that is it important to isolate the guerilla. O'Neill indicates that more outside support is better.

Some feel it is more important that that. Joes is very clear that they need to isolate the combat area, and that it is one of the three most important elements (the other two being high force ratios and elections). Bernard Fall states: "In brute fact, the success of failure of all rebellions since World War II depended entirely on whether the active sanctuary was willing and able to perform its expected role. . . . A guerilla's logistical requirement may be simpler than that of a large regular force, but it has some rock-bottom needs which must be filled through outside support, or it dies."

POLITICAL CONCEPT OF THE INSURGENCY

The political concept of an insurgency was a definition developed by *The Dupuy Institute*, and therefore, not surprisingly; few of the earlier theorists addressed this. This included Manwaring, Trinquier, Joes and Clutterbuck.

On the other hand, several theorists considered the insurgent cause to be important or essentially important. O'Neill states: "Aside from this essentially nationalist variation, the general effectiveness of esoteric appeals as a method of gaining popular support should not be overemphasized." The BDM report favored insurgencies based upon "nationalism." Kitson stressed cause and focused on nationalism as one such example. Fall very much focused on cause and focused on nationalism as a cause in his writings. Galula very much stressed cause as one of the two most important parts (cause and counterinsurgent administrative weakness were his two major parts).

STRUCTURE OF THE INSURGENCY

The structure of the insurgency was also definition developed by *The Dupuy Institute*, and as expected, few of the earlier theorists addressed this, including Trinquier, Joes, Galula, Clutterbuck, Fall and Kitson.

Only the American school picked on this issue, with Manwaring stressing unity of effort, with more structure is assumed to be better. Both O'Neill and the BDM report indicated the more structure and organization was better. This is somewhat different the finding we presented in Chapter Eight.

STRATEGIC APPROACH

Strategic Approach was based upon a Bard O'Neill definition and as such, was not really addressed by any of the other theorists. O'Neill defined it, rather than analyzed it, but it appears he favors the category he called Protracted Popular War (PPW). Our analysis supported that.

TYPE OF INSURGENCY

The Type of Insurgency was also based upon a Bard O'Neill definition, and as such, was not really addressed by any of the other theorists. O'Neill defined it, rather than analyzed it. By default, since he favors insurgencies based upon nationalism, then his secessionist category favors the insurgents. His secessionist category is similar to our political concept based upon a central idea (usually nationalism). In his case, though his secessionist category includes a number of insurgencies conducting by minorities in countries that were looking to secede from that country. We usually code those as "limited' or "regional". What we did find was that we obtained better fits using our political concept definitions than we were able to obtain using Bard O'Neill's definitions.[4] This was primarily because the definitions were created for different reasons. Ours were specifically created for analysis, while his were more intended to be explanatory.

SUMMARY

To summarize the viewpoints on these five factors that are indicative of the basic nature of insurgencies:

THEORIST	DEGREE OF OUTSIDE SUPPORT	POLITICAL CONCEPT OF THE INSURGENCY	STRUCTURE OF THE INSURGENCY	STRATEGIC APPROACH	TYPE OF INSURGENCY
Manwaring	Important	N/A	Important	N/A	N/A
Trinquier	N/A	N/A	N/A	N/A	N/A
Joes	Important!	N/A	N/A	N/A	N/A
Galula	Sometimes	Important	N/A	N/A	N/A
Clutterbuck	N/A	N/A	N/A	N/A	N/A
Fall	Important	Important (nationalism)	N/A	N/A	N/A
Kitson	N/A	Important (nationalism)	N/A	N/A	N/A
O'Neill	Important	Nationalism	Important	PPW is best?	Secessionist?
BDM	N/A	Nationalism	Important	N/A	N/A
The Dupuy Institute	Not important	Important (central idea)	Not important	PPW is best	Secessionist

E. MEASUREMENTS OF BURDEN

The Dupuy Institute as part of its Task 11 report (and is discussed in Chapter Fifteen of this book) measured the impact of the burden of fighting an insurgency per 100,000 home population. This was calculated for commitment (average number of troops committed per-year-per-100,000 population) and intensity (average troops killed-per-year-per-100,000 population). These measurements were then evaluated for intervening forces, indigenous government forces, insurgents, civilian casualties and total forces. Each of these issues is addressed below. As the Measurements of Burden was work, that as far as we know, was unique to *The Dupuy Institute*, not surprisingly, it is rarely addressed by most of these authors.

INTERVENING, GOVERNMENT, INSURGENT OR TOTAL FORCE COMMITMENT

Manwaring did not address the burden of fighting these wars, but does say, "The need to 'stay the course' remains constant." The other eight authors did not address this issue of the burden of force commitment.

The Dupuy Institute's findings on this are a little complex, but the following two conclusions were reached, albeit with questionable statistical support,

> *III.A.2. It appears that when the average level of commitment by an outside power exceeds more than 0.1% of the population of the intervening country, then the insurgency wins in two-thirds of the cases.*
> *III.B.2. It appears that when the average level of commitment by the indigenous government exceeds more than 1% of the population of the indigenous country, then the insurgency succeeds in almost two-thirds of the cases.*

See the Task 11 report for more details. The issue of "staying the course" is specifically addressed in Appendix IX of this book.

INTERVENING, GOVERNMENT, INSURGENT INTENSITY

None of the nine authors specifically addressed the burden of losses on maintaining an insurgency or counterinsurgent effort.

The Dupuy Institute findings on this are a little complex, but the following conclusion was reached with some statistical support:

> *IV.A.2. It appears that when the average intervening forces killed facing an insurgency exceeds more than 0.001% of the population of the intervening country, then the insurgency succeeds in over two-thirds of the cases.*

The parallel conclusion concerning indigenous forces and overall population are not well supported. See the Task 11 report for more details.

F. OPERATIONAL DETAILS—ACTIVE SANCTUARIES, BORDER CONTROLS AND POPULATION RESETTLEMENT

The Dupuy Institute as part of Tasks 5 & 8 report under the CAA contract conducted a preliminary analysis of Sanctuaries, Border Barriers, and Population Resettlement. We did not find a strong relationship between presence of Sanctuaries and outcome. Still, the insurgents won 52% of the time when there was a sanctuary vice 31% of the time when there was not one. In the case of border barriers, there was a statistical correlation, but that was that border barriers favored the insurgency. The insurgents won 69% of the time when there was a border barrier vice 30% of the time when there was not one. We suspect that there is another factor at work here (border barriers are usually built in response to large, intractable insurgencies). In the case of population resettlement, there was again a statistical correlation that showed that population resettlement favored the insurgency. The insurgents won 80% of the time when there was population resettlement vice 30% of the time where there was not. Again, we suspect that there is another factor at work here.

These results in some respect were surprising and sometimes counterintuitive. A number of theorists have discussed this aspect in depth, so let's walk though each.

SANCTUARY

Manwaring, Kitson and the BDM report do not discuss the value of Sanctuaries. Clutterbuck does not really address them other than in the context of Malayan insurgency history.

O'Neill takes a very nuanced look at the subject with: "But, while one might agree with the general thrust of this proposition, three qualifications should be kept in mind when examining external support. First, there are exceptions where the insurgents accomplished their goal with minuscule or no sanctuaries; second, the presence of sanctuaries may be less important in explaining development than other factors; and, third, the specific contributions of sanctuaries vary from case to case."

On the other hand, the French school tends to see them as very important. Galula states that "The length of the borders, particularly if the neighboring countries are sympathetic to the insurgents, as was the case in Greece, Indochina, and Algeria, favors the insurgent."

Bernard Fall states: "Still, special geopolitical conditions may bring about a situation particularly favorable to the sustenance of a revolutionary war. Probably the most important such condition is the existence of what—for want of a better term—-I call an active sanctuary . . . In brutal fact, the success or failure of all rebellions since World War II depended entirely on whether the active sanctuary was willing and able to perform its expected role. . . . As long as the problem of the active sanctuary is not solved politically as well as militarily, the West might as well settle down to a long losing streak of 'brushfire wars'."

Trinquier seems to be even more adamant than Fall in the statement: "The destruction or neutralization of enemy bases on foreign territory is essential if we are to hasten the end of hostilities and ensure a durable peace."

Joes considers that isolating the combat area is one of his three most important points. "If it is believed impossible to cut off, or at least greatly impeded, outside help to the guerillas, the wisest course may be to decline to undertake a counter-guerilla effort."

Joes is one of the few theorists to suggest that if you cannot create favorable conditions, then perhaps you should decline to undertake the counterinsurgency.

BORDER BARRIERS

Border barriers are closely related to sanctuaries, in that this is one of the primary ways of isolating them. Clutterbuck, Kitson and the BDM report do not address border barriers, which is not surprising as they also do not address sanctuaries. Galula does not address them either, which is surprising considering that he does address sanctuaries, and the Algerian war he participate made extensive and almost successful use of them.

O'Neill leaves you wonder what his position is on border barriers while Manwaring provides a very limited statement: "The logical need to isolate belligerents from sources of support is obvious in any number of contemporary cases."

Both Trinquier and Fall don't have a strong view of the importance of border barriers. Trinquier states: "No doubt the barrier has a certain value, but it has no effect on the combat potential the enemy can rally together with impunity along the frontiers." In the end, he concludes that you need to conduct cross-border attacks at enemy bases by using guerilla forces.

Fall states: "And while the complete closing of the South Vietnamese border to infiltrators certainly remains a worthwhile objective, to achieve it along 700 miles of jungle-covered mountains and swamp would just about absorb the totality of South Viet-Nam's 1964 forces of 250,000 regulars and 250,000 paramilitary troops of various kinds."

It is hard to determine what Joes believes on border barriers, but in like of "isolating the combat area" being one of his three most important points, it is suspected he provides some qualified support for them.

It is interesting to note that as much as several theorists considered sanctuaries to be a critical factor, not one of them considered border barriers to be the obvious answer.

POPULATION RESETTLEMENT

Population resettlement has become a major effort in several different wars (Malaya, Algeria and Vietnam), and certainly played a very prominent part in our early efforts in Vietnam with the strategic hamlets program. Only Manwaring did not address them.

Trinquier clearly favored creating Strategic Hamlets, Clutterbuck appears to favor it for both Malaya and Vietnam. Joes did not address the subject in his paper. A review of his book, *The War for South Viet Nam*[5] indicates that he thinks they are a very good idea. Kitson seems to favor them and was our impression with O'Neill's writing. BDM seemed ambililent about them

On the other hand Galula clear states: "Resettlement clearly is a last-resort measure, born out of the counterinsurgent's weakness. It should be undertaken only if the trend of the war definitely shows no prospect for the counterinsurgent forces to deploy safely to the required level. If such is the case, resettlement must first be carefully tested in a limited way in order to detect the problems arising with the operation and to get the necessary experience." Bernard Fall was clearly not impressed with the idea except as it applied to the situation in Malaya.

SUMMARY

To summarize the viewpoints on these three factors on operational details:

THEORIST	SANCTUARY	BORDER BARRIER	POPULATION RESETTLEMENT
Manwaring	N/A	Yes?	N/A
Trinquier	Yes	Maybe?	Yes
Joes	Yes?	Yes?	Yes
Galula	Maybe?	N/A	No
Clutterbuck	N/A	N/A	Yes?
Fall	Yes!	Maybe?	No
Kitson	N/A	N/A	Yes?
O'Neill	Maybe?	Maybe?	Yes?
BDM	N/A	N/A	Maybe?
The Dupuy Institute	Maybe?	Negative	Negative

G. SCORECARD

If we make the gross and potentially erroneous assumption that our analytically derived conclusions are correct, we can score all the theorists based upon how close they match across the 17 categories we examined.[6] Let us say that a match is worth 2 points, somewhat of a match is worth 1 point, and no match at all is zero points. If the issue is not addressed, it is assumed to mean that it is unimportant or not a factor. This will produce a total number of points indicating a degree of agreement with *The Dupuy Institute* (for example, Galula basically agrees with *The Dupuy Institute* in 6 out of the 7 points on the subject of terrain). They are listed below in five categories. The total is simply the total of points, which by default gives significant weight to terrain. If all categories are given equal weight, and every one is valued as a percent of the *The Dupuy Institute* value (i.e. 12 out 14 points = 0.86), then we get a degree of agreement weighted by category.

THE SCORECARD

THEORIST	TERRAIN	RULES	FORCE RATIOS	NATURE	OPERATIONAL	TOTAL	WEIGHTED BY CATEGORY
The Dupuy Institute	14	6	2	6	6	34	5.00
Galula	12	3	2	5	6	28	4.19
Fall	6	4	2	4	4	20	3.43
Clutterbuck	7	6	0	4	3	20	2.67
BDM	6	6	0	3	4	19	2.60
Kitson	6	3	0	6	3	18	2.43
Joes	6	5	2	0	1	14	2.43
O'Neill	12	2	0	1	3	18	1.86
Trinquier	6	1	0	4	2	13	1.59
Manwaring	6	0	0	0	3	9	0.93

While this is admittedly a poor way to evaluate these authors, it does provide a nice quantified summary and some insights. Obviously, shorter works leave lots of details out, and that lowers their score. This clearly affected Joes' score. Fall was similarly affected by the fact that his was not a theoretical, doctrinal work, so some issues were not addressed in depth. Still, this does indicate our general sense that the works of Fall and Galula most closely parallel our own. There are good discussions on terrain in Galula and O'Neill. In general, there are lot of areas of disagreement as to what issues should be addressed in the BDM report, O'Neill, Trinquier and Manwaring. There are some fundamental disagreements (force ratios) with Kitson and Clutterbuck.

If you fundamentally think our analysis of insurgencies is correct, then we would recommend you read Galula and Fall. If you think what we have presented here in this book is fundamentally wrong, then there is a list above seven other authors that you can consult.

II. ACTUAL STRATEGIES TO BE MEASURED (LARGER THEORETICAL CONSTRUCTS TESTED)

The second comparison of our work with the other theorists consisted of testing any larger theoretical constructs they proposed to our data. What we chose to focus on were the clear, overarching theoretical constructs that each of them chose to develop. At some point in their writings, they would summarize what these are in two important points (Fall), or three (Joes), or four (Galula), or six (Manwaring) or 14 (the BDM report). These constructs are very useful as they could be a basis for building a model of insurgencies. The first question is: Are they right? Let's walk through each of them.

A. MANWARING'S LARGER THEORETICAL CONSTRUCT

His basic construct is that all six of these elements must be present to some degree to be able to win (counterinsurgent win):

1. Moral Legitimacy
2. Appropriate use of military force
3. Isolate belligerents
4. Stay the course
5. Intelligence
6. Unity of Effort

Looking at each of these separately, we evaluated his conclusions into one of three categories (yes, some and no) so we could compare them to ours.

1. Moral Legitimacy—His focus here is on the moral legitimacy of the insurgents. In effect, less moral legitimacy of the insurgents is good for the counterinsurgency. We do have an existing measure that overlaps with this category to some extent, which is "Political Concept," which is "limited" (yes), "central" (no) and overarching (some).
2. Appropriate use of military force—The author favors restricted rules of engagement. Therefore, we will take the measure "Rules of Engagement" and treat "polite" and "strict" as yes, "restricted" as "some", and "unrestricted" and "brutal" as "no."
3. Isolate belligerents—The author favors isolation of the guerillas. Therefore, we will take the measure "primarily indigenous" as "yes," "some outside support" as "some" and "considerable outside support" as "no."
4. Stay the course—Not sure what this really means. Therefore, we simply chose to tie it to duration of the insurgency (which is kind of an after the fact measurement). Durations of greater than 14 years is "yes," duration of 7–14 years is "some" and durations of less than 7 years is "no." These durations are based upon our previous analysis of the data.
5. Intelligence—We have no way of specifically measuring this, so this factor is ignored for now.
6. Unity of Effort - The author favors unified counterinsurgent command. This is measureable but we did not measure it in our work.

The hypothesis to test is: "To the extent that these factors or dimensions are strongly present in any given strategy, they favor success. To the extent that any one is absent, or only present in a weak form, the probability of success is minimal." Basically, all five of the measurable factors have to be "yes" to favor success in this construct.

The Dupuy Institute tested three of these factors independently, that is "Appropriate Use of Military Force," "Isolate Belligerents" and "Stay the Course," and has effectively tested "Moral Legitimacy." In the case of the second one (Isolate belligerents), we determined that this is not a significant factor. This subject is discussed in depth in Chapter Ten of this book and our CAA Task 5 & 8 report. In the case of

"Stay the Course," this is a red herring, in that as measured by people killed per 100,000 population, the insurgencies are favored once the level of violence goes up to the rather low level of 8 killed per 100,000 per year. There is a strong tendency for longer duration insurgencies to result in blue wins. That means the insurgency must last longer than 14 years (15.52 actually). Let's look at the data for a moment:

DURATION VERSUS RESULTS

DURATION	INSURGENCY CASES	BLUE WINS	RED WINS	GRAY RESULTS	OTHER CASES	BLUE WINS	RED WINS	GRAY RESULTS
0–7 Years	25	9	13	3	17	11	3	3
7–14 Years	25	11	11	3	2	1	0	1
14+ Years	12	10	2	0	2	1	0	1

As can be seen, insurgencies win as often as not until such time as they last longer than 15.52 years. Yet this is misleading and was therefore examined in depth in Appendix IX, especially as the "stay the course" argument comes up in various forms in the writings of the authors (for example, Trinquier). Therefore, we needed to look in depth at exactly what that entailed. What we did in Appendix IX was focus only on those insurgencies that has outside intervening forces (INS/I and INS/C) as the INS/NI appeared to have different patterns to them. Our analysis in Appendix IX showed that is was probably not the duration of the insurgency that mattered, but its intensity and cost. Quite simply, once insurgencies with outside intervening forces totaled more the 0.59 killed per 100,000 population of the home country, they lost in 75% of the cases (12 out of 16). The other four cases included one unresolved case (U.S. in Iraq), two cases of counterinsurgent victory that included a withdrawal by the intervening power, and only one real exception (Cuba in Angola). This appeared to be relatively disconnected from the issue of duration. The upper limit of "staying the course" appeared to be around 30 cumulative deaths out of 100,000 population, regardless of the nature of the regime (democratic, dictatorship or communist) and regardless of the situation. There simply appears to be an upper limit to staying the course. As our database includes all the major insurgencies (bloodiest) against intervening forces since World War II, then one is left with no examples of anyone staying the course past a level of 10 killed per 100,000 population and only one real case (possibly more as we have not studied every post-World War II insurgency) of a Blue win past the rather low figure of 0.59 cumulative killed per 100,000 population.

Therefore, the "stay the course" option suggested by Manwaring and also Trinquier is a request for an action that to date only one country has been able to do. Above the level of 10 killed per 100,000, no country has been able to do so since World War II. **Essentially, they are suggesting a strategy for a country that does not exist.** The real world data indicates that this is no strategy at all and in the long run effectively doomed to failure, as there is almost no country, whether democratic, dictatorial or communist, whether French, Russian or American, whether large or small, that will be able to sustain such a strategy once the level of pain in an outside intervention exceeds 0.59 cumulative casualties per 100,000.[7] While "staying the course" may be perceived by some as a valid strategy for horse racing and slots, it is not one for an outside intervening force that faces an insurgency that can cause enough accumulated casualties over time.

Still, "staying the course" is a valid approach as long as the insurgency is not too intense or as long as it is strictly internal (INS/NI), but intensity not duration, seems to be the bigger issue here.

Finally, by default, the measurement of "Moral Legitimacy" is effectively covered by "Political Concept of Insurgency" where those based upon a central idea are considered "morally legitimate." As such, these win 68% of the time, compared to 28% for "limited" and 30% for "overarching."

So, out of the six factors in his construct, we were effectively able to measure four. Of those, two are clearly not a major factor across insurgencies in general, and two are significant (moral legitimacy and appropriate use of military force). With half the measurable elements of his construct in considerable doubt, we did not see any reason to further test this construct.

B. TRINQUIER

Trinquier was the first book-length treatise we reviewed, and one of the more original ones. For example, he raised the issue of the use of torture (or nature of interrogation), which we tested by default and is discussed in Chapter Nine. He also talked about such things as the need for the blue side to initiate the combat actions, the degree of freedom of the press, use of internal passports, size and extent of blue side intelligence organization, the legal environment, and types of strategic plans. We didn't specifically test any of these, although we feel that they all need to be tested at some point. He also talked about participation in local defense organizations, which we did not test specifically but for all practical purposes tested in the much larger sense (percent mobilized).

In our Task 11 report, we note that: "It appears that when the average level of commitment by an outside power exceeds more the 0.1% of the population of the intervening country (more than 141 per 100,000 home population), then the insurgency wins in two-thirds of the cases."

Now, this is only built upon 13 cases, where 4 were blue wins and 9 were red wins, but it does appear to be part of a larger pattern, where once the level of commitment to fighting an insurgency gets high, the insurgents tend to win. Therefore, it makes one wonder if a mass mobilization scheme serves as a useful aid in fighting insurgencies or whether the need for it is an indicator that the government is facing a much bigger problem (lack of popular support).

He also talked about taking action against border sanctuaries, which we did not test specifically, although we discuss the whole issue of outside support and barriers in some depth in Chapter Ten and Tasks 5 & 8, where it is addressed to some extent in the Outside Support variable. In this particular case, we note that:

1. A lack of outside support does not necessarily doom an insurgency
2. Considerable outside support does not mean an insurgency will win
3. There appears to be little correlation between the degree of outside support for an insurgency and the outcome of the insurgency.

Beyond testing specific recommendations, there was no clear overarching theory that we could test in the case of Trinquier. His work is fundamentally a tactical and operational discussion, and as such, it may have value in those realms, but it was not directly comparable to the other books referenced in this study, which tended to also look at the strategic picture. More analysis of specific tactics and operational approaches proposed by Trinquier needs to be conducted.

C. JOES

Joes's article being only four pages left out many of the details that are probably in his more extensive books and focused primarily on his overarching construct. His larger theoretical construct was ". . . [S]haping the strategic environment consists of (1) isolating the combat area, (2) committing sufficient forces, and (3) offering the population of the contested region a peaceful path for the alleviation of grievances." According to Joes, the counterinsurgent needed all three to win, and a shortfall in one (or at least in isolating the combat area) leads to defeat.

This construct has been tested to some extent in each of its individual parts. As outlined in Chapter Six, force ratios do matter when facing an insurgency based upon a central or overarching idea. They need to be greater than 5-to-1 to win (there are no exceptions in our data). Between 5-to-1 and 10-to-1, they win 46 percent of the time. Above 10-to-1 (actually above 10.67-to-1), they win 8 percent of the time. Clearly this is a dominant factor.

In the case of isolating the combat area, our analysis of outside support in Chapter Eight and as discussed in some depth in the CAA Tasks 5 & 8 report, shows that this is really not critical. While always helpful, it does not guarantee that the insurgents will lose (as shown in spades by Algeria). Therefore, we do not think that this should be one of three major parts of an overarching construct. Like Manwaring, Joes may have been overly influenced by the U.S. experience in Vietnam.

For the issue of Free Elections, there is some basis for believing that it is a clear factor for those insurgencies where there are no significant outside interventions (primarily domestic insurgencies), but the situation is not as clear for insurgencies with significant outside interventions (insurgencies against foreigners). We examine this issue in depth in Chapter Twelve of this book. In that chapter we concluded that:

One notes a significant trend across this data which is:

1. For those insurgencies with significant outside interventions (insurgencies against foreigners). We note that

    a) Indigenous government type has no significantly measurable influence. In fact, in all but five cases the indigenous government is a dictatorship.

    b) Intervening government type does not seem to matter.

    c) Elections do not seem to matter.

2. For those insurgencies without significant outside intervening forces (primarily domestic insurgencies)

    a) Having the indigenous government as a Democracy or Troubled Democracy clearly favors the Blue side. This result is statistically significant.

    b) Having elections favor the Blue side. This result is statistically significant.

One wonders if the process of intervention undercuts the benefits of democracy.

This is clearly an area that needs to be studied further. We specifically looked at the government type of the indigenous government in the insurgency, the government type of the intervening forces and whether elections were held. It does indicate that there are some bases for Joes' comments, but it is not clear if this is indeed one of the three main points.

Therefore, with two of the three major factors of this construct in question, we do not feel this is a very useful construct. Still, we choose to give it a fair try and test all three elements of the construct across all 62 insurgencies. The data is provided in Appendix X.

Joes specifically stated the variable was to "isolate the combat area," vice the degree of outside support, but it becomes somewhat difficult to measure this unless we create a new set of rules of how to measure that, assign values (i.e. "yes," "maybe," or "no"), and then go through the 62 insurgencies and make the judgment calls. We suspect that the calls would pretty much parallel our existing variable "Degree of outside support," so we used that instead. Still, it is somewhat different that what Joes discussed, so one must be aware that this is a not a perfect test. Joes does note in his writings that Malaya and Algeria would qualify as cases where they were isolated ("yes"), while Vietnam and Afghanistan would qualify as cases where they were not ("no"). One notes that only one of these (Malaya) is a blue win.

In the case of elections, our election variable is whether or not elections were held. We did not determine if they were free or not, and in fact, some were decidedly not free. By Joes' own statements, Greece, Malaya, South Vietnam and Northern Ireland were free elections (and failed insurgencies). We rated the government type as democracies in two of these cases, troubled democracy in one and a dictatorship (a colonial) government in the case of Malaya. We also consider Vietnam to be a successful insurgency, unlike Joes. Still, we are comfortable using indigenous government type as a substitute for whether there were free elections or not. There are three common options, democracy, troubled democracy and dictatorship.

As Joes specifically states that one needs all three conditions, in this case interpreted as high force ratios (above 5 to 1), isolated insurgents (primarily indigenous) and elections (democracy or troubled democracy), we note that we have only five cases out of 62 that fit this description. Four are blue wins, and one is a gray result (the democratic government was overthrown and replaced a dictatorship). All are INS/NI's (no significant outside intervening forces) and "Latin American" in a sense. If one expands the list to include "some outside support," then one ends up with nine additional cases, of which six are blue wins, two are gray results (draw or ongoing) and one is a red win. Eight are INS/NI. If one looks at all the INS/NI above 5-to-1 force ratios, then one notes that there were 17, of which 13 of them are blue wins and only one is a red win. More to the point, of those 17 cases, 13 of them are democracies or troubled democracies with 10 of them being blue wins, while four of them are not democracies with three of them being blue wins. Certainly, this provides no argument to support Joes' theme past the issue of force ratios. Clearly government type is not an issue when it comes to the high force ratio. None of the INS/NI has considerable outside support.

The high force ratio INS/I and INS/C examples consists of 13 cases, of which only one is indigenous or only some outside support and democratic or troubled democracy (U.S. in Iraq 2003 to present). The other twelve cases either have considerable outside support and an indigenous dictatorship or theocracy. Of those, eight are blue wins.

To summarize for the high force ratio cases:

TYPE	LITTLE OR SOME OUTSIDE SUPPORT	DEMOCRACY OR TROUBLED DEMOCRACY	CASES	BLUE WINS	GRAY RESULTS	RED WINS
INS/NI	Yes	Yes	13	10	2	1
INS/NI	Yes	No	3	1	1	1
INS/NI	No	Yes	0	0	0	0
INS/NI	No	No	1	1	0	0
INS/I or C	Yes	Yes	1	0	1	0
INS/I or C	Yes	No	9	5	0	4
INS/I or C	No	Yes	2	2	0	0
INS/I or C	No	No	1	1	0	0

So, we have 14 cases that sort of meet Joes' requirements and 16 cases that do not. To express the comparison in a table:

TYPE	CASES	BLUE WINS	GRAY RESULTS	RED WINS
May Meet Joes' Requirements	14	10	3	4
Clearly does not meet Joes' Requirements	16	10	1	5

While the difference of 71% blue wins for those meeting Joes' requirements may be better than the 63% blue wins for those that do not, it is certainly not significant. The major difference is in the red wins, which clearly favor those that may meet Joes' requirements.

So, while this data clearly does not support Joes' construct beyond the issue of force ratios, this does not mean that these is no value to isolating them from outside support or no value to attempting democratic reforms; it just means that they are a second order effect when compared to force ratios.

More to the point, only two data points actually fulfill Joes' ideal requirements (high force ratio, primarily indigenous, and democracy). One is a blue win (Puerto Rico 1950–1954, a truly insignificant insurgency), and one is a gray result (Uruguay 1963–1973). There are 28 other blue wins out of our 62 classic insurgencies. Of those 28 other blue wins, 9 are with low force ratios, 6 are in the face of considerable outside support and 15 are with the indigenous government being a dictatorship or theocracy. Clearly there is no basis for accepting James Joes' three-point construct.

JOES' SEVEN BASIC COMPONENTS

As Joes states:

> With the above three conditions securely in place, an insurgency is already strategically defeated, and might well fizzle out with little actual fighting. But assuming the insurgency persists, the second part of the strategy—defeating the guerrillas on the ground—has seven basic components: (1) practicing rectitude toward civilians, prisoners and enemy defectors; (2) emphasizing the key role of intelligence; (3) establishing civilian security; (4) separating guerrilla leaders from their followers; (5) offering timely and well-aimed amnesties; (6) draining the rebellious area(s) of weapons; and (7) interdicting guerrilla food supplies.

Most of these seven basic components have not been tested by us. In the case of "rectitude," this has been examined in depth in Chapter Nine. On this the data appears to be in agreement with Joes. We have found no easy way of testing intelligence. In the case of civilian security, we note in our Task 11 report that we have civilian casualty data from 39 out of 83 cases but only for 28 out of 62 insurgencies. Our analysis of this data seems to indicate that there is a correlation between percent of civilians killed and outcome (more killed favored the insurgents), but everything we found was far from statistically significant. Therefore, we have no clear results to support or contradict this point. Separating guerilla leaders is another one that is difficult to determine without going back through each of the 62 insurgencies and making a judgment call as to whether this was done or not. In the case of Amnesty, this is addressed in two fields in our data bases. One of those fields is Amnesty during Fighting and the other is Amnesty during Settlement. These fields are coded as "none," "limited," "general" and "complete."

In the case of Amnesty during Fighting, which is the closest equivalent to what Joes is addressing, we have 56 out of the 62 cases coded. Of those 56 cases, 23 are coded as "none," 15 of those are coded as "limited," 14 of those are coded as "general" and 4 of those are coded as "complete." To compare them to each other for the 62 insurgencies:

AMNESTY DURING FIGHTING	CASES	BLUE WINS	GRAY RESULTS	RED WINS
None	23	9	4	10
Limited	15	7	1	7
General	14	9	1	4
Complete	4	2	0	2
Total	56	27	6	23
Not Coded	6	2	0	4

If there is any relationship it is between general amnesty and outcome. Is the tendency for more blue wins to involve general amnesty because general amnesty increases the chance of a blue win, or because an insurgency being won by the counterinsurgent have the luxury or develop the equanimity to offer amnesties?

And, for the other 21 cases (not classic insurgencies):

AMNESTY DURING FIGHTING	CASES	BLUE WINS	GRAY RESULTS	RED WINS
None	11	7	2	2
Limited	3	1	1	1
General	2	0	2	0
Complete	4	4	0	0
Total	20	12	5	3
Not Coded	1	1	0	0

210 AMERICA'S MODERN WARS

We do not see any clear relationships in this data. Still, it is not hard to imagine that some form of amnesty will speed the end of a war.

We have yet to look at either draining weapons or interdicting food supplies. These should probably be tested at some point.

Overall, we have not found that a lot of Joes work is supported by our data and in some cases, is probably not supportable. Some points appear to be overrated in their importance in the overall picture. We do not believe the Joes serves as a good theoretical basis for understanding insurgencies.

D. GALULA

David Galula's 1964 106-page book definitely covers a wide range of variables and issues. Some of these have been addressed above, and as Galula influenced Joes, his variables related to civilian losses and force ratios have been addressed in our discussion on Joes. There is still a need to look at the strategy (Galula recommends "ink blot") and a host of other factors that Galula discussed such as Nature of Command (Committee, Integrated Civilian-Military Staff, Integrated Military-Civilian Staff versus Primarily Military), Timing of Reforms (Before the insurgency, Early in the insurgency, Middle of the insurgency, End of the insurgency, After the insurgency, or Never), Billeting of Troops (Among the population, In camps in the villages, Outside of the villages or in Central Strongholds), Control of Villages (Strict, Restricted, Unrestricted), Degree of Public Works (Limited and local, Some counterinsurgent help, Considerable Counterinsurgent help), Local Government (None, Appointed by Counterinsurgents, Appointed by non-democratic National Government, Appointed by elected national government, Locally elected separate (before) from national elections, Locally elected after (or in conjunction) with national elections) and a number of other issues. Still we have looked at a wide range of issues that Galula addressed.

Some of his other variables that were addressed include Percent of Urban Population, which was measured as the actual percent urban population in a country. This was tested and is discussed above in Chapter Thirteen and in the CAA Task 12 report. The issue of Nature of the Insurgent Cause (No real cause, Captureable cause and Unique dynamic cause) is addressed to some extent in Chapter Five and the CAA Task 4 & 7 report with the analysis of the Political Concept behind an insurgency. The nature and type of reforms (i.e. Land redistribution, Income redistribution, Anticolonialism, Independence, Communism, Socialism, Free Market, Democracy, Political Reform, "Throw the Rascals Out," ethnic differences) is addressed to some extent in the CAA Task 4 & 7 report. The Protection of the Population is addressed in the discussion above of Joes as one of his seven basic components.

Galula did offer a larger theoretical construct, one of only two that we feel has real value. This was based upon four major points:

1. Insurgents need a cause
2. A police and administrative weakness
3. A non-hostile geographic environment
4. Outside support in middle to late stages

He specifically states that: "The first two are musts. The last is a help that may become a necessity."

This was the most interesting construct that *The Dupuy Institute* found besides those tangentially proposed by Bernard Fall. In this case the cause of the insurgent can be measured by *The Dupuy Institute* created variable called Political Concept. We have no measurement for "administrative weakness." On the other hand, if one substitutes force ratios for "administrative weakness," then one is back to the *The Dupuy Institute* model of the two most important factors being force ratio and cause. As Galula says that the two most important factors (factors that are a "must") are 1) "insurgents need a cause" (or "nature of insurgent cause") and 2) "administrative weakness," then these two constructs are not far apart.

The third point, which is a "non-hostile" geographic environment, we think does have some basis as discussed in our chapter on terrain. This clearly plays some role, and there is clearly some terrain that favors insurgencies (large rural populations and overhead cover) and some that do not (small islands).

While his fourth point was not established, he specifically limited the discussion to middle and late stages. We have not examined that issue in depth, and there may be some value to it.

In general, Galula is one of two theoretical constructs we have seen that we believe has a sound basis. The rest we believe can be dismissed.

One could specifically test Galula using his terms. In this case we would have to develop a variable on Nature of the Insurgent Cause (No real cause, Captureable cause or Unique dynamic cause). This is similar to the variable suggested from our analysis of Manwaring called "Morale Legitimacy of the Insurgency."

Unfortunately, we are not sure how to test the second point on administrative weakness. An administrative weakness could be any number of things. A shortage of troops is an obvious one, and one that is easily measured by force ratios. But, an administrative weakness can be something other than just troop shortfalls. It could be shortfalls in training, it could be shortfalls in morale and motivation, it could widespread corruption, it could be inability for the government to reform, or it could be any number of other things. Galula did not list what these are, so we are in fact forced to measure this based upon the most obvious measure, force ratios.

The third point is discussed in some depth in Chapter Thirteen and the Task 12 report. Still, in that report, it was specifically oriented to finding environments that favor blue or red. The requirement here is the much less demanding 'non-hostile' geographic environment. As discussed on page 25 of Galula and in the Task 12 report, this would certainly include a small island with little overhead cover. Beyond that, no particular environment dooms an insurgency, although some environments (primarily overhead cover) favors insurgencies. As such, this is a factor that only comes into play in the most extreme of cases.

To address the fourth point would require us to look at degree of outside support in the middle to late stages of an insurgency. We have not coded for insurgency support over time, although it would not be impossible to code it for the last third of the duration of an insurgency, or to code its change (more, the same, less) in the last third of the duration of an insurgency. Still, while this was obviously a significant factor in the Chinese Civil War and the Vietnam War, we are not going to see it systematically across the data for a large number of cases.

Therefore, in some sense we are comfortable in reducing Galula's overarching construct down to the first two points that he said are a must and making those two options measured by force ratio compared to political concept. This is, in effect, the same overarching construct that was proposed by Fall.

One does note that Galula is very clear that there are some insurgencies that you cannot win and some in which the outcome is decided in advance. *The Dupuy Institute* feels that these are very important points that no other theorists bother to address. One gets the impression, especially from the British authors, that the process of defeating an insurgency is simply one of proper application of tactics. There was a reason we proposed the hypothesis in our original Iraq briefing given in January 2005 that "Insurgencies succeed or fail based upon their own merits, not due to any particularly clever application of counterinsurgent strategy and tactics."

Galula did list the Greek Insurgency and the Indo-China Counterinsurgency as cases that were decided in advance. He states that China, Cuba and Algeria were not decided in advance.

In our original Iraq briefing back-of-the envelope analysis of this subject we simply tested this hypothesis by taking five points for measuring the success of failure of an insurgency (area, population, border length, political concept, and size of insurgency) and rating them as 0 (favorable), -1 (not as favorable) or -2 (unfavorable). We then added up the scores, and insurgencies with a value of -6 or worse were doomed to failure (in 12 out of 14 cases), and insurgencies with a value of -3 or better were successful insurgencies (also in 12 out of 14 cases). The same comparison is done here for these five cases:

COUNTRY	AREA	POPULATION	BORDER LENGTH	POLITICAL CONCEPT	SIZE OF INSURGENCY	TOTAL
Greece	−2	−1	−2	−1	−1	−7
Indochina	0	0	0	0	0	0
China	0	0	0	−1	0	−1
Cuba	−2	−1	−2	−1	−1	−7
Algeria	0	0	0	0	0	0

In this construct, Greece and Cuba should have clearly been blue wins (Cuba was a red win), while Indochina, China and Algeria should have clearly been red wins (as they were). Obviously, a more sophisticated measurement could be developed.

E. CLUTTERBUCK

Clutterbuck's book is an analysis and explanation of the British victory in Malaya. Unfortunately, being based upon a single case, it often goes astray when he compares and contrasts to other insurgencies. His book produced many of the same prescriptions as the French theorists (Trinquier and Galula) in that he stresses intelligence, census, suspension of civil liberties (favored by Trinquier), and use of small unit tactics. He also stresses the need for early intervention and in contradiction to Trinquier, strongly objects to the use of torture. He disparages the discussion of force ratios, even though the British always had very favorable force ratios in Malaya.

Clutterbuck summarizes his conclusions in a simple one-page chart on page 175. This is repeated in its entirely below. It is labeled "Figure 7: A Pattern of Counter insurgency:"

COMMUNIST PLAN	GOVERNMENT COUNTERMEASURES	EFFECT ON COMMUNISTS
Organize underground support among the people, with parallel hierarchy to control them	Good local government and intelligence system	Prevents establishment of popular base
Rioting, sabotage, intimidation, *coup d'état* if possible	Emergency regulations, including registration of population and powers of detention	Prevents *coup d'état*, forces leaders and armed Communists out of towns and villages
If coup fails, take to jungle or mountains	Protect and control population, harass big guerilla units to make them split up	Guerilla warfare on a falling scale

Thereafter:

	IF LOSING GROUND	IF WINNING GROUND	
Guerilla warfare on rising scale	Try to retain police posts and local government in every village. Take advantage of guerillas' concentrating into big units to find and destroy them. If government control is lost in a large area, re-establish it village by village, dealing with the easiest first. Then resume wining cycle.	Develop intelligence system	Revert to terror and subversion to keep hold on people until government loses determination

Form "liberated" areas	Concentrate pressure to clear easiest areas first	Growing flow of intelligence and increasing guerilla surrenders
Build up conventional forces	Patient determination and progressive government; lift restrictions as each area is cleared	Collapse of public support, area by area.
Defeat government forces		

The following appears to be the simplest, most complete strategic statement from Clutterbuck:

Try to retain police posts and local government in every village. Take advantage of guerillas' concentrating into big units to find and destroy them. If government control is lost in a large area, re-establish it village by village, dealing with the easiest first. Then resume winning cycle. (page 175)

While this is tactical, it again appears to rely on having sufficient troops available to make it work. His conclusions emphasize a number of other points:

These big units must be destroyed without irrevocably alienating the population. (page 176)

There must, above all, be absolute determination to establish and retain a government police post intact and uncorrupt in every inhabited village. (page 176)

If whole areas become untenable, then the rest of the country must be held; authority must be re-established patiently, village by village, into the `liberated' area, dealing the easiest areas first. (page 176)

It would appear that all of this was done or at least seriously tried in the unsuccessful Algerian and Vietnamese counterinsurgent efforts. The weakness of Clutterbuck is that he tells what was done in Malaya without contrasting it to failed counterinsurgencies, which often tried the same thing.

Finally, Clutterbuck provides a guidebook to tell if you are wining.

People directing a counterinsurgency are often in need of indicators of progress—or danger signs—to guide their actions. I believe that the insurgencies in North Vietnam, Malaya, and South Vietnam have produced four such reliable indicators of progress against the Mao Tse-tung plan.

The first is the degree to which the local government is able to do an honest job and enforce the rule of law. It is quite easy to detect when reassuring reports are false. Where the local government and police can survive only by turning a blind eye to the enemy, that village is a Communist village.

Second is the size in which guerilla units live and operate. In North Vietnam they grew, declined, and grew again—up to divisional strength. In Malaya, they declined—to platoon strength. In South Vietnam, they have grown from year to year. Though air power may keep them from growing above battalion or regimental strength, both of these are much too big for village defenses to hold off. It is at company strength (100) that they become dangerous, and so long as they can live in company groups, they will tend to grow bigger all the time, until massive conventional operations are needed to deal with them.

Third is the flow of information from the people. This is both an indicator of confidence and a battle-winning indicator.

So, too, is the fourth—the rate of surrender of genuine guerillas. This can be a misleading indicator if the temporary compliance of previous hostile villages is credited as surrender. As a battle-winning factor, it can quickly be thrown away if the surrendered guerillas are not handled well. (pages 177–178)

He then concludes:

So far all these indicators—excepting sometimes the fourth—have pointed depressingly in the wrong direction throughout both the wars in Vietnam—against the Vietminh and against the Viet Cong—so both wars have escalated. (page 178)

The decisive element in doing all these things in Malaya was the police force; counterinsurgency is a matter of restoring law and order, and law and order is a matter for policemen with the training and the lawful status for the task—not for part-time armed villagers. (page 178)

The quickest way to get immediate information from a captured guerilla or from an arrested supporter is by torture, but this is a fatal mistake in the long run. (page 178)

The quickest way to stop a village supplying guerillas is to shoot ten hostages, take ten more, and tell the people that this will continue until they stop. They will stop, but they will hate the government that did this to them—not only for a few years but for a whole generation. The village will be ready to welcome anyone who will rid them of that government in the future. (page 178)

Chin Peng in Malaya, like Mao Tse-tung in China, will assuredly try to come back. Had we been more ruthless in our methods, the government we helped to establish would have inherited the blame. The people would then have welcomed the returning Chin Peng as a savior; in the end, we would have made quite sure of losing the war. (page 178)

We choose the other way. It took us a long time to win, but I believe that Malaya is now inoculated against Communism for many years to come. If Chin Peng comes back and pokes his nose out of the jungle fringe, a prosperous people will tell him to go away— and then they will inform the police. That is the real measure of a victory over insurgency. (pages 178–179).

Still, this does give us some basis for a testable overarching theory. We could summarize it as:

FACTORS	CLUTTERBUCK	*THE DUPUY INSTITUTE* TESTS
Good Intelligence	Yes	Not tested
Emergency Regulations	Yes	Not tested
Control Population	Yes	Not tested, but related to Force Ratios
Harass Big Guerilla Units	Yes	Not tested, but related to Force Ratios
Importance of Police	Yes	Not tested
Use of Torture	No	No
Takes Time	Yes	Yes

It is clear that to test the details of Clutterbuck's analysis, *The Dupuy Institute* needs to develop some way of measuring the quality of the intelligence organization, some way of testing the effectiveness of emergency regulations (this is easy and is discussed in Appendix I.E. of our OTI report),[8] and some way of testing good versus bad police organizations. In the end, Clutterbuck offered a series of tactical and operational prescriptions that are useful, but he only partly analyzed the strategic issues. As such, there is not a good overarching counterinsurgency theory to test here.

F. FALL

Bernard Fall did not propose a clear overarching construct, but an extensive reading of his work makes clear the elements he thought were important. Elements of his work are extracted and discussed in Appendix I.F. of our OTI report while the chapter "The Theory and Practice of Insurgency and Counterinsurgency" from *Last Reflections on a War: Bernard B. Fall's Last Comments on Vietnam* clearly laid out his theoretical ideas.

Basically, Fall believed that the two most important elements were Force Ratios and Cause. This parallels our current thinking on the subject.

Fall also addresses the restrictive use of firepower (he does not discuss the use of torture) and recommended tight restrictions on its use. This parallels Clutterbuck and is in line with our analysis.

Fall also discusses active sanctuaries, making the statement that: "In brutal fact, the success or failure of all rebellions since World War II depended entirely on whether the active sanctuary was willing and able to perform its expected role." (*Street Without Joy*, page 376). This we did test in our Task 5 & 8 report and saw no such clear relationship.

Fall also discusses the tactic of gridding as opposed to Ink Spot in page 222 of *Last Reflections*. He clearly favors the former, as is recommended in other French works. In many respects, this is what the U.S. did in Baghdad in 2007 with its surge strategy. We have not tested these various strategic approaches.

As we noted in our discussion above on Galula: **Galula and Fall are the two theorists we have seen that are mostly supported by the data and analysis we have collected. The rest we believe can be dismissed.**

G. KITSON

Frank Kitson eventually arose to command the British Army. His book parallels Clutterbuck's book and is mostly focused on the details of how to conduct operations. It is more a tactical primer and does not add much to the analytical framework. As such, it has limited value for this study. His stated purpose makes this pretty clear:

> *The purpose of this book is to draw attention to the steps which should be taken now in order to make the army ready to deal with subversion, insurrection, and peace-keeping operations during the second half of the 1970's. The book is slanted towards the situation and needs of the British army in so far as it outward form is concerned, but the analysis of past campaigns and prediction of the likely nature of future operations from which the specific recommendations are made, is relevant to the armies of most countries, as indeed are many of the recommendations themselves, including all of the important ones.* (page 2)

Kitson's book is known for its discussion of pseudo-gangs and pseudo-operations. This is a tactical issue that is too small to be effectively analyzed in this broad-based top-level type of analysis. But, beyond a range of often well thought out tactical prescriptions, there is no overarching theory of insurgency offered. The closest he comes is in Chapter 1, where he focuses on cause and the importance of cause. He does not relate this to any other factors. It may be that he considers this the single most important factor. Unfortunately, his concluding Chapter 11 does not offer summary of his ideas or something that could be identified as an overarching construct. As such, our analysis of Kitson must be limited to what was done earlier in this chapter, and the comments and back-of-the-envelope analysis done in Appendix I.G of our OTI report.

H. O'NEILL

Bard O'Neill's book on insurgencies has been around under various titles since 1990. It has been revised, updated and republished twice. The latest version dates from 2005, although our review of his work comes from the final draft manuscript dated 2005. O'Neill is a professor at the National Defense University in Washington, D.C. He served with the U.S. Army in Vietnam.

The book is clearly oriented towards training intelligence analysts. As such, the first half of this work reads like a basic textbook on insurgencies and a very good one at that. It is the second half of his book that we have some problems with.

It is clear from the preface and other comments that his starting point was Ted Gurr's *Why Men Rebel*. This is a probably one of the better places to start. Still, the first half of his work is not theoretical, but primarily descriptive. As he states on page 18: "Although there is a continuous effort throughout the study to identify, define, and suggest relationships among the factors, there is no pretense that the framework is a formal theory or model."

Having stated in the beginning of the book that he was not going to present a formal theory or model, he does end his book with the statement that: "Each of the factors represents an area of inquiry that may be crucial for explaining the course of events in insurgencies. How important the factors are varies from case to case and can only be determined by careful empirical investigation. Since numerous studies give ample evidence that combinations of important factors vary considerably between cases, there is no one model that can be applied in all cases."

The statement that there is no one model that can be applied in all cases not only argues against any form of overarching construct but would also lead one to believe that the author does not believe that one is possible. Still, he notes: "While acknowledging that the differences between insurgencies do exist, it is important to recognize that there may also exist similarities that permit particular lessons to be transferred from one case to another."

Regardless, there is no overarching theory here to analyze. There is considerable advice to the analyst as to what elements to look for and their importance. In some cases, we agree, and as shown earlier in this chapter, in some cases we clearly do not agree.

The problem is that in some areas of analysis, with the heavy influence of the lesson of Vietnam, a reading of O'Neill's book may cause the analyst to overrate certain factors, including organization and support. This creates the danger of negative learning and misanalysis of the seriousness of the situation. If the analyst does not see a hierarchical communist-like structure for the insurgency, should the analyst then assume that all these clan-based central Asian militia are not particularly dangerous as an insurgent threat? There is a potential problem here in training if O'Neill's book has overly influenced the training approach for U.S. intelligence analysts.

I. BDM

The BDM report was authored by Douglas S. Blaufarb and Dr. George K. Tanham. Blaufarb served as a CIA intelligence officer in Greece during 1950–1956, Vietnam 1956–1958, Singapore 1958–1961, and Laos 1964–1971, when he retired to work for RAND, while Tanham was a RAND analyst who had served as an AID rural development officer in Vietnam and then was special assistant for counterinsurgency at the U.S. Embassy in Bangkok.

The report usually does not reach its opinions analytically, even though there is a considerable body of historical examples described in narratives. The ideas in the report appear to be a synthesis of these two authors' opinions based upon examination of a variety of cases and their own experience. They state that their experience is a primary research tool, along with their ten case studies (including two that they served in). Their appendix shows 10 cases (vice the 83 cases we examined). Of those 10, we have done 7. The three they have examined that we have not are the Philippines, 1946–1954, Thailand 1961 to present (1984), and Venezuela, 1958–1968. We agree that these are all good cases worthy of further examination.

In effect, this is the same methodology as used by all the other authors examined. One does note that even though the report has an extensive bibliography, they appear to have somehow managed to avoid Bernard Fall's writings entirely.

They state that: "The purpose of this study is to provide a framework of analysis to help the analyst determine whether or not a government threatened by insurgency can prevail and, if that is in some doubt, what foreign assistance is required to make success more likely." (page EX-I)

This is similar to O'Neill's work in that it is supposed to allow some predictive analysis of the outcome or threat of an insurgency. Like O'Neill's work, for this to be of value, negative learning and false lessons need to be avoided.

The authors then note that: ". . . . the study is concerned only with left-wing insurgencies with some communist involvement." (EX-I) We note that these cases make up a minority of the 62 cases we code as an insurgency. They also note:

There are, of course, other types of insurgency which have been or are today in evidence such as ethnic separatist movements or those that are anti-communist and conservative or traditionalist in motivation. (Afghanistan, Nicaragua, etc.) These are not dealt with here since it is the left-wing insurgencies that are of greatest concern to the U.S. and present the most difficult problems for analysts. (IN-1)

And state that:

Effective counterinsurgency against either of these two strategies [people's war or foco] calls for government actions, behaviors, and programs which are identified and described in the study and number 14 in all.

The 14 government actions, behaviors and programs are:

1. *Military Leadership*
2. *Unconventional tactics and strategy*
3. *Competent military intelligence*
4. *Discipline, behavior and military civic action*
5. *Air and naval operations*
6. *Civil-Military relations*
7. *Establishments of a popular militia*
8. *Police Operations*
9. *Intelligence Operations*
10. *Psychological Operations*

11. *Unified management of counterinsurgency activities*
12. *The Political framework*
13. *Programs to improve rural conditions and administration*
14. *The legal framework* (page EX-I)

This is not, unfortunately, a complex-14 point overarching theory. It is a series of points, very much parallel to those of Clutterbuck, which need to be individually addressed. We have done this to some extent in Appendix I, part I of the OTI report. As we noted with Clutterbuck, "In the end, Clutterbuck offered a series of tactical and operational prescriptions that are useful, but he only partly analyzed the strategic issues. As such, there is not a good overarching counterinsurgency theory to test here."

Other then being structured for training analysts, *The Dupuy Institute* is not sure what is the advantage of this report over Clutterbuck. They do prioritize the 14 points, with the three military-related points of Military Leadership, Unconventional tactics and strategy and competent military intelligence being give the first priority.

J. COMPARING AND CONTRASTING THE THEORISTS

This chapter addressed how each theorist addressed specific points and addressed which points they considered the most important. For example, while David Galula spends considerable time in his book discussing terrain, intelligence and details of operations, when he puts together his four-point overarching construct, none of those are among those four points. In three cases, the theorists never did provide an overarching construct. We flagged a few points for the table below from Trinquier's writing, while Kitson seems to mention only one thing of paramount importance (cause). O'Neill clearly does not want to provide an overarching theory and may believe that it is not possible.

To attempt to compare them across the major points of importance that they emphasized, the following table had been constructed. Anything coded as "I" means that it is included as a factor. The situation is greatly complicated by people saying somewhat similar things in different ways.

IDEA	MANWARING	TRINQUIER	JOES	GALULA	CLUTTERBUCK	FALL	KITSON	O'NEILL	BDM
Moral	I								
Legitimacy									
Appropriate use of military force	I					I			
Isolate belligerents	I		I*	I**					
Stay the course	I				I "Takes Time"				
Intelligence	I	I			I				I
Unity of Effort	I			***					I
Use of Torture		I							
Peak Force Ratios			I				I		
Free Elections Held During									

Insurgency		I					
Insurgents need a cause			I		I	I?	
A Police and administrative weakness			I				
A non-hostile geographic environment			I				
Emergency Regulations				I			
Control Population				I			
Harass Big Guerilla Units			I				
Importance of Police				I			I
No use of Torture				I			
Active Sanctuaries					I		
Gridding	I		****		I****		
Military Leadership							I
Unconventional Tactics							I
Discipline, behavior and military civic action							I
Air and naval operations							I
Civil-Military Relations							I
Establishment of popular militia							I
Intelligence Operations							I
Psychological Operations							I
The Political Framework							I
Programs to improve rural conditions and administration							I
The Legal Framework							I

I = Included as a factor

* Joes addressed it as Counterinsurgency isolated the combat area

** Galula addresses this as the insurgent receiving outside support in middle to late stages

*** One would be tempted to incorporate Galula's "A police and administrative weakness" in this, but it is more far reaching in concept than just "Unity of Effort"

**** This is effectively stated also by Galula although it is not part of his overarching theory.

It is hard to determine much from this table except that there is very little agreement as to what are the most important factors across the nine theorists. Considering that the five of these theorists (Manwaring, Joes, Kitson, O'Neill and BDM) primarily built their work from the other four theorists (Trinquier, Clutterbuck, Galula and Fall), this is surprising. The only ones that show up more than twice across the 9 theorists are Isolate Belligerents (3 cases), Cause (3 cases) and Intelligence (4 cases). There is clearly no common thrust although there is often wide agreement on a number of points (the importance of intelligence, value of small unit operations, systematic clearing, being patient, etc).

In the end, it shows that a significant number of these studies are idiosyncratic and probably overly influenced by the particular events of the wars the authors participated in and their actual functions during those wars. This indicates both a strong need for further study and that there is not a strong basis for developing a model of insurgency before such further study is conducted.

K. SUMMARY

In general, Galula and Fall are the two theoretical constructs we have seen that we believe have a sound basis to it. The rest we believe can be dismissed.

This rather blunt and tactless statement is very much driven by our concern over negative learning. In the case of the intelligence community, it could be developing an understanding of insurgencies that would cause them to misappreciate the danger and virulence of proto-insurgencies that they are evaluating. We feel this danger is the worse with O'Neill's work (which has many positive points also) and the BDM report (which we do not feel adds much to the discussion).

In the case of people interested in application, there are of course useful lessons to be learned from Clutterbuck, Kitson, Trinquier, and others, but the lack of a clear overarching construct in these works reduce them to useful operational and tactical primers only. One can't help but note in the early years in Iraq War (2003 to present) that many mistakes could have been avoided that later had to be rectified. Still, we are uncertain if the general course of the Iraq War would have been changed if these theorists were read and followed, as they miss what appears to be one of the more important points—you need enough troops. Perhaps a reading of Clutterbuck and Kitson would have forced the U.S. Army to argue forcefully for bringing one or more of its Military Police brigades to help in the occupation of Iraq in 2003.

Still, a reading and proper application of Galula and Fall would not have corrected many of the problems encountered in Iraq, but at least in the case of the Fall, it would have forced consideration of the proper level of troops needed to do the job, and in the case of Galula and Fall would have forced the planners to address the size and capabilities of the forces they have, and also, the nature and motivation of the insurgents. While we have not done any systematic analysis of how the theorists applied to Iraq would have changed the outcome of the contest (and this would be a useful test to do), it is hard to ignore such a significant and recent case of misapplication of military force.

We believe that at least three of the four points of Galula's construct are supported by the data and we have not established how much merit his fourth point has (Outside support in middle to late stages). The problem is determining what is really meant by his second point, and police and administrative weakness. We choose to interpret this as force ratio, which we were able to test. In the case of Fall, the two factors he considers the most important (force ratios and cause) appear to be supported by the data. Certainly this is demonstrated in Chapter Six of this book.

All the other theorists touch on some of these points, but none assemble the picture from elements that are entirely supported. For example, with Manwaring we were only able to establish two of his six points as having validity, while two of three main elements of Joes' construct are not supported. The British theorists (Clutterbuck and Kitson) ignore force ratios. This may be because it was not an issue to them, as the British always had favorable force ratios in all the insurgencies these soldier-scholars served in (Malaya, Mau Mau and Northern Ireland).

Therefore we concluded from this analysis that: 1) There is a strong need for further study of these issues, 2) There is a considerable danger of negative learning, 3) there is not a strong basis for developing a model of insurgency before such further study is conducted, and 4) There are sometimes limitations with developing theories based primarily upon personal experience.

NOTES

1. Original source not identified.
2. See Task 12 report, section K for more details.
3. Only covered terrain was addressed.
4. See our Task 6 & 9 report: Examination of Factors Influencing the Conduct of Operations in Guerilla Wars: Task 6: Examine Forms of Warfare & Task 9: Study the Leadership, Organization, and Political System (Annandale, VA.: The Dupuy Institute, 22 February 2008).
5. Anthony James Joes, The War for South Viet Nam, 1954–1975 (Westport, Conn.: Praeger, rev. ed., 2001), 63–65.
6. We ignore the two categories based entirely on O'Neill's definitions and that based solely on Galula's discussion of location.
7. The one or two exceptions (Cuba and possibly Morocco) are rather exceptional cases. See Appx. XI of The Analysis of the Historical Effectiveness of Different Counterinsurgency Tactics and Strategies: Final Report (Annandale, VA.: The Dupuy Institute, 31 Mar. 2008) for further discussion of these.
8. The OTI report is The Analysis of the Historical Effectiveness of Different Counterinsurgency Tactics and Strategies: Final Report (Annandale, VA.: The Dupuy Institute, 31 Mar. 2008). The acronym refers to the department we did the report for.

CHAPTER 18

The Other Side[1]

My fighting gospel is T.E. Lawrence's Seven Pillars
of Wisdom. I am never without it.

—General Vo Nguyen Giap in 1946[2]

Warfare is always a struggle between at least two sides. Yet, the theoretical study of insurgencies always seems to be written primarily from the standpoint of one side, the counterinsurgents. We therefore briefly looked at what the other side was saying to see if there were any theoretical constructs that were proposed or supported by them. They obviously know as much about insurgencies as the counterinsurgents.

We examined the writings and interview transcripts of eight practitioners of insurgency to see if what they had said was important. The eight insurgents we chose for analysis were (in order they were examined):[3]

1. Chin Peng, or Ong Boon Hua. He was the leader of communist insurgency in Malaya from 1948 through 1960. His book was written in 2003.

2. General George Grivas or "Dighenis." He was the leader of the Cyprus Rebellion from 1955 to 1959. He then became the Minister of Defense for Cyprus. His book was first published in Greek in 1962. The first English edition was published in 1964.

3. General China or Waruhiu Itote. He was the senior commanding general of the Mau Mau from 1952 to his capture in early 1954. His book was written in 1967.

4. Amilcar Cabral. He was the leader of the revolutionary Partido Africano da Independencia da Guiné e Cabo Verde (PAIGC) in Portuguese Guinea from 1956 to 1973. He was assassinated in 1973. His texts are based upon interviews conducted during the insurgency in Portuguese Guinea.

5. Truong Nhu Tang. He was the one of the founding members of the National Liberation Front (NLF) and was the NLF's senior agent in Saigon during the Vietnam War until his arrest in 1967. He was later Minster of Justice

for the South Vietnamese government in the jungle that was established by the NLF. His book was written in 1985.

6. António Agostinho Neto. He was the most prominent political leader and theorist of the revolutionary Popular Movement for the Liberation of Angola (MPLA), serving as the party's first president and, eventually as the first president of newly-liberated Angola (1975–79). In the later stage of the Angolan War, he became embroiled in conflict with Chipenda. His texts are based upon a compilation of his speeches and messages to his comrades.

7. Daniel Júlio Chipenda. He was a leader of the revolutionary MPLA. His texts are based upon an interview conducted in Lusaka, Zambia in 1969.

8. Floribert Monimambu or "Spartacus." He was a senior commander in the MPLA military, responsible for the Eastern Region, or Front, in Angola. His texts are based upon an interview conducted in Dar es Salaam, Tanzania in 1968.

One notes that of these eight theorists, five of them were effectively in overall charge of the revolt (Peng, China, Grivas, Cabral and Neto), two of them were at very senior levels in the political organization (Tang and Chipenda), and one was a regional military commander (Monimambu). Five of them were involved in wars that the insurgents won (Cabral, Tang, Neto, Chipenda and Monimambu). One of them was involved in a war that clearly failed (Peng). Two of them were involved in wars in which it is hard to determine if they actually succeeded or failed militarily or politically (Grivas and China), although in our MISS database, the Cyprus Revolt and Mau Mau Rebellion are both coded as counterinsurgent wins. Of the practitioners, one is European, five are sub-Saharan African (all but two either of mixed race or *assimilado* background), and two are Southeast Asians. Concerning religion, three or more of them were raised as Protestant Christian, two nominally Confucian. Almost all had been exposed to Christianity during their schooling. None of them were raised Muslim.

SUMMATION OF THE INSURGENTS' IDEAS

A brief summation of the main points of each of the insurgent leaders is provided below:

Chin Peng—An extremely intelligent and moderately educated writer, this leader thought very much of the bigger picture over time. As such, many of his own decisions early in the insurgency come under scrutiny and criticism in his book. The main reason he gives for the defeat of the Malayan insurgency was the Briggs Plan. Basically, he contends that the population resettlement and control of food effectively isolated them from the food. This forced the units to break into smaller groups and concentrate their efforts on finding food, vice conducting operations. With the added harassment of the constant patrolling by the British, the insurgency was thrown on the defensive, reduced to survival and reaction, and slowly died. Finally, at Malayan independence in 1957, one of the primary causes was cut out from under the insurgency, finally killing it.

Peng goes out of his way to stress that is was the Briggs Plan, vice Templar's command and actions, which won the war for the British. Whether this reflected his biases, or was in fact a sound analysis of the situation has not been determined. Still, he does give considerable credit late in the insurgency to the British intelligence efforts. By default, because of the constant patrolling and the number of British deployed, he does in passing almost address the issue of force ratios, but never directly addresses it. He does address the issue of cause and says that one of their big mistakes was to make the insurgency a communist insurgency, vice a nationalist one. To summarize:

Of primary importance in defeating the insurgency:

1. Briggs Plan
   a. Population resettlement
   b. Cutting off food

2. British patrolling
   a. Force ratio addressed in passing

Also of importance:

1. Not having a nationalist cause vice a communist one.

Of importance late in the insurgency

1. Good intelligence
2. Defections
3. Malayan independence (under-cutting the cause)

General Grivas—A brilliant, well-educated military man, with wide experience in the Greco-Turkish War (1920–1922), World War II and the Greek Civil War, not only as a regular officer but also as a leader of partisans, Grivas produced a memoir of the Cypriot independence war, in which he led the insurgents, that was at once a detailed primer on the preparation and conduct of guerrilla war and a recommendation in effect to NATO to incorporate guerrilla warfare into its defense plans for western Europe.

Grivas' book not surprisingly meets the requirement for "completed staff work" in the subject area and emphasizes thorough pre-operational planning, secrecy, surprise, leadership, security operations, the continuous offensive, attrition and wearing down the enemy. It may be said that Grivas is the only one of our subjects who (practically) views guerrilla warfare as a set-piece battle. Since part of his military education was in France, it may be that he had been exposed to the thoroughness of French interwar officer training curricula and had internalized the maxim of the great French Marshal-General Turenne that "nothing may be considered done while anything remains undone."

General China—Although he possessed a limited education and was much more the active leader as opposed to the theorist, China's (that is, Waruhiu Itote's) book is basically a poorly-written account of his experiences. Still, it is clear that he understood the situation and kept records, as demonstrated by his order of battle, rules of conduct, and details on weapon and ammunition captures. He was nominally the senior military commander of the Mau Mau until his capture. The Mau Mau did not have any significant political leaders in the field, as they were all arrested at the start of the war.

His book addresses a wide-range of tactical and operational issues, including execution of informers and traitors, supply, obtaining weapons, rules of conduct, etc. What his book does not offer is any grand strategic views. There is no discussion of the British plans and actions. There is little discussion of what the insurgent strategy was and why. It is mostly a poor retelling of the events by someone who was clearly a very able commander. As such, there is little of theoretical value here.

Amilcar Cabral—The Portuguese-educated Guinean leader was one of the few insurgents that actually led an almost classic Maoist campaign, in the sense of developing liberated areas (something Chin Peng could never do), developing a shadow government in those areas, and slowly building and expanding his control of the countryside until the opposition collapsed. He was the overall commander of the insurgency and its political leader from the beginning until his assassination less then two years before the end. The interview was conducted in 1968, while the insurgency was matured but had not yet won. The interview obviously contains elements of propaganda.

Cabral's interview addresses the limitations of urban terrorism, his overall strategy (effectively, what O'Neill characterizes as "Protracted Popular War"), forcing the Portuguese to disperse forces, terrain, strategic hamlets and his own reforms.

Truong Nhu Tang—Highly educated (French masters degree in law) and very intelligent, this writer had the additional advantage that he was never a communist and broke from the Viet Cong in the end. As such, his book is truly unencumbered by propaganda. On the other hand, he was not at the senior levels of command and therefore could only discuss things in and around Saigon as they related to the political situation and the NLF.

His main point was that the support for unification of Vietnam was pretty close to universal. The Diem government and subsequent versions had very little support from the average Vietnamese. Diem's actions had systematically made enemies of many major groups of people and eventually they all turned on him. As such, his focus was primarily on cause. Oddly enough, there is little on the U.S. intervention, except for the damage that they did. It does not connect these two issues into an overall theory, but it is clear that his focus is on cause, the lack of moral legitimacy of the South Vietnamese government (to use Manwaring's terms, vice Tang), and use of firepower by the U.S.

António Agostinho Neto—The poet-philosopher-physician president of the MPLA was, despite appearances, a ruthless revolutionary and realist, undoubtedly hardened by years in Portuguese jails. In the end, it was his vision for the MPLA and Angola that triumphed over divisions within his own movement (as exemplified by the Chipenda faction) and within the broader anti-colonialist movement, particularly the more tribalist parties of Holden Roberto and Jonas Savimbi. Neto's texts emphasize the broad base of the MPLA and its multiracial character, as opposed to the relatively narrow foundations of Roberto's Revolutionary Government of Angola in Exile (GRAE) and Savimbi's National Union for the Total Independence of Angola (UNITA). In addition, he stressed the importance of protracted popular war, outside support and the development of civil administration in the liberated areas. As the principal leader of the MPLA, it is clear that he was concerned also with the longer term and looked beyond the war to the problems that would confront an independent Angola.

Daniel Júlio Chipenda—One of several faction leaders of the MPLA, he rose to senior political leadership. His interview was also conducted while the war was underway.

Most of his discussion centers on the early phases of the insurgency while it was still establishing itself. He refers to the manifold problems of leading the insurgency from outside the country during that phase. It was only when the active sanctuary of Zambia became available in 1964 that the MPLA could finally develop a functioning armed presence inside Angola. This was an insurgency that concentrated first on developing its base in the rural areas. It was classic people's war or protracted popular war. He stresses the need to force the Portuguese to disperse their forces and the need to maintain outside support, although he points out that many of his units supported themselves without any outside support. It appears that he considers it useful but not entirely essential.

Spartacus Monimambu—A young man, but a senior faction leader of the MPLA, his interview is more straightforward and tactical in its emphases than Chipenda's.

He clearly indicates that forcing the Portuguese to disperse was important, and he had no qualms about the importance of outside support (unlike Chipenda). He was not impressed with Portuguese efforts at developing protected villages. His interview indicates the critical importance of the struggle to claim and maintain the support of indigenous population.

COMPARISON OF THE INSURGENTS' CONCEPTS

To summarize the insurgents' main points into a single look-up table:

	PENG	GRIVAS	CHINA	TANG	CABRAL	NETO	CHIPENDA	MONIMAMBU
Force ratios	Maybe*	Maybe*	N/A	N/A	Maybe*	Maybe*	Maybe*	Maybe*
Cause	Yes	N/A	N/A	Yes	Maybe*	Yes	Maybe*	Maybe*
Terrain	N/A	Yes	N/A	N/A	Yes	N/A	N/A	N/A

Counterinsurgent Tactics & Operations

Population								
resettlement	Yes	N/A	N/A	No	No	No	N/A	No
Cutting off food	Yes	Yes	N/A	N/A	N/A	N/A	N/A	N/A
Continued								
patrolling	Yes	N/A	N/A	N/A	N/A	N/A	N/A	N/A
Good intelligence	Yes **	Yes	N/A	N/A	N/A	N/A	N/A	N/A
Defections	Yes**	N/A	N/A	Maybe*	N/A	Yes	N/A	N/A
Under-cutting								
the cause	Yes	N/A	N/A	N/A	N/A	Yes	N/A	N/A
Use of firepower	N/A	N/A	N/A	No ?	No	N/A	N/A	N/A
Other issues								
Outside support	N/A	Yes	N/A	N/A	N/A	Yes	***	Yes
Fracture lines	U	N/A	U	NA	N/A	Yes	Tried to unite	N/A

N/A = not addressed
U = Unresolved
* By inference, we suspect that the author considers this important. For example, in the case of Cabral, he discussed his fundamental tactical principle being to force the Portuguese to disperse their forces to control an area. This would imply that the Portuguese had insufficient forces. Chipenda and Spartacus make the same point.
** Peng indicates that effective British intelligence and Peng's problems with defections only occured later in the insurgency. He does not seem to indicate that is was a major issue before then.
*** Useful but not essential

SUMMATION

Looking at the list of items that the insurgents seem to consider important, it is worthwhile looking at not only what they said but what they did not say.

Force Ratio—One notes that no one actually said it was important. On the other hand, it could be inferred that 6 out of 8 of the insurgents considered it important.

Cause—It is probably important for 6 out of the 8 insurgents, if not all. In almost all cases, the cause is effectively nationalism.

Terrain—Only discussed by two insurgent leaders, both of whom had to work with very poor terrain (Cyprus and Portuguese Guinea). Otherwise, it did not seem to be a major issue.

Population resettlement—Clearly considered effective by one leader, ineffective by four and not addressed by three.

Cutting off food, continued patrolling, good intelligence, defections, undercutting the cause—In all cases, only mentioned by one insurgent, and this was Chin Peng (Malaya). Chin Peng, before he wrote his account, researched the British side of the insurgency, including archival research at the Public Record Office in London. This certainly influenced the subjects that he addressed. His was the most scholarly of books on their experience.

Defections are not an issue with three of the insurgents (Peng, Tang and Neto).

Undercutting the cause is only addressed by two (Peng and Neto). These other issues are really not mentioned by the other insurgents, other than logistics and good intelligence by Grivas. Clearly, other insurgent leaders were concerned with food and supplies and discussed it (Itote, Cabral, Chipenda and Sparatacus), but it was never an issue for them. It appears to have only been a major problem for the Malayan insurgency. Yet, these solutions make up a significant part of the tool box of counterinsurgent theorists like Clutterbuck, Trinquier, Galula and Kitson.

Use of firepower—Two insurgents consider the heavy-handed approach of their opponents to have been to their advantage. One gathers that Chin Peng, with his extended criticism of Templar's command in Malaya, may lean the same way.

Outside support—Only three insurgents considered it important.

Fracture lines in society—This was a concern with four of the insurgent leaders, of which only two were able to make any significant progress in correcting.

Other factors—With the exception of Grivas, most of the leaders don't discuss the military aspects of insurgencies in detail. As our eight cases above include five political leaders, this is not too surprising. Still, the real focus of the discussion of even military leaders like General China and Spartacus is more on logistics and organization than it is on operations.

We note that several things were hardly discussed analytically at all. For example, several of the leaders were tortured, yet there is no discussion on the value or lack thereof of using torture. Some other major issues not really addressed include population size, structure of the insurgency, indigenous government type, elections, specific government reforms, and the counterinsurgents "staying the course." This list of factors that is not discussed in depth vastly exceeds that which is discussed in depth.

COMPARISON TO COUNTERINSURGENT THEORISTS

To place this work in context, it is probably worthwhile to look at what the counterinsurgents think is important compared to what the insurgents think is important—in effect a comparison of the blue view of the world to the red view.

1. TERRAIN AND GEOGRAPHIC CONSIDERATIONS

Several counterinsurgent theorists consider terrain to be important. This certainly includes Galula, O'Neill and *The Dupuy Institute* (see our Task 12 report). Clutterbuck (who served in Malaya) also discussed the importance of covered terrain. On the other hand, none of the insurgents raised the issue of terrain except for Grivas, Cabral and Peng. Peng only raised it to the extent that he was addressing the need for overhead cover in the base camps to protect them from British air reconnaissance. Grivas believed that mountainous terrain provided security for his guerrillas.

Cabral was well aware of the terrain limitations of his small, swampy country. He directly addresses it and claims that to compensate for not having rough terrain, he had to use the people as his "mountains" and hide in the jungle and swamps. This may be more rhetoric that realistic analysis. As *The Dupuy Institute* is favoring "covered" terrain over "rough" terrain (see our Task 12 report), then swamps and jungles may have been sufficient for his purposes.

These limited discussions on terrain by the insurgents may be because they did not really have a choice and had to fight when and where their support was.

2. RULES OF ENGAGEMENT AND DEGREES OF BRUTALITY

Most of the counterinsurgent theorists encourage the restricted use of force. The attitude seems to be to severely restrict it in the case of Clutterbuck, Fall, the BDM report, *The Dupuy Institute* and possibly Joes. The attitude is that there needs to be some restrictions, but with flexibility by Galula, O'Neill and possibly Joes. Trinquier advocates the use of torture.

The insurgent leaders occasionally touch on this. After the Malayan insurgency had developed unfavorably for several years, Peng gave orders to reduce the amount of killings and assassinations, as he felt it was working against them.

In the case of General China (Itote), his war committee in late 1953 reviewed the issue of killing women and children and resolved, ". . . . that no women or children whatsoever should be killed because such actions limit the future growth of our population."[4] He then states that "The Committee then votes on the resolution, which was supported, ten to five. From that time on, we avoided the killing of women and children."[5] He also puts forward in late 1953 six steps that are needed to strengthen their movement. Step four was "Villages should not be burnt, first because this would anger the people and second because if the Government thought it was protecting the people it would leave them alone; if the people turned against us, we would be defeated."[6] This is also an Appendix to the book on the "Rules of Conduct in the Forest" that were codified January 4, 1954, and listed 52 different rules, some of them addressing treatment of civilians. [7] These were clearly changes from what had gone on before that were being made 18 months into the insurgency.

Clearly, in these two cases, after the excesses of the early part of their insurgency, they were taking steps to control and limit the amount of violence conducted by their forces.

Cabral pointed out that the Portuguese after their experimentation with the "art of repression," tried to work politically. This would imply that he felt that repressive approaches were not very successful.

Reading between the lines, Tang clearly feels too much American airpower was used in Vietnam but does not connect this complaint to the outcome.

3. FORCE RATIOS

Joes, Galula, Fall and *The Dupuy Institute* consider force ratios to be important. Clutterbuck, Kitson and O'Neill clearly do not consider them important, and the theorists like Manwaring, Trinquier and the BDM report do not address them.

It could be inferred from Peng that the large number of forces the British deployed did matter. He notes the British build-up and complains about the incessant British patrolling. The issue is not addressed by General China (Itote) and Tang.

Cabral addresses it only to the extent that he points out that a major tactical plan of theirs was to force the Portuguese forces to disperse their forces to control an area. This would imply that the Portuguese had insufficient forces. Chipenda and Spartacus make a similar point.

4. NATURE OF INSURGENCIES

Here, *The Dupuy Institute* and Fall focused on the cause being extremely important. We gather that Galula, Kitson, O'Neill and the BDM report all consider it to be important also. Specifically Fall, Kitson, O'Neill and the BDM report focus on nationalism as a cause being important, as does by default, *The Dupuy Institute* with its categorization of insurgencies based upon a central idea, like nationalism.

Peng also considered the cause of nationalism to be important and specifically states on page 238 that: "In hindsight, I think we made another critical mistake here. What we should have done was to announce our aim of fighting for the broad concept of independence." Furthermore, he clearly considers that the undercutting of his cause hurt his insurgency on page 395 with the statement: "With the assurance of Malayan independence in 18 months, the core of our armed struggle had been abruptly extracted."

General China does not discuss cause much except as part of his personal motivation, which was clearly for Kenyans to rule Kenya. Truong Nhu Tang indicates in many passages in his book that what they wanted was a unified Vietnam. He indicates this for himself, for the people in the provinces that he associated with and the general majority of people in South Vietnam.

With Cabral, steeped in Maoist rhetoric, it is hard to separate his real feelings on cause and motivation from the propaganda. He clearly is pursuing a protracted popular war strategy. Neto, Chipenda and Spartacus are probably similar in concept.

Clearly, cause, and that cause being nationalism, was of paramount important to Peng, Tang and probably Cabral and Neto. It was the reason General China took up arms also.

5. BURDEN

None of the counterinsurgent theorist indicates that the overall cost and burden of the war was a significant factor. *The Dupuy Institute* believes it is and addresses this subject in our Task 11 report. It was not addressed by Chin Peng, General China or Cabral. On the other hand, Tang was very aware of the decreasing U.S. interest in pursuing the Vietnam War as casualties mounted.

6. OPERATIONAL DETAILS—ACTIVE SANCTUARIES, BORDER CONTROLS AND POPULATION RESETTLEMENT

While Fall and Joes consider an active sanctuary to be important, it was merely the retreat place for Chin Peng after he was already losing the war in Malaya. There was none for General China, and while Truong Nhu Tang lived in one of the biggest and most conveniently located active sanctuaries in any guerilla war (the "Parrots Beak" in Cambodia), at no point did he state that this was a significant factor in winning the war.

In the case of border controls, while Manwaring and Joes consider it important, none of the insurgents we reviewed ever had to deal with effective border controls, other than the invasion of Cambodia in 1970.

In the case of population resettlement, Trinquier, Joes, Clutterbuck, Kitson and O'Neill all consider it important. In the case of Peng, he clearly states that is was the single most significant factor in his defeat, as it cut him off from his food sources, forcing him to break into smaller units, and handing the initiative to the Brtish. Food was a severe problem during the Malayan insurgency, unlike the Mau Mau or the Vietnamese. Cabral noted that the Portuguese protected villages had not produced the expected results. Both Neto, Chipenda and Spartacus are also dismissive of the Portuguese efforts. Tang was also dismissive of the resettlement efforts in Vietnam. In the case of General China, resettlement is only addressed as part of the post-war prisons and concentration camps the British used.

7. OVERARCHING THEORIES

Various overarching theories and larger theoretical constructs are proposed by Manwaring, Joes, Galula, Fall and BDM. The two that we felt had the most value was Galula and Fall. Galula offered a larger theoretical construct based upon four major points:

1. Insurgents need a cause
2. A police and administrative weakness
3. A non-hostile geographic environment
4. Outside support in middle to late stages

He specifically states that. "The first two are musts. The last is a help that may become a necessity."

Fall was similar and much simpler; he focused primarily on force ratios and cause being most important.

In the case of Peng, his views clearly support the importance of cause (or the lack thereof in his case), and one could infer that the British troop strength was important. Peng also points out the venality and corruption of the British administration of Malaya in the second half of the 1940s as being a real issue. This certainly plays to Galula's second point (an administrative weakness). But, the real reason Peng considers he was defeated was the Briggs Plan that created the new villages for the Chinese squatters and cut off the food supply to the insurgency. The inability of the insurgency to obtain food completely eviscerated the insurgency. Peng states on page 268, ". . . we realized we were facing nothing less than a crisis of survival." The effect was probably greatly magnified because as Peng stated on page 270 "Malaya, we realized was not a food-growing country." Therefore, one could claim that Galula's third point, a non-hostile geographic environment, comes into play here, although Galula never discussed it in terms of fertility, food supplies, etc. Still, as we could not get any strong indication of the significance of population resettlement and food supply across multiple insurgencies, and it may be an issue that was fairly unique to Malaya because of an export-driven economy, squatters, and heavy food importation. Therefore, if that issue is set aside, Peng is probably not in opposition to Galula and Fall in their overarching theories.

In the case of General China, there was clearly no overarching theory or such construct presented.

In the case of Cabral, we infer that he might have considered cause and force ratios to be important, although it is impossible to determine if he considered them of primary importance, and if he did not, then what did he consider of primary importance? The same may be said for Chipenda and Spartacus.

Truong Nhu Tang clearly considered the cause to be overwhelming in the case of Vietnam. As he comments in referring to the cancelled elections of 1956: "It seemed to me that the sentiment for national unity was so powerful that some way would have to be found to accommodate it."[8] He never discussed force ratios or the size of force needed to fight the insurgency.

FINDINGS

A review of eight insurgent leaders found that the following was considered important by the majority, if not all of them:

1. Cause

In almost all cases, the cause is effectively nationalism.

The majority may have also considered the following important:

1. Force ratios

The following items were considered important by three or four of the insurgents:

1. Use of firepower in general (by either side)
2. Fracture lines in society
3. Outside support
4. Defections to the counterinsurgency

The following items were only considered important by one or two of the insurgents:

1. Terrain
2. Population resettlement by counterinsurgents
3. Cutting off food by counterinsurgents
4. Continuous patrolling by counterinsurgents
5. Good intelligence by counterinsurgents
6. Under-cutting the cause by counterinsurgents
7. Burden
8. Active sanctuaries
9. Insurgent use of firepower
10. Counterinsurgent use of firepower

The following items were not really addressed:

1. Value of the use of torture
2. Population size
3. Structure of the insurgency
4. Indigenous government types
5. Elections
6. Specific government reforms
7. The counterinsurgents "staying the course"
8. Gridding, ink blot strategies, etc.

The list of factors that is not discussed in depth vastly exceeds that which is discussed in depth.

CONCLUSIONS

This review of the insurgents shows an entirely different focus as to what is important in an insurgency than one gets from reading the "classical" counterinsurgent theorists. In the end, the insurgent is primarily focused on the cause. The military aspects of the insurgency seem to be secondary concerns. When looking at some of the things that the counterinsurgents discuss in depth (for example, gridding, ink blot strategies, unit sizes, etc.), one wonders about the importance and priority of some of these factors. As the insurgents with a theoretical bent tend to be political polemicists and have only knowledge of the one war they fought in, they are a weaker source for understanding insurgent and counterinsurgent theory, but they clearly are a source that needs to be examined and tapped for insights.

On the other hand, the majority of the insurgents we reviewed actually won and or managed a favorable result from their war in the long run (this certainly applies to Grivas and Itote). Perhaps their focus on the political cause, with the military aspects secondary, is an indication of the correct priorities.

One final observation: It is hard not to be impressed with the dedication, motivation, courage and intelligence of many of these insurgent leaders. In most cases, what they suffered for their cause is much more challenging than that endured by the vast majority of their opponents.

NOTES

1. I was helped considerably by C. Curtiss Johnson in this task. The chapter is effectively coauthored by him.
2. Giap was the commander of the People's Army of Vietnam in both the Indochina and Vietnam wars. He was victorious in both wars. The quote is from a conversation with General Raoul Salan of France.
3. C. Curtiss Johnson reviewed four of the insurgents' writings, and I reviewed four.
4. Itote, op. cit., 129.
5. *Ibid.*, 138. There is also a claim by General China that the government side had begun to limit the carnage after considerable slaughter, but this needs to be further investigated. See pp. 131-132.
6. *Ibid.*, 150.
7 *Ibid.*, 285–291. Specific rules addressing treatment of civilians included: "(20) There is no authority to kill any person under eighteen years, for this would show us to be unwise". (21) No one may be killed without the approval of village leaders, for they are responsible for reporting traitors. . . . (24) There is no permission to beat civilians for that will turn them against us. (25) Soldiers have no authority to collect any tax without the permission of their commander. (26) Attacks on any prison are not permitted unless the prisoners and prison families are firmly united behind the action; such actions otherwise are dangerous, for the Government will take stern measures against the villages and relatives of the prisoners. (27) No hospital should be attacked, but wounded people in hospital may be recovered and returned to the forest; nurses should not be harmed for they are friendly to all; any solider found molesting a nurse will be punished severely. (28) Villages under construction should not be burned, for people will turn against us. (29) There is no authority to burn any school, even though ours were burnt buy the Europeans and their agents. (30) No child should be hindered from going to school. (31) There is no authority for any solider to rape a girl or a woman."
8 Tang, 35.

CHAPTER 19

Withdrawal and War Termination

As this long and difficult war ends, I would like to address a
few special words to . . . the American people: Your steadfastness
in supporting our insistence on peace with honor has made
peace with honor possible.

—Richard M. Nixon, 1973[1]

The missing piece of analysis in both our work and in that of many of the various counterinsurgent theorists is how does one terminate or end these wars, and what is the best way to do so? This is not an insignificant point. We did propose doing exactly such a study in several of our reports, briefings and conversations, but no one expressed a strong interest in examining war termination.

Obviously, if the insurgents are driving tanks through the streets of the capital city, the war has ended, and not favorably for the counterinsurgents. But many insurgencies end with some form of negotiated settlement. Many insurgencies end with the slow collapse and disintegration of the insurgency. Many of them end with some form of political compromise. Most of them end with some form of negotiation and political agreement, regardless of victor.

We did look at this briefly in our original Iraq Casualty estimate. First of all, an insurgent win was easy to determine. Usually it means that the insurgents took control of the capital and the government.[2]

Counterinsurgent wins were a little more nuanced. For example, in 4 of our original 14 original cases of counterinsurgent wins, there was neither stability nor complete success in the long run. In the Mau Mau rebellion, 7 years after its suppression, the intervening power handed over control of the country to the independence movement. Many of the leaders that the British arrested at the start of the rebellion, including Jomo Kenyatta, ended up in charge of the country in 1963. In the case of Cyprus, the head of the insurgency, General Grivas, ended up as the defense minister of the new Cypriot government, and while EOKA did not achieve its goal of unification with Greece, it did achieve independence for the country. Still, Cyprus has gone through several more rounds of violence since then and remains to this day a divided island. Katanga Province has remained the source of continuous revolts and violent movements over the years, and is still in violence today.[3] Chad erupted into a later civil war, required multiple French interventions and is still in violence today. Kashmir, which is not counted among the four cases above, is still in violence; although at a much lower level that before.

Three of the 14 counterinsurgents wins were resolved through political compromise, including Cyprus, which formed an independent nation, vice unifying with Greece, Yemen, where the central government moderated to be much less radical government, and Lebanon, where after over 15 years of warfare, they finally constitutionally adjusted the balance of power between Christians and Muslims and achieved a fragile peace. One might argue that Northern Ireland was also in that category, except that the insurgents had clearly lost the struggle before they negotiated a peace that included allowing them to participate in the government.

Still, a significant number of cases were finally resolved by modifying the political balance in the country: Cyprus, Yemen, Lebanon, to an lesser extent Northern Ireland, and seven years after the insurgency was defeated, Kenya. Malaya also was granted its independence during the course of the insurgency, which helped undercut the insurgents' cause.

Many others were resolved with a peace settlement (including the Vietnam War). These peace settlements were to end the violence which had become pointless because one side had clearly won (for example, the Malaysian peace settlement with Chin Peng in 1989), to allow for a final resolution, or a graceful ending for one side or the other.

The Vietnam peace settlement is unique in that some of the participates actually thought it would work somehow, and it led to U.S. Secretary of State Kissinger and Le Duc Tho winning a Nobel Peace Prize less than two years before South Vietnam was overrun. Le Duc Tho of North Vietnam refused his prize.

We know what an insurgent win is. Those are fairly easy to determine. Counterinsurgent wins appears to be unclear in about one-third of the cases. One could interpret our original statistics to mean that of the 28 insurgencies, the intervening power or government power was ultimately successful in only 10 cases (35 percent).

We have not looked at the issue in more depth with our database of 83 cases, but in general, it is safe to say that around one-third of counterinsurgent wins are clouded, or somewhat less than clear victories.

FORCE DRAW DOWN

We also looked at force draw down in our original Iraq casualty estimate. This was not for the purpose of examining war termination, but for the purpose of making an estimate as to force strengths during the life of an insurgency. Still, the results of that examination are significant for addressing war termination also.

In our initial look at 28 cases, we found only three cases where the counterinsurgents were able to reduce or choose to significantly reduce force strength during the course of an insurgency. These are Malaya, Northern Ireland and Vietnam. With our expanded database of 83 cases, these are still the only three cases of such.

Let us look at each in turn. The case of Malaya is illustrated below:

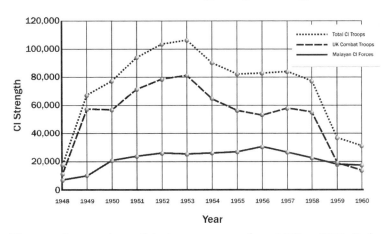

The most intense phase of the insurgency was from 1958 to 1952. Peak counterinsurgent deaths were 488 in 1951, with 272 in 1952 and only 95 in 1953. Over the course of 1959 and 1960, there were only three deaths.

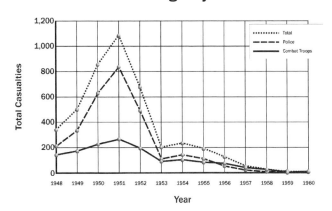

When one looks at counterinsurgent force strength over that period, one notes a large decline in strength, but in fact, it is a decline in militia strength. Commonwealth troop strength peaked at 29,656 in 1956, consisting of UK troops, Gurkhas and Australians. It declined to 16,939 in 1960. Basically, even with no combat occurring for two years, the troop strength of the intervening forces ("UK Combat Troops" on the first graph) was reduced by one half and only during last couple of years. The decline is Malayan strength is primarily due to police force declining after 1953 and the "Special Constabulary" declining after 1952 and eventually being reduced to zero. There was also a Malayan Home Guard that was briefly up to 300,000 people, but most of them were never armed and were eventually disbanded.

This is the best case we have of a force draw down, and it was only done to any significance late in the war, where the insurgency was pretty much reduced to 400 or so fighters sitting across the narrow border with Thailand and scattered remnants being policed inside of Malaya.

Northern Ireland is another case in which the degree of activity was very intense early on. For example:

Counterinsurgency Casualties

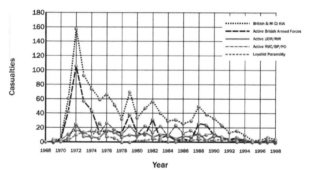

On the other hand, force strength does not draw down much.

Counterinsurgent Strength

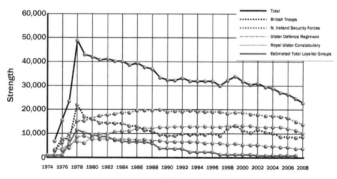

In this case the peak counterinsurgent strength was 48,341 in 1972, and the counterinsurgent strength is still 22,691 in 2002. These two cases show the limitation of a draw down.

In the case of Vietnam, there was a four-year-long massive build up, and then four years of equally hasty withdrawal. This is clearly not the way to conduct a war and is discussed in more depth in Chapter Twenty-Two. Vietnam is clearly is not a good example of a successful force drawn down.

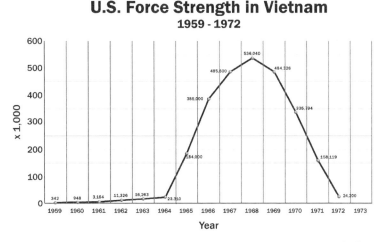

Besides these three cases, we do not have any other good examples of a force draw down except that which occurs in the last year of the war, and agreements are reached and the war ended. In general, this strongly indicates that draw downs are not very practical until you have resolved the war.

A basic examination needs to be done concerning how insurgencies end, how withdrawals are conducted, and what the impact of various approaches towards war termination is. This also needs to address long-term outcome, that is, what happened following war termination.

We have nothing particularly unique and insightful to offer in this regard. Therefore, we will avoid the tendency to pontificate generally and leave this discussion for later. Still, we are currently observing with Afghanistan and Iraq two wars where the intervening power is withdrawing or has withdrawn. These are both interesting cases of war termination strategies, although it we do not yet know the outcome in either case.

NOTES

1. From the televised broadcast to the American people on January 23, 1973, after the signing of the ceasefire agreement between the North Vietnamese, the Viet Cong, and the South Vietnamese.
2. Two of our Vietnam cases–Vietnam I (1956–1960) and Vietnam II (1961–1964)–were adjudicated as insurgent wins, because if the U.S. had not significantly increased its commitment, the insurgents clearly would have taken control of the government within a short time.
3. Katanga Province was also called Shaba Province and as of 2009 had been divided into four provinces.

CHAPTER **20**

Relating a Force Ratio Model to Iraq

If we can stay the course over here for another
year or so, the insurgency will wear itself out.

—Colonel Dusty Rhoades, a Marine intelligence
office in Iraq, August 2004[1]

In December 2009, the U.S. lost no soldiers to combat in Iraq for that month. This was the first time in the 81 months that the U.S. had been in Iraq that we had gone through a month without a combat loss. This is in contrast to the situation three years earlier (December 2006), when the U.S. lost 112 soldiers and marines in a month, 95 of them from combat. The U.S. had been suffering significant losses for the 45 months before then, month after month, with more than 20 killed each month, with no clear resolution in sight. December 2006 was the last month before the implementation of the new surge strategy.

The U.S. strategy in Iraq had gone through several shifts over time. First was the original occupation in March 2003, where we went in with 92,000 troops and somehow or the other expected everything to settle down quickly after that. But Iraq did not seem to settle down, and a very low level of losses continued through 2004. The U.S. forces were forced to increase their size in the face on the continue insecurity and problems. It was during this time that we prepared our Iraq Casualty estimate. This was also the time when the U.S. made the two assaults on Fallujah in April and November 2004, which were viewed by some as breaking the back on the insurgency. Most of the northern Iraqi city of Mosul was also briefly overrun by the insurgents in November 2004.

When we were briefing in early 2005, we were informed of a new strategy, which apparently was to keep U.S. troops base bound in an attempt to limit U.S. losses and to instead quickly replace the U.S. forces in the field with Iraqi troops. This was attempted but this new strategy really did not settle Iraq down. The insurgents effectively were given a free hand to conduct mayhem while it was quickly shown that we could not create an effective Iraqi Army overnight. The development of an effective allied army was a problem similar to what we had in Vietnam and similar to what we would

243

have in Afghanistan. The U.S. Army was then forced to come back out of its bases and once again engage in guerilla war. This of course, was accompanied by increased U.S. losses and what was appearing to be an open ended and extended commitment. With the increasing losses and no end in sight, in 2006 the war in Iraq was beginning to develop into a very familiar but depressing pattern.

Very late in 2006, the "surge" strategy was proposed. The idea here was to increase U.S. forces in Iraq by 30,000 troops to help calm down the insurgency, and then we would be able to withdraw. With its increased deployments in early 2007 until the end of 2009, U.S. losses peaked in May of 2007 and then declined until we reached the point in December 2009 where we went through a month with no U.S. losses in combat.

There is no question by the end of the surge, the Iraq war looked like a success story. Still as of 2009, this was success with 134,000 U.S. troops deployed and 150 U.S. troops being killed that year.[2] Regardless, this is far better than it has been, and the level of violence in Iraq had declined to a much lower level compared to what it used to be. Control of most operations had been transferred to the Iraqis, their army had taken over the security mission and the U.S. withdrew completely at the end of 2011.

DOES THIS MEAN THAT . . .

- There may be no clear easy lever to tip the war in the right direction?
  - Controlling the borders is good, but is probably not a panacea
  - Revised rules of engagement may be meaningful
  - Political compromise (Sunni political security) may be useful
- We are fundamentally reduced to an attrition strategy?
  - With a later political settlement after many years
  - There is also the Foreign Insurgent (Jihadist) issue (not negotiable?)
- Our only major lever is to increase force size?
  - Up to 500,000 troops based upon 20 troops per 1,000 population
  - Up to 500,000 troops based upon 25-to-1 force ratio
- Regardless, this all supports at least a straight-line casualty estimate

---

Our data in 2004 was not showing a positive picture. In fact, not only was our estimate based upon a straight-line casualty estimate, but up until the end of 2006, the U.S. Army pretty much lost the same number of people each year. That was 849 U.S. killed in 2004, 846 killed in 2005 and 822 killed in 2006. This appeared to be regardless of who was in command or what strategy they were using.

And then, from outside the normal channels of command at the Pentagon, a new strategic approach was developed, in part by General Raymond Odierno, in part by General David Petraeus, in part by retired General John Keane and with help from the conservative analyst Frederick W. Kagan and the American Enterprise Institute, and by several others.[3]

We saw the American Enterprise Institute briefing on this in January 2007.[4] Our initial reaction was that this looked to be a good thing, but we were not convinced it was a panacea. In fact, the surge was not. As noted by David Kilcullen, an advisor to General Petraeus, "the tribal revolt was arguably the most significant change in the Iraqi operating environment in several years."[5] There were other major factors that made the "surge" effective.

Looking at our previous slide, we note that, "Controlling the borders is good, but is probably not a panacea." The U.S. had attempted to control the entry points with Syria but avoided the temptation to try to control all 3,650 linear kilometers of foreign borders that Iraq had, especially the 1,458 kilometer one with Iran, which was probably not controllable. Therefore, we avoided the effort to try to win the insurgency by locking the insurgents out. In light of the effectiveness of such previous efforts (see Chapter Ten), this was probably wise.

Our second point, "Revised rules of engagement may be meaningful," is indeed what was done in Iraq. We did tighten our rules of engagement, use of firepower and how we treated the local Iraqis. This last point is significant. As Thomas Ricks points out about a conversation he had with General Petraeus, when they talking about the treatment of the Iraqis, the general began singing a classic Aretha Franklin song as, "R-E-S-P-E-C-T, find out what it means to the Iraqis."[6] Ricks also points out the contrast in behavior of General Odierno's command when he commanded the 4th Infantry Division (Mechanized) in Iraq in 2003–2004 and later when he returned as commander of the Multi-National Corps-Iraq in Iraq in 2006–2008.[7]

While none of our work has yet to look at the effects of "respect" or treatment on the local population, we do not think this is an issue entirely separated from "rules of engagement" and certainly not from "use of firepower." See Chapter Nine for our conclusions concerning those subjects.

Our next point through is really the crux of the matter, which was "Political compromise (Sunni political security) may be useful." What actually happened in Iraq was significant. We were facing an insurgency that *The Dupuy Institute* estimated had at least 20,000 fighters and probably more like 60,000 fighters. We then talked to this enemy, dealt with them, found a common cause with them, co-opted them, paid them off, and turned them! By 10 December 2007, the U.S. had signed up 73,397 men as part of the Sunni Awakening Councils or Son of Iraq.[8] The Awakening Councils were local armed Sunni forces, led by local or tribal leaders that the U.S. was now paying to help patrol and keep the peace in their areas. The Sunnis were a minority in Iraq, but they made up the large majority of the insurgents. The Sunni Awakening Councils certainly contained some former insurgents! The Awakening Councils would eventually grow to be over 100,000 men.

We bought off the insurgents, pure and simple. It was a very cheap and effective solution. So, the situation we faced at the end of 2006 was that we had 140,000 U.S. troops, 15,200 allied troops and 132,700 Iraqi army troops facing 60,000 insurgents.[9] This was a 4.8-to-1 force ratio. Using the "limited" line in our model (and we always stated in our briefings that we considered Iraq to be a very large regional or factional insurgency), it indicates that our odds of winning would be 86 percent. While this is clearly very favorable, no one was in the mood to continue losing over 800 Americans a year in this venture.

Instead, we bought off 100,000 potential insurgents. Now, the math gets a little fuzzy here in that you have bought off 100,000 potential insurgents from a pool of an estimated 60,000 insurgents, but this again shows the nebulous nature of counting insurgents. Not every armed man is an insurgent, not every armed insurgent is an insurgent all the time, and certainly not every member of an Awakening Council is a former insurgent. Still, the end of result of this is that we had set aside 100,000 potentially dangerous people, and that left us with maybe 20,000 actual insurgents to deal with. This is now a much more tractable problem. So, instead of having 287,900 troops facing 60,000 insurgents, you now had a force ratio of 14-to-1, with the much more favorable odds of a 99 percent chance of winning.

But more than simply increasing the odds of winning, it clearly removed from the battlefield two-thirds of the people who were trying to kill us. This resulted, after almost a year of heavy and serious fighting in a decline in U.S. losses down to 23 killed for the month of December 2007, 14 of them from combat from a peak of 126 killed in May 2007. It was all very clever and effective. It was almost by accident.

The U.S. surge plan was not specifically based upon the effective buy-out of the opposition. In the original Kagan briefings of December 2006 and January 2007, they simply never addressed the subject of Awakening Councils in the 56 pages of the briefing. It did not discuss any plans to talk to or negotiate with the Sunnis or the sheiks. There was not a single line in the briefing even vaguely hinting at such an approach. The plan was clearly for the "surge" to defeat the problem, and the plan made no provisions to buy out the insurgents.

The original contacts with the Sunni Iraqis started coming to fruition in September 2006 with the founding of the Anbar Salvation Council. In August 2006, in one of the most violent provinces in Iraq, an Iraqi sheik named Abdel Sittar Baziya approached the local U.S. brigade commander in Ramadi, Colonel Sean MacFarland. Even though the effort was opposed by some in the U.S. armed forces and in the Shiite dominated Iraqi government, these contacts were developed so that during the fall of 2006, the violent city of Ramadi was slowly brought under control with the help of local Sunni Iraqis, many of whom joined the police, and three locally raised militia "emergency battalions."[10]

This was an effort that was independent of the "surge." In reality, the long-term results in Iraq would have been similar if there was no surge, although I think that the surge did help in the overall implementation of the plan and in the long-term helped reduce costs (U.S. casualties). One of the other values of the surge was that it gave the Bush administration a year of breathing space politically, and this breathing space allowed the Awakening Councils to fully develop and be proven. By the end of 2007, with U.S. losses in decline and insurgent activity lower, a precipitous withdrawal from Iraq no longer was seriously considered by most politicians.

Therefore, to go back to my previous slide, "Does this mean that there may be no clear easy lever to tip the war in the right direction?" Well, there clearly was, but it was an option that only presented itself in 2006 and was brought to us by the Iraqis. It was a unique opportunity that resulted in a rather sharp decline in violence in Iraq. In 2006, there were 45,330 incidents in Iraq. In 2009, there were less than 1,000 incidents a month.[11] It is a tribute to the working level of the army that they were able to explore and expand upon this option. This was a plan that did not come from above.

The next question, "Does this mean that we are fundamentally reduced to an attrition strategy with a later political settlement after many years?" Well, the hope was that we dodged this line of development. We dodged the need to attrite the insurgents until they were slowly ground down and exhausted and were willing to negotiate. Instead, we bought them off. From a practical point of view, we went from 904 U.S. dead in 2007, to 314 dead in 2008, to 150 dead in 2009, to withdrawal in 2011. This appears to be success by any measure.

Now, there were still dangers here, because Iraq still had its Sunni Awakening Councils, 100,000 armed men not under government control, and there were still an estimated 20,000 or so insurgents out there.[12] They did have the potential to return to the field at any time and reboot the insurgency. What happened as the U.S. withdrew and the insurgency declined was that the Awakening Councils were slowly dissolved. They were down to 51,900 in January 2011 and around 30,000 in June 2012 and by 2013 were dissolved.[13] If the insurgency was truly ended, then this process makes sense. If the insurgency was dormant, or the Sunnis were being released without reintegration into the governance of the country, then this reduction potentially could lead to a revitalization of the insurgency. In fact, this appears to be a part of what occurred, and in 2014 the insurgents suddenly sweep across and took large parts of northwestern and northern Iraq. As this occurred after the U.S. withdrawal, then the "surge" strategy in Iraq began looking more like the "Vietnamization" strategy tried by the U.S. from 1969–1973, where we managed to withdraw, and then lost the country. Was the "surge" strategy just another failed attempt to shortcut a counter-insurgency effort?

The final point in our slide was, "Does this mean that our only major lever is to increase force size?" Well, in fact that is what happened. By the end of 2007, the U.S. had in Iraq 160,000 troops, 10,961 allies and 141,991 Iraqi Army troops. This is a total of 312,952. Added to that are 17,208 defense support forces, 1,075 Air Force, 1,106 Navy, 142,138 Police Service, 32,517 National Police, 31,376 Border Enforcement, 2,578 Special Operations for a total of 540,950. This is not far from the 500,000 we were estimating on that chart back in January 2005! Of course, our estimates usually do not include police unless they are police forces primarily dedicated to fighting the insurgency. Also, one could claim that the 103,000 Sunni Awakening Council forces are anti-insurgent forces[14] The U.S. also had 180,000 contractors including 20,000 that were private security guards. These contractors were usually performing tasks that in the past were done by uniformed military. As such, they could also be counted as part of the deployed tail of the U.S. Army.[15] Regardless of who and how you count it, in the end, you can't get away from the fact that you need "boots on the ground," or in our terminology, favorable force ratios. That is what was done in Iraq.

Finally, the Sunni Awakening Councils (vice the surge) did have an effect on our casualty estimate. The U.S. did pretty much run a straight line casualty loss rate from 2004 through 2007. U.S. casualties then dropped more than half in 2008 and by half again in 2009. As such, we ended up bumping into the bottom of part of our original estimate of 5,000 to 10,000 U.S. killed (all causes) vice landing somewhere dead in the middle of it. On the other hand, our duration estimate is pretty much on target, in that we figured on around ten (or more) years. Our involvement lasted almost nine years.

There are other reasons that losses declined. As the surge ended we reduced our participation in intense combat operations and left that work to the Iraqis (of course, this is the point). We pulled our troops back from the cities and safely sequestered them back in their bases. For 2009, the U.S. losses in Iraq were around one troop killed per 1,000 deployed.[16] Just for comparison, the U.S. losses in Vietnam from 1970 through 1973, during the phase we were withdrawing, was consistently running more than 10 troops killed per 1,000 deployed. So even during the withdrawal and Vietnamization of the Vietnam War, the intensity of combat was more than ten times higher in Vietnam than it is in Iraq. South Vietnam fell to the North Vietnam 27 months later.

Clearly, Iraq is not Vietnam, but it does provide a yardstick for comparing a hopefully successful withdrawal to a withdrawal that was clearly not successful. In this case, the level of intensity for the U.S. in Vietnam was more than ten times higher than it was for the U.S. in Iraq in 2009. Furthermore, there was a large hostile armed conventional force, with armor, sitting across the border and also inside South Vietnam, waiting for us to withdraw. Clearly, we were not facing the same conditions in Iraq. Still, low losses do not automatically indicate that the situation is under control. They can also be achieved by simply not engaging the insurgency.

This was done once before. In 2005, the U.S. Army indeed adopted a strategy in Iraq of pulling our troops back into their base camps, outside of the cities, and safe from harm. While they were doing that, the Iraqi insurgency continued to escalate to even higher levels, for effectively the U.S. had handed the playing field over to the insurgents. Part of the surge strategy was to pull the U.S. troops out of their base camps and put them back into the cities. This was a very useful and essential part of the plan.

Now, as the levels of violence went down considerably, it was considered safe to pull them back, unlike in 2005. But, the difference is that we had brought the situation back under control before starting to withdraw, unlike what was done in Iraq in 2005 or Vietnam from 1969 to 1973.

The withdrawal from Iraq started in June 2009. The plan was not to withdraw completely, but to leave behind a force of tens of thousands after 2011 to provide training and advice to the Iraqis. This step did not happen, in part because of the Iraqi government refusal to accept American troops unless they could be tried in Iraq courts for crimes committed in Iraq. The U.S. insisted on some degree of immunity from Iraqi law as part our condition to remain. So instead of having a continued presence there as trainers and advisors for several years after 2011, we completely withdrew. Still, at the time of withdrawal, it appeared that the situation in Iraq was being brought under control.

At that point, the war in Iraq had been turned around by two things, increased force ratios and buying off the insurgents. These two are linked to some extent. Still, if the dynamics between the Sunni, Shiites, and other factions were worked out properly, this could be a war that the U.S. could claim to have won. On the other hand, if the country broke into civil war or sustained factional violence continues, then we would be left with something less than victory.

In 2014, the situation on the ground dramatically changed again, with Sunni insurgents again sweeping across northwestern and northern Iraq like they did in 2004. This time they took Mosul completely, with the Iraqi army collapsing and retreating. Their ability to expand beyond the Sunni areas of Iraq was limited though. They did not attempt to expand into Kurdish controlled areas and their much heralded march on Baghdad did not really amount to much. As of the time of this writing (June 2014), the Iraqi Army has retaken Tikrit and may eventually reclaim Mosul. Still, it appears that the insurgency has been renewed with considerable virulence.

What happened in the interim, where we went from a seemingly successful withdrawal, to a situation that briefly looked a whole lot like the end of the Vietnam War in 1975? Well, a couple of events over the last few years empowered the insurgency. First, the Shiite dominated government never really incorporated or effectively included the Sunni's into the government of Iraq. As such, the divide between them remained and even further widened. Just as the U.S. was able to bring the insurgency under control through the establishment of the Awaking Councils, we now find that since the U.S. left, the Awaking Councils have disappeared and their people were not successfully incorporated into the Iraqi Army or any other organizations. Instead, the potential insurgents were once again left un-tethered.

Added to that there developed a civil war in Syria, and this helped revitalize the most extreme elements of the insurgency. This new organization, the Islamic State of Syria and the Levant (ISIL),[17] evolved from the earlier Al-Qaeda affiliated Iraqi groups. Its leader, Abu Bakr al-Bahgdadi (meaning "from Baghdad") is from Iraq.[18]

So with the insurgency revitalized and with the Awakening Councils gone, the situation was ripe for another shift in the war in Iraq. As we have done no analysis of these recent developments, I will limit my comments to how it reflects on the lessons from the previous ten years in Iraq.

First, it clearly shows the value of the Awakening Councils, in that Iraq was much more peaceful when they were there, and much less peaceful when they ceased operating. In fact, it would appear that some of the Sunnis have accepted ISIL as a better alternative than the current Shiite dominated government in Iraq.

Second, it shows that the United States almost certainly did withdraw from Iraq too early. We are now back in Iraq, although with only a force of around 500 men, but we back nonetheless. For the purposes of our estimate, were we in Iraq for only 8.7 years, or has the clock indeed started ticking again?

Third, it is clear that "Sunni political security" needs to be addressed, or one can certainly loose a war that was looking like it was won. As a minimum, the Iraqi government needed to maintain the support of the local Sunni tribal chiefs, the Awakening Councils and other Sunnis, and needed to make sure they were included in the government and armed forces. It appears that over time, the government did the reverse, and a renewed insurgency is the clear result of that.

Fourth, it again shows the limited value of decapitating an insurgency. In 2004, the group, known informally as Al Qaeda in Iraq was headed by Abu Musab Al-Zarqawi. He was killed by a targeted U.S. air strike in June 2006. The organizations subsequent leaders, Abu Abdullah al-Rashid al-Baghdadi and the Egyptian Abu Ayyub al-Masri were both killed in April 2010 in a joint operation by the U.S. and Iraq. But as always, if the insurgency has a cause, new leaders and new forces will arise. Headhunting alone is probably not enough to end an insurgency. This is a concern as the use of drones and the targeting individuals with air strikes seems to have become our preferred way of war.

Lastly, we still stand by our conclusion that the Iraq war is winnable by the government. While the insurgents have made significant gains in the first half of 2014, that they are mostly Sunnis facing a Shiite government has meant that they have not been able to seize the capital, have not been able to control large areas of Shiite or Kurdish populated areas, and remain fundamentally a regional or factional insurgency. As such, the future of Iraq remains one where a Shiite or coalition government will control Baghdad. We do not believe that there will be a Sunni-based caliphate established in that city. The current government of Iraq still has a chance to regain control of all of Iraq. In the long-run, there appears to be two options, Iraq will either be under control of a central government with considerable Shiite representation, or it will break up into three component states (Shiite Arab, Sunni Arab and Kurdish). It does not appear that there will be any Sunni dominated government, or Al-Qaeda related government, or Islamic Caliphate operating out of the much more secular city of Baghdad. Still, it does appear that the Iraqi government was thrown away an opportunity to develop a more peaceful democratic multi-national and multi-religious state and instead is going to face continued warfare. It does appear that the Iraq insurgency will continue for some time now and with considerable violence. It does raise the question as to how "gimmicky" was the surge, in that we temporarily boosted troop strength, withdrew those forces, and then went home early. Just as we almost threw away a chance to successfully control Iraq with our poor handling of the early stages of the war, have we also mishandled the later stages of this war?

NOTES

1. Jim Michaels and Charles Crain, "Insurgents Showing No Sign of Letting Up." *USA Today* (22 Aug. 2004).

2. The strength figure is from May 2009. For 2009, there were 73 killed in action, 76 accidental deaths and one death from illness.

3. See Thomas E. Ricks, *The Gamble* (New York: The Penguin Press, 2009), 106–124.

4. The version we saw was "Choosing Victory: A Plan for Success in Iraq: Phase I Report" by Frederick W. Kagan, The American Enterprise Institute, 4 Jan. 2007. This was widely distributed, available on the web, and includes the Dec. 2006 briefing that they prepared.

5. David Kilcullen, *The Accidental Guerrilla: Fighting Small Wars in the Midst of a Big One* (New York: Oxford University Press, 2009), 179. The entire quote is, "The tribal revolt represented very significant political progress toward reconciliation at the grassroots level, and major security progress in marginalizing extremists and reducing civilian deaths. It also did much to redress the lack of Coalition forces that had hampered previous counterinsurgency approaches, by throwing tens of thousands of local allies into the balance, on our side. For these reasons, the tribal revolt was arguably the most significant change in the Iraqi operating environment in several years. But the significance of this development was initially overlooked to some extent, because it occurred in ways that were neither expected nor accounted for in our 'benchmarks'. . . ."

6. Thomas E. Ricks, 10 Feb. 2009, on Jon Stewart's *The Daily Show.*

7. Ricks, *The Gamble*, 107–110.

8. Alissa J. Rubin and Stephen Farrell, "Awakening Councils by Region." *The New York Times* (22 Dec. 2007). Of those 73,397, about 65,000 were receiving monthly salaries from the U.S.

9. The Iraqi Army figure is for both actives and those in training. There were 94,788 Iraqi Army troops rated as Level I or Level II (the highest levels) in Nov. 2006. There were also 900 Iraqi Air Force and 1,100 Iraqi Navy in the Defense Ministry Forces. Reporting to the Interior Ministry were 332,260 police, including 159,400 Iraqi National Police (active and in training) and144,000 Iraqi Facilities Protection Forces (active and in training).

10. See Mark Kukis, "Turning Iraq's Tribes against Al-Qaeda." *Time Magazine* (26 Dec. 2006) and Ricks, *op. cit.*, 66–72.

11. See *Measuring Security and Stability in Iraq: June 2009 Report to Congress* (US Department of Defense), 22. Their chart, "Overall Weekly Security Incident Trends, January 3, 2004 – 29 May, 2009," shows some number less than 200 for every week in 2009, or roughly

an average of 150 a week. Multiplied by 52, this would be almost 8,000 incidents per year. This is not a complete recording of incidents, as it notes "coalition reports only" (meaning it does not include Iraqi reports). We do not know how comprehensive the coalition reports are.

O'Hanlon has a chart on page 6 of his report called, "Enemy-Initiated Attacks against the Coalition and its Partners, by Week." This chart is currently updated through 13 Nov. 2009. It shows around 200 incidents per week.

12. The last estimate of insurgent strength we have seen is 3,150 from Jan. 2008. In light of the number of incidents in 2009, this figure seems low.

13. See Derek Harvey and Michael Pregent, "Who's to Blame for the Iraq Crisis", CNN, June 12 2014. To quote: "By 2013, the Sons of Iraq were virtually nonexistent, with thousands of their sidelined former members either neutral or aligned with the Islamic State of Iraq and Syria in its war against the Iraqi government."

14. As noted by Kilcullen, "Another key benefit [of the tribal revolt] is to force ratios and Coalition troop numbers . . . the fact that 95,000 former insurgents and tribal fighters are now on our side and fighting the enemy is worth a great deal, because it indicates that more Iraqis are lining up with the government and against extremism. It simultaneously increase our forces, improves our reach into the population, reduced the enemy's recruiting pool and active forces, reduces the number of civilians who need to rely on protection from Coalition (hence cuts the demand for our security services), and erodes the enemy's ability to intimidate and control the population. All these things have a positive effect on the overall correlation of forces in the theater (Kilcullen, *op. cit.*, 181).

15. See Ricks, *op. cit.*, 187 and 311. A more precise figure of 103,536 Sons of Iraq is reported for June 2008, in Michael E. O'Hanlon and Ian Livingston, *The Iraq Index: Tacking Variables of Reconstruction & Security in Post-Saddam Iraq* (Washington, D.C.: The Brookings Institution, 11 Dec. 2009). This figure has not been updated since then.

16. For 2009, 150 killed; 142,000 troops deployed as of Jan. 2009 and 115,000 as of Nov. 2009.

17. Also known as ISIS (Islamic State of Iraq and Syria).

18. This is a nom de guerre. His real name is Awad Ibrahim Ali al-Badri al-Samarrai, and he was born in Samarra.

CHAPTER 21

Relating a Force Ratio Model to Afghanistan

People often ask me, 'How long will this last?' It may happen tomorrow, it may happen a month from now, it may take a year or two, but we will prevail.

—President George W. Bush, 2001, in response to questions in his first new conference 96 hours after the war in Afghanistan had begun.[1]

Afghanistan in an unusual case, as the central government (controlled by the Taliban) was overthrown in 2001 by the U.S. and their Afghan allies, with the U.S. allied with and helping the anti-Taliban insurgents! The U.S. then installed a new government and a new insurgency developed against this U.S. supported government. Still, this insurgency appeared to lie fallow until 2005, when the incidents and violence began cycling upwards and finally exploding into a full scale insurgency by 2008 that now appears to be difficult to control.

The initial U.S. intervention in Afghanistan was conducted by a very small force of 3,850 U.S. and allied troops,[2] with the main ground force being around 22,500 local Afghan forces that were labeled the Northern Alliance. This limited U.S. intervention was keeping in line with Secretary of Defense Donald Rumsfeld's transformation ideas of minimizing the size of deployed U.S. ground forces. This campaign relied heavily on the use of U.S. airpower, with a limited U.S. presence on the ground. The bombing campaign continued for almost four weeks without a clear result and was punctuated by the oddly humorous claim by Donald Rumsfeld that "we're not running out of targets, Afghanistan is!"[3] Finally, in early November, with a shift to providing direct air support to the Northern Alliance, we saw the Afghani Army collapse quickly, Taliban dominated government fold up, and on 14 November, the Northern Alliance marched into Kabul and by middle of December had effective control of the entire country. This was, once more, an example of a successful insurgency in Afghanistan, although it was an insurgency that had the benefit of U.S direct support and massive U.S. air power. It was a relatively cheap intervention for the U.S.

It was also a test of Rumsfeld's ideas of using minimal ground force in these campaigns, like he would do again in Iraq in 2003. In this case it worked, but left us relying on local forces to help envelop the trapped Al Qaeda leader, Osama bin Laden, in the Tora Bora region in eastern Afghanistan. Unfortunately, the Al Qaeda leader waltzed out of that encirclement and into Pakistan, resulting in one major embarrassing failure in this campaign. He remained at large for almost ten years. So, while the campaign was successful in removing the Taliban dominated government of Afghanistan, it failed to eliminate the most senior leaders of Al Qaeda or the Taliban.

Still, the Taliban had been ousted, scattered across Afghanistan and chased into Pakistan. Their international terrorist allies, Al Qaeda and its leaders also decamped for Pakistan, where we suspect they remain. It has also been a cheap campaign, as the U.S. had suffered only 12 dead from all causes (4 from combat) in Afghanistan from October through December 2001.

After that, a new supposedly democratic government was established under the leadership of Hamid Karzai in December 2001 and now the former insurgents had control of the government and the previously ruling Taliban became the new insurgents.

From 2002 through 2006, the war continued at a very low level. The U.S. presence remained low, with about 9,000 troops in 2002 slowly growing to 22,100 in 2006. Our allies and other international forces started with about 6,527 troops in 2002 and expanded to 18,966 troops in 2006, with the UK providing the largest portion of these troops. The Afghan government slowly built up its army to 36,000 in 2006 and its police force to 37,000 in 2006. This gave the counterinsurgents a force of around 114,066 troops in 2006.

On the other hand, insurgent activity was operating at a very low level with less than 70 U.S. troops being killed in action each year. This was from a low of 17 killed in action in 2003 to over 60 in 2005 and 2006. Our allies lost less then 10 people killed in action each year until 2006, when it rose to 65. The Afghan army losses remained similarly low, below 70 killed each year. But, the warning signs of a developing insurgency could clearly bee seen in the Afghan police forces, from a reported 9 killed in 2003, to 92 killed in 2004, to 138 killed in 2005 to a threatening 412 Afghan police killed in 2006. It was clear that they were taking the brunt of Taliban and other insurgents' actions and that the insurgency had indeed gotten serious and deadly.

Open source U.S. estimates of insurgent strength at that time though remained low. The coalition provided and estimate of only 1,000 insurgents in 2003[4], although by 2006 the estimate had grown to a range between 2,000 and 5,000.[5]

Still, this was a developing insurgency and while our combat troops were not seriously threatened, there were clear warning signs that it was heading in the wrong direction. The most obvious sign was the losses of Afghan police. Their losses escalating with 412 killed in 2006. It is clear that someone was systematically establishing their control over the country side, and with those hemorrhaging loses, it was clearly not the Afghan police.

This left the U.S and allies in 2006 with 114,066 counterinsurgents facing allegedly only 2,000 to 5,000 insurgents and suffering 65 U.S. killed in action (as opposed to killed from all causes), 65 coalition killed in action, 63 Afghan Army and a rather significant 412 police. Were the counterinsurgents loosing control of the war at that point, only securing those spots they most cared about, and handing over control of the rest of the country to the insurgents? That appears to be the case.

From there, the war tipped rapidly out of control, with 2007 seeing 83 U.S. killed in action, 99 coalition troops killed in action, 385 Afghan Army and a stunning figure of 925 police killed. The following year was a no better, with 133 U.S. killed in action, 125 coalition killed in action, 226 Afghan Army and 880 police killed. The years of 2009 and 2010 have only been worse.

So, what happened and how did the U.S. loose control of the situation? Unfortunately, *The Dupuy Institute* was not doing any work on the subject at the time. But, we do note to start with that the estimates of insurgent strength again appear low, as was the case with Iraq. In 2006 it was estimated that the insurgents had between 2,000 to 5,000 troops. The U.S. and coalition forces also claimed to have killed 600 insurgents and captured 1,200 more. That is pretty significant casualties if the insurgency really only had 2,000 fighters. One wonders how so few guerillas managed to keep the insurgency going with such losses.

By 1 January 2008 the NATO-led International Security Assistance Force (ISAF) had upped its estimate to between 7,000 and 20,000 guerillas, which is much better, but when one considers that the guerillas had been doing over 6,000 incidents a year since 2006, it appears that the public estimates were still catching up with the reality on the ground.

In December 2008 we flagged this concern about guerilla force size in a briefing we gave. We noted that the incidents in Afghanistan were on the rise.

Total Incidents

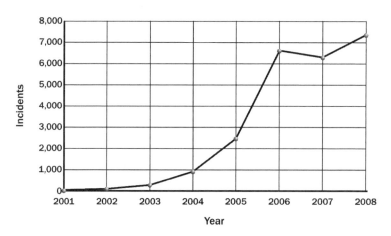

We then noted that insurgent strength had to be at least 13,192 based upon 500 incidents per thousand insurgents per year, for example as in Algeria 1955 (which was still building up to higher levels of violence at the time) or Malaya 1952 (which was on a downward slide in incidents and violence at that time). On the other hand, if an estimate was based upon 333 incidents per thousand insurgents per year, which was higher than in Algeria from 1958–1962 and Malaya 1953–1960, then insurgent strength was more like 19,788. Still, Algeria and Malaya were only two cases, and were two cases with highly organized and motivated insurgents. A better figure for estimation might be 250 incidents per thousand insurgents per year, this is still better than the worst years of Colombia (1966, 1972, 1976–78, 1994 and 1997. which remained below 200 incidents per thousand insurgents throughout their insurgency). Still, if we use a figure of 250 incidents, then we are looking at an estimated insurgent strength as high as 26,384. This is still based upon a performance that may have been better than what the insurgents were doing in Iraq! We are probably looking at an insurgent force strength that is greater than 20,000 and had been that way for the three years of 2006 to 2008.

Our tentative conclusion from our back-of-the-envelope analysis was the insurgent strength has to be at least in the range of 15,000 to 25,000. Still for the rest of our analysis we choose the mid-point of the U.S. provided figures for an estimated 14,500 insurgents. They were facing between 110,790 counterinsurgent forces with the police not counted, or 151,757 counterinsurgent forces with the police counted. This comes out to a 7.64 or a 10.47 force ratio.

Looking once again at our logit regression model, if the insurgency is regional or factional, then the counterinsurgency has 93.1 to 96.8 percent chance of winning. If the insurgency is broadly based (national) then the counterinsurgency has a 28.9 to 48.1 percent chance of winning.

With the United States withdrawn, we are now seeing whether a peaceful, democratic and stable Iraq can emerge from this war. This has not been the case so far. As we noted in early 2005:

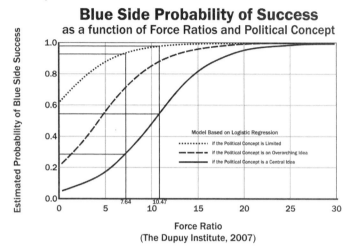

Blue Side Probability of Success
as a function of Force Ratios and Political Concept

Estimated Probability of Blue Side Success

Model Based on Logistic Regression
・・・・・・・・・・・ If the Political Concept is Limited
– – – – If the Political Concept is an Overarching Idea
——— If the Political Concept is a Central Idea

Force Ratio
(The Dupuy Institute, 2007)

So, again we are back to the same two questions that we face in Iraq, what is the size of the insurgency and is it a regional or factional insurgency?

In a December 2008 briefing I posed that question after presenting this data. I then asked the room full of analysts whether the insurgency in Afghanistan regional or factional, or was it broadly based. I was concerned that is might be broadly based because:

1. The insurgents came from the majority tribe in Afghanistan, the Pashtun. So unlike the situation in Iraq where the insurgents came from a group that was 20–30% of the population, while the Government came from a group that was 60–70% of the population of the country, here the situation was reversed, with Pashtun being the largest ethnic group in the country and making up over 40% of the population of Afghanistan. Of course, the situation was not as simple as in Iraq in that both the government and the insurgency were lead by Pashtun.
2. It appears that the open source estimate of insurgent strength was again low.
3. It appeared that things were getting worse.

At the time of that briefing, we had 110,790 troops there. *The Dupuy Institute* estimated insurgent strength between 15,000 and 25,000, with us leaning towards the higher figure. So if the insurgency was a regional or factional insurgency, then even at a force ratio of 4.43 to 1 (assuming 25,000 insurgents), we had an 84 percent chance of winning. Yet, it did not appear that we were winning.

So, the question went around the table, and two or three people there strongly opined that is was clearly a regional or factional insurgency. There was certitude in the voices. I was not sure, but was not ready to argue it at the time.

The danger is that if the insurgency is a broadly based, and there were indeed something like 25,000 insurgents, then at a 4.43 to 1 force ratio, then according to our logit regression model, the chance of the blue side winning was only 14 percent. To push the odds up to a more reasonable level of 80 percent would mean that we needed a force ratio of more like 15.5 to 1, meaning an additional 276,710 troops, and most likely the majority of them would have to come from America! Needless to say, as the U.S. was hesitant to build up to 160,000 troops in Iraq, then such a number for Afghanistan was going to be difficult to sell.

We received no substantive response to our briefing and meanwhile the war in Afghanistan continued. Finally in early 2009, we wrote an unpublished op-ed piece that said in part:

Right now, in Afghanistan we have very roughly 30,000 U.S. Troops, 30,000 other international troops, 60,000 operational Afghani Army troops and maybe 60,000 active Afghani Police. The effectiveness of the Afghani army and police are open to debate, but the police have been losing almost 1,000 people a year. Public estimates have put insurgent combat strength (who are more than just the Taliban), at an estimated 7,000–22,000. This insurgency has been generating 6,000 or more violent incidents a year, including around 8,000 for this last year. We believe, based upon our research into the relationship between insurgent incidents and insurgent strength, that the insurgency has between 16,000 to 32,000 active full-time and part-time insurgents. This is not addressing the 180,000 or so people that are considered as part of illegal armed groups.

Looking at the graph above, if there are 16,000 insurgents, and the political concept behind the insurgency is limited (regional or factional), then this produces a force ratio of 11.25-to-1 and a chance of counterinsurgent victory of 97% given enough time and no significant changes in the environment. If there are 32,000 insurgents, then the force ratio drops to 5.63-to-1 and the chance of counterinsurgent victory is 88%. Yet, things are getting worse. Clearly either the Afghani forces are particularly ineffective, or there are more insurgents than most estimates have established, or it is much more broadly based and supported that most people assume. Assuming widespread weaknesses in the Afghani forces, then if our effective strength in Afghanistan is reduced to 60,000 troops, then we are looking at forces ratios of 3.75-to-1 (81% chance of counterinsurgent victory) if there are 16,000 insurgents, and forces ratios of 1.88-to-1 (72% chance of counterinsurgent victory) if there are 32,000 insurgents. This appears to better represent the situation.

This argues, regardless of everything else currently going on, that US need to add between 30,000 to 60,000 troops to Afghanistan. Anything less is too little to give us the best chance of a favorable outcome. At 60,000 more, then pushes the force ratio back up to a more comfortable 3.75-to-1 ratio even if there is 32,000 insurgents and one does not count the Afghani army or police.

This is assuming that we fully understand the nature of the Afghan insurgency. If this insurgency is much more broadly based (i.e. based upon nationalism), then we are looking at even higher force levels being required. We note that our current force levels should be sufficient to handle the insurgency if there are only 16,000 insurgents and they are based upon a limited political concept. Yet the insurgency keeps expanding and getting stronger. This raises the concern that the insurgency is much more broadly based or much stronger than current public estimates.

Therefore, we recommend pushing U.S. force levels up another 60,000 more for this next year while continuing to aggressively search for a political solution and while continuing to develop the Afghani National Army and the Afghani Police. If this increase and a potential political solution noticeably changes the conditions on the ground, then this has worked. If not, then in the long run we will want to back out of any major ground commitment in Afghanistan sooner rather than later.

This quantitative analysis of Afghanistan offered by this small think tank was never published. Instead, we have presented it here for the first time for context.

In the interim, the Obama administration came up with its own response to the developing Afghan crisis, which was its own surge. Under this plan, announced in December 2009, another 30,000 or so troops were added as part of a surge, having reached the peak of the surge in the later half of 2010. They then set a withdrawal date of the middle of 2011, which they were unable to achieve.

So, more than five years after we wrote the February 2009 unpublished op-ed piece, does it still stand up? In the Report of Secretary-General of the United Nations for March 2014, they record that as of mid-January 2014 there were 145,199 Afghan National Police and 193,427 Afghan National Army soldiers.[6] The "surge targets" were 152,000 and 195,000 respectively. So, this is between 193,427 to 338,626 counterinsurgents (depending on how you count police). This is certainly enough strength to counteract a force 20,000 insurgents.

The U.S. force is drawing down and is disengaged from any active combat role as of 2015. The force peaked from about 100,000 in 2010 down to 66,000 as of the start of 2013. Over the course of 2013, 34,000 of these troops were to be withdrawn, with the U.S. involvement to end sometime in 2015. The coalition forces have already mostly left. As such, this Afghan force of over 300,000 troops is the primary counterinsurgent force for the future. It is certainly a much more impressive force than the 114,066 that we tried to prosecute the war with back in 2006.

On the other hand, the level of violence continued to rise during the buildup of the Afghan Army. This can be shown with the reporting by the U.N. Department of Safety and Security (UNDSS) of security incidences in Afghanistan:

PERIOD	SECURITY INCIDENCES	INCIDENCES PER MONTH
2008	8,893	741
2009	11,524	960
2010	19,403	1,617
2011	22,903	1,909
Jan–July 2012	10,019	1,431
16 August–15 November 2012	4,639	1,546
16 November 2012–15 February 2013	3,783	1,261
2013	20,093	1,674

The 2013 figure of 20,093 incidents a year does argue for a significant insurgency force. If we use a conservative figure of 333 incidents per thousand insurgents, then we are looking at more than 60,000 full-time and part-time insurgents. The number of security incidences has declined slightly since 2011. This would indicate that either we are slowly bringing the insurgency under control or that they are simply waiting until the U.S. leaves before they get more serious. Still, the level of violence is higher than it was in 2009, before the surge started, and the level of violence in 2013 is not significantly less than it was in 2011. Even with the erratic reporting for 2012,[7] it does appear that the level of violence has been pretty much the same for the last four years. It certainly appears we are a long way from getting the situation under control, and leaves open the question as to what will happen once the United States completes it withdrawal.

We still do not know for sure if Afghanistan is a regional or factional insurgency or whether it is broadly based. But if it is a regional or factional insurgency, then according to our regression model, we should be winning. Yet we only appear to be winning during the surge. In 2009 there were 11,524 security incidents (they reported 8,893 security incidents in 2008)[8] and 266 U.S. troops killed (as opposed to 132 in 2008). In 2010 there were 69% more security incidents[9] and 451 U.S. troops killed in combat by the end of the year. In 2011 it was a rather staggering 22,903 incidents a year but there were less U.S. troops killed in combat, down to 367. The year 2012 brought some relief with maybe around 17,000 incidents a year, but it went back up for 2013 to 20,093. This has been in the face of 251 U.S. troops killed in combat in 2012 and 85 in 2013. Still, the incidence figures indicate the insurgency is still operating with about the same level of virulence for the last four years.

There are other indicators that send mixed signals as to the trends. For example, 2012 was the first time in six years that civilian casualties declined. Still the decline in 2012 was only 4 percent compared to 2011. Furthermore, civilian deaths from anti-government forces increased by 9 percent compared to 2011.[10] So the decline in civilian deaths is primarily due to less civilian casualties caused by coalition forces. If civilian deaths by anti-government forces are increasing, does this indicate that the insurgents are expanding their control of the population?[11] For 2013, the number of civilian deaths increased by 7% to 2,959.[12] This is not an encouraging trend.

There are also "administrative weaknesses", to use David Galula's phrase. For example, bribery is widespread. The UN reports that total bribes paid to public officials in 2012 were $3.9 billion, and increase of 40 percent since their previous survey of 2009. They did a survey of 6,700 Afghans (of whom 42 percent were women), and half had paid a bribe to public officials.[13] When one considers that women rarely do public business in Afghanistan, then this pretty much means that anyone who was doing public business in Afghanistan was paying bribes.

Opium poppy cultivation for the south, west, center and east parts of Afghanistan, where most of the fighting is going on, has increased for three consecutive years. There are 154,000 hectares of opium poppy cultivation in Afghanistan in 2012, 18 percent more than in 2011, although production is down due to plant diseases and bad weather. [14] As of 13 November 2013, it was estimated that there were 209,000 hectares under cultivation.[15] Again it raises the question of who has control of the countryside.

There are still nearly three million Afghan refugees living in Iran and Pakistan. This is a man-power pool out of reach of the counterinsurgents. Furthermore, there were more than 124,000 people newly displaced in 2013.[16] This certainly provides for fertile recruitment grounds.

With the insurgency is able to threaten and kill more civilians, the government riddled with corruption and bribery, opium poppy cultivation expanding in the areas currently being fought over, and large numbers of people displaced and continuing to be displaced, this all paints a picture of an insurgency that is not only not under control, but it actually expanding its influence.

If this is a broadly based insurgency then at the current force levels our chances of winning still appear to be low. To push the ratios up to a level where we have good chance of winning it would require another 100,000 or more troops (almost certainly from the U.S.) plus the commitment of time and losses for several more years while it is turned around![17] In effect we would have to go back to the force levels we had in 2010.

Clearly, at this stage, the U.S. is very hesitant to make such a commitment. Our first withdrawal date was July 2011. Still, this date turned into the date that we are going to start building down, with the actual withdrawal date now being 2015. Even after 2015 it would appear that we are going to maintain tens of thousand of trainers, but effectively end our combat role. Very similar to what we tried to do in Iraq, even though the situation on the ground is very different, and the withdrawal is now much more extended.

The extension of our withdrawal date appears to have been connected to a desire to use the extension to pressure the Taliban to negotiate with the current government.[18] This would appear to be a tacit admission that the original July 2011 date was a mistake, as it gave the Taliban all the reason to believe that it did not need to negotiate and could simply wait out the U.S. But three years since that date, it appears that no significant progress has been made on negotiation of any type of settlement. If the Taliban and other insurgents are not willing to negotiate, then this appears to be because they still believe they can win this.

The interesting parallel here was the various U.S. bombing campaigns during the Vietnam War that were done against North Vietnam in an attempt to bring them to the negotiating table. That effort was not successful, even through more than one U.S. president tried to make it work. It is clear in retrospect that it was never going to work. Is the U.S. heading down the same path, trying to force the insurgents to the negotiating table by increasing their pain, but not doing what it takes to truly resolve or even defeat the insurgency?

If our model is correct and the insurgency is indeed broadly based, then it is going to take more than time to defeat it. It is going to take more force than we currently have. Theoretically this can come from the Afghan Army, but they do need to be raised, trained, motivated, and made effective. This is a major long-term program and because of the backgrounds and education levels of the people involved, is much harder to do than in Iraq. We also got a slower start on it than in Iraq. This growth has been with problems, as would be expected, including insurgent infiltration into the forces.[19] So, most likely the troops for any more significant increases will have to come from the U.S. or NATO. Right now there are about 300,000 counterinsurgents in Afghanistan.

How many Taliban and other insurgents are there? If there are around 30,000[20] then we are still looking at a 10-to-1 ratio, and if this is a broadly based insurgency, then there is only a 44.7% chance of counterinsurgent success. Does this give us enough force after 2015 to actually win the war? It does not look like this is the case.

If this insurgency is broadly based, then the surge we did up to 100,000 U.S. troops in 2010 and the building up of the Afghan army was probably good enough to turn the tide. The fact that incidents appear to have declined in 2012 indicates that this may have been working, but incidents are back up for 2013. The problem is if this insurgency is broadly based, then those surge forces needed to stay in place for the next ten years, with the expected continued losses and expenses.

If the insurgency is regional or factionalized, then we do have the force to defeat it. This is an awfully big insurgency to be simply regional and factionalized and we have few regional or factional insurgencies coded in our data base as such that are anywhere near this size. We remain very concerned about the direction of this insurgency. It does drive home the need for a better understanding of the nature and strength of insurgencies.

DUELING SURGES

Afghanistan shows that a surge and good tactics alone do not win insurgencies. It was claimed by some that this is what turned around Iraq, but in fact, what was most important in correcting Iraq was the buying off of the insurgents and forming the Iraq Sunni Awakening Councils. Without a successful buy off in Afghanistan, the surge and good U.S. tactics have not turned the situation around and by itself, will not. In the end, you still need to have sufficient troops on the ground to control the terrain, protect the population, and contain the insurgents. There are few short-cuts that allow you to avoid the basics.

Let us look for a moment, in a very big picture view, of how the surge actually occurred in Iraq versus the Afghanistan. In the case of Iraq, in December 2006, there were 140,000 U.S troops in Iraq, 15,200 allied troops and 132,700 Iraqi troops (active or training). By October of 2007, the surge had built up to 171,000 U.S. troops for a grand total of 346,168 counterinsurgent troops in Iraq.[21]

U.S casualties in 2006 were 822 killed from all causes for the year. For the year of 2007 it was 904 killed from all causes, and for the following year it was only 314 dead. The most intense period was from January to September 2007 where to U.S. lost 806 dead in those nine months. U.S. dead then dropped to below 40 a month starting the next month, and mostly remained there. Then in October 2008, dropped to below 20 killed a month (all causes) and has mostly remained below that level ever since then. Starting July 2009, U.S. dead dropped to below 12 a month and has not gone above that figure since. In effect, the surge had arrived and significantly resolved the fighting in Iraq in only nine months.

So, for an increase of 22 percent in U.S. strength and losses of 806 over a nine month period, the situation was very notably improved. In 2009 the U.S casualties of 150 dead were 18 percent of what they were in 2006. This is success by any stan-dard, although we primarily credit that success to the development of Sunni Awak-ening Councils, vice the surge.

In the case of Afghanistan, in December 2008, there were 26,612 U.S. troops there, 29,178 coalition troops, and 68,000 Afghani Army troops. During 2009, the U.S. added 21,000 more troops and then in December 2009, President Obama announced the addition of another 30,000 troops. This is a 48 percent increase in strength in U.S. and coalition troops, making the Afghanistan surge relatively more significant than the Iraqi surge.

U.S. casualties for 2008 were 155 killed from all causes for the year and coali-tion forces lost 140. For the year of 2009 it was 317 killed for the U.S. and 204 for the coalition forces. For 2010, it has been 499 killed (all causes) and 212 for the coalition forces. The year of 2011 saw a decline in U.S. casualties with 418 killed from all causes, along with 148 coalition forces, but an increase in the num-ber of security incidents, meaning the level of violence had not declined. So, 36 months into start of the strength increases done by President Obama, there is no drop in the level of violence. Only in 2012, after it was clear that the U.S. and coalition forces were withdrawing, does the level of violence drop. In contrast the surge in Iraq achieved a measurable result in nine months.

The difference between the two is striking and clearly makes the point that the whole strategic situation needs to be fully addressed and these problems cannot be solved by simply applying a technique from one war to the next. The surge in Afghanistan is simply larger, more sustained and has achieved less dramatic results when compared to the rather limited and brief surge in Iraq.

LESSONS AND OBSERVATIONS

There are five final lessons or observations that we wish to make about this war. First, it is clear that the new government did not establish control of the country-side in 2002 through 2004. The Northern Alliance and other armed groups totaled only around 60,000 people, at best.[22] U.S. and international commitment remained at low levels, below 30,000 troops. The Afghan National Army was slowly developing, also reporting only 8,000 operational troops in December 2004 and the Afghan police forces had less than 30,000 police in 2004, almost all of them raised that year. Both the Afghan Army and Afghan police were newly raised and poorly trained. Part of the reason the reported level of violence against these forces were low up through 2004 was that there was not a whole lot of forces in the countryside to commit violence against. As the Secretary General of the United Nations noted in August 2005; "From 2002 to 2004, powerful commanders and their militias, dominated the security environment. Narcotics trade and related criminal activities also expanded rapidly. More recently, there have been troubling indications that remnants of the Taliban and other extremist groups are reorganizing."[23]

In 2005 the Afghan police expanded to over 50,000, and their losses went up from 9 in 2003, to 92 in 2004, to 138 in 2005. In 2006 the Afghan police continued to develop and expand and their losses grew to 412 in that year. We see the losses more than doubled in 2007 (925 killed) and have continued at even higher levels since then.[24] It is clear that police force presence led to increased police force losses, indicating that significant parts of the country were never under control of the central government.

Second, we question the wisdom on concentrating and giving priority to developing the Afghan police forces ahead of the Afghan army. Some of this appears to have been inspired by the British example of counterinsurgencies, which leaned heavily on using police as part of its counterinsurgent forces. This worked in part because they also had sufficient ground troops (usually 25-to-1 or greater ratios) and were facing very small insurgencies. When we did our analysis of insurgencies, including the logit regression model, we did not count police forces in the counterinsurgent forces in the data or the model. We felt that most police were not dedicated to the task of counterinsurgency most of the time and had many other duties and tasks to perform. As such, we did not count the traffic cops in Saigon as part of the war effort against the Viet Cong. Now, if there were portions of the police force clearly set aside with a primarily counterinsurgency mission, we did count those, but in most of our cases, we did not include them in our data and our calculations.

As such, we did not include them in our analysis of Afghanistan, and we still believe that this is the best representation. But, the U.S. by focusing on building up the Afghan police, and there were more Afghan police than army from 2003 through 2006, probably did not provide the government with the tools it needed to secure the country side. Isolated police stations simply do not establish government control. As such, we believe that the U.S. learned the wrong lessons from its review of UK counterinsurgency doctrine because they did not properly and fully understand the context in which they were conducted: which was with the UK having overwhelming military force. We therefore tried to substitute police for army. We also did the same thing early in Iraq also.

The third lesson concerns the value of these "little surges" that the U.S. did in Iraq and is doing in Afghanistan. Whether or not the surge in Afghanistan succeeds or fails may be determined by whether they can buy off, negotiate a settlement with, or otherwise co-opt significant numbers of insurgents. So while the increased troop strength obviously helps, it clearly drives home the point that the actual surge, by itself, did not resolve Iraq and a similar surge, by itself, will not resolve Afghanistan. It was a reduction in the number of insurgents that resolved Iraq. For a "surge" to be truly effective, it would have to be more in the order of 100,000 or more troops, not just 30,000. And, if no significant insurgent forces were co-opted, then this would have to be a long-term commitment or at least a commitment until such time as a large number of insurgents stood down.

The fourth observation concerns the issue of rules of engagement. Even under the tightly controlled rules of engagements the U.S. was using, the United Nations were reporting over 1,500 civilians killed in 2007. In 2008, we had a determination from the UN as to who was responsible, with their claim being that there were 2,118 civilian casualties in 2008, of which 55% those killed were caused by the insurgents and 39% were of those killed were caused by the counterinsurgents. There were 6% that were not attributed as to who caused that death. This is actually very good on the part of the counterinsurgents, as in most insurgencies, the majority of civilian deaths are caused by the counterinsurgents. But, 34% of the civilian casualties were caused by indiscriminate suicide bombers, a weapon only used by the insurgents. So, if one removes the casualties caused by this relatively new weapon, then one is looking at 21% of the civilian deaths caused by the insurgents (excepting suicide bombers) versus 39% done by the counterinsurgents. If effect, this pattern matches what we have seen elsewhere where almost two-thirds of the losses (excluding suicide bombers) are accounted for the counterinsurgents.

But, the U.S. and other international forces did tighten the rules of engagement, and for 2009 the UN reports 2,412 civilian deaths, with now 67% accounted for by the insurgents and only 25% accounted for by the counterinsurgents (and 8% unattributed). This only got better in 2010, with the first six months there being 3,268 conflict related civilian casualties (deaths or injuries). Of those, the insurgents were responsible for 76% of them, while the counterinsurgents were responsible for only 12%. The Secretary General notes that they are " . . . the result of a significant decline in deaths and injuries caused by air attacks."[25]

It is clear that they are getting favorable results from the tighter rules of engagement although it is harder to determine how much these tighter rules are helping to actually win the insurgency. Still, our own work (see Chapter Nine) points to tighter rules of engagement helping the counterinsurgents win in the long run, so this is an effort we support wholeheartedly support.

One adjunct issue to the rules of engagement issue is the U.S. forces, the contractors and other coalition forces habit of driving through the urban areas at higher speeds for their own safety. While this does increase force security, it also brings attendant problems. For example, on 29 May 2006 a riot broke out as a result of the U.S, traffic accident caused by this aggressive driving. When it was over at least 25 people died in the riot. This is not the only situation like this.[26] Clearly, there is a trade off here between force protection and maintaining support in the local population.

Finally, one must ask the question, did the United States almost loose the war in Afghanistan, or at least seriously compromise its position there, with its gross undercommitment in 2001–2004. Did we simply "mis-estimate" the situation and because we were not taking casualties, fail to commit the energy and effort required to secure the area and keep an insurgency from developing? As noted in Chapter Twenty-four on recommendations for the future, we need to understand better the early stages of an insurgency and how they develop, and how to recognize a developing insurgency. Usually by the time we realize we have a problem, we have a big problem, not a little one. Did we make the same mistake both in Afghanistan and in Iraq?

POLITICAL WILL

The United States has lost 499 killed from all causes in Afghanistan in 2010.[27] Compared to Vietnam, this does not seem like much, but when compared to all insurgencies; it is enough losses to favor the insurgents.

As we point out in Chapter Seventeen, the Burden of War:

> *It appears that when the average intervening forces killed exceeds more the 0.0001% of the population of the intervening country (more than 0.12 per 100,000 home population), then the counterinsurgency, intervention or peacekeeping operation fails in over two-thirds of the cases.*
>
> *Furthermore, it appears that if the average intervening forces killed*

exceeds more than 0.00001% of the population of the intervening country (more than 0.01 per 100,000 home population) that the chances of failure rises to around 50% (p-value =0 .0006)

The average intervening forces killed data basically falls into three groupings:

		BLUE WINS	GRAY RESULTS	RED WINS
0	18 cases	16	0	2
0.01–0.09	17 cases	8	2	7
0.12–4.08	14 cases	3	1	10
		27	3	19

Or, to put in another format:

	PERCENT BLUE WINS	PERCENT RED WINS
Low intensity cases	89%	11%
Medium intensity cases	47%	41%
High intensity cases	21%	71%

A nation with a population of 300 million would produce thresholds of 360 killed a year for .12 per 100,000 and only 30 killed per year for a value of .01 per 100,000. The U.S. population is a little over 300 million. As such, we were at the medium level of intensity for Afghanistan since 2002, and as of 2010, have crossed over to join the high intensity cases. Just for comparison The U.S. in Iraq during 2004–2007 was between 0.22 to 0.25 killed (KIA) per 100,000 population. The U.S. peak in Vietnam was over 7 killed per 100,000 population (population as of 1968).

Does this mean we will now lose? What is means is that in the 14 cases we have were losses were so high, the counterinsurgents only won in three of them. Let us look at the data for a moment, just the cases where more than 0.12 were killed per 100,000 home country population:

CASE	AVERAGE KILLED PER YEAR PER 100,000 HOME COUNTRY POPULATION	
Palestine	0.12	
Iraq	0.20	data through 2007
USSR in Afghanistan	0.38	
Angola Civil War	0.57	

Tanzania in Uganda	0.69
Angola	0.84
Indonesia	0.88
Portuguese Guinea	0.92
Mozambique	1.02
Hezbollah War	1.67
Vietnam War	2.46
Indochina War	2.75
Algerian War	3.07
Yemen	3.62

Where are the three counterinsurgent wins? They are Angola Civil War, Tanzania in Uganda, and Yemen, with Iraq still unresolved. An examination of each of those cases provides cold comfort. In the case of the Angola Civil War, the Cuban army was heavily supplemented by Soviet aid, as was the entire nation of Cuba. Part of the reason they were getting such aid was to allow them to intervene in Africa. So while they were paying the cost of the war in casualties, they were not paying the rest of the cost of the wars. Furthermore, Cuba kept the losses hidden from most of their population. Tanzania in Uganda was a successful intervention and overthrow of the government of Ugandan strong man Idi Amin and then stabilizing the government against his limited and furtive attempts to return to power. Perhaps they could even be considered to be the insurgents. Regardless, they did withdraw a year later and the Ugandan government seized power in violation of the election results. That government was later overthrown by insurgents lead by the legitimate head of state. Yemen was an Egyptian intervention, which by 1967 was already withdrawing and hastened that withdrawal when they became embroiled in a war with Israel. The war continued for several more years after Egypt withdrew and the government eventually reached an agreement with the rebels in 1970 and effectively defeated the insurgency.

The U.S. has now stepped over the threshold of 0.12, although one could easily argue from the data above that the threshold should be higher (0.38 or greater) or lower (0.06).[28] But, regardless of the exact break point, we are now at an uncomfortable threshold where the insurgents win in 70% of the cases. This does not mean that this is the case for Afghanistan, but it does indicate that we are now at a level of losses that forces nations to evaluate their levels of commitments to these wars. In some respects, this harkens back to the point made in Chapter Three, that the track record for winning large wars is not very good. Afghanistan is at the lower threshold of being a larger insurgency.

Now, the current administration's has been withdrawing since July 2011. This has dropped our loss rates in 2012 down to 310 killed from all causes, or down below the threshold point (assuming it is not as low as 0.05). Losses in 2013 were much lower (127 killed from all causes) and the levels of commitment and losses in 2014 are even less. So, it appears that the issue of U.S. losses has been resolved by lowering the level of commitment, but it does not resolve the concern as to whether there is now sufficient force to suppress the insurgency.

CONCLUSIONS

One cannot but help compare Iraq to Afghanistan. In the case of Iraq, we faced a regional or factional insurgency mostly based upon the minority Sunnis, we installed a government from the majority Shiite faction and then backed that with force ratios sufficient to suppress a regional or factional insurgency. We then bought off the Sunni insurgents by the tens of thousands bringing the violence rapidly under control, while at the same time conducted a surge. The end result was to create a very favorable situation on the ground, allowing us to withdraw and leaving behind trainers in a much more stable environment, and then withdraw entirely in 2011. Still, the effort has been far from perfect, and the insurgency appears to be now renewed.

In the case of Afghanistan the government is under control of the majority ethnic group, with minority representation. The insurgency is also drawing mainly from that same majority ethnic group. The insurgency primarily appears to be domestically based. As the United Nations noted September 2006; "The insurgency is being conducted mostly by Afghans operating inside Afghanistan's border. However, its leadership appears to rely on support and sanctuary from outside the country."[29] The attempts to buy off the insurgents have not met with much success. The current surge has created a force ratio that should be sufficient to control a regional or factional insurgency, given sufficient time.

On the other hand, if this insurgency is broadly based, then we do not have a sufficient force ratio regardless of time. So, in that case, if we cannot buy of the insurgents, then our only option is to add another 100,000 to 200,000 troops to the war and invest several more years, with the attendance casualties and costs, trying to turn the war into our favor. Obviously this precludes meeting any set withdrawal date.

Still, in all reality the current administration is not going to commit another 100,000 to 200,000 troops to Afghanistan for the next five or more years. This is not in discussion. It does not appear to be in consideration by the U.S. opposition party either.

Given our unwillingness to step up our commitment, then the only question is whether a slower withdrawal will provide more tangible benefits than a fast withdrawal. This we have not examined. Still, this is not "winning" the war in any sense of the word winning. It is withdrawing with the situation on the ground unresolved and a government that is far from democratic or stable. We will be leaving behind trainers and other support people, but limited combat troops. If history is a guide, then this government will be replaced one way or the other several years after we withdraw. What will replace it is hard to determine, but will probably include a return to some extent of the Taliban, or perhaps with them leading the new government. It is also distinctly possible that the country will return back into civil war. None of this fulfills our objectives.

NOTES

1. Mark Thompson, "Can Obama, McChrystal Agree New Afghan War Strategy." *Time Magazine* (7 Oct. 2009).
2. The force consisted of around 2,000 U.S. 1,700 UK and 150 Australians.
3. Transcript of 9 October 2001 press conference provided by the *Washington Post* at: http://www.washingtonpost.com/wp-srv/nation/specials/attacked/ transcripts/rumsfeld_100901.html
4. Coalition estimate made as of February 2004 that probably reflected the best estimate of the end-year 2003 strength of the Taliban "hard-core" (Mark Sedra Foreign Policy in Focus).
5. Roggio quoting, "Coalition and Afghan sources", gave a range of 2,000–5,000 as of mid-year with 600 killed and possibly 1,200 wounded, however, a later U.S. DOS Fact Sheet (20 September 2006) quoted Coalition estimates of Taliban strength in Operation MEDUSA alone as 3,000–4,000 with 1,000–1,500 killed, which would imply 2,000–3,000 wounded. Given that the strength estimates did not vary on average and the large number of killed estimated, it seems likely that the higher strength averages are probably correct.
6. *Report of the Secretary-General: The situation in Afghanistan and its implications for international peace and security* (7 March 2014), A/68/789–S/2014/163, page 5. These figures do not include prison personnel (7,430 in December 2012) or 27,000 Afghan Local Police. The National Army figure includes 7,300 Afghan Air Force personnel. The Army's "attrition rate" was reported to be 34 percent!
7. See Rod Nordland, "Study Finds Sharp Rise in Attacks by Taliban" in the *New York Times* (20 April 2013).
   In part, it states that: "One of the closest-kept secrets in Afghanistan these days is data about how active the insurgents have become in their spring offensive this year." The article also notes that: "The American military, which last year publicized data on enemy attacks with meticulous bar graphs, now has nothing to say. 'We're just not giving out statistics anymore,' said a spokesman, Col. Thomas W. Collins, suggesting that the Afghan Ministry of Defense might do so. The article does provide some figures "According to a respected independent group, the Afghanistan NGO Safety Office, the recent increase in violence has been dramatic, based on data for the first quarter of 2013, which the organization released Thursday. There were 2,331 attacks by armed opposition groups in the first quarter, compared with 1,581 in the same period last year, an increase of 47 percent, the statistics show."
   Related to our discussion on insurgent strength it notes: "In addition, the official said, the data showed that Afghan forces had killed 4,664 enemy fighters that year, and captured 6,401. Since most Western estimates are that the Taliban's active strength is on the order of 20,000 to 25,000 fighters, that would represent more than half of the insurgents' total numbers, which seems unlikely given the increased tempo of insurgent attacks."
   Our security incident figures all come from the UN Secretary-General Reports, although we have had a problem finding data for the second half of 2012.
8. *Report of the Secretary-General: The situation in Afghanistan and its implications for international peace and security* (10 March 2010), A/64/705-S/2010/127, page 7.

9. *Report of the Secretary-General: The situation in Afghanistan and its implications for international peace and security* (14 September 2010), A/64/911-S/2010/463, page 4. My math says 68% more security incidents.

10. In 2012, conflict-related violence killed 2,754 civilian and injured 4,805. Anti-government elements were responsible for 2,179 deaths and 3,952 injuries. Pro-government forces were responsible for 316 deaths and 271 injuries. This last figure is a decrease of 46 percent compared to 2011. See *Report of the Secretary-General: The situation in Afghanistan and its implications for international peace and security* (5 March 2013), A/67/778–S/2013/133, pages 7, 8 and 24.

    Between 1 February and 30 April 2013 the U.N. records a 25 percent increase compared with the same period in 2012, with 553 civilian deaths and 882 civilian injuries.

11. For example, targeted killing of civilians deemed to be supporting the government resulted in 158 civilian deaths between 1 February and 30 April, an increase of 88 percent compared with 2012. See *Report of the Secretary-General: The situation in Afghanistan and its implications for international peace and security* (13 June 2013), A/67/889–S/2013/350, page 8.

12. *Report of the Secretary-General: The situation in Afghanistan and its implications for international peace and security* (7 March 2014), A/68/789–S/2014/163, page 7.

13. *Report of the Secretary-General: The situation in Afghanistan and its implications for international peace and security* (5 March 2013), A/67/778–S/2013/133, page 10.

14. *Report of the Secretary-General: The situation in Afghanistan and its implications for international peace and security* (5 March 2013), A/67/778–S/2013/133, pages 12, 31 and 32.

15. *Report of the Secretary-General: The situation in Afghanistan and its implications for international peace and security* (6 December 2013), A/68/645-S/2013/721, page 12.

16. *Report of the Secretary-General: The situation in Afghanistan and its implications for international peace and security* (7 March 2014), A/68/789–S/2014/163, page 10.

17. I would recommend the rather caustic article by Michael Scheuer, "Get Nasty or Go Home: The go-light strategy in Afghanistan is a joke," 12 October 2009 on the Foreign Policy web magazine (http://www.foreignpolicy.com/articles/2009/10/12/go_big_or_go_ home). In that article he makes the statement that "military victory would require 400,000 to 500,000 additional troops."

18. According to the head of the NATO mission, Anders Fogh Rasmussen: "I consider it of utmost importance to continue our military operations because the fact is it is the increasing military pressure on the Taliban and the Taliban leadership that has stimulated the reconciliation talks." See "NATO sees no alternative to Afghan operations", *Reuters* (November 15, 2010). The Taliban leadership immediately issued a statement opposing any such talks. See "Afghan Taliban reject talks again", *Reuters* (November 15, 2010).

19. For example see "Afghan police officer kills 6 U.S. service members" by Heidi Vogt and Rahim Faiez, *Associated Press* (20 November 2010).

20. For example, "Obama War Review: Taliban, Al-Qaida diminished" by Ben Feller, *Associated Press* (16 December 2010), states "They face an estimated 25,000–30,000 Taliban guerillas and other rebels."

21. Allied forces declined to 11,668 while the Iraqi Army expanded to 163,500 troops active or in training.

22. The UN later reported 63,380 militia were demobilized by 7 July 2005. Some estimated of Northern Alliance strength in 2001 was in the 20,000 to 25,000 range.

23. *Report of the Secretary-General: The situation in Afghanistan and its implications for international peace and security* (12 August 2005), A/60/224-S/2005/525, page 14.

24. "On 29 October [2013], a senior Ministry of the Interior official was quoted in the media as stating that 1,273 Afghan National Police and 779 Afghan Local Police personnel had died since April." See page 6, *Report of the Secretary-General: The situation in Afghanistan and its implications for international peace and security* (6 December 2013), A/68/645-S/2013/721.

25. *Report of the Secretary-General: The situation in Afghanistan and its implications for international peace and security* (14 September 2010), A/64/911-S/2010/463, Page 13. In their 23 September 2008 report they noted that "air strikes remain responsible for the largest percentage of civilian deaths attributed to pro-Government forces." See A/63/372-S/2008/617, page 13.

26. For example, a recent accident by Dyncorps International employees in July of 2010 that killed four Afghanis and generated a small riot.

27. Compared to 12 in 2001, 49 in 2002, 48 in 2003, 52 in 2004, 99 in 2005, 98 in 2006, 117 in 2007, 155 in 2008 and 317 in 2009.

28. The rest of the cases above 0.01 include:

CASE	AVERAGE KILLED PER YEAR PER 100,000 HOME COUNTRY POPULATION
Grenada	0.01
Panama	0.01
Operation Tacaud	0.01
UN Somalia	0.01
Borneo	0.01
U.S. in Afghanistan	0.01
Aden	0.02
Mau Mau	0.02
French Intervention in Chad	0.03
Vietnam II	0.03
Northern Ireland	0.03
Cyprus	0.04
Malaya	0.04
Cameroun	0.05
PK Lebanon	0.06
Timor	0.06
Namibia	0.07

These last two cases were insurgent wins as was Cameroun.

29. *Report of the Secretary-General: The situation in Afghanistan and its implications for international peace and security* (11 September 2006), A/61/326-S/2006/727, page 2.

CHAPTER 22

Relating a Force Ratio Model to Vietnam

Its going to be difficult for us to very long prosecute effectively a war that far away from home with the divisions we have here, and particularly the potential divisions, and what's really had me concerned for a month and I'm very depressed about it is that I see no program from either defense or state that gives me much hope of doing anything except just praying and grasping to hold on during the monsoon and hope they'll quit. I don't believe they are ever going to quit. I don't see how . . . how . . . that we have anyway of either a..either a plan for victory dip. . . . . militarily or diplomatically.

—President Lyndon Johnson to Defense Secretary Robert McNamara, 10 July 1965.[1]

Westmorland, uh, says that the offensive that he has anticipated, that he has been fearful of, is now on and he wants people as quickly as he can get them. My judgment is, and I am no military man at all, but I study it every day and every night and I read the cables, and if we get 150 [thousand troops] we'll have to have another 150 [thousand troops] and then they've have to have another 150 [thousand troops]. To me its, its shaping up like this, you either, you either, get out or you get in. I don't think there is much more neutral. I think we have tried all the neutral things and we think they are winning. Now if we think they are winning you can imagine what they think.

—President Lyndon Johnson to Senator Mike Mansfield, 15 July 1965.[2]

By the end of the summer of 1973 I thought it was virtually impossible for South Vietnam to survive. How in the heck could they?

—General William Westmoreland, Commander of the Military Assistance Command, Vietnam, 1964–1968.[3]

These graphs, from our original Iraq briefing, show the charge to victory and the sudden withdrawal that defined the U.S. commitment in Vietnam. We spent four years trying to win the war, and then four years trying to make a graceful exit. In the end, we did neither.

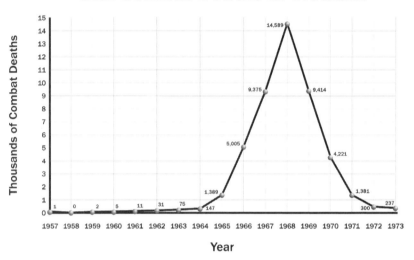

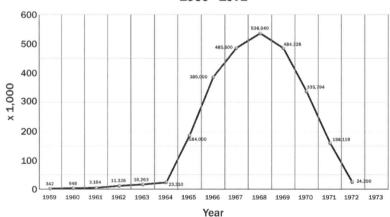

The question that still remains open is how the United States could have won in Vietnam. Was it just a matter of staying the course, was it an issue of using the right tactics and operations, or were there some other fundamental issues at stake here?

Let's go back to our force ratio and cause model. In this case, I think we can now safely say that the insurgency was fundamentally broadly based. It was a communist insurgency, but one that was so clearly wrapped up in nationalism, that I am tempted to use that line on the regression line. So, let us run the figures through for 1968, when the U.S. was at its peak commitment and the war was at its most violent.

On 31 December 1967, the U.S. had 485,600 troops in Vietnam. They were supporting the ARVN (Army of the Republic of Vietnam) which was contributing 776,041 troops of all types. [4] Between the army, the regional forces, the popular forces, civilian irregular defense groups, and the police, the Republic of Vietnam (South Vietnam) was mobilizing some 4.6% of its manpower for the war. This is a very high degree of mobilization. For comparison, the U.S. mobilized 10.6% of its people for World War II. Still, the Republic of Vietnam was pretty close to mobilizing up to the limit of its manpower, especially when you consider that its population was also supporting an insurgent army of 200,000 to 300,000. There were also allied troops there totaling 59,450, including 47,829 South Koreans in two divisions, 6,818 Australians, some 2,205 Thai troops that would eventually grow to one small division, 2,020 from the Philippines, 534 New Zealanders and 44 from China (Taiwan) and Spain. Not a large "coalition of the willing" but, significant additional support nonetheless. This is a grand total of 1,321,091 counterinsurgents.

Opposing them was a reported 261,500 insurgents. This is a figure from the history provided by the Peoples Republic of Vietnam (originally referred to as North Vietnam) and is in line with U.S. estimates.[5] This included 79,900 from the Peoples Army of Vietnam (PAVN or North Vietnamese Army or NVA), probably as many as 67,000 Peoples Liberation Army (PLA or Viet Cong) main forces, and probably around 170,351 regional and militia troops. These last two figures are from the Peoples Republic of Vietnam but for 1966.[6] They, added to the PAVN figure, produce a larger number than 261,500. At this stage, the Viet Cong (VC) were not entirely composed of South Vietnamese. For example, in 1967, the North sent down 94,243 PAVN.

This means that the combined counterinsurgent forces had a force ratio of 5.05-to-1 in their favor. Comparing that back to our model based upon the type of insurgency, if the Vietnam insurgency was regional or factional, there would be an 86% chance that it would win at that force ratio. If the insurgency was based upon an overarching idea, like communism, then there was a 53% chance that it would win at that force ratio. If the insurgency was based upon a central idea, like nationalism, then there was a 16% chance that it would win at that force ratio.

As the Tet offensive was about to occur in February 1968, I think we can reasonably conclude that it was simply not just a very large regional or factional insurgency. If it was an insurgency that was broadly based, and fundamentally based upon nationalism or anti-colonialism, then we clearly did not have enough force in the country at that point in time. As such, the model tells us that even at 500,000 American troops deployed; we needed more forces in country to tip the balance to our favor.

Peak U.S. troop strength in Vietnam was 543,482 as of 30 April, 1969. Still, this peak strength figure is a misrepresentation of the U.S. commitment. We were only above 500,000 troops in Vietnam for a little more than 18 months, and above 400,000 troops for only around 42 months.[7] Our deployment was almost a flash in the pan, although a very, very large flash. From the period of the war covering from the beginning of March 1965 until the end of January 1973, a total of 95 months that many consider to be the period of the U.S. phase of the Vietnam War, the U.S. forces were below 200,000 for something like 28 of those months. The average U.S. strength figure for those 95 months was around 300,000.[8] This is a real "surge" strategy, but not one that is integrated into anything that looked like a strategic plan. We never really had a long-term strategic plan for Vietnam and were pretty much making it up as we were going along. While it is convenient to blame the politicians for this, in the end the Joint Staff or the U.S. Army did not offer up any such plan either. As General Bruce Palmer, Westmoreland's deputy, states:

Finally, there was one glaring omission in the advice the JCS provided the president and the secretary of defense. It is an obvious omission, but more importantly, a profoundly significant one. Not once during the war did the JCS advise the commander-in-chief or the secretary of defense that the strategy being pursued most probably would fail and that the United States would be unable to achieve its objectives. The only explanation of this failure is that the chiefs were imbued with the "can do" spirit and could not bring themselves to make such a negative statement or to appear to be disloyal.[9]

One must keep in mind that this insurgent army was as tough as any insurgency that anyone had faced. They were organized into over 200 combat battalions, and armed with a full range of modern weapons, including large 122 mm mortars, rockets and artillery. This is in contrast to some place like Malaya, where the insurgents were limited to operating in squads (9–12 men) or at best platoons (40 men) and did not have any operable mortars or other indirect fire weapons!

One notes that even after the Tet offensive, the U.S. was still recording on 19 June 1968 the following:[10]

Deployment of Opposing Maneuver Battalions by Corps Tactical Zone
As of 19 June 1968

CORPS ZONE	NVA	VC	TOTAL COMMUNIST	ARVN	U.S.	FREE WORLD	TOTAL ALLIED
I	58	18	76	34	54	4	92
II	35	15	50	28	18	18	64
III	20	35	55	56	33	4	93
IV		23	23	42	5		47
Total	113	91	204	160	110	26	296

About 70% of the communist troops in the south, including 30% of the VC were NVA.

Now, just looking at "boots on the ground," these do not seem to overwhelmingly favor the counterinsurgents. It is a 1.45 to 1 force ratio, assuming all battalions are equal. Certainly, U.S. combat maneuver battalions were more capable in conventional combat than the NVA and VC battalions. On the other hand, it is less clear in the case of the ARVN versus the NVA and VC. Furthermore, in Corps Zones I and II, there was almost parity. In Corps Zone IV there were almost no U.S. battalions.

So, even after the military disastrous Tet offensive (at least for the VC), according to U.S. intelligence, it does not appear that the counterinsurgency forces had a dominant advantage in "boot on the ground" in Vietnam.

To convert the entire, dreadful "rise and crash" scenario into force ratios provides an interesting picture:

YEAR	U.S. FORCES	ALLIED FORCES	ARVN FORCES	TOTAL	INSURGENTS
1965	184,314	22,404	651,885	858,603	212,000
1966	338,568	52,566	714,359	1,155,493	267,351
1967	485,600	59,450	776,041	1,321,091	261,500
1968	536,040	65,802	946,981	1,548,823	290,000
1969	474,819	68,889	1,080,732	1,624,440	236,800
1970	335,794	67,444	1,142,009	1,545,247	213,800
1971	170,079	54,497	1,159,940	1,384,516	197,700
1972	24,000	42,082	1,208,739	1,274,820	243,000

To convert this to force ratios:

YEAR	FORCE RATIO	PERCENT CHANGE OF VICTORY: IF LIMITED	IF OVERARCHING	IF CENTRAL IDEA
1965	4.05	83%	45%	13%
1966	4.32	84	47	13
1967	5.05	86	53	16
1968	5.34	87	55	17
1969	6.86	91	65	24
1970	7.23	92	68	27
1971	7.00	92	66	25
1972	5.25	87	54	17

As can be seen from the force ratios, the insurgency appeared to be losing ground from 1968 through 1971. As the U.S. withdrew though, it reestablished itself at a force ratio it could live with. These of course, are forces in and around South Vietnam. It ignores the giant red elephant standing outside of the room, which was an increasingly larger and well-armed conventional North Vietnamese Army.

This does not seem to change the overall strength on the part of the counterinsurgency force in a favorable direction over time. Furthermore, after 1968, it is replacing the U.S. forces with less capable Vietnamese forces, while the overall force strength is declining. These are all negative trends.

But the point is, there was never really the force in place to defeat and control the insurgency. We were bringing it under control once we got it up above a five-to-one ratio, but that period lasted only three years (1968–1970). As shown earlier in this book, you need to plan on being there at least 12 years at fairly high force levels. We did not do that.

What Vietnam was left with after the U.S. withdrawal was around 1.2 million troops and 35,000 South Korean allies. By 1972, the Republic of Vietnam was probably maxed out in deployment, with something like 6.2% of its population under arms, not counting the VC. The insurgency had grown to around 376,000 troops in 1973, including 176,000 PAVN and 200,000 PLA mainforce (which at this point had significant numbers of North Vietnamese). This does not count any surviving regional and militia forces. By 1973, the force was more like 3-to-1, and the ARVN simply could not defeat this insurgency. With a North Vietnam Army looming across the border, the situation was fragile indeed. It is pretty obvious at this stage what the outcome would be.

So how could we have won this war? Well, let's look at three approaches. One is just to continue the war as is from sometime in the early 1970s (go long), another is to look at the strategic suggestions made by General Bruce Palmer and endorsed by Colonel Harry Summers, and the other is to simply use more force (go strong).

First, looking at continuing the war as is, let us assume that the 5-to-1 to 7-to-1 ratios that we had developed from 1968 to 1971 were sufficient to win the war. We certainly had the countryside under much better control than ever before. Roads were more open, and violence was down. In 1972, the U.S. only lost 300 killed. Still, the South Vietnamese lost almost 40,000 troops that year, roughly equally split between regular army and regional and provincial forces.[11]

But 1972 was the second bloodiest year of the war for the counterinsurgents. It was only slight less deadly than 1968. In 1968, total counterinsurgents killed in action were 43,461. The counterinsurgent losses had steadily declined to a low of 24,566 for 1971 and then went back up to 40,330 for 1972. In 1968, U.S. killed in action were 14,567, South Vietnamese were 27,915, and our other allies were 979. In 1972, it was only 300 Americans, 443 allies (mostly South Koreans) and 39,587 killed from South Vietnam. This was the bloodiest year of the war so far for the South Vietnamese. Clearly in 1972, the war was far from over, even if the U.S. losses were low.

Still one could postulate that if we held our force levels at the current levels for the next 12 years, we could have eventually brought this to a favorable conclusion. This brings us to 1984.[12] This would be a smaller U.S. commitment of 24,000 troops and 300 killed a year. If this is all that it would have taken, then it was certainly a price we could have afforded and were probably willing to afford. This of course, ignores the reality on the ground.

With the U.S. withdrawing, the North Vietnamese and Viet Cong were rebuilding. They launched a major offensive in the spring of that year that the South Vietnamese were barely able to hold against. South Vietnam lost Quang Tri Province entirely and lost a provincial capital for the first time in the war! It was not a very encouraging sign, and was done when the U.S. still had a large number of advisors, some troops and a massive amount of airpower.[13] Still, the South Vietnamese were able to rally later in the year, retook Quang Tri City and most of the province. It is clear that the situation 1972 was not anything that looked liked a victory. The South Vietnam had survived and that was about it. It was helped considerably by massive doses of American airpower. This did not stop the United States from negotiating a peace arrangement with North Vietnam in January 1973 and completing its withdrawal.

Obviously, to have sufficient force to stabilize the situation we need to therefore look back at least to end-of-year figures for 1971 of 170,079 U.S. troops and 1,302 killed in action (953 died of other causes). This means that if the forces in South Vietnam were sufficient to hold the country at the end of 1971 (and we do not know that that was the case), then to be able to "win" the war required a commitment of roughly 200,000 U.S. troops for another 10 to 20 years. Using our 12-year figure, this would be at the cost of potentially another 27,000 U.S. dead.

Clearly this was not going to happen, especially considering the political dynamics in the U.S. at the time. Therefore, simply staying the course at lower force levels (say 200,000 U.S. troops) was probably no longer a war winning strategy. Anything less (and what we did was much less) was definitely not a war winning strategy.[14]

The other alternative was the solution recommended by General Palmer and endorsed by Colonel Summers. The strategy Palmer proposed in 1977 (a little late!) was that the U.S. Army should have occupied a line across Laos to Thailand and permanently cut the Ho Chi Minh Trail. Palmer estimated that it would take 2 U.S., 2 ROK and 1 ARVN divisions to isolate the DMZ, plus 3 U.S. divisions in Laos (which was thrice the length of the DMZ area).[15] Taking this assessment as correct, then we are looking at a deployment of at least 100,000 troops to cut the Ho Chi Minh Trail and probably much more than that. This included moving three divisions into Laos. It may have been possible to start doing this in late 1965–early 1966.

Certainly, the forces in Laos would taken some losses—from NVA forces, any Pathet Lao forces, and the Disease and Non-Battle Injuries (DNBI) expected from operating in an underdeveloped countryside. There would also have been a supply line to those troops, wandering through Vietnam and Laos that would be vulnerable to guerillas. We also would have had to make sure Thailand was properly reinforced and certainly would have not received reinforcements from them during the war. The Thais would have to make sure, possibly with American aid, that their part of the border was closed.

An additional problem is that the North Vietnam did have a number of conventional force divisions, and these could have be mobilized and deployed against us in Laos. This certainly would have led to some losses and possibly incomplete closure of the Ho Chi Minh Trail. It is possible that as the NVA attempted to break the American stranglehold on the trail, that the war would have expanded into Thailand.

Such a plan was first suggested in 1965 by ARVN General Vien Cao Van, Chairman of the South Vietnamese Joint General Staff, 1965–75 and Minister of Defense, 1967–75. His proposed line went along the 17th parallel from Dong Ha, Vietnam (near the coast in Quang Tri province) to Savannakhet, Thailand. This is around 160 miles. Similar types of plans, but less ambitious, were discussed by the JCS in August 1965 and proposed by Westmoreland in April 1967.

Still, one notes that the area from the Vietnamese border to the Thai border is actually three times the width of the DMZ, so, it can be argued that in fact more that three U.S. divisions would be needed, especially as the NVA could deploy more forces in that area. If we were looking at five divisions to cover the DMZ, then why are we only considering three divisions to cover an area three times that width?

Furthermore, even if successful it would not cut off all aid to the Viet Cong. The North Vietnamese were moving supplies down the coast by sampans and other ships. While we did have a naval interdiction program in place, it was, like everything in warfare, not perfect. Also, the North Vietnamese could still be able to do some limited infiltration from the north regardless. They were able to cross the DMZ regularly during the war and certainly would have had some ability to cross the much larger patrolled area of Laos. Furthermore, they were getting supplies from Cambodia. This did become a major transshipment point during the war. Much of it was by ship, indicating the limitations of naval interdiction. Finally, they were always able to obtain local supplies in South Vietnam, from the areas they controlled, from their sympathizers and agents in South Vietnam, and in some cases, directly from the U.S. armed forces. So, while much of their supplies would be cut off by such an effort, not all of it would be.

In concept, the idea is that the U.S. would protect the border, like we did in Korea, and let the South Vietnamese fight the insurgency. If this strategy was implemented, it would have changed the nature of the war.

The problem is that five U.S. divisions was a significant portion of the U.S. commitment at that time. In 1970s planning inside the Pentagon, people often discussed "division slices," where there were the 15,000 men in the division, backed up by all the various air, artillery, engineer and other combat support forces, plus all the logistical support personnel. A division slice was 45,000 people, consisting of one 15,000-man division. So, five division slices would be 225,000 troops committed to the borders. Just for reference, at our peak in Vietnam, we deployed around nine full divisions and over 500,000 troops.[16] In the Palmer construct, the U.S. would guard the border and the Vietnamese would fight the war. Still, U.S. commitment would be high, for in addition to the 225,000 on the borders, in 1966 there were 6,910 advisors assigned to the various Vietnamese forces, there were 19,953 U.S. Navy and Coast Guard, plus 52,397 U.S. Air Force, and 9,472 miscellaneous DoD and Joint Staff troops. [17] This was probably a commitment of about 310,000 troops. U.S. troop levels at the end of 1965 were 184,314 and grew to 388,568 by the end of 1966.

So, assuming only five U.S., two ROK and 1 ARVN divisions was needed and that this would effectively shut down the trail, what would that mean for the rest of the war?

Let's assume that the U.S. somehow manage by the start of 1966 to have dropped the North Vietnamese reinforcement down to a more controllable trickle, with effectively most of the U.S. Army deployed across the border arc of South Vietnam and Laos, connecting to Thailand and supporting Thailand. Therefore, only tens of thousands of North Vietnam are infiltrating to South Vietnam each year. While this may be enough to keep the PLA active (the Viet Cong), let us assume that it precludes deploying PAVN main force battalions in the area. So, this leaves the Viet Cong in 1966 with a PLA main force of 67,000 and regional and local troops of 170,351 (data from April 1966). This is 237,351 troops not counting the PAVN forces of 30,000. With the South Vietnamese Army of 714,359 (1966 figure) engaged with them only, while the U.S. Army guards the borders only), this leads to a force ratio of three-to-one. This could appear to not be enough. Even if it was a regional or factional insurgency, this is only up to a 78% chance of winning.

Now, over time the South Vietnamese Army got stronger. Eventually it peaked at around 1.2 million. So, if the VC could maintain the field at around 200,000 (which is roughly where they were at the end of 1968), then this is a six-to-one ratio. This still does not quite do the trick, as it gives only a 20% chance of counterinsurgent victory if the insurgency is broadly based. It does give them a 89% chance if it is regional of faction and a 59% chance if it is communist based.

Let's play this scenario out to its natural conclusion. The U.S. would maintain a holding force of around five divisions (lets say around 225,000 troops) across Vietnam and Laos and bolster Thailand. This would probably shut down a lot but not all of the infiltration. The issue of infiltration through Cambodia would have to be addressed more successfully too. This blockade would probably have to remain in place for at least 20 years. That would bring a permanent deployment in Vietnam at least until 1986. There would probably also have been other troops elsewhere in Vietnam, primarily to support the Vietnamese Army. At this point, world changes may have rewritten the conflict, as Gorbachev came to power in 1985, initiated Perestroika in 1987, Glasnost in 1988, the Berlin Wall fell in 1989, the Warsaw Pact was dissolved in 1990 and the Soviet Union was dissolved in 1991.

These forces would have taken losses. As they were in a more conventional mode, then those losses may have actually been lighter than what might have been experienced doing search and destroy operations. Let's say they would lose 10 troops per

1,000 troops deployed a year. The loss rate of the U.S. forces in Vietnam in 1970 was around 15–18 killed per thousand.[18] Over the course of 20 years, this is potentially 45,000 killed, not counting losses to troops elsewhere in Vietnam. The real figure would probably be lower, but considering we lost 58,000 as it was, it might fall into the range of acceptable losses.

This assumes that the South Vietnamese Army can maintain the war for the next 20 years as it builds up to a six-to-one or so ratio. Then we are looking at reaching a point in the late 1980s where you can finally reach an agreement and a peace settlement with the Viet Cong that was probably more helpful than the 1973 Paris Peace Accords.

On the other hand, to win it probably required a little bit more. Let's say that on top of that, we provided the South Vietnam Army with an additional 200,000 troops. This boosts the starting ratio up to 4-to-1 in 1966 and the eventual ratio up to 7-to-1. This improves the situation, and as the U.S. was making progress from 1968–1971 when the force ratio was above 5-to-1, gives some hope.

This still does not look decisive, but let's say it leads to resolving the internal insurgency in ten or so years (say 1976). With the Viet Cong defeated, then there is a clear basis for a negotiated settlement that will allow this force to go home, the violence to end, and by the early 1980s, the internal U.S. force to withdraw, although the force protecting the border would have to remain.

As the internal force of 200,000 would take casualties at 20 per 1,000 troops for 10 years and the external force of 225,000 would take casualties at 10 per 1,000 troops now for only 10 years (as violence would probably stop once there was no Viet Cong to support from North Vietnam), then were are looking at 62,500 U.S. dead to win the war. The real figure would probably be lower, as the death rate would decline as the war neared its end. Still, there is probably no way to win without looking at losses in the 40,000–60,000 killed range.

More to the point, we are looking at more than 400,000 troops deployed in Vietnam for 10 years and 200,000 remaining for at least another 10 years before a complete resolution. This is a considerably larger commitment than the 42 months we spent at 400,000 or greater. Would the United States have accepted such a deployment at that time? Doubtful. But with a plan for victory and victory in sight, perhaps they may have. As the approach that was used clearly did not work very well, then this is nominally, in hindsight, a better approach.

This of course, assumes that everything works out as planned. Levels of commitment could be higher if more than three divisions are needed to cover Laos. If the war expands to Thailand, this could also increase the levels of commitment. Also, we really need to be able to cut the supply from Cambodia, which was significant. Overall, this option appears to have been better than what was done, but still far from a clear and simple success.

Of course, the interesting aspect of Palmer's plan was that no one seriously pushed for such an approach during the war.

In 1965, journalist and military affairs expert Hanson W. Baldwin, estimated that we needed a million American troops to provide for an adequate saturation ratio.[19] This certainly is in line with our models. The force ratio in 1966 would have shot up to seven-to-one and, as the South Vietnamese Army grew to 1.2 million, would have pushed the force ratio up to nine-to-one.[20] This gives us 95% chance of winning a regional or factional insurgency, and a 38% chance of winning a nationalist one. Considering the capabilities of the U.S. Army at that time (which was quite good) and the morale boost it would have given to the ARVN, then given 10 years at that level, it probably could have turned it into a win. Even if the model does not quite give the answer desired, the idea of being able to the fight the Vietnam War with twice as many American troops as we used makes it hard to believe that significant progress would not have been made.

This may have been at the cost of at least 50% more casualties. Would the U.S. have accepted such a large deployment and the additional losses that would have gone with it? Perhaps they may have, if the American people were comfortable that we were going to win the war. It was the sense, driven home by the Tet offensive, that we were in a long, drawn-out war that we could not win that led the majority of the American people to turn against the war in 1967 and 1968. As we are a democracy, their opinion was the deciding factor.

The problem with all three scenarios offered is that while they may be potentially war winning, they all offer higher stress than the original (failed) approach. The approach of carrying on with about 200,000 troops from the early 1970s (go long approach) leads to an extended duration and more casualties. Fortifying the border and cutting the Ho Chi Mihn Trail leads to a long, permanent deployment and heavy casualties. Adding in a million troops leads to even higher casualties. If the U.S. breaking point was reached in 1968,[21] then what are the chances, given that it was a heavily conscripted army, that the Americans would have accepted these commitments and losses even if they promised victory? We recommend rereading Chapter Seventeen to understand the full implications of this.

So, was the Vietnam War unwinnable? Close. To have won it would have required strategies and approaches that would have led to considerably higher levels of commitment over time than the U.S. was willing to sustain. I have yet to see a suggested strategy that would have resulted in U.S. victory for the same or less commitment than we took to lose it. In the end, winning the war required considerably more commitment. If the U.S. government had a clear plan to victory and the confidence of the American people, then maybe they might have accepted those losses. The U.S. government had neither.

In the end, the U.S. needed to make a commitment for probably twice what it did to win the war.[22] It does not appear that there was an easy and simple strategic, operational or tactical adjustment that could have significantly changed the outcome. One of the big problems is that we were facing over 250,000 insurgents. This was a large number, much larger than any other post-World War II example we have.

The only advantage that our theoretical constructs and the attendant model provide in relation to this discussion is to show that we really were not quite at the level we needed to be. We effectively fought a war with half the people we needed.

NOTES

1. Quote transcribed by author from the recorded conversations of President Johnson.
2. Quote transcribed by author from the recorded conversations of President Johnson.
3. Original source not identified.
4. We have 324,637 for the Army, 15,963 for the Navy, 7,561 for the Marine Corps, 16,161 for the Air Force, 152,549 for Regional Forces, 151,945 for Popular Forces, 36,964 for Civilian Irregular Defense Groups, and 70,261 for the National Police.
5. The MACV Intelligence estimate for 1967 was 115,150 combat and support troops (NVA and PLA Main Force Combat and Support Troops), 71,700 local militia, 37,725 Political Cadre and Administrative Troops, and 3,425 miscellaneous for a total of 228,000, including an estimated 55,674 NVA personnel. The total estimate for 1966 was 280,600, and for 1968, it was 259,000.
6. See *Victory in Vietnam: The Official History of the People's Army of Vietnam*, 1954–1975 (Lawrence, Kansas: University Press of Kansas, 2002).
7. These are estimates. U.S. troop strength was 498,000 at the beginning of 1968, 537,000 as of July 1969 and was in decline. U.S. troop strength was 385,000 at the beginning of 1967 and was 404,000 as of July 1970.
8. For example, calculating by year, based upon strength on 31 Dec. of each year = 318,652 (184,314 for 1965, 338,568 for 1966, 485,600 for 1967, 536,040 for 1968, 474,819 for 1969, 335,794 for 1970, 170,079 for 1971 and 24,000 for 1972.)
9. General Bruce Palmer, Jr. *The 25-Year War: America's Military Role in Vietnam* (New York: Touchstone, 1985), 46. He notes in a footnote that, "This omission on the part of the JCS was first pointed out to me by General H. K. Johnson, Army chief of staff and a member of the JCS for four years (1964–68), and he too could offer no logical rationale for this apparent lapse."
   Bruce Palmer was commander the II Field Force and deputy commander in Vietnam 1967–68. He was Vice Chief of Staff of the Army from 1 Aug. 1968 to 30 June 1972 and acting Chief of Staff of the Army from 1 July to 11 Oct. 1972.
10. Table drawn from Micheal Clodfelter, *Vietnam in Military Statistics: A History of Indochina Wars, 1772–1991* (Jefferson, North Carolina: McFarland & Company, Inc. 1995), page 128.
11. We have the ARVN losses for 1972 at 19,735, the RVN RF/PF KIA at 18,962, and the RVN Paramilitary KIA at 890.
12. There is no question that without a peace settlement, the North Vietnamese, with the support of the Soviet Union, would have continued the war at some level through at least 1984, and likely even later than that. Gorbachev did not come to power until 11 Mar. 1985, did not start his "Perestroika" (restructuring) reforms until the middle of 1987, did not introduce Glastnost (openness) until the following year and did not withdraw the Soviet Union from Afghanistan until Feb. 1989. Clearly, at some point after 1984, events outside of Vietnam would have put pressure on the Vietnamese government to negotiate a settlement.
13. 66,300 on May 1, according to Clodfelter, *op. cit.*, 201.

14. The claims made by some political commentators that Congress' reducing aid in Aug. 1974 from $1.26 billion to $700 million doomed the South Vietnamese simply ignores the obvious fact that they were doomed long before then. It appears the Nixon-developed plan of withdrawal and Vietnamization simply had no means to succeed.

15. See Harry G. Summers, Jr., *On Strategy: A Critical Analysis of the Vietnam War* (New York: Ballantine Books, 1995 [1982]), pages 122–123. Also see General Bruce Palmer Jr,, *The 25-Year War: America's Military Role in Vietnam* (New York: Touchstone, 1985), pages 182–188. Palmer claims on page 185 that "The Viet Cong, cut off from sustained outside support, would be bound to whither on the vine and gradually become easier for South Vietnam to defeat on its own."

16. This included the 1st and 3rd Marine divisions, 1st Cavalry Division (Airmobile), the 101st Airborne Division, and the 1st, 4th, 9th, 23rd (Americal) and 25th Infantry divisions. There were also numerous brigade and regiment-size forces that would certainly have added up to another division, including the 1st Brigade, 5th Infantry Division (Mechanized), the 3rd Brigade of the 82nd Airborne Division, the 173rd Airborne Brigade, the 199th Infantry Brigade (Light) and others.

    There were a total of 440,029 troops (Army and Marines) in Vietnam at the end of 1968, including 359,313 Army and 80,716 Marines. Of those, 11,596 were MACV advisors.

    To give another example of a division slice: the U.S. Marine Corps at the end of 1968 had 80,716 Marines in two divisions.

17. These are all end of year figures for 1966.

18. That is, 4,183 killed in 1970 (1,841 died of other causes), compared to an end of year strength of 335,794. The end of year strength for 1969 was 474,829. It is 15 per 100,000, if the average strength of these two points is used.

19. Fall, *Last Reflections*, 182. Hanson Baldwin was a contemporary of Trevor N. Dupuy and was involved in several of his reports and studies.

20. End of 1966 strength of 714,359 ARVN, 52,566 allies and 1,000,000 U.S. = 1,766,925 versus 267,351.

21. See *Examination of Factors Influencing the Conduct of Operations in Guerilla Wars, Task 11: Examine Measurement of Popular Support* (Annandale, VA.: The Dupuy Institute, 25 Feb. 2008), 40–42.

    It concludes that: **In sum, American support for the Vietnam War declines throughout the conflict. The polls indicate that public opposition to the war overtook public support for the war in the period just prior to the Tet Offensive and increased as American force strength peaked at 546,040 in 1968.**

22. Twice as long or twice as many troops, with the appropriate increases in losses.

CHAPTER 23

Conclusions

A conclusion is the place where you got tired thinking.
—Physician and writer Martin H. Fischer1

Our conclusion from this exercise is that Force Ratios and Insurgent Cause are extremely significant factors. We can build a model based upon only these two factors that will explain the outcome of 80% of the 83 cases we have examined. This is quantitative analysis of the largest and most detailed insurgency database that we are aware of. This doesn't mean we're convinced that we're correct, but we will argue that it has at least as much support as any other suggestion made and more support than most. Still, it is clear that more work needs to be done.

The issue of having sufficient forces or underestimating the virulence and motivations of the insurgents has been a continued problem for counterinsurgents. If an army entered a conventional war with half the strength of the other side, in most cases, the outcome would be pre-ordained, and the leadership would be considered complete fools. On the other hand, nations repeatedly engage in counterinsurgencies with half or less of the forces that they need. This was certainly the case for the French in Indo-China, and this error has been repeated many times by other nations. The fact that the insurgents actually can't "win" the war in a conventional sense, seduces the counterinsurgent leadership into believing they have the situation under control. There is a large gap between being able to maintain a conventional force in a hostile country and having control of the situation.

As far as underestimating the virulence, determination and motivation of the insurgents, well that seems to happen all the time. Just look at Chapter Five of this book at Galula's comments about Vietnam or Kitson's comments about Northern Ireland. These are commentators who should have known better, not the ramblings of political hacks. In part, because of differences in organization, military professionalism, economic development, and some old-fashioned racism, counterinsurgents often depreciate who and what the insurgents represent and their motivations.

So, from a strategic sense, what this "model" tells you is that you first need to understand the nature and motivation of the insurgency you are facing. You need to understand their "cause." Then, you need to produce a realistic estimate of their forces (a process that always seems to fall short). Finally, you need to determine what level of forces you need.

This does not guarantee you the win, and it certainly does not guarantee that you won't be there a very long time. What it does do is allow you to play the game. Without that, you will probably not be able to achieve anything approaching a clear victory and will simply be putting troops into harm's way for no clear achievable goal.

FINDINGS

Our findings related to insurgencies are summarized below. These mostly repeat the findings presented in different chapters of this book.

FORCE RATIOS

1. While high force ratios are not required to win an insurgency, intervention or peacekeeping operation, force ratios above 10-to-1 pretty much guarantee a counterinsurgency victory.
2. While high force ratios are not required to win an insurgency, force ratios above 10-to-1 pretty much guarantee a counterinsurgency victory.
3. While low force ratios do not preclude a win for the counterinsurgency, force ratios below 2-to-1 greatly favor an insurgency victory.

Here the pattern is very clear, higher force ratios help win an insurgency. This may be the single most important variable.

FORCE RATIO VERSUS CAUSE

Facing Limited Insurgencies (36 cases):

1. When a force is facing a limited insurgency, that force will win the insurgency, intervention or peacekeeping operation at least 73% (24 out of 33) of the time, as long as they have a favorable force ratio.
2. When a force is facing a limited insurgency, that force will win the insurgency at least 79% (15 out of 19) of the time as long as they have a favorable force ratio.
3. A force facing a limited insurgency will not win if they do not have a favorable force ratio (based on 3 cases).

Facing Insurgencies based upon a central idea (27 cases):

1. When a force is facing an insurgency based upon a central idea, that force will lose the insurgency, intervention or peacekeeping operation if they do not have at least a 5-to-1 force ratio (12 cases, or 14 cases, if one counts Vietnam II and Vietnam War as based on nationalism).

2. When a force is facing an insurgency based upon a central idea, that force will lose the insurgency if they do not have at least a 5-to-1 force ratio (12 cases, or 14 cases, if one counts Vietnam II and Vietnam War as based on nationalism).

3. When a force is facing an insurgency based upon a central idea, that force will win the insurgency, intervention or peacekeeping operation 44% of the time, if they have a force ratio between 6-to-1 and 10-to-1 (5.71 to 10.28 to one). This is based upon 9 cases.

4. When a force is facing an insurgency based upon a central idea, that force will win the insurgency 43% of the time, if they have a force ratio between 6-to-1 and 10-to-1 (5.71 to 10.28 to one). This is based upon 7 cases.

5. When a force is facing an insurgency based upon a central idea, that force will win the insurgency 67% of the time if they have a force ratio grater than 10-to-1 (greater than 10.67 to one). This is based upon 6 cases.

Facing insurgencies based upon an overarching idea (13 cases)

1. When a force is facing an insurgency based upon an overarching idea, that force will win the insurgency, intervention or peacekeeping operation 62% of the time, regardless of force ratio (or 73% of the time, if Vietnam is not counted).

2. When a force is facing an insurgency based upon an overarching idea, that force will win the insurgency 58% of the time, regardless of force ratios (or 70% of the time, if Vietnam is not counted). This is based upon 12 cases.

3. One cannot rule out that the force ratios when facing overarching insurgencies are following the same rules as for insurgencies based upon a central idea (below 5-to-1 insurgent victory, between 5-to-1 and 10-to-1 it could go either way, above 10-to-1 mostly counterinsurgent victory).

Facing Insurgencies based upon a central idea or an overarching idea (40 cases):

1. When a force is facing an insurgency based upon a central or overarching idea, that force will lose the insurgency, if they do not have at least a 5-to-1 force ratio. This is based upon 14 cases.

2. When a force is facing an insurgency based upon a central or overarching idea, that force will win the insurgency 50% of the time, if they have a force ratio between 6-to-1 and 10-to-1 (5.71 to 10.28 to one). This is based upon 12 cases.

3. When a force is facing an insurgency based upon a central or overarching idea, that force will win the insurgency 73% of the time, if they have a force ratio greater than 10-to-1 (greater than 10.67 to one). This is based upon 11 cases.

The bigger picture:

1. Force ratios, within reason, are not an issue when facing regional or factional insurgencies.
2. When facing insurgencies that have a broad base of support, one needs at least a 5-to-1 force ratio and preferably a 10-to-1 force ratio.
3. It appears that the two most important factors in determining the outcome of an insurgency are the force ratio and the nature of the cause of the insurgency.

NATURE OF INSURGENCIES

1. There is a clear correlation between the political concept underlying the insurgency and its outcome.
2. A lack of outside support does not necessarily doom an insurgency.
3. Considerable outside support does not mean an insurgency will win.
4. There appears to be little correlation between the degree of outside support for an insurgency and the outcome of the insurgency.
5. A disorderly insurgency is not necessarily a doomed insurgency.
6. An orderly insurgency will not necessarily be a successful insurgency.
7. There appears to be little correlation between the structure of an insurgency and the outcome of an insurgency.
8. Protracted popular war is clearly the best insurgent strategy to employ against a foreign force.

The political concept underlying an insurgency is a significant (if not the most significant) factor in an insurgency.

RULES OF ENGAGEMENT AND DEGREES OF BRUTALITY

There is a clear, consistent pattern which, in the face of no other data on the subject (and we are not aware of any other data collection that addresses this subject), produces a powerful argument that there is some correlation between rules of engagement and outcome, and that there might be a cause-and-effect relationship between rules of engagement and outcome.

In general, there seems to be a pattern where insurgencies win more often if the number of civilians killed compared to the number of insurgents killed is greater than ten, but there is no statistical support for such an assumption.

Therefore, we tentatively conclude that increased levels of brutality favor the insurgency when the number of civilians killed each year averages more than 8 per 100,000 in the population.

The inverse is that it is to the long-term advantage of counterinsurgent forces to limit damage to civilian populations, whether caused by their own or by insurgent actions. This means tightly controlling rules of engagement and probably requires a strictly limited use of artillery and airpower. It also means properly protecting the host population, which would probably require the deployment of significant security forces as part of the total counterinsurgent force.

OPERATIONAL DETAILS—ACTIVE SANCTUARIES, BORDER CONTROLS AND POPULATION RESETTLEMENT

The Dupuy Institute conducted a preliminary analysis of Sanctuaries, Border Barriers, and Population Resettlement. We did not find a strong relationship between the presence of Sanctuaries and outcome. Still, the insurgents won 52% of the time when there was a sanctuary vice 31% of the time when there was not one. In the case of border barriers, there was a statistical correlation, but that was that border barriers favored the insurgency. The insurgents won 69% of the time when there was a border barrier vice 30% of the time when there was not one. We suspect that there is another factor at work here (border barriers are usually built in response to large, intractable insurgencies). In the case of population resettlement, there was again a statistical correlation that showed that population resettlement favored the insurgency. The insurgents won 80% of the time when there was population resettlement vice 30% of the time where there was not. Again, we suspect that there is another factor at work here.

INDIGENOUS GOVERNMENT TYPE AND ELECTIONS

One notes a significant trend across this data, which is:

1. For those insurgencies with significant outside interventions (insurgencies against foreigners), we note that:

   a) Indigenous government type has no significantly measurable influence. In fact, in all but five cases the indigenous government is a dictatorship.

   b) Intervening government type does not seem to matter.

   c) Elections do not seem to matter.

2. For those insurgencies without significant outside intervening forces (primarily domestic insurgencies):

   a) Having the indigenous government as a Democracy or Troubled Democracy clearly favors the Blue side. This result is statistically significant.

   b) Having elections favor the Blue side. This result is statistically significant.

One wonders if the process of intervening undercuts the benefits of democracy.

TERRAIN

From our examination of terrain, we concluded that there was some correlation between covered terrain and outcome and covered terrain and duration. There might also be a correlation between rough terrain and outcome. Our 'tentative conclusions" were:

1. Covered terrain appears to favor the insurgents and this is supported statistically in the majority but not all of the various tests that we conducted.
2. As our data set probably includes more than a third of all significant insurgencies since World War II and almost all insurgencies against outside forces, including all major cases, then the failure to obtain a tight statistical result does not mean we should assume a null hypothesis (there is no relationship) is correct if there exists a visible pattern.
3. Rough covered terrain (or simply covered terrain) appears to increase the chances of the red side winning.
4. Covered terrain appears to increase the duration of insurgencies.
5. The value of covered terrain may be related to airpower. This needs to be examined further.
6. Terrain may be a more significant factor for insurgencies against outside powers than for civil wars.
7. Otherwise, there is no strong indication that there are any differences between level terrain, rough terrain, mountainous terrain, urban or any other significant terrain type as far as their strategic effect on determining outcome.
8. There is no indication that accessibility of the terrain is the issue here (isolated v. not isolated).

LOCATION

Galula stated that naturally isolated country or a locale situated among countries that opposed the insurgency favored the counterinsurgent. In Task 12 we looked at countries with small border areas and found that: "Out of these 15 cases, we still note 5 wins, or 33%. This is clearly not enough to claim that islands, island-like nations, or isolated nations are noticeably less successful at insurgencies than otherwise. One may be able to argue, based upon 4 cases, that small islands (less than 70,000 square kilometers) always produce blue wins."

MEASUREMENTS OF BURDEN

The Dupuy Institute measured the impact of the burden of fighting an insurgency.

This was based on burden per 100,000 home population and was measured as commitment (average troops committed per year per 100,000 population) and as intensity (average troops killed per year per 100,000 population). These different measurements were then evaluated for intervening forces, indigenous government forces, insurgents, civilian casualties and total forces.

The tentative rules on commitment are:

1. It appears that when the average level of commitment by an outside power exceeds more the 0.1% of the population of the intervening country (more than 141 per 100,000 home population), then the insurgency wins in two-thirds of the cases.

2. It appears that when the average level of commitment by the indigenous government exceeds more the 1% of the population of the indigenous country, then the insurgency succeeds in almost two-thirds of the cases.

3. It appears that when the average level of commitment by the insurgents exceeds more the 1% of the population of the indigenous country, then the insurgency succeeds in more than two-thirds of the cases.

4. It appears that when the average level of commitment by the government and insurgents exceeds more the 1% of the population of the indigenous country, then the insurgency succeeds in almost two-thirds of the cases.

The rules for intensity are:

1. It appears that when the average intervening forces killed facing an insurgency exceeds more the 0.00001% of the population of the intervening country (more than 0.01 per 100,000 home population), then the insurgency succeeds in over two-thirds of the cases.

2. It appears that when the average government forces killed facing an insurgency exceeds more the 0.001% of the population of the country (more than 1.11 per 100,000 home population), then the insurgency succeeds in around half of the cases. This is a very tentative conclusion with little statistical support.

3. It is clear from this data that government forces facing an insurgency are not as casualty sensitive as intervening forces facing an insurgency. The casualty sensitivity of intervening forces is clearly supported by statistics, while that of the government forces is not.

4. It appears that when the average insurgent forces killed exceeds more the 0.001% of the population of the country (more than 1.05 per 100,000 home population), then the insurgency succeeds in around half of the cases.

5. It appears that when the average insurgent forces killed exceeds more the 0.01% of the population of the country (more than 10.67 per 100,000 home population), then the counterinsurgency fails in more than half of the cases. This is a very tentative conclusion not statistically supported.

6. It appears that when the average indigenous people killed facing an insurgency exceeds more the 0.001% of the population of the country (more than 1.00 per 100,000 home population), then the insurgency succeeds in almost half of the cases. This is a very tentative conclusion not statistically supported.

OTHER THEORISTS

In general, Galula and Fall are the two theoretical constructs we have seen that we believe have a sound basis. The rest we believe can be dismissed.

We therefore conclude from this analysis that:

1. There is a strong need for further study of these issues.
2. There is a considerable danger of negative learning.
3. There is not a strong basis for developing any model of insurgency before such further study is conducted.
4. There are sometimes limitations with developing theories based primarily upon personal experience.

Note, the analysis that *The Dupuy Institute* has conducted is primarily focused on analyzing and understanding a developed insurgency. Different factors may be in play if one is looking at an early or proto-insurgency or if one is analyzing conditions before an insurgency develops. Each probably needs to be subjected to an independent line of analysis.

Furthermore, our primary focus has been the importance of these factors on determining the outcome of the insurgency. We have found much less correlation between these factors and the duration and have not seriously examined such issues as intensity and combat value of these factors. Clearly, there is more that needs to be done.

NOTES

1. In Charlie Walker, *My Few Wise Words of Wisdom* (Walker, 2008), page 151.

CHAPTER 24

Where Do We Go From Here?

Reports that say that something hasn't happened are always interesting to me, because as we know, there are known knowns; there are things we know we know. We also know there are known unknowns; that is to say we know there are some things we do not know. But there are also unknown unknowns—the ones we don't know we don't know.

—Secretary of Defense Donald Rumsfeld, 2002[1]

I consider this work to be a good start. It is far from the end-all-and-be-all of analysis of insurgencies. Yet I think there is enough here that it needs to be brought forward and presented. The analysis presented in this book represents our work up until early 2008. After that, all analytical work effectively stopped, although we continued to research and expand our data. These were hundreds of additional tasks, pieces of analysis and other things that we wanted to do. But, we had reached a stopping point, and there was no more budget to do anything further. My attention had to shift to other tasks.

Many years ago, I had the pleasure of having a series of meetings with Professor Ivo Feierabend. I was taking a graduate course in Econometrics at San Diego State University (SDSU). I decided that for my class paper, I would do something on the causes of revolution. The two leading efforts on this, both done in the 1960s, were by Ted Gurr and the husband and wife team of Feierabend and Feierabend. I reviewed their work, and for a variety of reasons, got interested in the measurements and analyses done by the Feierabends, vice the more known work by Ted Gurr. This eventually led me to Dr. Feierabend, who still happened to be at San Diego State University much to my surprise. This was some 20 years after he had done what I consider to be ground-breaking work on revolutions. I looked him up and had several useful and productive meetings with him.

In the 1960s, he had an entire team doing this work. Several professors were involved, and he had a large number of graduate students coding events of political violence. In addition, he had access to mainframe computers, offices, etc. The entire effort was shut down in the 1960s, and he had not done anything further on this in almost 20 years. I eventually asked him why he didn't continue his work. His answer, short and succinct was, "I had no budget."

This was a difficult answer for a college student to understand. But, it is entirely understood by me now. To do these types of analytical projects requires staff, resources, facilities, etc. They cannot be done by one person, and even if they could, that one person usually needs a paycheck. So, the only way one could conduct one of these large analytical projects is to be funded. In the case of the Feierabends, that funding came from the government, as did ours. Their funding ended after a few years, as has ours. Their work could be described as a good start, but there was so much more that needed to be done. Intellectually, one is mystified why someone would not make sure that this work was continued. Yet, in the cases of Ted Gurr and the Feierabends, it did not.

The problem lies in that the government (or at least the parts that I dealt with) sometimes has the attention span of a two-year-old. Not only that, it also has the need for instant gratification, very much like a two-year-old. Practically, what that means is that projects that can answer an immediate question get funding (like the Bosnia and Iraq casualty estimates). Larger research efforts that will produce an answer or a product in two to three years can also get funding. On the other hand, projects that produce a preliminary answer in two to three years and then need several more years of funding to refine, check, correct and develop that work, tend to die. This has happened repeatedly. The analytical community is littered with many clever, well thought-out reports that look to be good starts. What is missing is a complete body of analysis on a subject.

We have already outlined in big picture terms in Chapter Two the development of U.S. counterinsurgency studies and analysis through Vietnam. It is no accident that Dr. Andrew Birtle's second book on U.S. counterinsurgency doctrine ends in 1976. There isn't much after that. When we started the Iraq study in 2004, I asked one employee to assemble a list of counterinsurgency experts and cells in the U.S. Army. There were no cells, or groups of experts. There were a few individual academics, mostly pursuing it out of their own passion. That was it. There were general military affairs experts who had recently re-badged themselves, but there was no significant grouping, or body of experts. One analytical agency openly admitted to me in private conversation that they had no one on their staff of over 100 people that was a counterinsurgency expert.

Now, the picture has changed somewhat. One can argue that we now have hundreds of thousands of counterinsurgency experts, many with very real and personal experience, and the scars to show for it. Still, we have relatively fledgling analytical efforts going on for insurgencies, or irregular war, to use the latest muddying-the-water term.[2] We still do not have a very clear doctrine, even though we are having considerable success in Iraq. Still, this plan for "the surge" in Iraq did not come out of the structure of the Army, but was a somewhat improvised back-channel effort that involved a retired general officer, a right-wing think tank, and active duty officers.[3] This is a rather bizarre way to do business, but as it was successful, it does show a certain amount of resilience in the system. But, overall the system was doing a poor job, which is why it had to be done outside of normal channels.

We pay a lot of taxes for a government. These people are paid good salaries. I expect them to be thinking about our long-term interests, focused on the long-term problems, and addressing all aspects of military affairs. This is simply not the case. I don't have all the answers to correcting this and putting realistic analysis and realistic, soundly-based, long-term vision back in the Defense Department. But, I think it needs to be done. Having been rattling around the industry for a couple of decades, I am all too aware of DoD's ability to get enthralled with the next new toy, the next great single idea, the next neat theory to win all wars by some superlative methodology, the next new set of buzz words, all reinforced by the ability to ignore what is not immediately in front of it, the ability to claim that it does not do certain missions (even though history clearly says that they invariably do) and the tendency to send the funding off chasing the next new fad. I think we can do better than that.

So, let me take a moment to make a few recommendations of where this work should go from here. While all criticism has value, criticism with proposed solutions is more valuable. These are general recommendations. I have produced lists of more specific ones, most of which seemed to have fallen on deaf ears.

First, future analysis should be focused, so that it addresses one of the three distinct time frames:

a. Before an insurgency starts (pre-insurgency)
b. In the early stages of an insurgency (proto-insurgency)
c. As an insurgency has clearly developed (developed insurgency)

Currently our work primarily addresses developed insurgencies. As such, it only addresses what to look at and what to do once you're already up-to-whatever in alligators, to paraphrase an old expression. It does not say how to recognize and deal with an insurgency that had not reached the stage of increasing violence, or how to recognize and deal with a potential insurgency. Corrective action is probably much cheaper in those stages.

As such, the defense and intelligence community needs three sets of quantitative predictive tools. These are not intended to replace current approaches but to supplement them. The three sets of tools are:

a. A model that predicts the chances of political violence across all nations. This is, in effect, readdressing the Gurr and Feierabend & Feierabend work and would be extended to address all the data that has accumulated in the 40 years since they did their analysis. This is not a small effort (pre-insurgency model).

b. A model or set of procedures that predicts the chances of and analyzes the nature of insurgencies in their early stages (proto-insurgency model).
c. A model or set of procedures that predicts the chances of and analyzes the nature of insurgencies that are clearly developing. This is effectively what our Iraq Casualty Estimate did in January 2005 (developed insurgency model).

Second, training tools need to be revamped to consider current understandings and to remove past biases.

a. The political concept, motivation and cause of insurgencies needs to be seriously addressed.
b. The structure of the insurgency needs to be addressed. The current material appears to be overly influenced by the U.S. experience in Vietnam.
c. The issue of outside support needs to be addressed. The current material appears to be overly influenced by the U.S. experience in Vietnam.

There is considerable concern over negative learning in this case. Our inability early on to come to terms with Iraq because we were too wedded to the example of Vietnam is a classic case of not basing our education on a broad and deep enough set of cases. In the end, there are well more than 100 post-World War II insurgencies to learn from.[4] We should probably be expanding our range beyond the same half-dozen case studies that everyone seems to use.

There is considerable value in Galula and Fall. The other theoretical works raise the specter of negative learning. The over reliance on Malaya in the study of counterinsurgency has clearly led to some negative learning. One needs to make sure that case studies are being used for what they are best for, while the bigger issues need to be addressed more analytically.

While *The Dupuy Institute* considers everything in this book to be fundamentally hypothetical, it is still strongly supported by data. There is considerable material out there that is given more weight than the data used to support it warrants. There is considerable material out there that is credited for having theoretical value that probably should only be considered hypothetical. The word hypothesis should be used a lot more than it is, and the word theory should be used a lot less.

Training materials, manuals, text books and books used as textbooks should be reviewed to make sure that the conclusions in them that may lead to negative learning are flagged as such. Material used in the analysis of insurgencies need to be reviewed for the same reasons. Any insurgency or combat model designs need to be reviewed for the same reasons.

Third, analysis needs somehow to be able to parse the study of insurgencies to their appropriate levels, from strategic concerns (most important), to operational concerns to tactics. Each level needs to be studied separately and at some point, interrelated. Our work tended to be focused on the strategic level, as that was the simplest, and in our mind, the most important to address.

Related to the above points, databases need to be constructed for analytical uses that address the appropriate levels and the appropriate time frames. Right now, the existing databases do not address proto-insurgencies, or the events leading up to an insurgency (pre-insurgency). These are all significant, separate efforts.

Finally, we recommend a study of the changes in violence caused by climate change. While people are measuring and arguing over the degree and extent of climate change, the actual impact such change will have on political violence, intensity of violence, etc., is not known and has not been systematically studied. Right now, it is not known if in the long run climate change will result in more political instability or in fact less violence. The degree is also not known. The current databases serve as a convenient starting point for measuring the impact of any long-term climate change on degree and extent of violence. As a minimum an analysis based upon seasons and climate areas can provide some useful insights.

NOTES

1. Remark is from a Department of Defense briefing given on February 12, 2002. See "Rum remark wins Rumsfeld an award", *BBC News*, 2 December 2003.
2. For example, in December 2009, people from several agencies were meeting to review the analytical support behind Quinliven's ideas. This is five years after I first flagged the issue, and twelve years after he first proposed it.
3. See Thomas E. Ricks, The Gamble: General David Petraeus and the American Military Adventure in Iraq, 2006–2008 (New York: The Penguin Press, 2009).
4. This is a rough estimate. Our database eventually covered over 80 of them, including most major ones. We estimate the entire population of post-World War II insurgencies to be some number between 150 and 200, depending on how you define them. We have not tried to count them more precisely.

CHAPTER 25

A Tale of Two Books

The lesson from history is that no one learns from history.
—Anonymous[1]

T his book was intended to be a theoretical work based upon the studies and analysis that *The Dupuy Institute* did for the Defense Department and intelligence agencies. This is the primary purpose of the book and is still its intended purpose.

But, since the beginning of the writing process, a second book or purpose has crept in, which is far less theoretical and much more oriented towards addressing the issues here and now. This was the discussion on the failures of the studies and analysis community, the U.S. Army, and the national defense leadership to properly study, understand and appreciate the complexities of guerilla warfare. Initially, the wars in Iraq and Afghanistan were conducted with so little preparation that they have had a very amateurish look. While there were many individuals who performed above and beyond the call of duty, the overall plans, execution, expertise and understanding were sorely lacking.

The Army and the national defense community have made a number of changes since then. But even if the glass is half full, the American serviceman and the American taxpayer have every right to demand that the glass be completely full.

It is also important to understand that these are America's wars. They are not George Bush's wars. He was elected by the majority of the Electoral College votes, which is closely tied to the popular vote. It was the American voter who had the responsibility to review his credentials, experience, knowledge and capabilities before the election. His actions were overseen and approved by Congress. Not a penny is spent on these wars without the approval of the elected representatives of Congress. Those congressmen are elected by the majority votes of the each and every American voter in their district or state. They are not the U.S. armed forces' wars, as in the end, they are simply a department of the government under command of the executive branch and funded and ruled by the legislative branch. By the same token, these wars do not belong to Donald Rumsfeld, Dick Cheney, Karl Rove, Dick Armey, Trent Lott,

General Franks, General Petraeus, Barack Obama, William Gates, Nancy Pelosi, Harry Reid, the military-industrial complex, big oil, Halliburton, AIPAC or any other single convenient person to blame. These wars belong to the voters, citizens, and taxpayers of the United States. They are the ones responsible for who actually runs our government and ensuring that it is run properly. One can argue about how good a job they have done over the last twelve years.

The wars in Iraq and Afghanistan are not resolved, although we are disengaging. They may yet be resolved in a favorable manner. They may not. Regardless, their execution was flawed and improvised. The fact the U.S. Army and defense authorities may have been able to recover from a bad start does not remove the demand that there should not have been a bad start to begin with, nor does it remove the demand that actions need to be taken to make sure that there is not a bad start in the future. Unfortunately, if there is any theme in U.S. military history, it is that we often don't get a good start. This was clearly shown at Detroit in 1812, at Manassas in 1861, in the invasion of Cuba in 1898, Pearl Harbor in 1941, Kasserine Pass in 1942, at Chosin and Kunuri in Korea in 1951, with the defeat of the U.S. in Vietnam (1965–1973), at Tang Island in 1975, with the confused operation in Grenada in 1982, and now of course, both Iraq and Afghanistan. I think the U.S. citizens have a right to demand that both the national command authorities (the civilians) and the U.S. armed forces be prepared for all types of wars and to be able to initiate them with considerable competence. They have done it before (for example World War I and the Gulf War), and sadly enough, some of our opponents have also done it before.

So this second book or theme, as harsh as it is presented, is intended to hopefully generate some reforms in the studies and analysis community, and the U.S. Army and the defense community as a whole. It is intended to hopefully help with the education of officers and civilians in the chain of command, and maybe even a few voters. It is not intended to be aimed at any particular party, ideology, or individuals. All this writer really wants is good government and good decision-making. I do not feel, from my vantage point, that we have always gotten that.

It would take yet another book or study to address what those changes are, and this author does not have his finger on the pulse of every department or initiative in the government. There are always various improvement programs going on, and of course, some areas that never seem to quite fix themselves.

But, what is needed at least in the analytical community is a clear, long-range program to analyze and understand every aspect of warfare. While individuals in the government may be able to point to departments that are responsible for doing that, I can point out that they are not actually really doing that to the depth and extent needed. While individuals in the government may be able to point to their latest improvement initiatives, I have seen many of these before, and very few achieve permanent traction.

What has been done theoretically on insurgencies is sparse, and when we look at things like peacekeeping operations, interventions, occupations, nation-building and all those messy missions that people don't like to analyze, the record is even worse. I am not aware of any significant corrective actions.

Of course, the long-term solution is not a corrective program, or a newly-funded program, but an analytical community structured to be able to take on long-term independent research, and to be able to discuss and present such research. It requires the right mix of independent-minded and creative analysts who have both the skills and the expertise to do the work. Right now, I cannot point to an analytical center inside of the DoD that I feel does that. What is needed is a long-term study plan and the steady funding to implement such a plan.

We will see over the next few years how Iraq and Afghanistan resolve themselves. Hopefully, the sacrifices made by our servicemen and women there will be used to make sure that the next time we enter into these types of wars, we enter with a much better start. Hopefully, their sacrifices will finally force the national security apparatus and the Defense Department to fully understand and analyze the complexities of these types of interventions. Hopefully, their sacrifices will be used to educate future political leaders and the voters. I can honestly say that this was not the case for Vietnam.

NOTES

1. I have no idea where this saying originally came from.

Briefing Slides from January 2005

SALIENT POINTS

- Insurgent force strength is probably between 20,000–60,000
- This is a major insurgency
  - It is of medium intensity
- It is a regional or factionalized insurgency and **must** remain that way
- U.S. commitment can be expected to be relatively steady throughout this insurgency and will not be quickly replaced by indigenous forces
- It will last around 10 or so years
- It may cost the U.S. 5,000 to 10,000 killed
  - It may be higher
  - This assumes no major new problems in the Shiite majority areas

---

UNLESS THERE IS A SUDDEN CHANGE ON THE GROUND IN THE NEXT MONTH

- U.S. losses are **not** likely to be **less than** 3,000 killed
  - It is already half of that
- May well be in the 5,000 to 10,000 range
- May be higher
- Duration is likely to be around 10 years
  - Lets say 63% chance between 7 to 13 years
  - Lets say 37% chance of being 15 years or longer
- U.S. & Allied force size is likely to be a constant (for the estimate)
  - U.S. Force Size is likely to remain fairly high
  - Iraqi government force size is growing

DETERMINING WINNERS AND LOSERS
Percent of Cases the Insurgents Won

CATEGORY	LOW	MEDIUM	HIGH	IRAQ CATEGORY
Country area	14%	43%	71%	High
Population	27	40	100	High
Border Length	18	63	78	Medium or high
Outside Support	56	54	33	Medium
Political Concept	0	75	50	Low or medium? (probably low)
Orderliness	73	36	33	Low
Intervening Force Size	50	39	71	High
Insurgent Force Size	22	47	86	Medium or high? (possibly high)
Casualty Rate	40	86	50	Medium
Force Ratios	0	66	47	Medium

POSSIBLE SWEEPING CONCLUSIONS

1. It is difficult to control large countries (above 290,079 sq. km.)
   - Iraq is 437,072 square kilometers
2. It is difficult to control large populations (above 9,529,000 people)
   - Iraq is 24,001,816+
3. It is difficult to control an extended land border (above 3,477 kilometers in length
   - Iraq's land borders total 3,650 kilometers
   - The U.S./Mexican border is 3,141 kilometers

Iraq is a large country, with a very large population and a large land border. As such, it would be expected to be difficult to control

MORE SWEEPING CONCLUSIONS

4. "Limited outside support" does not doom an insurgency
5. "Disorderly" insurgencies are very intractable and often successful insurgencies (for example Afghanistan)
6. Insurgencies with a large intervening forces (above 95,000) are often successful insurgencies
7. Higher combat intensities do not doom an insurgency

THREE AREAS FOR CONSIDERATION

8. Insurgent Political Concept
   - Is it "limited developed political thought"or based upon a "central political idea"
9. Insurgent Force Size
   - Is it above 20,000 insurgents?
10. Force Ratios
    - What is their influence and how should they be measured?

POLITICAL CONCEPT OF INSURGENCY

- If the insurgency in Iraq is (and remains) a factional or regionally based rebellion, then based upon our 8 other examples, it should fail.
- If Iraq is (or becomes) a nationalist revolt against the intervening powers, then based upon 15 examples, it should succeed
- Therefore, the critical issue here: is the U.S. facing a regionally and factionally based insurgency in Iraq or facing a widespread anti-intervention insurgency
- For the purpose of estimating casualties, we may need to consider whether this is a locally based insurgency or a national one, and we may need to estimate the duration and losses from the outside foreign insurgency separate from the indigenous insurgents

OPEN QUESTION: WHAT IS THE BASIS
OF THE IRAQI INSURGENCY?

SO WHAT IS THE SIZE OF THE INSURGENCY (CONCLUSION)?

Therefore based upon counterinsurgency casualties (killed)
8,472 to 13,464 (Vietnam)
Or 12,567 to 25,133 (Malaya & Algeria)
Or 19,842 to 145,000 (aggregate data)
Or 48,645 (based on average rate from aggregate data)

Based upon incidents
35,632 to 89,080 (Feb 2004–Jan 2005)
Or 61,107 to 152,767 (Sep 2004–Jan 2005)
Or others

This leads one to suspect that insurgent force size is from 20,000 to 60,000

- And is probably greater than 20,000
- And is clearly greater than 5,000
- And it may represent the highest category in our analysis (50,000 or greater)
- This does not parse the insurgents into "full-time"and "core" insurgents versus "part-time"and "support"

DURATION VERSUS OUTCOME (CONCLUSION)

Therefore, for the sake of estimating the duration of an insurgency, one should determine first if it is:

1. A **short successful** counterinsurgency of 1,037 days (2.8 years) in length (7 cases)

2. An **extended successful** counterinsurgency of 5,614 days (15.4 years) in length (7 cases)

3. An **early withdrawal** (unsuccessful) intervention of 1,555 days (4.3 years) in length (3 cases)

4. A **typical successful** insurgency of 4,256 days (11.7 years) in length (9 cases)

THERE IS A TENDENCY FOR COUNTERINSURGENCY CASUALTIES TO BE STEADY OR STEADILY INCREASING

- Early Peak (3 cases)
- Later Peak (1 real case—Vietnam War)
- Steady state (4 cases)
- Increasing (10 cases)
  - Eight clearly are
  - Two are suspected to be
- Steadily Decreasing (5 cases)
  - Two clearly is
  - Three are suspected to be
- Unknown (5 cases)

For further "refinement" of our estimate, this needs to be measured as casualty rates

THERE IS A STRONG TENDENCY FOR COUNTERINSURGENCY FORCE STRENGTH TO BE STEADY OR STEADILY INCREASING

- Early Peak (1 case—Malaya)
- Later Peak (1 real case—Vietnam War)
- Steady state (5 cases)
  - One clearly is
  - Four are suspected to be
  - Some of these increase rapidly in the first year
- Increasing (20 cases)
  - Twenty clearly are
- Unknown (1 case)

There are no cases of significantly decreasing counterinsurgency force strengths besides Malaya and late Vietnam

TENTATIVE CONCLUSIONS

- Early Peak insurgencies are rare
  - And appear to be small and successful counterinsurgencies
  - This case may not apply to Iraq
  - Regardless, force strength still tends to be constant
- In other insurgencies, counterinsurgent casualties may steadily decrease, remain steady or increase steadily
- In other insurgencies, counterinsurgent force strengths tend to remain steady or increase
  - This appears to be true for 23 out of our 26 cases

TIPPING POINTS (CONCLUSION)

- Occurs in 6 of the insurgencies (two successful)
  - Six others defeated militarily (two conventional)
  - Four others resolved by negotiation
- In four out of the six tipping points, control of borders was a factor
  - This was definitely the case with Greece and Kashmir
    - Although in both cases, it was a decision to withdraw support that really mattered, not a physical closing of the borders
    - In the case of Greece, it only shortened a failing insurgency
  - Less so with Malaya and Algeria
- In one case, rules of engagement was a factor (but not in the other five cases)
- In two or three cases, enemy "bloodiness" was a factor
  - Militarily headstrong insurgents in Vietnam and Greece
- Elections do not seem to have been a major factor

APPENDIX II

The Bosnia Casualty Estimate

Bosnia has never been a single nation. If they're trying to marry (three sides) together, it's not going to work. The U.S. could be in for a long, messy period . . . When you're asking Americans to die, you have to be able to explain it in terms of the national interest. I see no vital United States interest to support a combat mission there.

—Former Secretary of State Henry Kissinger, as told
    to CNN in November 1995[1]

On 1 November 1995, the leaders of three parts of the former Republic of Yugoslavia met in Dayton, Ohio to hammer out an accord that would bring peace to the warring factions of the former Yugoslavia. That same day, *The Dupuy Institute* was asked to apply its historical expertise on combat casualties to the estimation of fatalities that U.S. forces might experience in a projected twelve-month intervention in Bosnia. So that its report would contain independent thinking, *The Dupuy Institute* was given no briefing regarding any detailed plans or assumptions of the intervention, only that it would comprise 60,000 troops, 20,000 of whom would be U.S., and that some reasonable peace posture would be a precondition.

One of the central issues of the Dayton conference was that someone needed to deploy between the warring factions to establish and keep the peace. Being located in Europe, next to NATO countries, those forces clearly had to come from NATO, with the U.S. Army front and center. So, the U.S. Army was looking at inserting itself between three warring factions that had been fighting each other for five years and had managed to kill over 100,000 people. This was not an enviable task.

Within two weeks, *The Dupuy Institute* delivered its estimate, based on its analysis of a large number of contingencies and peacekeeping operations and on its own judgments about how such an operation might be run. We produced two casualty estimates. One was based on a compact deployment, intended to minimize fatalities in the face of worst-case behavior by nationalist forces. It estimated 11 to 29 U.S. fatalities with a pessimistic result (90%) of 17 to 42 fatalities. Obviously, even worse things can happen than the 90 percentile results; for example, a transport plane crashes with 200 troops on board.

In the case of an extended deployment (which is what was done), it was estimated that there was a 50% chance that U.S. killed from all causes in Bosnia in the first year would be below 17 (12 combat deaths and 5 non-combat fatalities) and a 90% chance U.S. killed would be below 25.[2] These numerical results were based upon two separate sets of analysis, a constructive analysis of incidents and a historical analysis of selected contingency operations and peacekeeping operations.

To quote from the last paragraph of the executive summary:

The current operational relevance of these estimates is their impact on risk thresholds, contemplated by U.S. decision makers. This estimate is accurate enough to support conclusions that a "few"—that is, at least 10 or 20, and even possibly 50 American soldiers,—will be at significant risk. At the same time, this study clearly shows that the probability of death for more than 100 U.S. soldiers is highly unlikely—if history and experience are to be a gauge.[3]

JCS Chairman General John Shalikashvili had the draft executive summary of the Bosnia casualty estimate with him in the meeting with President Clinton during which the decision was made to commit U.S. forces to the peace mission.[4]

The Dayton conference would continue until 17 November, when agreement was reached. This agreement was signed by the heads of Serbia, Croatia, and Bosnia and Herzegovina on 14 December 1995. The United States and other nations of NATO then deployed significant forces into the region as part of a peacekeeping effort that continues to this day.

As always with such short-term projects, the original data was provided in the form of briefings. The actual first draft of the report was provided to JCS on 28 November 1995, with a final version of the report delivered later.

Over the course of the year, the deployment was in fact more peaceful than many people expected. Actual U.S. casualties from all causes in the first year in Bosnia were six, and there were no combat deaths, unless one counts the soldier who picked up an unexploded mine as a combat death. This was within the range of the casualty estimate and certainly fit into our estimate that we were looking at 10 or 20 killed, vice some of the more frightening scenarios some were envisioning.[5]

But behind this estimate was considerable concern on our part over the data and methodologies. Before coming to us, the Joint Chiefs of Staff asked the Deputy Under Secretary of the Army for Operations Research (DUSA-OR) if he could provide an estimate of the potential losses in Bosnia. They were informed that there was no methodology to estimate casualties in an "Operation Other than War (OOTW)".[6]

They then turned to us, giving us three weeks to assemble an estimate of casualties for Bosnia. The contract was issued on 1 November 1995, and our first briefing was provided ten working days later. *The Dupuy Institute* decided to make use of two separate sets of analysis to construct this estimate: a constructive analysis of incidents and historical analysis of selected counterinsurgency operations and peacekeeping operations.

The first part of the briefing was the constructive analysis of incidents. In this case, a senior operations research analyst sat down with a group of retired military officers (including two general officers) and walked through the entire scenario. This included preparation, entry, operational deployment, maintaining piece and retirement (withdrawal). They then systematically looked at the type of threats during each phase and produced an estimate of possible losses from each threat. This included such things as harassment, land mines, withdrawal of recalcitrant units, mortar attacks, attack or ambushes by renegade units, terrorist attacks, surface-to-air and anti-aircraft fire, and of course, non-combat losses (accidents). For combat calculation, we used our combat model, the TNDM, for a series of battalion-level engagements. For other events, like mortar attacks, we estimated their frequency and lethality. The constructive analysis was then assembled from each of these parts to produce a percentage range of casualties.

This was nothing new. It was classic back-of-envelope operations research. While it gave an answer, there was no way of really knowing if that answer was correct. It also was susceptible to analysts overlooking critical factors, misestimating critical factors, and it could be influenced by analyst bias.

The second part of our analysis was our historical analysis of selected counterinsurgency operations and peacekeeping operations. This dual track result developed because we could not agree on how best to approach the problem. So we did both! This had the advantage that if the estimates overlapped, our confidence in our approach would certainly be increased. Fortunately, they did overlap.

This action involved data collection on 144 contingencies and minor insurgencies drawn primarily from a 1985 HERO report, UN sources and other secondary sources. Analysis was done on 90 of those operations including all 38 UN peacekeeping operations preceding the intervention in Bosnia. It was only possible to have even done this analysis because of the material collected in 1985 by HERO.[7] Even then, as we went through the data, we had questions as to the accuracy or meaning of some of it. Having no time to check, we threw out the questionable data and continued forward with the data that we had some confidence in. In the case of the UN, we were able to get a steady stream of data on their operations faxed directly to us from their offices. We then dumped all this data into a simple database and did a few cuts on it. This produced a series of charts looking at total killed in each operation compared to force size. For example:

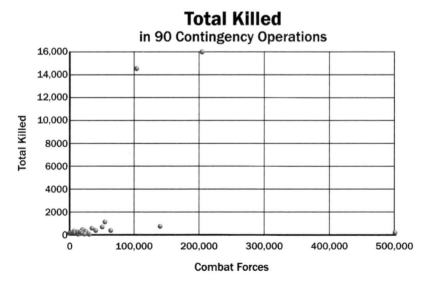

Total Killed
in 86 Contingency Operations

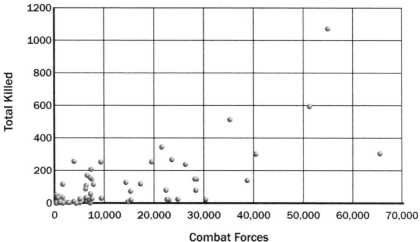

Total Killed
in 42 Peacekeeping Operations

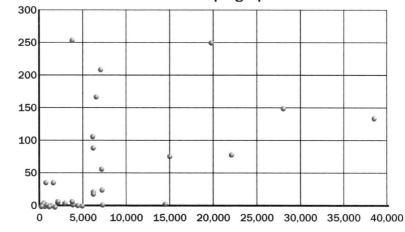

We then converted them into a standard measurement of killed per year. This produced the following:

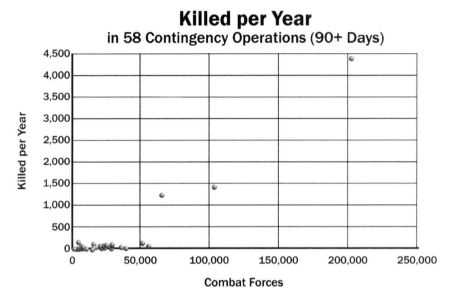

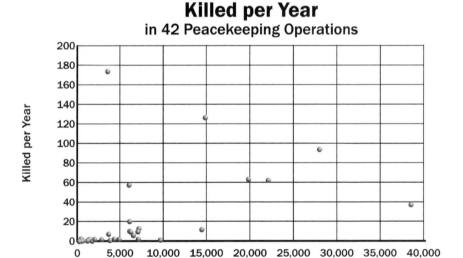

We then went through and selected those operations that had similar size forces and calculated their rates for a one year. This was 15 cases. With a little regression analysis provided (mathematical correlation), we ended up with an estimate of U.S. losses paralleling our constructive analysis estimate.

Killed per Year
in 15 Contingency Operations (90+ Days)

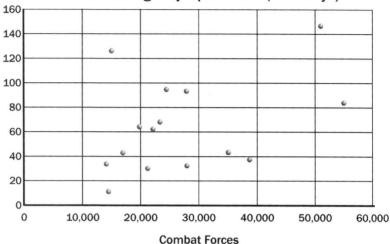

We summarized the data as follows:

Historical Data Summary
of Fatalities

Per Operation

* Average Killed Per Operation (90 Operations): — 421
* Average Killed Per Operation (less Afghanistan
  and Greek Civil War — 88 Operations): — 85
* Average Killed Per Peacekeeping Operation (42 Operations): — 42

Per Year

* Average Killed Per Year Per Operation, 90+ Days (58 Operations): — 143
* Average Killed Per Year Per Operation, 90+ Days, (less 3 major combat
  operations: Greece, Afghanistan, Lebanon — 55 Operations): — 24
* Average Killed Per Year Per Peacekeeping Operation (42 Operations): — 17
* Average Killed Per Year In 15 "Representative" Operations: — 64

THE DUPUY INSTITUTE

This turned out to be powerful evidence, and some of this data was used in General Shalikashvili's testimony to Congress.[8] It clearly showed that unless these operations turned into a significant insurgency, the casualty cost was affordable, provided the political will and desire were there.

The fact the average killed per year per peacekeeping operation matched the exact number our constructive estimate was using as its center point was just a lucky accident.

We then added a series of slides called "The Inevitable Vietnam Comparison":

The Inevitable Vietnam Comparison

- **The Bosnian peacekeeping mission is *not* similar to Vietnam**
  - **Population and size differences**
    - Yugoslavia has 20+ million people, Indochina has 55+ million
    - Yugoslavia is .26 million square miles, Indochina is .75 million
  - **Peacekeeping verses major insurgency**
  - **US is not the primary enemy**
  - **Level of intensity is lower**

But, since everyone makes the comparison...

THE DUPUY INSTITUTE

VIETNAM FATALITIES

	THE ADVISORY PERIOD				THE U.S. COMBAT PERIOD		
YEAR	PEAK STRENGTH	ANNUAL KILLED	KILLED PER 1,000	YEAR	END OF YEAR STRENGTH	ANNUAL KILLED	KILLED PER 1,000
1961	3,164	11	3.5	1965	154,000	1,636*	10.6
1962	11,326	31	2.7	1966	389,000	4,771	12.3
1963	16,263	78	4.8	1967	480,000	9,699	20.2
1964	23,310	147	6.3	1968	536,040	14,437	26.9
				1969	484,326	6,727	13.9
				1970	335,794	7,171	21.4
				1971	158,119	942	6.0
				1972	24,200	531	21.9

*since January 1961

IF BOSNIA ACHIEVES VIETNAM LEVELS OF VIOLENCE
(Based on 20,000 U.S. troops)

	ESTIMATED KILLED PER YEAR	
	1961–1964 FIGURES	1965–1972 FIGURES
Low	54	120
Average	87	333
High	126	538

Of course, this all presupposed that our commitment was not going to exceed 20,000, but as this was the parameter given to us by the customer, this is what we worked with. Inevitably, the Vietnam comparisons would come again in 2003–2004.

This was all assembled into a brief final report of 12 pages backed up by 75 briefing slides. For the record the people that worked on this were: Richard Anderson, David Bongard, Dr. William Bradford, Joseph A. Bulger (LtCol, USAF, ret.), Dr. George A. Daoust (LtCol., USAF, ret.), Dr. Richard W. Harrison, Jay Karamales, John Kettelle, Nicholas Krawciw (MG, USA, ret.), Christopher A. Lawrence, Dr. Joseph E. McCarthy (Brig.Gen. USA, ret.), and Robert E. Schmaltz. John Kettelle headed the team that did the constructive analysis, I headed the team that did the historical analysis and General Krawciw headed the overall study.

NOTES

1. Jack Kelly, "'Amicable divorce' could turn nasty experts say", *USA Today* (22 November 1995).
2. *Peacekeeping in Bosnia Fatality Estimates* (McLean, VA.: The Dupuy Institute, 1995).
3. *Ibid.*
4. As described by General John Shalikashvili in private conversations with Nicholas Krawciw (MG, USA, ret.), who, at the time was president of *The Dupuy Institute*.
5. Usually with a reference to Vietnam, for example see Cal Thomas, "Another Vietnam?", *The Baltimore Sun* (October 19, 1995) or Garry Wills, "Beware Bosnia Becoming Another Vietnam, *Chicago Sun-Times* (November 26, 1995).
6. OOTW was the then-current buzzword for anything that was not a full-scale conventional war. It had replaced past buzzwords like SSCO (Small Scale Contingency Operations) and "unconventional war." The current buzzword is "irregular warfare." While the concepts do not change significantly, the words used to describe them seem change every decade or so.
7. HERO was the Historical Evaluation and Research Organization, one of the organizations that Colonel Trevor N. Dupuy established before he started *The Dupuy Institute*. The study in question had been funded by the Army's CAA (Concepts Analysis Agency, now Center for Army Analysis).
8. This was noted in one of the hearings in November 1995.

APPENDIX III

List of Cases

The data base used for the analysis in this book was first assembled into a series of Excel spread sheets and was known as the MISS (Modern Insurgency Spread Sheets). The version of the MISS that was used for the analysis in this book had 83 cases in it, of which 62 were classified as insurgencies. Since then the data base has been updated to 109 cases by *The Dupuy Institute*. The analysis presented in this book is based on the 83-case version of the data base. At the end of September 2007, the list of 83 insurgencies, interventions and peacekeeping operations consisted of:

1. UK in Palestine (1944–1948)
2. Ukrainian Independence Movement (1944–1954)
3. Indonesia (1945–1949)
4. Greek Civil War (1946–1949)
5. Indochina War (1946–1954)
6. La Violencia (1948–1958)
7. Malaya (1948–60)
8. Puerto Rican Independence Movement (1950–1954)
9. Mau Mau Revolt (1952–1956)
10. Algerian War (1954–1962)
11. Cyprus (1955–59)
12. Cameroun (1955–1960)
13. Tibetan Revolt (1956–1974)
14. Soviet Intervention in Hungary (1956)
15. Cuban Revolution (1956–1959)
16. Oman (1957–1959)
17. Vietnam I (1957–1960)
18. La Menos Violencia (1958–1964)
19. UN Peacekeeping in Congo (1960–1964)
20. Guatemala (1960–1996)
21. Vietnam II (1961–1964)
22. Angola (1961–1974)
23. Katanga War (1961–1963)
24. Yemen (1962–1970)
25. Portuguese Guinea (1963–1974)
26. Borneo (1963–1966)
27. Tupamaro Insurgency (1963–1973)
28. Aden (1963–1967)
29. Colombian Civil War (1964–present)
30. Mozambique (1964–1974)

31. Vietnam War (1965–1973)
32. Dhofar Rebellion (1965–1976)
33. Chad Civil War (1965–1969)
34. Rhodesia I (1966–1972)
35. Namibia (1966–1989)
36. Guevara Guerilla Campaign (1966–1967)
37. Sandinistas (1967–1979)
38. Cabanas Insurgency (1967–1974)
39. Northern Ireland (1968–1998)
40 French Intervention in Chad (1969–1971)
41. Argentina (1969–1983)
42. Rhodesia II (1972–1979)
43. Polisario Rebellion (1973–1991)
44. Angola Civil War (1975–1988)
45. Lebanon (1975–1990)
46. Indonesia in Timor (1975–1999)
47. Mozambique Civil War (1976–1992)
48. Operation Tacaud (1978–1980)
49. Tanzania in Uganda (1978–1980)
50. Cambodia (1978–1989)
51. El Salvador (1979–1992)
52. Uganda Civil War (1979–1986)
53. USSR in Afghanistan (1979–1989)
54. Shining Path in Peru (1980–1999)
55. Contras in Nicaragua (1981–1990)
56. Tamil Insurgency (1983–2002)
57. U.S. Invasion of Grenada (1983)
58. First Intifada (1987–1993)
59. Kashmir Insurgency (1988–present)
60. UN Peacekeeping in Angola (1988–1999)
61. Afghan Civil War I (1989–1992)
62. U.S. Invasion of Panama (1989)
63. Peacekeeping in Liberia (1990–1997)
64. Peacekeeping in Lebanon (1990–present)
65. UN Peacekeeping in Cambodia (1991–1993)
66. Peacekeeping in Former Yugoslavia (1992–present)
67. UN Humanitarian Mission to Somalia (1992–1995)
68. UN Peacekeeping in Mozambique (1992–1994)
69. UN Peacekeeping in Rwanda (1993–1996)
70. First Chechen War (1994–1996)
71. Chechen Disorder (1996–1999)
72. Afghan Civil War II (1992–1996)
73. Peacekeeping in Sierra Leone (1997–2005)
74. Second Chechen War (1999–present)

75. Peacekeeping in Congo (2000–present)
76. Second Intifada (2000–2005)
77. U.S. in Afghanistan (2001–present)
78. Peacekeeping in Cote d'Ivoire (2002–present)
79. Iraq (2003–present)
80. Second Peacekeeping Effort in Liberia (2003–present)
81. UN Peacekeeping in Burundi (2004–2006)
82. Hamas War (2006–present)
83. Hezbollah War (2006)

These 83 cases provided the bases for the analysis done in this book.

As of 31 December 2009, we have added the following to develop the database to 109 cases:

1. Huk Rebellion (1946–1954)
2. Tunisian Independence War (1952–1956)
3. Moroccan Independence War (1953–1956)
4. Venezuela (1960–1963)
5. Naxalite Conflict (1967–present)
6. Chile (1973–1989)
7. Kurdish Rebellion (1974–1975)
8. Chad Civil War (1980–1982)
9. Kurdish Rebellion vs Turkey (1984–1999)
10. Croatian Independence War (1991–1995)
11. Bosnian War (1991–1995)
12. Peacekeeping in Croatia and Bosnia (1992–present)
13. Algerian Civil War (1992–1999)
14. Violence in Israel and the Occupied Territories I (1993–2000)
15. Peacekeeping in Kosovo and fYROM (1995–present)
16. Afghan Civil War III (1996–2001)
17. Nepal People's War (1996–2008)
18. Kosovo (1998–1999)
19. Niger Delta Conflict (1998–present)
20. Ethnic Insurgency in Macedonia (fYROM) (2001)
21. Peacekeeping in Macedonia (2002–2006)
22. Darfur (2003–present)
23. Yemen Al–Houthi Insurgency (2004–present)
24. Violence in Israel and the Occupied Territories II (2005–present)
25. Somali Civil War (2006–present)
26. Mexican Narcowars (2006–present)
27. Pakistan (2007–present)

The data in some of the original 83 sheets was also revised or further developed and one case broken into multiple cases.

Force Ratios

NAME	FORCE RATIO	PEAK INSURGENT STRENGTH	DURATION (YEARS)	WINNER	CLASSIFICATION
63. Peacekeeping in Liberia (1990–1997)	0.38	31,000	7.11	Insurgents	INS/I
70. First Chechen War	0.61	62,000	1.73	Insurgents	CONV/INS becomes INS/NI
65. UN PK in Cambodia (1991–1993)	0.70	27,000	2.08	Intervening Force	PEACE
48. Operation Tacaud (1978–1980)	0.75	19,400	2.21	Insurgents	INS/I
49. Tanzania in Uganda (1978–1980)	1.07	26,200	2.01	Intervening Force	CONV/INS becomes INS/I
23. Katanga Wars (1961–1963)	1.09	12,400	1.36	Intervening Force	CONV
67. UN Mission to Somalia (1992–1995)	1.09	32,000	2.47	Insurgents	VIOLENCE
2. Ukraine (1944–1954)	1.12	40,000	10.24	Government	INS/NI
3. Indonesia (1945–1949)	1.13	160,000	4.33	Insurgents	INS/C
26. Borneo (1963–1966)	1.25	22,000	3.34	Intervening Force	GUERINV
5. Indochina War (1946–1954)	1.28	350,000	7.67	Insurgents	INS/C
75. UN PK in Congo (2000–present)	1.28	89,250	7.85	Intervening Force	PEACE
78. PK Ivory Coast (2002–present)	1.28	52,564	5.28	Intervening Force	PEACE
42. Rhodesia II (1972–1979)	1.34	33,500	7.01	Insurgents	INS/I
80. Second PK in Liberia (2003–present)	1.52	42,604	4.41	Intervening Force	PEACE
24. Yemen (1962–1970)	1.55	40,000	7.55	Intervening Force	INS/I
1. UK in Palestine (1944–48)	1.58	55,500	4.29	Insurgents	INS/C
66. UN PK in Yugoslavia (1992–present)	1.57	219,000	15.87	Intervening Force	PEACE
33. Chad Civil War (1965–1969)	1.60	5,000	3.42	Insurgents	INS/NI
62. U.S. Invasion of Panama (1989)	1.61	16,980	0.12	Intervening Force	CONV
12. Cameroun (1955–1960)	1.82	3,000	4.48	Insurgents	INS/C

57. U.S. Invasion of Grenada (1983)	1.82	5,002	0.03	Intervening Force	CONV
64. PK in Lebanon (1990–present)	2.09	37,700	17.22	Ongoing	PEACE
21. Vietnam II (1961–1964)	2.26	261,710	4.00	Insurgents	INS/I
53. USSR in Afghanistan (1979–1989)	2.28	110,000	9.15	Insurgents	INS/I
40. French in Chad (1969–1971)	2.30	5,000	2.21	Intervening Force	INS/I
69. UN PK in Rwanda (1993–1996)	2.37	20,000	2.43	Insurgents	PEACE
60. UN PK in Angola (1988–1999)	2.45	65,600	10.19	Intervening Force	INS/I
44. Angola Civil War (1975–1988)	2.56	68,550	13.87	Intervening Force	INS/I
73. PK in Sierra Leone (1997–2005)	2.71	21,000	8.61	Intervening Force	CONV/INS becomes INS/I
35. Namibia (1966–1989)	2.84	14,000	22.68	Insurgents	INS/C
16. Oman (1957–1959)	3.14	630	1.54	Intervening Force	INS/I
19. UN PK in Congo (1960–1964)	3.18	17,244	3.96 3.96	Intervening Force	PEACE
25. Portuguese Guinea (1963–1974)	3.35	9,560	11.26	Insurgents	INS/C
17. Vietnam I (1957–1960)	3.52	75,017	3.40	Insurgents	INS/NI
52. Uganda Civil War (1979–1986)	3.73	11,000	6.80	Insurgents	INS/NI
50. Cambodia (1978–1989)	4.06	64,000	10.78	Insurgents	CONV/INS becomes INS/I
47. Mozambique Civil War (1976–1992)	4.08	20,000	16.60	Government	INS/I
37. Sandinistas (1967–1979)	4.18	4,000	12.50	Insurgents	INS/NI
31. Vietnam War (1965–1973)	4.32	376,000	8.08	Insurgents	INS/
77. U.S. in Afghanistan (2001–present)	4.68	25,000	6.13	Ongoing	INS/I
22. Angola (1961–1974)	4.89	13,900	13.23	Insurgents	INS/C
45. Lebanon (1975–1990)	5.67	28,000	15.52	Intervening Force	INS/I
43. Polisario Rebellion (1973–1991)	5.71	21,000	18.34	Intervening Force	INS/I
9. Mau Mau Revolt (1952–1956)	5.97	12,000	3.44	Intervening Force	SUP/INS becomes INS/C
55. Contras in Nicaragua (1982–1990)	6.38	12,000	8.41	Government	INS/NI
51. El Salvador (1979–1992)	6.39	9,000	13.04	Government	INS/NI

27. Tupamaro Insurgency (1963–1973)	6.67	4,200	9.92	New Government	INS/NI
32. Dhofar Rebellion (1965–1976)	6.75	2,000	10.90	Intervening Force	INS/I
28. Aden (1963–1967)	6.75	4,000	3.98	Insurgents	INS/C
30. Mozambique (1964–1974)	7.00	10,000	9.87	Insurgents	INS/C
29. Colombian Civil War (1964–present)	8.03	38,100	43.62	Government	INS/NI
18. La Menos Violencia (1958–1964)	8.32	8,100	6.29	Draw	VIOLENCE
14. Soviet Intervention in Hungary (1956)	8.90	15,000	0.05	Intervening Force	SUP
4. Greek Civil War (1946–1949)	8.97	25,700	3.55	Government	INS/NI
20. Guatemala (1960–1996)	9.28	6,000	36.15	Government	INS/NI
15. Cuban Revolution (1956–1959)	10.00	3,000	2.09	Insurgents	INS/NI
83. Hezbollah War (2006)	10.00	3,000	0.09	Insurgents	GUERINV
46. Indonesia in Timor (1975–1999)	10.20	3,000	24.03	Insurgents	CONV/INS becomes INS/I
10. Algerian War (1954–1962)	10.28	61,100	7.67	Insurgents	INS/C
13. Tibetan Revolt (1956 – 1964)	10.47	21,006	18.59	Intervening Force	INS/I
8. Puerto Rico (1950–1954)	10.67	402	3.34	Government	SUP/INS becomes INS/NI
6. La Violencia (1948–1958)	11.23	6,000	9.85	Draw	VIOLENCE
68. UN PK in Mozambique (1992–1994)	11.79	20,538	1.98	Intervening Force	PEACE
7. Malaya (1948–1960)	12.91	8,200	12.13	Intervening Force	INS/I
58. First Intifada (1987–1993)	12.95	14,050	5.77	Insurgents	INS/NI
79. Iraq (2003–present)	15.39	27,000	4.79	Ongoing	CONV/INS becomes INS/I
34. Rhodesia I (1966–1972)	15.96	1,360	6.72	Government	INS/I
56. Tamil Insurgency (1983–2002)	16.40	7,500	18.60	Government	INS/NI
81. UN PK in Burundi (2004–2006)	18.69	3,000	2.62	Intervening Force	PEACE
41. Argentina (1969–1983)	22.81	5,700	14.53	New Government	INS/NI
76. Second Intifada (2000–2005)	22.85	7,900	4.36	Draw?	INS/NI
39. Northern Ireland (1968–1998)	24.56	1,500	29.53	Intervening Force	INS/NI

54. Shining Path in Peru (1980–1999)	29.50	6,000	19.17	Government	INS/NI
36. Guevara Guerilla Campaign (1966–1967)	37.41	54	0.92	Government	INS/NI
59. Kashmir (1988–present)	40.00	10,000	19.43	Government	INS/NI
38. Cabanas Insurgency (1967–1974)	105.89	350	7.55	Government	INS/NI
11. Cyprus (1955–1959)	162.73	273	3.89	Intervening Force	INS/C

At the time we did not yet have force ratio data for the following cases:

NAME	FORCE RATIO	PEAK INSURGENT STRENGTH	DURATION (YEARS)	WINNER	CLASSIFICATION
61. Afghan Civil War I (1989–1996)			7.62	Insurgents	INS/NI
71. Chechen Disorder (1996–1999)			3.06	None	GUERINV
72. Afghan Civil War II (1996–2001)			5.13	Insurgents	INS/NI
74. Second Chechen War (1999–present)			8.28	Ongoing	CONV/INS becomes INS/NI
82. Hamas War (2006)			0.43	Draw?	GUERINV

Force Ratios as Divided by Political Concept

Limited (Regional or Factional)

NAME	FORCE RATIO	PEAK INSURGENT STRENGTH	YEARS	WINNER	CLASSIFI-CATION
63. Peacekeeping in Liberia (1990–1997)	0.38	31,000	7.11	Insurgents	INS/I
70. First Chechen War	0.61	62,000	1.73	Insurgents	CONV/INS becomes INS/NI
48. Operation Tacaud (1978–1980)	0.75	19,400	2.21	Insurgents	INS/I
49. Tanzania in Uganda (1978–1980)	1.07	26,200	2.01	Intervening Force	CONV/INS becomes INS/I
23. Katanga Wars (1961–1963)	1.09	12,400	1.36	Intervening Force	CONV
67. UN Mission to Somalia (1992–1995)	1.09	32,000	2.47	Insurgents	VIOLENCE
2. Ukraine (1944–1954)	1.12	40,000	10.24	Government	INS/NI
26. Borneo (1963–1966)	1.25	22,000	3.34	Intervening Force	GUERINV
75. UN PK in Congo (2000–present)	1.28	89,250	7.85	Intervening Force	PEACE
78. PK Ivory Coast (2002–present)	1.28	52,564	5.28	Intervening Force	PEACE
80. Second PK in Liberia (2003–present)	1.52	42,604	4.41	Intervening Force	PEACE
24. Yemen (1962–1970)	1.55	40,000	7.55	Intervening Force	INS/I
66. UN PK in Yugoslavia (1992–present)	1.57	219,000	15.87	Intervening Force	PEACE
33. Chad Civil War (1965–1969)	1.60	5,000	3.42	Insurgents	INS/NI
64. PK in Lebanon (1990–present)	2.09	37,700	17.22	Ongoing	PEACE
40. French in Chad (1969–1971)	2.30	5,000	2.21	Intervening Force	INS/I
69. UN PK in Rwanda (1993–1996)	2.37	20,000	2.43	Insurgents	PEACE
60. UN PK in Angola (1988–1999)	2.45	65,600	10.19	Intervening Force	INS/I

44. Angola Civil War (1975–1988)	2.56	68,550	13.87	Intervening Force	INS/I
73. PK in Sierra Leone (1997–2005)	2.71	21,000	8.61	Intervening Force	CONV/INS becomes INS/I
16. Oman (1957–1959)	3.14	630	1.54	Intervening Force	INS/I
19. UN PK in Congo (1960–1964)	3.18	17,244	3.96	Intervening Force	PEACE
52. Uganda Civil War (1979–1986)	3.73	11,000	6.80	Insurgents	INS/NI
47. Mozambique Civil War (1976–1992)	4.08	20,000	16.60	Government	INS/I
77. U.S. in Afghanistan (2001–present)	4.68	25,000	6.13	Ongoing	INS/I
45. Lebanon (1975–1990)	5.67	28,000	15.52	Intervening Force	INS/I
55. Contras in Nicaragua (1982–1990)	6.38	12,000	8.41	Government	INS/NI
51. El Salvador (1979–1992)	6.39	9,000	13.04	Government	INS/NI
18. La Menos Violencia (1958–1964)	8.32	8,100	6.29	Draw	VIOLENCE
13. Tibetan Revolt (1956–1964)	10.47	21,006	18.59	Intervening Force	INS/I
6. La Violencia (1948–1958)	11.23	6,000	9.85	Draw	VIOLENCE
68. UN PK in Mozambique (1992–1994)	11.79	20,538	1.98	Intervening Force	PEACE
79. Iraq (2003–present)	15.39	27,000	4.79	Ongoing	CONV/INS becomes INS/I
56. Tamil Insurgency (1983–2002)	16.40	7,500	18.60	Government	INS/NI
81. UN PK in Burundi (2004–2006)	18.69	3,000	2.62	Intervening Force	PEACE
59. Kashmir (1988–present)	40.00	10,000	19.43	Government	INS/NI

Central Idea (like nationalism)

NAME	FORCE RATIO	PEAK INSURGENT STRENGTH	YEARS	WINNER	CLASSIFI CATION
3. Indonesia (1945–1949)	1.13	160,000	4.33	Insurgents	INS/C
5. Indochina War (1946–1954)	1.28	350,000	7.67	Insurgents	INS/C
42. Rhodesia II (1972–1979)	1.34	33,500	7.01	Insurgents	INS/I
1. UK in Palestine (1944–48)	1.58	55,500	4.29	Insurgents	INS/C
12. Cameroun (1955–1960)	1.82	3,000	4.48	Insurgents	INS/C

NAME	FORCE RATIO	PEAK INSURGENT STRENGTH	YEARS	WINNER	CLASSIFICATION
53. USSR in Afghanistan (1979–1989)	2.28	110,000	9.15	Insurgents	INS/I
35. Namibia (1966–1989)	2.84	14,000	22.68	Insurgents	INS/C
25. Portuguese Guinea (1963–1974)	3.35	9,560	11.26	Insurgents	INS/C
17. Vietnam I (1957–1960)	3.52	75,017	3.40	Insurgents	INS/NI
50. Cambodia (1978–1989)	4.06	64,000	10.78	Insurgents	CONV/INS becomes INS/I
37. Sandinistas (1967–1979)	4.18	4,000	12.50	Insurgents	INS/NI
22. Angola (1961–1974)	4.89	13,900	13.23	Insurgents	INS/C
43. Polisario Rebellion (1973–1991)	5.71	21,000	18.34	Intervening Force	INS/I
9. Mau Mau Revolt (1952–1956)	5.97	12,000	3.44	Intervening Force	SUP/INS becomes INS/C
28. Aden (1963–1967)	6.75	4,000	3.98	Insurgents	INS/C
30. Mozambique (1964–1974)	7.00	10,000	9.87	Insurgents	INS/C
29. Colombian Civil War (1964–present)	8.03	38,100	43.62	Government	INS/NI
14. Soviet Intervention in Hungary (1956)	8.90	15,000	0.05	Intervening Force	SUP
83. Hezbollah War (2006)	10.00	3,000	0.09	Insurgents	GUERINV
46. Indonesia in Timor (1975–1999)	10.20	3,000	24.03	Insurgents	CONV/INS becomes INS/I
10. Algerian War (1954–1962)	10.28	61,100	7.67	Insurgents	INS/C
8. Puerto Rico (1950–1954)	10.67	402	3.34	Government	SUP/INS becomes INS/NI
58. First Intifada (1987–1993)	12.95	14,050	5.77	Insurgents	INS/NI
34. Rhodesia I (1966–1972)	15.96	1,360	6.72	Government	INS/I
76. Second Intifada (2000–2005)	22.85	7,900	4.36	Draw?	INS/NI
39. Northern Ireland (1968–1998)	24.56	1,500	29.53	Intervening Force	INS/NI
11. Cyprus (1955–1959)	162.73	273	3.89	Intervening Force	INS/C

Overarching Idea (like communism)

NAME	FORCE RATIO	PEAK INSURGENT STRENGTH	YEARS	WINNER	CLASSIFICATION
65. UN PK in Cambodia (1991–1993)	0.70	27,000	2.08	Intervening Force	PEACE

NAME	FORCE RATIO	PEAK INSURGENT STRENGTH	YEARS	WINNER	CLASSIFI CATION
21. Vietnam II (1961–1964)	2.26	261,710	4.00	Insurgents	INS/I
31. Vietnam War (1965–1973)	4.32	376,000	8.08	Insurgents	INS/I
27. Tupamaro Insurgency (1963–1973)	6.67	4,200	9.92	New Government	INS/NI
32. Dhofar Rebellion (1965–1976)	6.75	2,000	10.90	Intervening Force	INS/I
4. Greek Civil War (1946–1949)	8.97	25,700	3.55	Government	INS/NI
20. Guatemala (1960–1996)	9.28	6,000	36.15	Government	INS/NI
15. Cuban Revolution (1956–1959)	10.00	3,000	2.09	Insurgents	INS/NI
7. Malaya (1948–1960)	12.91	8,200	12.13	Intervening Force	INS/I
41. Argentina (1969–1983)	22.81	5,700	14.53	New Government	INS/NI
54. Shining Path in Peru (1980–1999)	29.50	6,000	19.17	Government	INS/NI
36. Guevara Guerilla Campaign (1966–1967)	37.41	54	0.92	Government	INS/NI
38. Cabanas Insurgency (1967–1974)	105.89	350	7.55	Government	INS/NI

Not Applicable

NAME	FORCE RATIO	PEAK INSURGENT STRENGTH	YEARS	WINNER	CLASSIFI CATION
62. U.S. Invasion of Panama (1989)	1.61	16,980	0.12	Intervening Force	CONV
57. U.S. Invasion of Grenada (1983)	1.82	5,002	0.03	Intervening Force	CONV

We do not have force ratio data yet for the following cases

NAME	FORCE RATIO	PEAK INSURGENT STRENGTH	YEARS	WINNER	CLASSIFI CATION
61. Afghan Civil War I (1989–1996)			7.62	Insurgents	INS/NI
71. Chechen Disorder (1996–1999)			3.06	None	GUERINV
72. Afghan Civil War II (1996–2001)			5.13	Insurgents	INS/NI
74. Second Chechen War (1999–present)			8.28	Ongoing	CONV/INS becomes INS/NI
82. Hamas War (2006)			0.43	Draw?	GUERINV

The first four of these are limited. Hamas War is based on a central idea (independent Palestinian state).

Facing Limited Insurgencies (36 cases):

1. When a force is facing a limited insurgency, that force will win the insurgency, intervention or peacekeeping operation at least 73% (24 out of 33) of the time, as long as they have a favorable force ratio.
2. When a force is facing a limited insurgency, that force will win the insurgency at least 79% (15 out of 19) of the time, as long as they have a favorable force ratio.
3. A force facing a limited insurgency will not win if they do not have a favorable force ratio (based on 3 cases).

Facing Insurgencies based upon a central idea (27 cases):

1. When a force is facing an insurgency based upon a central idea, that force will loose the insurgency, intervention or peacekeeping operation if they do not have at least a 5-to-1 force ratio (12 cases, or 14 cases if one counts Vietnam II and Vietnam War as based on nationalism).
2. When a force is facing an insurgency based upon a central idea, that force will loose the insurgency if they do not have at least a 5-to-1 force ratio (12 cases, or 14 cases if one counts Vietnam II and Vietnam War as based on nationalism)
3. When a force is facing an insurgency based upon a central idea, that force will win the insurgency, intervention or peacekeeping operation 44% of the time if they have a force ratio between 6-to-1 and 10-to-1 (5.71 to 10.28 to one). This is based upon 9 cases.
4. When a force is facing an insurgency based upon a central idea, that force will win the insurgency 43% of the time if they have a force ratio between 6-to-1 and 10-to-1 (5.71 to 10.28 to one). This is based upon 7 cases.
5. When a force is facing an insurgency based upon a central idea, that force will win the insurgency 67% of the time if they have a force ratio grater than 10-to 1 (greater than 10.67 to one). This is based upon 6 cases.

Facing insurgencies based upon an overarching idea (13 cases)

1. When a force is facing an insurgency based upon an overarching idea, that force will win the insurgency, intervention or peacekeeping operation 62% of the time, regardless of force ratio (or 73% of the time if Vietnam is not counted)
2. When a force is facing an insurgency based upon an overarching idea, that force will win the insurgency 58% of the time, regardless of force ratios (or 70% of the time if Vietnam is not counted). This is based upon 12 cases.

3. One cannot rule out that the force ratios when facing overarching insurgencies are following the exact same rules as for insurgencies based upon a central idea (below 5-to-1 insurgent victory, between 5-to-1 and 10-to-1 it could go either way, above 10-to-1 mostly counterinsurgent victory).

Facing Insurgencies based upon a central idea or an overarching idea (40 cases):

1. When a force is facing an insurgency based upon a central or overarching idea, that force will loose the insurgency if they do not have at least a 5-to-1 force ratio. This is based upon 14 cases.

2. When a force is facing an insurgency based upon a central or overarching idea, that force will win the insurgency 50% of the time if they have a force ratio between 6-to-1 and 10-to-1 (5.71 to 10.28 to one). This is based upon 12 cases.

3. When a force is facing an insurgency based upon a central or overarching idea, that force will win the insurgency 73% of the time if they have a force ratio greater than 10-to-1 (greater than 10.67 to one). This is based upon 11 cases.

APPENDIX VI

Results of Testing the Model Back to the Data

FORCE RATIOS	TRUE OUTCOME	CONCEPT	ESTIMATED PROB	PREDICTED OUTCOME
1.13	red	Central	0.0579	red
1.28	red	Central	0.0603	red
1.34	red	Central	0.0613	red
1.58	red	Central	0.0654	red
1.82	red	Central	0.0698	red
2.28	red	Central	0.0790	red
2.84	red	Central	0.0917	red
3.35	red	Central	0.1048	red
3.52	red	Central	0.1095	red
4.06	red	Central	0.1258	red
4.18	red	Central	0.1297	red
4.89	red	Central	0.1547	red
5.71	blue	Central	0.1885	red
5.97	blue	Central	0.2003	red
6.75	red	Central	0.2391	red
0.7	blue	Overarching	0.2395	red
7	red	Central	0.2525	red
8.03	blue	Central	0.3130	red
2.26	red	Overarching	0.3312	red
8.9	blue	Central	0.3697	red
10	red	Central	0.4466	red
10.2	red	Central	0.4610	red
10.28	red	Central	0.4668	red
4.32	red	Overarching	0.4739	red
10.67	blue	Central	0.4951	red
0.38	red	Limited	0.6209	blue
0.61	red	Limited	0.6365	blue
6.75	blue	Overarching	0.6459	blue
0.75	red	Limited	0.6459	blue
12.95	red	Central	0.6552	blue
1.07	blue	Limited	0.6668	blue
1.09	blue	Limited	0.6681	blue
1.09	red	Limited	0.6681	blue

1.12	blue	Limited	0.6700	blue
1.25	blue	Limited	0.6783	blue
1.28	blue	Limited	0.6802	blue
1.28	blue	Limited	0.6802	blue
1.52	blue	Limited	0.6952	blue
1.55	blue	Limited	0.6970	blue
1.57	blue	Limited	0.6983	blue
1.6	red	Limited	0.7001	blue
2.3	blue	Limited	0.7410	blue
2.37	red	Limited	0.7448	blue
2.45	blue	Limited	0.7492	blue
2.56	blue	Limited	0.7552	blue
2.71	blue	Limited	0.7631	blue
8.97	blue	Overarching	0.7765	blue
3.14	blue	Limited	0.7850	blue
3.18	blue	Limited	0.7869	blue
9.28	blue	Overarching	0.7936	blue
3.73	red	Limited	0.8125	blue
15.96	blue	Central	0.8200	blue
10	red	Overarching	0.8241	blue
4.08	blue	Limited	0.8275	blue
5.67	blue	Limited	0.8838	blue
6.38	blue	Limited	0.9034	blue
6.39	blue	Limited	0.9036	blue
12.91	blue	Overarching	0.9160	blue
10.47	blue	Limited	0.9684	blue
11.79	blue	Limited	0.9783	blue
24.56	blue	Central	0.9822	blue
16.4	blue	Limited	0.9942	blue
18.69	blue	Limited	0.9970	blue
29.5	blue	Overarching	0.9993	blue
37.41	blue	Overarching	0.9999	blue
40	blue	Limited	1.0000	blue
105.89	blue	Overarching	1.0000	blue
162.73	blue	Central	1.0000	blue

APPENDIX VII

Characteristics of Selected Modern COIN Barriers[1]

STATIC ELEMENTS OF SELECTED MODERN COIN BARRIERS

INSURGENCY	DESIGNATION	WIRE	MINES	WALLS	BERM	SURVEILLANCE MEANS	DETECTION MEANS
Second Italo-Sanusi War (1927–31)	"Border Fence"	x				Observation	
Algerian War	Morice Line	x	x			observation, radars	Radars
Algerian War	Morice/Challe Line	x	x			observation, radars	Radars
Algerian War	Sum of above	x	x				
Rhodesia II	"Corsan"	x	x			Observation	Alarms
Rhodesia II	"Mod Corsan"	x	x			Observation	Alarms
Rhodesia II	"Border Minefield"		x			Observation	
Polisario Rebellion	"The Berm"	x	x	x	x	observation, radars	Radars
Intifada 1.5	Gaza Barrier	x				Observation	buffer zone, sensors
Second Intifada	Gaza Barrier (II)	x		x		Observation	buffer zone, sensors
Second Intifada	"Separation Barrier"	x		x		Observation	sensors (incl thermal)
Hamas	Gaza Barrier (II)	x		x		Observation	buffer zone, sensors
Hezbollah War	Security Fence	x	x	x		observation, CCTV	sensors

ACTIVE ELEMENTS OF SELECTED MODERN COIN BARRIERS

INSURGENCY	DESIGNATION	FREE-FIRE ZONE	POPULATION CONTROLS	RAPID-REACTION FORCES	CROSS-BORDER OPS
Second Italo-Sanusi War (1927–31)	"Border Fence"	x	x	x	
Algerian War	Morice Line	x	x	x	
Algerian War	Morice /Challe Line	x	x	x	
Algerian War	Sum of above	x	x	x	
Rhodesia II	"Corsan"	x	x	x	x

Rhodesia II	"Mod Corsan"	x	x	x	x
Rhodesia II	"Border Minefield"	x	x	x	x
Polisario Rebellion	"The Berm"	x		x	
Intifada 1.5	Gaza Barrier				
Second Intifada	Gaza Barrier (II)	x			
Second Intifada	"Separation Barrier"				
Hamas	Gaza Barrier (II)	x			
Hezbollah War	Security Fence			x	x

CHARACTERISTICS OF SELECTED MODERN COIN BARRIERS

INSUR-GENCY	DESIG-NATION	LOCATION	DATE BEGUN	DATE ENDED	BORDER LENGTH (KM)	LENGTH (KM)	WIDTH (M/KM)	HEIGHT (M)
Second Italo-Sanusi War (1927–31)	"Border Fence"	Libya	Apr 1931	Sep 1931	1,115	270	9 / NA	1.5
Algerian War	Morice Line	Algeria-Morocco frontier	1956	1958	1,559	c460		
Algerian War	Morice/Challe Line	Algeria-Tunisia frontier	1957	1959	965	c700	NA / 60	
Algerian War	Sum of above		1956	1959	2,524	2,700		
Rhodesia II	"Corsan"	Rhodesia-Zambia border	1974	1976	3,066	179	25 / NA	
Rhodesia II	"Mod Corsan"	Umtali (now Mutare) on the Rhodesia-Mozambique border			3,066	18	300 / NA	
Rhodesia II	"Border Minefield"	Rhodesia-Mozambique border		1978	3,066	979	300/NA	
Polisario Rebellion	"The Berm"	Western Sahara	1980	1987	2,046	2,500		3
Intifada 1.5	Gaza Barrier	Gaza Strip	1994	1996	62	60		
Second Intifada	Gaza Barrier (II)	Gaza Strip	2000	2001	62	60		8
Second Intifada	"Separation Barrier"	West Bank	2002	Continuing	360	734	45 / NA	8
Hamas	Gaza Barrier (II)	Gaza Strip	2000	2005	62	60		8
Hezbollah War	Security Fence	Israel-Lebanon Border	2000	Continuing	120	120		3

NOTES:

1. These charts were the work of C. Curtiss Johnson.

Notes:

The barrage on the Algeria-Tunisia frontier was in effect a double line, with an immense no-man's land not only between the lines but also before and behind.

During the Algerian War, the sea frontier was patrolled as well.

"The Berm" is longer than the border because it extends into Morocco.

There were no barriers on the Rhodesia-Botswana border, which was declared a free-fire zone.

Gaza border extends over the Gaza coast, as well as buffering against Egypt and Israel. Gaza's border with Israel is 51km.

West Bank Separation Border is longer than the old Green line of the 1949 armistice accord because it crosses into and out of the West Bank at several points.

Hamas fence differs from Gaza Second Intifada fence in that the portion bordering Egypt was reinforced in 2005.

Definitions:

Active Elements: Actions taken by the defender to confront and destroy the enemy at (or behind) the barrier.

Berm: A long, relatively narrow, raised barrier, usually constructed of baked earth or sand.

Detection Means: Any and all means used to discover and locate enemy assets that are hidden or obscure.

Free-fire Zone: A designated area in which a military force may employ unrestricted firepower against its adversaries.

Static Elements: Emplaced, permanent or semi-permanent defensive means.

Population Controls: Any and all means used to prevent and control the interaction of the indigenous population with the insurgents. Typically, it may include inter alia removal, resettlement and concentration camps.

Surveillance Means: Any and all means used to observe an area continuously.

Walls: Any of several relatively narrow and long vertical constructions used to divide, enclose or protect.

Wire: A wire (usually barbed- or razor-wire) obstacle.

Sources:

Major General Doron Almog (23 December 2004). *Lessons of the Gaza Security Fence for the West Bank*. Jerusalem Center for Public Affairs.

http://www.vtjp.org/background/Separation_Wall_Report.htm

http://www.minurso.unlb.org/berm.html

http://members.tripod.com/selousscouts/rhodesian%20army%20coin%2072_79%20part1.htm

Cilliers, J. K. *Counter-Insurgency in Rhodesia*. London: Croom Helm, 1985.

Thein, Ben. "Is Israel's Security Barrier Unique?" *Middle East Quarterly*, Fall 2004.

Weiner, Justus Reid. "Israel's Security Barrier: An International Comparative Analysis and Legal Evaluation." *The George Washington International Law Review*, January 1, 2005.

Wilson, Scott. "Touring Israel's Barrier With Its Main Designer." *The Washington Post* (August 7, 2007), A1, A9.

APPENDIX VIII

List of all 83 Cases by Indigenous Government Type, the Presence of Elections, Duration, Winner and Type of Insurgency

NO.	NAME	TYPE	ELECT.	YEARS	WINNER	OPERATION
1	UK in Palestine	Dictatorship	No	4.29	Insurgents	INS/C
2	Ukrainian Ind. Movement	Dictatorship	Yes	10.24	Government	INS/NI
3	Indonesia	Dictatorship	No	4.33	Insurgents	INS/C
4	Greek Civil War	Democracy	Yes	3.55	Government	INS/NI
5	Indochina War	Dictatorship	Yes	7.67	Insurgents	INS/C
6	Colombia La Violencia	Dictatorship	Yes	9.85	New Gov't	VIOLENCE
7	Malaya (1948–1960)	Dictatorship	Yes	12.13	Int. Force	INS/I
8	Puerto Rico	Democracy	Yes	3.34	Government	SUP/INS became INS/NI
9	Mau Mau Revolt	Dictatorship	No	3.44	Int. Force	SUP/INS became INS/C
10	Algerian War	Dictatorship	Yes	7.67	Insurgents	INS/C
11	Cyprus	Dictatorship	Yes	3.89	Int. Force	INS/C
12	Cameroun	Dictatorship	Yes	4.48	Insurgents	INS/C
13	Tibetan Revolt and Insurgency	Theocracy	No	18.59	Int. Force	INS/I
14	Soviet Intervention in Hungary	Dictatorship	Yes	0.05	Int. Force	SUP
15	Cuban Revolution	Dictatorship	No	2.09	Insurgents	INS/NI
16	Oman	Dictatorship	No	1.54	Int. Force	INS/I
17	Vietnam I	Dictatorship	No	3.40	Insurgents	INS/NI
18	La Menos Violencia	Troubled Dem.	Yes	6.29	Draw	VIOLENCE
19	UN Peacekeeping in Congo	Dictatorship	Yes	3.96	Int. Force	PEACE
20	Guatemala	Dictatorship	Yes	36.15	Government	INS/NI
21	Vietnam II	Dictatorship	No	4.00	Insurgents	INS/I
22	Angola	Dictatorship	No	13.23	Insurgents	INS/C
23	Katanga Wars	Dictatorship	Yes	1.36	Int. Force	CONV
24	Yemen	Dictatorship	No	7.55	Int. Force	INS/I
25	Portuguese Guinea	Dictatorship	No	11.26	Insurgents	INS/C
26	Borneo	Dictatorship	Yes	3.34	Int. Force	GUERINV
27	Tupamaro Insurgency	Democracy	Yes	9.92	New Gov't	INS/NI
28	Aden	Dictatorship	Yes	3.98	Insurgents	INS/C
29	Colombian Civil War	Troubled Dem.	Yes	43.62	Government	INS/NI
30	Mozambique	Dictatorship	No	9.87	Insurgents	INS/C
31	Vietnam War	Troubled Dem.	Yes	8.08	Insurgents	INS/I
32	Dhofar Rebellion	Dictatorship	No	10.90	Int. Force	INS/I
33	Chad Civil War	Dictatorship	No	3.42	Insurgents	INS/NI
34	Rhodesia I	Troubled Dem.	Yes	6.72	Government	INS/I

35	Namibia	Dictatorship	Yes	22.68	Insurgents	INS/C
36	Guevara Guerilla Campaign	Dictatorship	Yes	0.92	Government	INS/NI
37	Sandinistas	Dictatorship	No	12.50	Insurgents	INS/NI
38	Cabanas Insurgency	Troubled Dem.	Yes	7.55	Government	INS/NI
39	Northern Ireland	Democracy	Yes	29.53	Int. Force	INS/NI
40	French Intervention in Chad	Troubled Dem.	Yes	2.21	Int. Force	INS/I
41	Argentina	Dictatorship	Yes	14.53	New Gov't	INS/NI
42	Rhodesia II	Troubled Dem.	Yes	7.01	Insurgents	INS/I
43	Polisario Rebellion	Dictatorship	Yes	18.34	Int. Force	INS/I
44	Angola Civil War	Dictatorship	Yes	13.87	Int. Force	INS/I
45	Lebanon	Troubled Dem.	Yes	15.52	Int. Force	INS/I
46	Indonesia in Timor	Dictatorship	No	24.03	Insurgents	CONV/INS became INS/I
47	Mozambique Civil War	Dictatorship	No	16.60	Government	INS/I
48	Operation Tacaud	Dictatorship	No	2.21	Insurgents	INS/I
49	Tanzania in Uganda	Dictatorship	No	2.01	Int. Force	CONV/INS became INS/I
50	Cambodia	Dictatorship	No	10.78	Insurgents	CONV/INS became INS/I
51	El Salvador	Troubled Dem.	Yes	13.04	Government	INS/NI
52	Uganda Civil War	Dictatorship	Yes	6.80	Insurgents	INS/NI
53	USSR in Afghanistan	Dictatorship	No	9.15	Insurgents	INS/I
54	Shining Path in Peru	Troubled Dem.	Yes	19.17	Government	INS/NI
55	Contras in Nicaragua	Troubled Dem.	Yes	8.41	Government	INS/NI
56	Tamil Insurgency	Troubled Dem.	Yes	18.60	Government	INS/NI
57	U.S. Invasion of Grenada	Dictatorship	No	0.03	Int. Force	CONV
58	First Intifada	Democracy	Yes	5.77	Insurgents	INS/NI
59	Kashmir	Democracy	Yes	19.43	Government	INS/NI
60	UN Peacekeeping in Angola	Dictatorship	Yes	10.19	Int. Force	INS/I
61	Afghan Civil War I	Dictatorship	No	7.62	Insurgents	INS/NI
62	U.S. Invasion of Panama	Troubled Dem.	Yes	0.12	Int. Force	CONV
63	Peacekeeping in Liberia	Dictatorship	Yes	7.11	Insurgents	INS/I
64	Peacekeeping in Lebanon	Troubled Dem.	Yes	17.22	Ongoing	PEACE
65	UN PK in Cambodia	Troubled Dem.	No	2.08	Int. Force	PEACE
66	UN PK in Former Yugoslavia	Dictatorship	Yes	15.87	Int. Force	PEACE
67	UN Mission to Somalia	Warlords	No	2.47	Insurgents	VIOLENCE
68	UN PK in Mozambique	Dictatorship	No	1.98	Int. Force	PEACE
69	UN PK in Rwanda	Dictatorship	Yes	2.43	Insurgents	PEACE
70	First Chechen War	Troubled Dem.	Yes	1.73	Insurgents	CONV/INS became INS/NI
71	Chechen Disorder	Dictatorship	Yes	3.06	None	GUERINV
72	Afghan Civil War II	Dictatorship	No	5.13	Insurgents	INS/NI
73	Peacekeeping in Sierra Leone	Dictatorship	No	8.61	Int. Force	CONV/INS became INS/I
74	Second Chechen War	Dictatorship		8.28	Ongoing	CONV/INS became INS/NI
	UN Peacekeeping					

75	in Congo	Dictatorship	Yes	7.85	Int. Force	PEACE
76	Second Intifada	Democracy	Yes	4.36	Draw?	INS/NI
77	U.S. in Afghanistan Peacekeeping	Troubled Dem.	Yes	6.13	Ongoing	INS/I
78	Ivory Coast	Troubled Dem.	Yes	5.28	Int. Force	PEACE CONV/INS
79	Iraq Second PK Effort	Troubled Dem.	Yes	4.79	Ongoing	became INS/I
80	in Liberia UN Peacekeeping	Dictatorship	Yes	4.41	Int. Force	PEACE
81	in Burundi	Dictatorship	Yes	2.62	Int. Force	PEACE
82	Hamas War	Democracy	Yes	0.43	Draw?	GUERINV
83	Hezbollah War	Democracy	Yes	0.09	Insurgents	GUERINV

The 36 examples we have of insurgencies with intervening powers:

NO.	NAME	GOV'T TYPE	DURATION	WINNER	
1	UK in Palestine	Democracy	4.29	Insurgents	INS/C
3	Indonesia	Dictatorship	4.33	Insurgents	INS/C
5	Indochina War	Democracy	7.67	Insurgents	INS/C
7	Malaya	Democracy	12.13	Int. Force	INS/I SUP/INS
9	Mau Mau Revolt	Democracy	3.44	Int. Force	bc INS/C
10	Algerian War	Democracy	7.67	Insurgents	INS/C
11	Cyprus	Democracy	3.89	Int. Force	INS/C
12	Cameroun	Democracy	4.48	Insurgents	INS/C
13	Tibetan Revolt	Dictatorship	18.59	Int. Force	INS/I
16	Oman	Democracy	1.54	Int. Force	INS/I
21	Vietnam II	Democracy	4.00	Insurgents	INS/I
22	Angola	Dictatorship	13.23	Insurgents	INS/C
24	Yemen	Dictatorship	7.55	Int. Force	INS/I
25	Portuguese Guinea	Dictatorship	11.26	Insurgents	INS/C
28	Aden	Democracy	3.98	Insurgents	INS/C
30	Mozambique	Dictatorship	9.87	Insurgents	INS/C
31	Vietnam War	Democracy	8.08	Insurgents	INS/I
32	Dhofar Rebellion	Dictatorship	10.90	Int. Force	INS/I
34	Rhodesia I	Democracy	6.72	Government	INS/I
35	Namibia	Democracy	22.68	Insurgents	INS/C
40	French Intervention in Chad	Democracy	2.21	Int. Force	INS/I
42	Rhodesia II	Democracy	7.01	Insurgents	INS/I
43	Polisario Rebellion	Dictatorship	18.34	Int. Force	INS/I
44	Angola Civil War	Dictatorship	13.87	Int. Force	INS/I
45	Lebanon	Dictatorship	15.52	Int. Force	INS/I CONV/INS
46	Indonesia in Timor	Dictatorship	24.03	Insurgents	bc INS/I
47	Mozambique Civil War	Dictatorship	16.60	Government	INS/I
48	Operation Tacaud	Democracy	2.21	Insurgents	INS/I CONV/INS
49	Tanzania in Uganda	Dictatorship	2.01	Int. Force	bc INS/I CONV/INS
50	Cambodia	Dictatorship	10.78	Insurgents	bc INS/I

53	USSR in Afghanistan	Dictatorship	9.15	Insurgents	INS/I
60	UN Peacekeeping in Angola	Democracy	10.19	Int. Force	INS/I
63	Peacekeeping in Liberia	Dictatorship	7.11	Insurgents	INS/I
					CONV/INS
73	PK in Sierra Leone	Troubled Dem.	8.61	Int. Force	bc INS/I
77	U.S. in Afghanistan	Democracy	6.13	Ongoing	INS/I
					CONV/INS
79	Iraq	Democracy	4.79	Ongoing	bc INS/I

Staying the Course (an analysis of duration of insurgencies)

One notes with great interest the following statistics from the 62 cases of insurgencies in our database of 83 insurgencies, interventions and peacekeeping operations:

DURATION[1]	INSURGENCY CASES	BLUE WINS	RED WINS	GRAY RESULTS
0–7 years	2	8	12	2
7–14 years	27	11	12	3
14+ years	13	10	2	1

The two-sided p-value from the Fisher's exact test is 0.1480 when using the blue, red and gray results in the test. When the gray results are omitted, the two-sided p-value is 0.0423, indicating that there may be some association between duration and outcome. This data shows that for the insurgencies, the insurgents are winning more often than not for those cases that lasted less than 14 years, while the situation dramatically reversed itself after 15.52 years.

The other 21 cases (not classic insurgencies) are provided below for completeness:

DURATION	OTHER CASES	BLUE WINS	RED WINS	GRAY RESULTS
0–7 years	16	11	3	2
7–14 years	3	1	0	2
14+ years	2	1	0	1

Still, this is not the whole story, as most of the insurgencies lasting longer than 14 years are primarily domestic insurgencies. The issue of "staying the course" is one that primarily refers to outside intervening powers as indigenous governments do not have a good alternative to "staying the course." So to just examine those cases where there were significant outside intervening forces (INS/I or INS/C):

DURATION	INSURGENCY CASES	BLUE WINS	RED WINS	GRAY RESULTS
0–7 years	12	5	6	1
7–14 years	18	7	10	1
14+ years	6	4	2	0

The pattern still appears to hold here but is extremely tentative. The two-sided p-value from the Fisher's exact test is 0.8140 when using the blue, red and gray results in the test. When the gray results are omitted, the two-sided p-value is 0.5909. This indicates that there may not be any association between duration and outcome.

The six exceptions (insurgencies longer than 15.52 years) probably need to be examined. The four blue wins are from 15.52 to 18.59 in duration. The two red wins are longer (22.68 and 24.03 years). The four blue wins are Lebanon (1975–1990), Mozambique Civil War (1976–1992), Polisario Rebellion (1973–1991), and the Tibetan Revolt and Insurgency (1956–1964). All four of these are rather unusual cases, and one would hard pressed to say these are good examples for establishing a rule. One of them was quite violent civil war (Lebanon), and two were resolved by a negotiated settlement that brought the insurgents into the government (Lebanon and Mozambique Civil War). One could argue in both of these cases that the result is "gray," vice blue. Tibet did not provide much of a burden on the Chinese government, while both Tibet and Morocco were neighboring areas that the country considered theirs by historical heritage. In that respect, they are similar in some respects to INS/NI cases.

The issue here may be burden of the war vice duration. This subject of "burden" is discussed in some depth in Chapter Seventeen. In that chapter we examined the "burden" of wars by looking at it measured as the average number of troops committed per 100,000 population and as the average number of people killed per year per 100,000 population.

In the case of commitment data, the figures for these six cases are:

NAME	INTERVENING FORCES PER 100,000 POPULATION	GOVERNMENT FORCES PER 100,000 POPULATION	INSURGENT FORCES PER 100,000 POPULATION	TOTAL INDIGENOUS PER 100,000 POPULATION
13. Tibetan Revolt (1956–1964)	18	N/A	106	106
46. Indonesia in Timor (1975–1999)	57	7,224	1,205	8,430
47. Mozambique Civil War (1976–1992)	59	251	109	328
43. Polisario Rebellion (1973–1991)	207	N/A	8,196	8,196
35. Namibia (1966–1989)	232	1,067	445	890
45. Lebanon (1975–1990)	284	568	1,006	1,574

The tentative rules on commitment from the Task 11 report are:

It appears that when the average level of commitment by an outside power exceeds more the 0.1% of the population of the intervening country (more than 141 per 100,000 home population), then the insurgency wins in two-thirds of the cases.

It appears that when the average level of commitment by the indigenous government exceeds more the 1% of the population of the indigenous country, then the insurgency succeeds in almost two-thirds of the cases.

It appears that when the average level of commitment by the insurgents exceeds more the 1% of the population of the indigenous country, then the insurgency succeeds in more than two-thirds of the cases.

It appears that when the average level of commitment by the government and insurgents exceeds more the 1% of the population of the indigenous country, then the insurgency succeeds in almost two-thirds of the cases.

We suspect that these four rules are what are having an impact on the outcome of these six cases, not some form of "staying the course" as measured by duration.

Assuming those rules are representative, then we will note below for six cases whether they follow the rules given above or not. "Yes" means that they are in the higher commitment category given above and are a red win or are in the lower categories where the blue side wins more often then the red side and are a blue win. No means that they are not.

NAME	INTERVENING FORCES PER 100,000 POPULATION	GOVERNMENT FORCES PER 100,000 POPULATION	INSURGENT FORCES PER 100,000 POPULATION	TOTAL INDIGENOUS PER 100,000 POPULATION
13. Tibetan Revolt (1956–1964)	YES	YES	YES	YES
46. Indonesia in Timor (1975–1999)	NO	YES	YES	YES
47. Mozambique Civil War (1976–1992)	YES	YES	YES	YES
43. Polisario Rebellion (1973 -1991)	NO	YES	NO	NO
35. Namibia (1966–1989)	YES	YES	NO	NO
45. Lebanon (1975–1990)	NO	YES	NO	NO

It is clear that the success in putting down the Tibetan Revolt and resolving the Mozambique Civil War can be explained by the low level of commitment. Indonesia in Timor is a red win, as would be expected from the high levels of violence there. Clearly the Polisario Rebellion and Lebanon stand out as being out of the norm. Namibia (a red win) is not entirely explained. Therefore, we may be looking at two cases where "staying the course" may have made a difference, except that the Polisario Rebellion is a very unusual case with many elements that favored the blue side, and the Lebanese Civil War was a general civil war in addition to an insurgency involving several outside intervening powers. These two cases are not the best basis for developing a rule about "staying the course." A similar exploration of intensity (people killed per 100,000 population) does not provide much support due to a shortage of good data. We only have good data for intervening forces killed in two cases, good data for government forces killed for four cases, good data for insurgent forces killed for three cases, good data for civilians killed in two cases, and good data for total indigenous people killed in three cases (the data in italics is poor or partial data and should not be considered).

NAME	INTERVENING FORCES KILLED		GOVERNMENT FORCES KILLED		INSURGENT FORCES KILLED		CIVILIANS KILLED		TOTAL INDIGENOUS PEOPLE KILLED	
	AVERAGE	TOTAL	AVERAGE	TOTAL	AVERAGE	TOTAL	AVERAGE	TOTAL	AVERAGE	TOTAL
47. Mozambique CW										
13. Tibet Revolt	*0*	*0*	0.03	0.63	*46.13*	*876.39*	*0*	*0*	*46.13*	*876.39*
46. Timor	0.06	1.48	0.20	5.11	13.05	326.17	624.16	15,615.14	637.86	15,946.43
43. Polisario	*0.07*	*1.24*	N/A	N/A	172.87	3,284.59	*0*	*0*	172.87	3,284.59
35. Namibia	0.07	1.66	0.12	2.93	22.35	536.47	*0*	*0*	22.48	539.40
45. Lebanon	*0.60*	*9.59*	*0.17*	*2.66*	*2.34*	*37.38*	38.93	622.89	41.43	662.92

Just for reference, the rules for intensity are:

It appears that when the average intervening forces killed facing an insurgency exceeds more the 0.00001% of the population of the intervening country (more than 0.01 per 100,000 home population), then the insurgency succeeds in over two-thirds of the cases.

It appears that when the average government forces killed facing an insurgency exceeds more the 0.001% of the population of the country (more than 1.11 per 100,000 home population), then the insurgency succeeds in around half of the cases. This is a very tentative conclusion with little statistical support.

It is clear from this data that government forces facing an insurgency are not as casualty sensitive as intervening forces facing an insurgency. The casualty sensitivity of intervening forces is clearly supported by statistics, while that of the government forces are not.

It appears that when the average insurgent forces killed exceeds more the 0.001% of the population of the country (more than 1.05 per 100,000 home population), then the insurgency succeeds in around half of the cases.

It appears that when the average insurgent forces killed exceeds more the 0.01% of the population of the country (more than 10.67 per 100,000 home population), then the counterinsurgency fails in more than half of the cases. This is a very tentative conclusion not statistically supported.

It appears that when the average indigenous people killed facing an insurgency exceeds more the 0.001% of the population of the country (more than 1.00 per 100,000 home population), then the insurgency succeeds in almost half of the cases. This is a very tentative conclusion not statistically supported.

Finally one must note in the case of "staying the course," that the insurgency won in 10 out of the 14 cases where the intervening force losses per 100,000 population were greater than an average yearly loss rate of 0.12 per 100,000. The three blue wins in that data are the Angola Civil War (the Cuban intervention), the invasion of Uganda by Tanzania and the Egyptians in Yemen. The one true exception there is the Cuban intervention in Angola, where the force took significant attrition over an extended time (total of 8.01 killed per 100,000 population).[2] Tanzania in Uganda was a conventional invasion followed by a couple of years of occupation and then a withdrawal. Tanzania was in Uganda for less than four years, generating a total killed of 2.06 per 100,000 population). The Egyptians in Yemen withdrew halfway through the war because of the high losses, yet the indigenous government won the war anyway.

If one looks at total casualties, one notes that once the cumulative total rises to 0.59 total killed out of 100,000 population, then out of 16 cases, of which are 3 are blue wins (the ones noted above) and only 1 is unresolved (the U.S. in Iraq). This cumulative total picks up the 2 extended red ones (Timor and Namibia), in addition to the 14 cases where the average intensity is above 0.12 per 100,000 per year. The other 12 cases are insurgent victories, whether they are democracies, dictatorships, military dictatorships, communist dictatorships, American, Soviet or French, and regardless of duration or intensity. The shortest of these red wins is Palestine at 4.29 years, while the longest is Timor as 24.03 years.

NAME	INTERVENING FORCES KILLED		GOVERNMENT FORCES KILLED		INSURGENT FORCES KILLED		CIVILIANS KILLED		TOTAL INDIGENOUS PEOPLE KILLED	
	AVERAGE	TOTAL	AVERAGE	TOTAL	AVERAGE	TOTAL	AVERAGE	TOTAL	AVERAGE	TOTAL
1. Palestine	0.12	0.59	N/A	N/A	2.23	11.16	12.19	60.96	14.42	72.12
79. Iraq	0.20	0.81	5.29	21.17	6.15	24.59	34.01	136.03	45.45	181.78
46. Timor	0.06	1.48	0.20	5.11	13.05	326.17	624.16	15,615.14	637.86	15,946.43
35. Namibia	0.07	1.66	0.12	2.93	22.35	536.47	0	0	22.48	539.40
83. Hezbollah War	1.67	1.67	N/A	N/A	11.62	11.62	16.62	16.62	28.24	28.24
49. Uganda I	0.69	2.06	0.41	1.22	2.71	8.14	0	0	3.12	9.36
53. Afghanistan	0.38	4.15	36.37	400.06	34.76	382.36	0	0	71.13	782.42
3. Indonesia	0.88	4.38	N/A	N/A	27.66	138.30	1.78	8.91	36.80	147.20
44. Angola Civil War	0.57	8.01	8.87	124.22	2.64	37.00	0	0	11.52	161.22

30. Mozambique	1.02	10.38	0.47	4.97	9.95	39.79	1.03	11.37	5.12	56.13
25. P. Guinea	0.92	11.05	3.60	43.19	156.94	*627.76*	*0*	*0*	55.91	*670.95*
22. Angola	0.84	11.82	0.22	3.11	15.44	61.76	0	0	4.63	64.87
31. Vietnam War	2.46	22.17	106.53	958.77	531.02	4,779.14	274.59	2,471.27	381.12	3,430.04
5. Indochina War	2.75	24.73	23.42	*70.26*	65.06	195.18	0	0	65.06	*265.44*
10. Algerian War	3.07	27.65	4.73	42.60	153.19	1,378.70	0	0	157.92	1,421.29
24. Yemen	3.62	32.60	*0*	*0*	*0.01*	0.05	2.78	25.00	2.78	25.05

This data strongly points that there is no country that is able to "stay the course" to the degree and extent that some theorists and writers desire. The only clear exception that actually stayed the course for an extended time under noticeable losses was communist Cuba. Cuba's overall commitment was even higher that what is shown for Angola, as they had troops scattered across Africa at the time.[3] But, Cuba was extremely sensitive to the casualties and kept them well hidden from its people. Cuba was receiving considerable financial support from the Soviet Union for doing this, and this aid was effectively underwriting their entire economy. This probably made the leadership willing to sustain a degree of losses that even the Soviet Union itself was unable to sustain in Afghanistan. Still the losses Cuba suffered were much less than the U.S. in Vietnam, the Portuguese in its three separate insurgencies in Africa, or the French in Indochina and Algeria.

NOTES

1. Note on breakpoints: The data in the 0–7 years category actually goes from 0.03 to 5.77. The data in the 7–14 years category goes from 6.13 to 13.87 years. There are four cases that are included in the 7–14 year category that lasted less than 7 years. At 6.13 is the U.S. in Afghanistan, which is dated until the end of 2007. We expect that this will continue for at least another year and will almost certainly end in the 7+ year category. At 6.29 is "La Menos Violencia," a bridging record to cover the lower level of violence between the 10 years of La Violencia and the 44 years of the Colombian Civil War. One could argue that this is a 60-year civil war. At 6.72 is Rhodesia I, which was immediately followed by continued warfare and is tracked on the 7-year Rhodesia II sheet. At 6.80 is the Uganda Civil War, which follows the 2-year Tanzania in Uganda sheet. It could be easily argued that all these conflicts are greater than 7 years, as are a number of other sheets like Vietnam I and Vietnam II.

2. Polisario and Lebanon may provide two other notable exceptions, except we currently do not have complete and reliable data for them. In the case of Lebanon, the data we have is for the marginal Israeli intervention, which eventually resulted in their withdrawal. This data with a total killed of 9.59 per 100,000 population fits into the pattern above. We do not have reliable casualty data for Syria, which remained in place in Lebanon for the duration of the war.

3. *In 1983–84, the Cubans had 57,220 military and 14,425 civilians in Africa. They were in 30 countries: 7 Arab and 23 sub-Saharan. The largest contingent was in Angola with 40,000 military and 6,000 civilians. The next largest was in Ethiopia with 12,000 military and 1,100 civilians. They officially lost 160 in Ethiopia, but the real number may have been as high as 2,000. See Juan F. Castro Benemelis, Subversión y terrorismo en Africa.* (Madrid: San Martín, 1988), 563.

APPENDIX X

Data on 62 Insurgences used for the Test of Anthony James Joes Theory

CASE NAME	FORCE RATIO	OUTSIDE SUPPORT	INDIGENOUS GOVERNMENT	YEARS	WINNER	CLASSIFICATION
63. Peacekeeping in Liberia (1990–1997)	0.38	Some	N/A	7.11	Insurgents	INS/I
70. First Chechen War	0.61	Indigenous	Troubled	1.73	Insurgents	CONV/INS becomes INS/NI
48. Operation Tacaud (1978–1980)	0.75	Considerable	N/A	2.21	Insurgents	INS/I
49. Tanzania in Uganda (1978–1980)	1.07	Some	N/A	2.01	Intervening Force	CONV/INS becomes INS/I
2. Ukraine (1944–1954)	1.12	Indigenous	N/A	10.24	Government	INS/NI
3. Indonesia (1945–1949)	1.13	Indigenous	N/A	4.33	Insurgents	INS/C
5. Indochina War (1946–1954)	1.28	Some	N/A	7.67	Insurgents	INS/C
42. Rhodesia II (1972–1979)	1.34	Considerable	Troubled	7.01	Insurgents	INS/I
24. Yemen (1962–1970)	1.55	Some	N/A	7.55	Intervening Force	INS/I
1. UK in Palestine (1944–48)	1.58	Considerable	N/A	4.29	Insurgents	INS/C
33. Chad Civil War (1965–1969)	1.60	Some	N/A	3.42	Insurgents	INS/NI
12. Cameroun (1955–1960)	1.82	Indigenous	N/A	4.48	Insurgents	INS/C
21. Vietnam II (1961–1964)	2.26	Some	N/A	4.00	Insurgents	INS/I
53. USSR in Afghanistan (1979–1989)	2.28	Some	N/A	9.15	Insurgents	INS/I
40. French in Chad (1969–1971)	2.30	Some	Troubled	2.21	Intervening Force	INS/I
60. UN PK in Angola (1988–1999)	2.45	Some	N/A	10.19	Intervening Force	INS/I
44. Angola Civil War (1975–1988)	2.56	Considerable	N/A	13.87	Intervening Force	INS/I
73. PK in Sierra Leone (1997–2005)	2.71	Some	?	8.61	Intervening Force	CONV/INS becomes INS/I
35. Namibia (1966–1989)	2.84	Some	N/A	22.68	Insurgents	INS/C
16. Oman (1957–1959)	3.14	Some	N/A	1.54	Intervening Force	INS/I
25. Portuguese Guinea (1963–1974)	3.35	Some	N/A	11.26	Insurgents	INS/C
17. Vietnam I (1957–1960)	3.52	Some	N/A	3.40	Insurgents	INS/NI
52. Uganda Civil War (1979–1986)	3.73	Some	N/A	6.80	Insurgents	INS/NI

50. Cambodia (1978–1989)	4.06	Some	N/A	10.78	Insurgents	CONV/INS becomes INS/I
47. Mozambique Civil War (1976–1992)	4.08	Considerable	N/A	16.60	Government	INS/I
37. Sandinistas (1967–1979)	4.18	Indigenous	N/A	12.50	Insurgents	INS/NI
31. Vietnam War (1965–1973)	4.32	Considerable	Troubled	8.08	Insurgents	INS/I
77. U.S. in Afghanistan (2001–present)	4.68	Some	Troubled	6.13	Ongoing	INS/I
22. Angola (1961–1974)	4.89	Some	N/A	13.23	Insurgents	INS/C
45. Lebanon (1975–1990)	5.67	Considerable	Troubled	15.52	Intervening Force	INS/I
43. Polisario Rebellion (1973–1991)	5.71	Considerable	N/A	18.34	Intervening Force	INS/I
9. Mau Mau Revolt (1952–1956)	5.97	Indigenous	N/A	3.44	Intervening Force	SUP/INS becomes INS/C
55. Contras in Nicaragua (1982–1990)	6.38	Some	Troubled	8.41	Government	INS/NI
51. El Salvador (1979–1992)	6.39	Some	Troubled	13.04	Government	INS/NI
27. Tupamaro Insurgency (1963–1973)	6.67	Indigenous	Democracy	9.92	New Government	INS/NI
32. Dhofar Rebellion (1965–1976)	6.75	Some	N/A	10.90	Intervening Force	INS/I
28. Aden (1963–1967)	6.75	Some	N/A	3.98	Insurgents	INS/C
30. Mozambique (1964–1974)	7.00	Some	N/A	9.87	Insurgents	INS/C
29. Colombian Civil War (1964–present)	8.03	Indigenous	Troubled	43.62	Government	INS/NI
4. Greek Civil War (1946–1949)	8.97	Some	Democracy	3.55	Government	INS/NI
20. Guatemala (1960–1996)	9.28	Indigenous	N/A	36.15	Government	INS/NI
15. Cuban Revolution (1956–1959)	10.00	Indigenous	N/A	2.09	Insurgents	INS/NI
46. Indonesia in Timor (1975–1999)	10.20	Indigenous	N/A	24.03	Insurgents	CONV/INS becomes INS/I
10. Algerian War (1954–1962)	10.28	Some	N/A	7.67	Insurgents	INS/C
13. Tibetan Revolt (1956–1964)	10.47	Some	Theocracy	18.59	Intervening Force	INS/I
8. Puerto Rico (1950–1954)	10.67	Indigenous	Democracy	3.34	Government	SUP/INS becomes INS/NI
7. Malaya (1948–1960)	12.91	Some	N/A	12.13	Intervening Force	INS/I
58. First Intifada (1987–1993)	12.95	Some	Democracy	5.77	Insurgents	INS/NI
79. Iraq (2003–present)	15.39	Some	Troubled	4.79	Ongoing	CONV/INS becomes INS/I
34. Rhodesia I (1966–1972)	15.96	Considerable	Troubled	6.72	Government	INS/I
56. Tamil Insurgency (1983–2002)	16.40	Some	Troubled	18.60	Government	INS/NI
41. Argentina (1969–1983)	22.81	Indigenous	N/A	14.53	New Government	INS/NI

76. Second Intifada (2000–2005)	22.85	Some	Democracy	4.36	Draw?	INS/NI
39. Northern Ireland (1968–1998)	24.56	Some	Democracy	29.53	Intervening Force	INS/NI
54. Shining Path in Peru (1980–1999)	29.50	Indigenous	Troubled	19.17	Government	INS/NI
36. Guevara Guerilla Campaign (1966–1967)	37.41	Considerable	N/A	0.92	Government	INS/NI
59. Kashmir (1988–present)	40.00	Some	Democracy	19.43	Government	INS/NI
38. Cabanas Insurgency (1967–1974)	105.89	Indigenous	Troubled	7.55	Government	INS/NI
11. Cyprus (1955–1959)	162.73	Indigenous	N/A	3.89	Intervening Force	INS/C

We do not have force ratio data yet for the following cases

CASE NAME	OUTSIDE SUPPORT	INDIGENOUS GOVERNMENT	YEARS	WINNER	CLASSIFICATION
61. Afghan Civil War I (1989–1996)	Some	N/A	7.62	Insurgents	INS/NI
72. Afghan Civil War II (1996–2001)	Considerable	N/A	5.13	Insurgents	INS/NI CONV/INS
74. Second Chechen War (1999–present)	Some	N/A	8.28	Ongoing	becomes INS/NI

Key:

Indigenous = Primarily indigenous

Some = Some outside support

Considerable = Considerable outside support

N/A under Indigenous Government indicates the government was effectively some type of dictatorship (including colonial governments)

Troubled = A troubled democracy, a very broad category that includes anything that is not clearly a functioning democracy and not clearly a dictatorship

Democracy = A functioning representative democracy

? = Unusual case where the indigenous government was a dictatorship that was overthrown by an intervening force, and the previous troubled democratic government was reinstated after which the insurgents were included as part of the government for part of that period.

Bibliography

1. The following reports and presentations by *The Dupuy Institute* (or previous organizations founded by Trevor N. Dupuy) were used to help create this book. They are listed in rough chronological order.

Casualty Estimates in Contingency Operations (Fairfax, VA.: DMSI, 1985)
    Volume I: The Draft Interim Report (8 February 1985)
    Volume II: Draft Final Report, Matrices of Casualty Rates (6 September 1985)
    Volume I: Final Report (15 November 1985)
    Volume II: Appendices (15 November 1985)

Dupuy, Trevor N., *Attrition: Forecasting Battle Casualties and Equipment Losses in Modern War* (Fairfax, VA.: HERO Books, 1990).

Dupuy, Trevor N., House Armed Services Committee. *Testimony of Col. T.N. Dupuy, USA, Ret.* (Washington D.C.: 13 December 1990).

Dupuy, Trevor Nevitt, *If War Comes, How to Defeat Saddam Hussein.* (McLean, VA.: Hero Books, 1991).

Peacekeeping in Bosnia: Preliminary Report (McLean, VA.: The Dupuy Institute, 1995).

Peacekeeping in Bosnia: Fatality Estimates (Preliminary and Final Reports (McLean, VA.: The Dupuy Institute, 1995).

Military Consequences of Landmine Restrictions (McLean, VA.: The Dupuy Institute, April 1996).

The Dupuy Institute's Research Study: Military Consequences of Landmine Restrictions (Washington, D.C.: Vietnam Veterans of America Foundation, Spring 2000)

Bellamy, Ronald F., MD and Christopher A. Lawrence, *Combat Mortality: Why is Marine Combat Mortality Less Than That of the Army* (Gray and Associates, 1998).

Military Consequences of a Complete Landmine Ban: The Dupuy Institute (Washington, D.C.: Vietnam Veterans of America Foundation, Summer 2001)

Capture Rate Study: Phase IV (part 2): EPWs in Small Scale Contingency Operations (McLean, VA.: The Dupuy Institute, March 27, 2001)

The Historical Combat Effectiveness of Lighter-Weight Armored Forces (McLean, VA.: The Dupuy Institute, 6 August 2001)

"Proposal for Casualty Estimation in the Iraq War." dated 20 April 2004.

Casualty Estimate for the Insurgency in Iraq: Final Report (draft report, never completed. File last dated 19 December 2005).

Casualty Estimate for the Insurgency in Iraq (Annandale, VA.: The Dupuy Institute, 28 February 2005). This is one of five briefings, dated September 2004, December 2004, January 2005, February 2005 and March 2005.

Users' Guide for the Modern Insurgency Spread Sheets (MISS), Phases I-IV (Annandale, VA.: The Dupuy Institute, 30 September 2007).

Examination of Factors Influencing the Conduct of Operations in Guerilla Wars: Task 3: Develop Estimate of Insurgent Force Size (Annandale, VA.: The Dupuy Institute, 19 October 2007).

Examination of Factors Influencing the Conduct of Operations in Guerilla Wars: Task 4: Factors That Increase and Decrease Insurgent Recruitment & Task 7: Examination of Government Reforms (Annandale, VA.: The Dupuy Institute, 24 October 2007).

Examination of Factors Influencing the Conduct of Operations in Guerilla Wars: Task 5: External Support & Task 8: Border Controls (Annandale, VA.: The Dupuy Institute, 8 February 2008).

Examination of Factors Influencing the Conduct of Operations in Guerilla Wars: Task 6: Examine Forms of Warfare & Task 9: Study the Leadership, Organization, and Political System (Annandale, VA.: The Dupuy Institute, 22 February 2008).

Examination of Factors Influencing the Conduct of Operations in Guerilla Wars: Task 10: Examination of Rotational Policies (Annandale, VA.: The Dupuy Institute, 30 September 2007).

Examination of Factors Influencing the Conduct of Operations in Guerilla Wars: Task 11: Examine Measurement of Popular Support (Annandale, VA.: The Dupuy Institute, 25 February 2008).

Examination of Factors Influencing the Conduct of Operations in Guerilla Wars: Task 12: Examining the Geographic Aspects of an Insurgency (Annandale, VA.: The Dupuy Institute, 4 February 2008).

Examination of Factors Influencing the Conduct of Operations in Guerilla Wars: Task 13: Insurgent Views of Tactics & Strategy (Annandale, VA.: The Dupuy Institute, 29 February 2008).

Examination of Factors Influencing the Conduct of Operations in Guerilla Wars: Task 14: Final Report (Annandale, VA.: The Dupuy Institute, 29 February 2008).

The Applicability of "Classical" Counterinsurgency Theory to Counterinsurgency Operations (Annandale, VA.: The Dupuy Institute, 31 January 2008).

The Analysis of the Historical Effectiveness of Different Counterinsurgency Tactics and Strategies: Final Report (Annandale, VA.: The Dupuy Institute, 31 March 2008).

2. The following other books and a few of the more significant reports and articles that were referenced and used for this book

Angola (International Documentation and Communication Centre (IDOC), 1975).

Barnett, Don, *Interviews in Depth. Angola—MPLA #2: Daniel Chipenda* (LSM (Liberation Support Movement), August 1969).

Barnett, Don. *Interviews in Depth. MPLA—ANGOLA #1: Spartacus Monimambu* (LSM (Liberation Support Movement), 1973).

Benemelis, Juan F. Castro, *Subversión y terrorismo en Africa.* (Madrid: San Martín, 1988).

Bickel, Keith B., Mars *Learning: The Marine Corps Development of Small Wars* Doctrine, 1915–1940 (Boulder, Colo: Westview Press, 2001).

Birtle, Andrew J., *U.S. Army Counterinsurgency and Contingency Operations Doctrine, 1860–1941* (Washington, D.C.: U.S. Army Center of Military History, 1998).

Birtle, Andrew J., *U.S. Army Counterinsurgency and Contingency Operations Doctrine, 1942–1976* (Washington, D.C.: U.S. Army Center of Military History, 2006).

Cabral, Amilcar, "Practical problems and tactics," in *Selected Texts by Amilcar Cabral: Revolution in Guinea, an African People's Struggle*, ed. and trans. Richard Handyside (London: Stage 1, 1969).

Callwell, C. E., *Small Wars Their Principles and Practice.* (Lincoln: University of Nebraska Press, 3rd ed. 1996 [1896, 1906]).

Campbell, Arthur, *Guerillas* (New York: The John Day Company, 1968).

Chabal, Patrick, *Amílcar Cabral: Revolutionary Leadership and People's War.* African Studies Series, 37. (Cambridge [Cambridgeshire]: Cambridge University Press, 1983).

Cilliers, J. K., *Counter-Insurgency in Rhodesia* (London: Croom Helm, 1985).

Clausewitz, Carl von, *On War* (Princeton: Princeton University Press, 1976)

Clodfelter, Micheal, *Vietnam in Military Statistics: A History of Indochina Wars, 1772–1991* (Jefferson, North Carolina: McFarland & Company, Inc. 1995).

Clodfelter, Micheal, *Warfare and Armed Conflicts: A Statistical Encyclopedia of Casualty and Other Figures, 1494–2007*, Third Edition (Jefferson, North Carolina: McFarland & Company, Inc. 2008).

Clutterbuck, Richard L., *The Long, Long War: Counterinsurgency in Malaya and Vietnam* (New York: Praeger, 1966).

Cohen, Robin, ed., *The Cambridge Survey of World Migration* (New York: Cambridge Univ. Press, 1995).

Fall, Bernard, *Last Reflections on a War: Bernard B. Fall's Last Comments on Vietnam* (Mechanicsburg, PA.: Stackpole Books, 2000 [1967]).

Fall, Bernard, *Street Without Joy* (Repr., Mechanicsburg, PA.: Stackpole Books, 1994 [1964]).

Fourteen Points: A Framework for the Analysis of Insurgency (McLean, VA.: The BDM Corporation, 31 July 1984).

Galula, David, *Counterinsurgency Warfare: Theory and Practice* (Praeger Security International, Westport, Conn., 2006 [1964]).

Geldenhuys, Gen. Jannie, *A General's Story* (Johannesburg: Johnathan Ball, 1995).

Grivas-Dighenis, Gen. George, *Guerrilla Warfare and EOKA's Struggle.* Tran. A. A. Pallis (London: Longmans, 1964).

Handyside, Richard, ed. and trans., *Selected Texts by Amilcar Cabral: Revolution in Guinea, an African People's Struggle* (London: Stage 1, 1969).

Horne, Alistair, *A Savage War of Peace: Algeria, 1954–1962* (Repr. New York: New York Review of Books, 2006).

Hull, Isabel V., *Absolute Destruction: Military Culture and the Practices of War in Imperial Germany* (Ithaca, N.Y.: Cornell Univ. Press, 2005).

Human Factors Considerations of Undergrounds in Insurgencies (CRESS, The American University, Washington, D.C., December 1966).

The Iraq Study Group Report: The Way Forward—A new Approach (Vintage Books, New York, 2006).

Itote, Waruhiu (General China), *"Mau Mau' General"* (Nairobi, Kenya: East African Publishing House, 1967).

Joes, Anthony James, *The War for South Viet Nam 1954–1975* (Westport, Conn.: Praeger, Revised Edition 2001).

Jomini, Baron de, *The Art of War. See Roots of Strategy: Book 2* (Harrisburg, PA.: Stackpole Books, 1987).

Kilcullen, David, *The Accidental Guerrilla: Fighting Small Wars in the Midst of a Big One* (New York: Oxford University Press, 2009).

Kitson, Frank, *Low Intensity Operations: Subversion, Insurgency, Peace-Keeping* (Mechanicsburg, PA.: Archon Books 1989 [1971]).

Klingaman, William K., *The First Century: Emperors, Gods, and Everyman* (New York: Harper Perennial, 1991).

Krivosheyev, G. F., *Grif Sekretnosti Snyat: Poteri Vooryzhennnyikh Sil SSSR v Voinakh, voyevyikh Deistviyakh I voyennyikh konfliktakh* (Moscow: Voyennoye Izdatelstvo, 1993),

Lawrence, T. E., *Revolt in the Desert* (New York: George H. Doran Co, 1927).

Lawrence, T. E., *Seven Pillars of Wisdom, A Triumph* (Garden City, NY: Doubleday, Doran & Co, 1935).

Lettow-Vorbeck, Paul von, *My Reminiscences of East Africa* (London: Hurst and Blackett, 1920).

Manwaring, Max G., *Internal Wars: Rethinking Problem and Response* (Carlisle, PA.: Strategic Studies Institute, September 2001).

Mao, Zedong, *On Guerrilla Warfare.* (Mineola, NY: Dover Publications, 2005).

Marcum, John, *The Angolan Revolution*, Vol. 2: *Exile Politics and Guerrilla Warfare (1962–1976)* (Cambridge, Mass.: M.I.T. Press, 1978).

Merom, Gil, *How Democracies Lose Small Wars State, Society, and the Failures of France in Algeria, Israel in Lebanon, and the United States in Vietnam* (Cambridge, UK: Cambridge University Press, 2003).

Morris, Michael Spence Lowdell, *Armed Conflict in Southern Africa: A Survey of Regional Terrorisms from Their Beginnings to the Present, with a Comprehensive Examination of the Portuguese Position* (Cape Town: Jeremy Spence, 1974).

Moyano, María José *Argentina's Lost Patrol: Armed Struggle*, 1969–1979 (New Haven [Conn.]: Yale University Press, 1995).

John A. Nagl, *Learning to Eat Soup with a Knife* (Chicago & London: University of London Press, 2005 [2002]).

Neto, Agostinho. *Messages to Companions in the Struggle*. Richmond, B.C., Can.: LSM Information Center, December, 1972).

O'Neill, Bard E. *Insurgency and Terrorism: From Revolution to Apocalypse*. (draft, Washington, D.C., 2005).

O'Neill, Bard E., *Insurgency & Terrorism: From Revolution to Apocalypse*, 2nd Ed., Rev. (Washington, D.C.: Potomac Books, Inc., 2005 [1990, 2001]).

Palmer Jr, General Bruce, *The 25-Year War: America's Military Role in Vietnam* (New York: Touchstone, 1985).

Partido Africano da Independencia da Guiné e Cabo Verde (PAIGC), *Guinea-Bissau: Toward Final Victory! Selected Speeches and Documents from PAIGC* (Liberation Support Movement, 1974).

Peckham, Howard H., *The War of Independence: A Military History* (Chicago: Univ. of Chicago Press, 1958).

Peng, Chin, *My Side of History: As Told to Ian Ward and Norm Miraflor* (Singapore: Media Masters, 2003).

Ricks, Thomas E., *Fiasco: The American Military Adventure in Iraq* (New York: The Penguin Press, 2006).

Ricks, Thomas E., *The Gamble: General David Petraeus and the American Military Adventure in Iraq, 2006–2008* (New York: The Penguin Press, 2009).

Record, Jeffrey, *Beating Goliath: Why Insurgencies Win* (Washington, D.C.: Potomac Books, 2007).

Sheehan, Neil, *A Bright Shining Lie: John Paul Vann and American in Vietnam* (London: Picador, 1990).

Small Wars Manual U.S. Marine Corps, 1940 (Washington, D.C.: U.S. G.P.O., 1940).

Spies, S. B., *Methods of Barbarism? Roberts and Kitchener and Civilians in the Boer Republics, January 1900–May 1902* (Cape Town: Human & Rousseau, 1977).

Stanton, Shelby L., *Vietnam Order of Battle* (New York: Galahad Books, 1986)

Summers, Harry G., Jr., *On Strategy: A Critical Analysis of the Vietnam War* (New York: Ballantine Books, 1995 [1982]).

Tapia, Carlos, *Las Fuerzas Armadas y Sendero Luminoso: Dos Estrategias y Un Final* (Lima: IEP Ediciones, 1997).

Thobhani, Akbarali, *Western Sahara since 1975 under Moroccan Administration: Social, Economic, and Political Transformation* (Lewiston, N.Y.: The Edwin Mellen Press, 2002).

Tone, John Leonard, *War and Genocide in Cuba, 1895–1898* (Chapel Hill, N.C.: Univ. of North Carolina Press, 2006).

Trinquier, Roger, *Modern Warfare: A French View of Counterinsurgency* (New York: Praeger, 1964; BDM Corporation).

Truong, Nhu Tang, with David Chanoff and Doan Van Toai, *A Viet Cong Memoir: An Inside Account of the Vietnam War and its Aftermath* (New York: Vintage Books, 1986).

Veuthey, Michel, *Guérilla et droit humanitaire* (Genève: Comité international de la Croix-Rouge, 1983).

Victory in Vietnam: The Official History of the People's Army of Vietnam, 1954–1975 (Lawrence, Kansas: University Press of Kansas, 2002).

Vines, Alex, *Still Killing: Land Mines in Southern Africa* (New York: Human Rights Watch, 1997).

Wilson, Jeremy, *Lawrence of Arabia: The Authorized Biography of T.E. Lawrence* (New York: Atheneum, 1990).

Windrow, Martin, The Last Valley: Dien Bien Phu and the French Defeat in Vietnam (Cambridge, MA.: Da Capo Press, 2004).

3. The following articles, reports and websites were used for this book

Charles-Robert Ageron, "Une dimension de la guerre d'Algérie: les `regroupments' de populations," in *Militaires et guerilla dans la guerre d'Algérie*, pp. 327–62. Edited by Jean-Charles Jauffret and Maurice Vaisse (Brussels: Editions Complexe, 2001).

Edward George McGill Alexander's M.A. thesis, *The Cassinga Raid* (Cape Town: Univ. of South Africa, 2003).

Major General Doron Almog (23 December 2004). Lessons of the Gaza Security Fence for the West Bank. Jerusalem Center for Public Affairs.

http://www.vtjp.org/background/Separation_Wall_Report.htm

http://www.minurso.unlb.org/berm.html

http://members.tripod.com/selousscouts/rhodesian%20army%20coin%2072_79%20part1.htm

"And now, the War Forecast: Can software really predict the outcome of an armed conflict, just as it can predict the course of the weather?" *The Economist Technology Quarterly*, 17 September 2005.

Ari Berman, "The Real Story of the Insurgency", *The Nation*, 3 March 2005.

Blaho, Justine and Lisa Kaiser, "A Predictive Model for Irregular Wars based on a Structured Historical Database" presented at the 48th Annual AORS Symposium, 14–15 October 2009.

"Bomb kills 1 U.S. service member, 4 Afghans in Kabul", *Associated Press* (January 17, 2009).

Borges Coelho, J. P. "African Troops in the Portuguese Colonial Army, 1961–1974: Angola, Guinea-Bissau and Mozambique," Portuguese Studies Review, 10: 1 (2002).

Peter Brush, "The Story Behind the McNamara Line," *Vietnam* (February 1996), 18–24. The Brush article is available on the web at http://chss.montclair.edu/ english/furr/pbmcnamara.html.

Stephen Budiansky "A Proven Formula for How Many Troops We Need," *The Washington Post* (May 9, 2004).

Lisa Burgess, Washington Bureau, "'Smart sanctions' policy will make U.S. look weak, policy experts claim." (FAS website, March 3, 2001).

Transcript: CNN Larry King Live: Interview with Dick Cheney, Lynne Cheney, aired May 30, 2005, 21:00 ET.

Cordesman, Anthony H., "Weapons of Mass Destruction in Iraq" (Center for Strategic and International Studies, Washington, 1999).

Cordesman, Anthony H., "The Military Threat from Iraq: The Gulf Military Balance, Iraqi Conventional Force and the Continuing Threat from Iraq's Weapons of Mass Destruction." (Center for Strategic and International Studies, Washington, March 2001).

Cordesman, Anthony H., "Iraq's Military Capabilities: Fighting A Wounded, But Dangerous, Poisonous Snake." (Center for Strategic and International Studies, Washington, December 3, 2001).

Cordesman, Anthony H., "If We Fight Iraq: The Lessons of the Fighting in Afghanistan (Center for Stategic and International Studies, Washington, December 7, 2001).

Cordesman, Anthony H., "Iraq's Military Capabilities in 2002: A Dynamic Net Assessment" (Center for Strategic and International Studies, Washington, September 2002).

Cordesman, Anthony H., "Biological Warfare and the 'Buffy Paradigm'" (Center for Strategic and International Studies, 20 September 2001).

Online discussion data February 18, 2003 with Anthony Cordesman, labeled *Iraq: Analysis.*

Cordesman, Anthony H., "Iraq and the Risk Posed by Weapons of Mass Destruction: Testimony to the Senate Armed Services Committee" (Center for Strategic and International Studies, 27 February 2002).

Cordesman, Anthony H., "Postwar Iraq: The New Old Middle East (Center for Strategic and International Studies, Washington, 16 April 2003).

Cordesman, Anthony H., "Iraq and Conflict Termination: The Road to Guerilla War? (Center for Strategic and International Studies, Washington, 25 July 2003).

Cordesman, Anthony H., "Iraq: Too Uncertain to Call" (Center for Strategic and International Studies, Washington, November 14, 2003).

Cordesman, Anthony H., "Development in Iraq at the End of 2003: Adapting U.S. Policy to Stay the Course" (Center for Strategic and International Studies, Washington, 7 January 2004).

Cordesman, Anthony H., "Fallujah, Sadr and the Eroding U.S. Position in Iraq" (Center for Strategic and International Studies, Washington, 3 May 2004).

Cordesman, Anthony H., "Iraq: What is to Be Done? (Center for Strategic and International Studies, Washington, 12 May 2004).

Cordesman, Anthony H., "The "Post-Conflict' Lesson of Iraq and Afghanistan" (Center for Strategic and International Studies, Washington, 19 May 2004).

Cordesman, Anthony H., "Iraq and After: Rethinking the Major Policy Issues in the Wider Middle East" (Center for Strategic and International Studies, Washington, 6 July 2004).

Cordesman, Anthony H., "The Failures of the CPA and the U.S. Effort in Iraq and

What Can Be Done to Salvage Them." (Center for Strategic and International Studies, Washington, D.C., 7 July 2004).

Cordesman, Anthony H., "Inexcusable Failure: The Progress in Training the Iraqi Army and Security Forces as of Mid-July 2004" (Center for Strategic and International Studies, Washington, 20 July 2004).

Interview on September 16, 2004 by Bernard Gwertzman, Council on Foreign Relations, "Cordesman: Stable Iraq Remains 'Doable' Goal But Odds for Success are Shrinking".

Interview by Bernard Gwertzman, Council on Foreign Relations, October 4, 2005 "Cordesman: No Compromise Possible With Zarqarwi, Other Extremist Insurgency Leaders".

Cordesman, Anthony H., "Iraq, Grand Strategy, and the Lessons of Military History", 2004 S. T. Lee Lecture on Military History, October 19, 2004).

Cordesman, Anthony H., "The Developing Iraqi Insurgency: Status at End-2004" (Center for Strategic and International Studies, Washington, 22 December 2004).

Cordesman, Anthony H., "The Middle East Crisis: Six "Long Wars" and Counting" (Center for Strategic and International Studies, 7 August 2006.

Defeating Insurgency on the Border, CSC 1985 SUBJECT AREA National Military Strategy, Executive Summary, TITLE: DEFEATING INSURGENCY ON THE BORDER at http://www.globalsecurity.org/military/library/report/1985/HJR.htm.

Defense Intelligence Agency Helicopter Loss database. Army Aviation Safety Center database. Survivability/Vulnerability Information Analysis Center Helicopter database. Also: OPERA, UH1P1, 01253, CRAFX, CASRP (Operations Report. Crash Facts Message. Casualty Report.) VHPA web site at: http://www.flyarmy.org/KIAINDEX.HTM.

Lawrence Devlin, Jacob Rinck, Christian Dennys and Idrees Zaman, *Conflict analysis: Kunduz city, Kunduz province* (CPAU—Cooperation for Peace and Unity, March 2009).

Gen. Maurice Faivre, "L'ALN extérieure face aux barrages frontaliers." *Revue internationale d'histoire militaire*, 76 (1997) http://www.stratisc.org/partenaires/cfhm/rihm/76/rihm_76_faivrewps.html.

Bernard Fall "The Theory and Practice of Insurgency and Counterinsurgency," *Naval War College Review* (April 1965), accessible at: http://www.au.af.mil/au/awc/awcgate/navy/art5-w98.htm.

James D. Fearon and David D. Laitin, "Ethnicity, Insurgency, and Civil War," *The American Political Science Review*, 97: 1 (February 2003).

IRNA, Berlin, August 30, 2008 "German Army Admits Civilian Shootings in Afghanistan".

"Iron Curtain, Episode 2" at http://www.gwu.edu/~nsarchiv/coldwar/interviews/episode-2/clifford3.html.

Gordon, Michael R. "Cracking the Whip," *The New York Times* (27 January 1991). http://query.nytimes.com/gst/fullpage.html?res=9D0CEED8163EF934A15752C0A967958260

Guardian Unlimited, 53 (Sept. 14, 2005) at: http://www.guardian.co.uk/pakistan/Story/0,2763,1569495,00.html

Lt. Col. Michel Goya and Lt. Col. Philippe François, "The Man Who Bent Events: 'King John' in Indochina," *Military Review* (Sept.-Oct 2007).

Peter Hart, "NYT Iraq War 'Debate' Excludes Critics: Paper's panel features nine hawkish 'experts'" June 2008, Fairness & Accuracy in Reporting website.

Andrew Hossack,, Ph.D. "Security Force & Insurgent Success Factors in Counter-Insurgency Campaigns" presented in spring 2007 at Cornwallis XII.

Anthony James Joes, "E-Notes: Recapturing the Essentials of Counterinsurgency," based on the W. W. Keen Butcher Lecture on Military Affairs (March 24, 2006), Foreign Policy Research Institute (May 30, 2006). http://www.fpri.org/enotes/20060530.military.joes.counterinsurgency.html

Seth G. Jones, "Pakistan's Dangerous Game." *Survival,* 49:1 (Spring 2007), 16, referencing John Gordon, et al., *The Challenge of Insurgency*, draft document, RAND, 2006.

Jumper, John. P. (Lieut. Gen) "In Guld War, Precision Air Weapons Paid Off," *New York* Times (14 July 1996). http://query.nytimes.com/gst/fullpage.html?res=9803EEDB1E39F937A25754C0A960958260

Jundanian, Brendan F. "Resettlement Programs: Counterinsurgency in Mozambique." *Comparative Politics*, 6:4 (July 1974).

Fred Kaplan, "The Army, Faced With its Limits," *The New York Times* (January 1, 2006).

Interview in *Le Figaro*, 7 September 2009 "Karzaï : «Je ne serai pas une marionnette des États-Unis»"

Johnathan F. Keiler, "Who Won the Battle of Fallujah", *Proceedings*, January 2005, citing Jackie Spinner and Karl Vick "Troops Battle for Last Parts of Fallujah", *The Washington Post* (14 November 2004).

Jack Kelly, "'Amicable divorce could turn nasty experts say", *USA Today* (22 November 1995).

Army pilot's 'suicide mission' kept enemy at bay, by Margo Rutledge Kissell, Staff Writer Updated 11:05 PM Saturday, May 23, 2009.

Knickerbocker, Brad. "Pentagon's Quietest Calculation: The Casualty Count," *The Christian Scientist Monitor* (28 January 2003). http://www.csmonitor.com/2003/0128/p01s02-woiq.html

Bran Knowlton, "Rumsfeld Speaks Cautiously on Strength of Insurgency, *International Herald Tribune*, June 26, 2005.

Interview with Ted Koppel on the evening news, March 1991.

Paul Krugman, "The Arithmetic of Failure," *The New York Times* (October 27, 2006).

Jim Lehrer, *Iraq: Military Briefing*, April 7, 2004.

Dana Milbank "Rumsfeld's order to end insurgency: Don't call it that: Enemies in Iraq 'don't merit the word,' he instructs" *Washington Post* (November 30, 2005).

Barbara Opall-Rome, "Raid Reveals Hole in Israeli Net," *Defense News* (July 17, 2006) http://www.defensenews.com

Pentagon Briefing on 30 June 2003, Secretary of Defense Donald Rumsfeld

O'Hanlon, Michael E. and Ian Livingston, *The Iraq Index: Tacking Variables of Reconstruction & Security in Post-Saddam Iraq* (Washington, D.C.: The Brookings Institution, 11 Dec. 2009).

Guy Pervillé, "La ligne Morice en Algérie, 1956–1962." Online version of "Des murs et des hommes." *Panoramiques*, 67 (2ème trimestre 2004), found at: http://guy.perville.free.fr/spip/article.php3?id_article=95

General David Petraeus, Interview on Fox News by Chris Wallace, 17 June 2007.

James T. Quinlivan, "Force Requirements in Stability Operations" in *Parameters,* Winter 1995.

James T. Quinlivan, "Burden of Victory: The Painful Arithmetic of Stability Operations (RAND, Summer 2003).

Jeffrey Record, "External Assistance: Enabler of Insurgent Success," *Parameters* (Autumn 2006).

Report of the Secretary-General: The situation in Afghanistan and its implications for international peace and security (12 August 2005), A/60/224-S/2005/525.

Report of the Secretary-General: The situation in Afghanistan and its implications for international peace and security (11 September 2006), A/61/326-S/2006/727.

Report of the Secretary-General: The situation in Afghanistan and its implications for international peace and security (10 March 2010), A/64/705-S/2010/127.

Report of the Secretary-General: The situation in Afghanistan and its implications for international peace and security (14 September 2010), A/64/911-S/2010/463.

Report of the Secretary-General: The situation in Afghanistan and its implications for international peace and security (5 March 2013), A/67/778-S/2013/133.

Report of the Secretary-General: The situation in Afghanistan and its implications for international peace and security (13 June 2013), A/67/889-S/2013/350.

Report of the Secretary-General: The situation in Afghanistan and its implications for international peace and security (6 December 2013), A/68/645-S/2013/721.

Report of the Secretary-General: The situation in Afghanistan and its implications for international peace and security (7 March 2014), A/68/789-S/2014/163.

"Rumsfeld doubt 'long war' in Iraq" *Washington Times* (1 February 2006).

Eric Schmitt, "The Conflict in Iraq: Troops; Rumsfeld See An Iraq Pullout Within 4 Years, *The New York Times* (December 7, 2004).

"Speech by Daniel Chipenda Commemorating the Eleventh Anniversary of the People's Movement for the Liberation of Angola." *Issue: A Journal of Opinion*, 2:3 (autumn 1972).

Spiegel Online International, 21 May 2008 "Interview with a Taliban Commander: What's Important is to Kill the Germans." Interview conducted by Susanne Koelbl and Sami Yousafzi.

Keith Sutton, "Population Resettlement—Traumatic Upheavals and the Algerian Experience," *J. Afr. Stud.,* 15:2 (June 1977).

Ben Thein, "Is Israel's Security Barrier Unique?" *Middle East Quarterly* (Fall 2004), http://www.meforum.or/article/652.

Time Magazine, 6 October 2009, "Can Obama, McChrystal Agree New Afghan War Strategy" by Mark Thompson.

Ann Scott Tyson, "Additional Deployment Not Announced and Rarely Noted", *Washington Post* (13 October 2009).

U.S. Department of Veterans Affairs. *Fact Sheet: America's Wars* (July 2007). http://www1.va.gov/opa/fact/amwars.asp.

"U.S. Declares insurgency "Broken"; Military also says bin Laden is cut off" by Rowan Scarborough, *The Washington Times* (19 November 2004).

U.S. National Archives and Records Administration, U.S. Army, Joint United States Military and Planning Group—Greece (JUSMAPG), *Brief History* and *History, 25 March 1949–30 June 1950.*

U.S. Defense Department Office of the Assistant Secretary of Defense (Public Affairs) News Transcript, dated 21 September 2004.

U.S. Defense Department News Transcript, "Secretary Rumsfeld Interview with George Stephanopoulos, ABC This Week", dated February 6, 2005, 0900 AM EST.

Weiner, Justus Reid, "Israel's Security Barrier: An International Comparative Analysis and Legal Evaluation." *The George Washington International Law Review,* January 1, 2005.

Wikipedia article on "German Armed Forces Casualties in Afghanistan."

Wikipedia article on the Gulf War discusses Trevor Dupuy's estimate compared to the others.

Scott Wilson, "Touring Israel's Barrier With Its Main Designer," *The Washington Post* (August 7, 2007).

Carlos L. Yordan, Ph.D. "Are More Troops Needed in Iraq?" *Small Wars Journal* (February 2006)

4. There are additional books and sources examined and referenced for use in the various reports done by *The Dupuy Institute*. These are not listed in this bibliography. There is a very large number of books and sources used to create our various database that are used to support these reports and this book, including the Iraq Casualty Data Base (ICDB), the MCODB (Modern Contingency Operations Data Base) the MISS (Modern Insurgency Spread Sheets) and the DISS (Dupuy Insur-

gency Spread Sheets). The sources for these data bases are not listed in this bibliography. Data bases used include:

The Dupuy Institute's Dupuy Insurgency Spread Sheets (DISS)

The Dupuy Institute's Iraq Casualty Data Base (ICDB).

The Dupuy Institute's Modern Contingency Operations Data Base (MCODB)

The Dupuy Institute's Modern Insurgency Spread Sheets (MISS)

The Dupuy Institute's Small Scale Contingency Operations Database (SSCO).

The Dupuy Institute's Warfare, Armed Conflict, and Contingency Operations Data Base (WACCO).

Iraq Coalition Casualty Count at icasulaties.org.